Allen Josephs

⇥ Ritual and Sacrifice

UNIVERSITY PRESS OF FLORIDA

GAINESVILLE · TALLAHASSEE · TAMPA · BOCA RATON

PENSACOLA · ORLANDO · MIAMI · JACKSONVILLE · FT. MYERS

in the Corrida

The Saga of César Rincón

Copyright 2002 by Allen Josephs
Printed in the United States of America on acid-free paper

07 06 05 04 03 02   6 5 4 3 2 1

Library of Congress Cataloging-in-Publication Data
Josephs, Allen.
Ritual and sacrifice in the corrida: the saga of César Rincón /
Allen Josephs.
p. cm.
Includes bibliographical references and index.
ISBN 0-8130-2462-5 (cloth: alk. paper)
1. Rincón, César. 2. Bullfighters—Colombia—Biography. I. Title.
GV1108.R56 J67 2002
791.8'2'092—dc21   2002016596
[B]

The University Press of Florida is the scholarly publishing agency
for the State University System of Florida, comprising Florida A&M
University, Florida Atlantic University, Florida Gulf Coast University,
Florida International University, Florida State University, University
of Central Florida, University of Florida, University of North Florida,
University of South Florida, and University of West Florida.

University Press of Florida
15 Northwest 15th Street
Gainesville, FL 32611-2079
http://www.upf.com

In memory of John Fulton
también se muere el mar

John Fulton, San Miguel de Allende, April 3, 1994.
This photograph was taken at a party to celebrate
John's retirement from the profession of matador de
toros. Earlier that afternoon he cut two ears, the maxi-
mum trophies, from the last bull of his career.

John Fulton. *Minotaur.* Commissioned piece, author's collection.

Am glad you liked the last chapter [of Death in the Afternoon]—*it is what the book is about but nobody seems to notice that.*
Ernest Hemingway to Arnold Gingrich, 4 December 1932

For that which befalleth the sons of men befalleth beasts; even one thing befalleth them: as the one dieth, so dieth the other; yea, they have all one breath; so that a man hath no preeminence above a beast: for all is vanity.
Ecclesiastes 3:19

The custom of killing a god in animal form . . . belongs to a very early stage of human culture, and is apt in later times to be misunderstood.
Sir James Frazer, *The Golden Bough*

A ritual can be defined as an enactment *of a myth. By participating in a ritual, you are actually experiencing a mythological life. And it's out of that participation that one can learn to live spiritually.*
Joseph Campbell, *The Power of Myth*

Proust Questionnaire: Which living person do you most admire?
Julian Schnabel: César Rincón.
Vanity Fair, February 2001

Contents

Figures

All figures are by the author unless otherwise noted.

Plates

A Note on Names, Terms, and Documentation

Jean Cau, a taurine writer who was for a time a collaborator of Jean-Paul Sartre, once refused to apologize to his French readers for the use of foreign—which is to say Spanish—terms in discussing tauromachy, what we call "bullfighting," itself a misguided term that I will not use. Instead I will use "tauromachy," and the Spanish term *toreo*. Jean Cau, in refusing to apologize, cited antecedents: Tolstoy sometimes wrote dialogue in French. The Parisian phenomenologists used German terms such as "weltanschauung" and other barbarisms. Besides, he concluded, "tauromachy is more complicated than philosophy" (*Por Sevillanas* 25).

Following Jean Cau's example, I will not apologize for the use of Spanish terms in this book—they simply are the only way to speak of certain taurine things. But I do want to explain how I will use them. Normally the first time a word appears it will be in italics, as with *toreo* above, thereafter as though it were in English, as with "toreo" in this sentence. Unless the meaning is very obvious, I will explain a term in the text or in an endnote. Also each term will appear in the index with the corresponding first-use page number. This is essentially the method employed by John McCormick in *The Complete Aficionado,* and I find it to be the most useful and least obtrusive method of dealing with taurine terminology, which McCormick described as "unusually vexing" (xi). Finally, I have usually put taurine usage in quotation marks; example: The matador was "below" the bull (that is, not up to the animal's level of quality).

Spanish names, especially taurine names, are not as troublesome for English readers as Tolstoyan names and their many diminutives, but they run a close second. For example, legendary torero (a word not in italics because it has been accepted into English, as have "matador," "corrida," "afi-cionado," and a few others) José Gómez Ortega, known as *Gallito*, was also known as *Joselito* and *Joselito el Gallo*, as well as "Joselito" or Joselito, and was often referred to simply as José. The recently deceased matador Luis Miguel González Lucas, on the other hand, was and is seldom referred to except as Luis Miguel Dominguín, as though "Dominguín," his *apodo* or "stage name," were his patronymic. For simplicity I will avoid italics or quotation marks except where necessary for clarity and will refer to toreros by the names most commonly in use. Thus José María Dols Abellán will be José Mari Manzanares, and my central subject, César Rincón—who was born Julio César Rincón Ramírez—is simply called César Rincón or César or Rincón.

Sources of direct quotes or important attributions are in parentheses, as for Cau and McCormick above, with short titles or authors' names when needed for reference to the bibliography. All translations are mine. For historical material I have depended particularly on four written sources: (1) The taurine weekly *6 Toros 6*, which I abbreviate *6T6*; (2) Javier Villán's *César Rincón: De Madrid al cielo*, abbreviated JV; (3) Geneviève Fondeviole-Stefanuto's *Le voyageur de San Jude*, abbreviated F-S; and 4) Juan Carlos Iragorri and Germán Bernate's *César Rincón: Perfil de un hombre de casta*, abbreviated I&B.

I have also drawn on hundreds of interviews and informal talks, some-times to try to straighten out contradictions in the historical sources. To include a note on every one would prove difficult and fruitless. Where im-portant or divergent information is involved, I have credited my sources, frequently in direct dialogue. And I have used videos of important corridas to supplement my notes and photographs and to refresh my memory.

Finally, there is the taurine rumor mill, the *malas lenguas* that sometimes prove correct and sometimes do not. Here I have had to use my judgment, and I have included as little from this source as possible. Still, it would be disingenuous not to acknowledge this very real, very unavoidable, and very taurine source of information and opinion. Taurine culture is, after all, far more oral than written.

Acknowledgments

The number of people who have helped me on this project is large, and many of them are cited directly in my text. Others who deserve mention for their patience, hospitality, helpfulness, and information are listed below, and I hope I have left no one out. I am indebted to the Program for Cultural Cooperation between Spain's Ministry of Culture and United States' Universities for a research grant and to the University of West Florida for my University Research Professorship, without which I would not have been able to complete this project.

Special thanks to Alfonso Alcázar, Aníbal Alfaro, Eloy Anzola, Phil Benton, Patrick Beuglot, Jolee Bohannon, Mario Botero, Jerry Boyd, Tony Brand, Juan Caballero, Eduardo Cabas, Curro Camacho, Paco Cano, Simón Casas, Miguel Angel Castander, Noel Chandler, Barnaby Conrad, Judy Cotter, Doug Day, Joe Distler, Gustavo Domínguez, Pepe Esteban, Valerie Etienne, Muriel Feiner, Betty Ford, Ken Ford, Carmelo Galindo, Ignacio Gómez, Angel González, Antonio González, Ian Gibson, Araceli Guillaume-Alonso, Claudio Guillén, Phil Hall, Rick Holmberg, Charles Jockelson, Don Junkins, Jerry Kuenn, Greg Lanier, Miguel Leal, Robert Lewis, Don and Mary Ann Long, Rodrigo Lloreda Mera, Bill Lyon, Georges Marcillac, Charo Martínez, Jean-François Mengelle, Pierre Miquel, Alvaro Molina, Phil Momberger, Lore Monning, Chris Morris, David Moss, Ray Mouton, Bradley Odom, Belarmino Pinilla, Irene del Prado, Carmen de Reparaz, Robert Ryan, Gastón Silva, Arantxa Sola Cía, Ed Stanton, H. R. Stoneback, Thomas

Sunday, Fernando Texidor, Dave Tuggle, Lee Turner, Ray Turner, Linda Uebelsteadt, Justo and Leonor Ulloa, Robert Vavra, John and Pam Wilkins, Mitzi Williams, and Dick Ziedman.

Very special thanks to Deborah Burlison for her manuscript management and to Ann Marlowe for her copyediting.

Prologue

Inspiration and Aspiration

A book, the axe to chop the frozen sea inside, as Franz Kafka once reputedly remarked, can have a strange and not altogether logical genesis. This one began in Madrid in an innocent conversation with taurine critic Michael Wigram one June evening in 1992. The conversation—about books in English on tauromachy—matters little, but a seed was planted and I made the decision to write a book with the Colombian matador César Rincón as the central subject (plate 1).

A year later, also in Madrid, I had a dream that made me realize how deeply the planted seed had been marinating inside the frozen sea. It was one of those lucidly intense dreams that make you feel you have been in some other dimension, and I wrote it down at once. This passage from my notes would prefigure much of the book:

> First César and I killed Bosch-like bird-people with high-powered BB guns. They were sacrifices, their roles were understood, the masks had fallen, and we had all assumed our proper roles. The war was over or the feria was over and everyone understood now what the ruses, the roles, and the rituals, which we had not understood before as rituals at all, meant.
>
> The dead—the sacrifices—had been surprised but had seemed to accept their roles as they died, finding themselves the same as brightly colored birds suddenly discovered at the edge of the wood.
>
> César, who sometimes seemed to be Theseus, was the supremely able killer who had come necessarily from poverty, not having understood early on what his real destiny was, but nonetheless having ful-

filled it intuitively to perfection. When he had fulfilled it, he understood it. I understood too. He was the doer. I was the recorder. Neither was complete without the other.

César-Theseus had no need of Ariadne any longer, for the thread had been woven into a tale. Now César would be legend. The little boy whose mother and sister had perished by fire as living sacrifices to the Virgin would no longer be afraid. The black bull of fear had made him into a hero, the only hero left, the last serious man in the world.

It was a strange dream, but it told me a few things, mainly that it was acceptable to my subconscious to proceed with the book, with this particular quest.

Six months later, at first light, I sweated through a Colombian dengue fever in a state of ecstatic insomnia at the Residencia Stein in Cali. As it grew gradually grayer outside, amid the outlandish songs of tropical birds, the structure of the book came to me all at once and full-blown as in some biblical visitation, or so it seemed in my deranged state. And that afternoon César Rincón, the crown prince of tropical heat, cut both ears[1] from an ugly gnu-shaped bull of Guachicono as Colombian flags waved and a deluge of hats filled the ring, and the crowd chanted in unison to their national hero: "¡To-re-ro! ¡To-re-ro! ¡To-re-ro! ¡To-re-ro! ¡To-re-ro!" I thought that afternoon I had the book all wrapped up, but I was sorely mistaken. The taurine reality I was dealing with was far more complex than febrile visitations and deconstructed dreams led me to believe.

In some regards this book is a sequel to *White Wall of Spain*, the title of which came from the verses of the Spanish poet Federico García Lorca:

¡Oh, blanco muro de España!
¡Oh, negro toro de pena!

Oh, white wall of Spain!
Oh, black bull of pain!

Originally in *White Wall* I had not planned to do a chapter on toreo. As I neared the end, however, I realized that such a chapter was necessary because it brought together all facets of the book. It would be impossible to discuss flamenco and religion and Andalusian culture without bringing in the creation of toreo, since all were part of the same sensibility. In fact, toreo was the key to the puzzle. Eventually I came to realize that any sequel to *White Wall* would have to be a book on toreo.

In all of Spanish and Hispanic culture, no subject generates more discussion or is more misunderstood in the non-Hispanic world. My intention is not to convert the "opposition" but to present a culturally and artistically oriented view of toreo. For the English-speaking world to understand it, tauromachy needs to be perceived as an integral and creative part of Spanish and Hispanic culture and art.

My treatment here, without avoiding technical questions, speaks to anyone concerned with the subject of toreo, including Hispanophiles and Hispanophobes, Hemingway fans and antifans, and anyone interested in spectacle, the performing arts, sacrifice, and ritual. It aspires to reach a wide audience, for it embraces the cultures of the eight active taurine countries—Spain, France, Portugal, Mexico, Venezuela, Colombia, Ecuador, and Peru—and tangentially, through aficionados, especially through taurine clubs such as the Club Taurino of New York and the Club Taurino of London, many other countries as well.[2]

Near the time I began mulling over doing such a book, a virtually unknown (in Spain) Colombian matador named César Rincón burst on the Spanish scene as possibly no one in the history of toreo had done. His story and his deeds as I watched him, studied him, and got to know him became the thread through the unformed labyrinth of my intentions, as I once again—as I had in *White Wall of Spain*—sought out the minotaur in his lair.

Many elements must come together to make a corrida, but the sine qua non is the Spanish fighting bull, the *toro bravo, bos taurus Africanus,* or perhaps more properly *bos taurus Ibericus,* a wild animal that bears only a family resemblance to domestic cattle. Along with the bull itself there must be fascination, veneration, awe, and love: fascination such as the cave painters at Lascaux and Altamira and Chauvet and Cussac felt; veneration such as the many Mediterranean and Near Eastern religions of antiquity have shown (including early Judaism: Moses slew thousands for backsliding into the cult of the "golden calf"); the utter awe, very close to terror, that runs through anyone—except (at least in theory) a trained professional—who gets close to the revered animal; and love. Although it may seem paradoxical at first, the corrida is based on all these elements, especially love of the animal, love of its physical beauty, its strength, its character, and above all love of its unmitigated wild bravery.

The fate of most bovines is to furnish food, on a continuous basis in milk products from dairy cows, and at one fell swoop as meat. Most beef cattle go somewhat pathetically to the slaughterhouse at about eighteen months.

Figure 1. The fate of all cattle. Before this bull—killed in Alcalá de Guadaira on April 29, 1995, by Colombian matador Vicente Salamanca—died, he lived the best possible bovine life on the ranch of former matador Miguel Báez, Litri. As with all such animals, the meat is highly prized and never wasted.

Some younger, some much younger. A toro bravo, its excellent and often prized meat always sold in advance, is killed in the ring at more than four years of age by law, and the breeding cows and stud bulls usually live out a full life. As Tom Booker in Nicholas Evans's novel *The Horse Whisperer* puts it: "Get born as a [domestic] bull and you've got a ninety-nine percent chance of getting castrated and served up as hamburger" (212).

A toro bravo, on the other hand, leads the best possible life as he is brought to maturity, one that leads naturally to his glorification through a complex and highly ceremonial ritual designed to reveal his best qualities. The death in the ring of a toro bravo is—or should be—the showcase of his virtues, and the whole spectacle of the corrida, when it is performed properly, reflects fascination, veneration, awe, and love. As García Lorca put it, "Toreo is the liturgy of the bulls, an authentic religious drama where, just as in the Mass, there is the adoration and sacrifice of a God" (3:316).

So this book starts from the point of view of one who loves the corrida and, through the corrida, the animals of which the corrida is a devoted artistic reflection. Without an abiding love and respect for the animals, one cannot be a true aficionado, much less a torero. If you love animals and especially if you love the bulls, read on; that is what the following pages are about. And remember that César Rincón, like most great matadors, usually considers the bull his collaborator, not his enemy.

If you think you hate "bullfights," read on anyway—some converts make great believers. Until you see one, you never know what your reaction to the corrida will be. Acclaimed naturalist Terry Tempest Williams spoke eloquently in her keynote address on July 21, 1996, at the Seventh International Hemingway Conference in Sun Valley, Idaho, about her first corrida. Watching the great young torero Enrique Ponce in his hometown of Valencia, she had been transfixed, transformed, and brought to tears, convinced she was watching a sacred ritual. Her husband was also moved to tears for quite the opposite reason. He left, she stayed, and afterwards they had what she called the worst quarrel of their marriage. Yet Terry Tempest Williams remains determined that what she experienced was one of the most important moments of her life.

And, if you are on the fence, kindly bear firmly in mind this ultimate paradox: Without the bull there would be no corrida, but without the corrida there would be no toro bravo. The "bravo" in toro bravo is not a matter of mood, it is a matter of *raza,* of race; that is, the toro bravo is the descendant of the wild, prehistoric *bos primigenius,* the aurochs of antiquity, precisely the bull that so fascinated the great cave painters of southern France and Spain.

The aurochs survived systematic destruction throughout southern Europe and the Mediterranean during antiquity, and the last herd was killed off in the 1600s in Austria. Near the cave of Lascaux at the park known as Espace Cro-magnon, the aurochs, or at least what looks like an aurochs, has been "back-bred" using Spanish and French bulls and other descendants of the aurochs. And while the breeders have gotten several perfect-looking imitations of the great bull of prehistory, there is one thing this faux aurochs lacks. When I asked the foreman of the park about the fascinating animals, he replied almost hesitantly, "No, monsieur, they are not bravo. They will not charge."

A prime toro bravo, on the other hand, will charge anything that moves, whether it be a hat thrown into the ring, a truck, or even a train. In the

Figure 2. Bos taurus. *Without the corrida these extraordinary animals would cease to exist.*

nineteenth century, as in antiquity, these bulls were matched against lions, tigers, bears, and elephants, opponents they usually killed—except the elephant, which reports say was merely beaten into submission.

Like the aurochs of antiquity, the once formidable herds of toros bravos—which ran wild and posed a definite threat to anything in their path— would have disappeared had there been no reason to corral and breed them on ranches and to guard vigilantly their survival. During the Spanish Civil War, as a case in point, herds were decimated and sometimes destroyed, eaten for meat and killed for vengeance, causing a dangerous shortage of stock that took years to replace. If there were no corrida, the indomitable but otherwise "useless" toro bravo, the Spanish fighting bull, *bos taurus,* would have no reason to exist. It would become an endangered species and in a short time would be extinct. Nonaficionados do not realize that the great hidden gift of the corrida—and ultimately the obscure purpose of the corrida—is and should continue to be the preservation of this magnificent species. The aim of this book is the understanding, hence the preservation, of the corrida as illustrated through the career of one of its most worthy celebrants, César Rincón.

The Novice Aficionado

Here follows a primer for beginning aficionados. It is, in simple terms, a brief explanation of the corrida, which is not simple at all but, as Jean Cau has forewarned us, more complex than philosophy. Such an explanation will present the novice with the requisite raw material, as well as allowing the introduction of technical terms, those Spanish words that drama and bull critic Kenneth Tynan called "the hard words" (19), many of which never appear in conventional dictionaries. Seasoned aficionados may amuse themselves searching for mistakes in my explanation—a favorite pastime of seasoned aficionados—or skip ahead to the next chapter.

Let us imagine we are in Madrid and let us go then, you and I, ere the evening is spread out against the sky like a matador's *capote*. Let us go through certain very crowded streets to the bar Los Clarines—named for the horns that announce the corrida—near the *plaza de toros*, the ring or arena,[1] of Madrid, called Las Ventas. In the noisy, smoke-filled bar, the aficionados come and go, speaking—passionately, for passion is the essence of *afición* or love of the corrida—of José Mari Manzanares or Francisco Ruiz Miguel, or one or another of a thousand matadors of time past and time present, and of the great bulls of Alvaro Domecq and Victorino Martín and other legendary breeders.

While we are here in Los Clarines, I will try to dispel certain mis- or preconceptions that the uninitiated sometimes harbor. To begin, we should remember that the corrida is based upon the animal's behavior, and especially on the fact that a toro bravo, unlike his domestic cousins, when isolated, will charge anything near him that moves. When a bull is alone his usual collective or herd instinct disappears, replaced by this instinct to charge. Fight replaces flight. The bull's defense is his offense, and his target is motion, not color (bulls are color-blind). This aggressiveness and the bull's lack of experience with a lure—the *capote* or cape used by the matador and his assistants, and the *muleta*, the smaller red cloth used by the matador alone—comprise the dynamics of the corrida. Both are required for the corrida to be a success.

If the bull has had experience with the capote or muleta, he will disregard the *engaño*, the trick or the lure of the cloth, and charge straight for the man. Bulls learn quickly, and if they have been previously caped, they remember and are said to be so smart they "know Latin." If they do not charge, becoming defensive from a stationary position and avoiding the engaño, they are said to be *manso*, literally peaceful or meek but, in the context of the corrida, un-bravo, not aggressive, even cowardly.

If, on the other hand, the bull charges frankly, aggressively, and happily at a gallop, he is called bravo. For aficionados there is nothing in the animal kingdom more beautiful than a toro bravo that charges repeatedly and from a distance, summoned by the matador's movement of the capote or muleta, usually coupled with a vocal call, "Jeje-toro-jeje," or "Toro-JAI, toro-JAI." A bull that charges repeatedly and without undue coaxing allows the matador to *ligar*, to link passes in a series that builds to a crescendo producing emotion and beauty and, when done perfectly so that the series themselves build in crescendo as well, even catharsis, as we shall see. No matador's performance can be judged or appreciated without taking into account the individual animal's behavior and characteristics. And no two animals are alike.

The matador's ability can vary as much as the bull's behavior. A good matador must be intelligent in a specialized way: he must be able to think in front of the bull. Thinking in front of the bull is not like the thinking I do as I write this sentence nor the thinking you do reading it. Neither the paper I write on nor the book you are reading can kill you in the blink of an eye. The matador must think so quickly about distance, about *terreno*, the bull's "territory,"[2] about the bull's past and present and future behavior that his thinking must seem automatic, virtually intuitive. He must also be in good physical shape and in complete command of his *trastos*, his tools or implements, the capote, the muleta, and the *espada* or sword, all of which are heavier and more difficult to manipulate than they appear. The matador must train constantly so that the use of his trastos becomes second nature.

I remember once César Rincón's *apoderado*, his manager, Luis Alvarez (plate 4a) saying to me: "There is no such thing as fear in toreo, only sitio and lack of sitio." *Sitio* is a difficult but important term to define, especially as Luis Alvarez was using it. It means, among other things, familiarity with the behavior of the animals, being comfortable (that is, not scared witless) in the presence of an animal that weighs five or six hundred kilograms and is trying to kill you, being able to think, to judge distances, to figure terrain—to understand instantly what space belongs to the toro, what to the torero—to stay calm no matter what the animal does, not "losing it," keeping your nerve, having the proper reflexes, and looking relaxed with the bull. It comes only from exhaustive training with the animals.

No matter how talented or valiant you are, if you are not *toreando*[3] frequently with live animals, you cannot have enough sitio for a difficult bull. And Luis Alvarez was right, especially from an apoderado's vantage. But my point here is, even though sitio can allay fear—in Spanish, fear is *miedo*—the fear exists. And one way or another, every matador must be able to deal with it. That item of control of fear separates many a would-be matador from the ranks of those who make a living at it. Luis Alvarez meant that enough sitio precludes fear, but very few matadors—one from thousands who begin and fail—ever achieve such enviable sitio. And fear haunts all toreros, even the ones with sitio, like fate itself.

If we put together the two wildly variable qualities of the animal's behavior and the man's ability, we can begin to appreciate the infinitely complex possibilities in any given corrida (bearing in mind that three matadors will kill six bulls on a usual afternoon). Consider, for example, a brave bull with an incompetent matador, a great shame since it means the animal's good qualities will not be sufficiently exhibited; or an able matador with a manso bull, a combination that often results in a frustrating experience for the matador and consequently for the spectators; or, finally, the best possible combination, a brave bull with a great matador. That ideal combination does not happen every day, but when it does happen, the result can be electrifying. All too frequently, however, it is as the old taurine saw has it: "When there are toros, there are no toreros; when there are toreros, there are no toros." To put it another way, a great afternoon is an exception, but it is an exception worth waiting for.

Eventually the aficionado comes to realize that the exceptional nature of the great afternoon is fundamental to the appeal of toreo. Routine greatness is not only an oxymoron, it is an impossibility in toreo, which is one reason toreros aim to maintain a high standard, *mantenerse*, rather than to achieve consistent greatness the way, say, a figure skater would. The ice is always more or less the same, the bull never is. And the bull, unlike the ice, is trying to kill the matador.

My description so far is a simplification, but it does provide a sort of sliding scale with which to approach the corrida. There are at least two other important variables that deserve mention here. The Colombian writer Antonio Caballero published a fine collection of taurine criticism titled *Toros, toreros y públicos*. That third element, the *público*, the spectators, the public, plays a very important role in the spectacle. The spectators should not be thought of as a passive presence, for without the público, the afición, there would be no *figuras*, no stellar performers, and eventually no corridas.

The other element is *arte*, the artistic ability of the matador with the bull, that transcendent and ineffable quality that gifted matadors sometimes possess that is capable of transporting twenty thousand people in a matter of seconds from boredom, idleness, indifference, and antipathy to a state of near delirium, through a collective catharsis, to a Dionysian ecstasy otherwise unimaginable in Western experience. Such a transformation is precisely what García Lorca had in mind when he called the spectacle "the only serious thing left in the world" (3:418).

This element of art precludes the spectacle of the corrida from being a sport. Everything that happens in the corrida, every technical movement and detail, from the moment the bull enters the arena, is performed with one purpose in mind: to kill the bull. The corrida is not a contest to see who wins. Fierce competition exists among matadors, but the bull must die. Although a battle of wills takes place between the bull and the man, the man is meant to kill the bull. If the matador is wounded, the next matador in line will kill the bull. If there is no one left to kill the bull, it will still be dispatched in the corrals behind the ring.

Even in those very rare instances when a bull's life is pardoned because of his extreme bravery (theoretically he may be used as a *semental*, a seed bull), he must first undergo all the preparations for his *muerte*, his death, including a symbolic killing. It is only by going through the preparation for being killed that he can be saved—like Abraham's son Isaac—and it is always the matador's task to make that death, whether real or symbolic, as graceful, as inspiring, and as beautiful as possible.

The matador, then, is not an athlete participating in a sporting contest. Think of him more as a high priest officiating at a ritual sacrifice, the hieratic nature of which inspired García Lorca to compare the corrida to the Mass. We can conceive of the matador, at the highest level, as the only mystagogue left from antiquity in the Western world. His performance is a ritual reenactment of the myth of the man-god who kills the bull-god, the hero who, through skill and art, conquers the primal force of nature. In so doing, he becomes "the first man of the world," as the critic Curro calls Juan Gallardo (played by Tyrone Power) in *Blood and Sand.*

Let us go on to the ring, to Las Ventas del Espíritu Santo, to give the Madrid ring its full name, for more specific matters. Many good books explain the technical aspects of the corrida—especially John Fulton's unique *Bullfighting,* the only such work in English by a matador who dedicated his entire life to the fiesta, as well as a number of books by the Dean of American Taurine Letters, Barnaby Conrad, John McCormick's erudite *The Complete Aficionado,* John Leibold's practical guide *This Is the Bullfight,* and of course Ernest Hemingway's classic *Death in the Afternoon*—and it is not my intention here to repeat much of that material. Still, to paraphrase Hemingway in *Death in the Afternoon,* there are a few practical matters to be considered.

The corrida divides into three *suertes* often compared in English to the "acts" of a tragedy. These suertes are the *suerte de varas* or the picking or piking of the bull from horseback with a long metal-tipped wooden pike;[4] the *suerte de banderillas* in which the matador or his assistants place three pairs of *banderillas,* decorative barbed wooden shafts, in the bull's withers; and the *suerte de matar,* in which the matador kills the bull with a sword. Each of these suertes—also called *tercios* or thirds—makes up part of the killing of the bull, and the first two are necessary for the third to take place. To make matters less simple, *suerte* also means luck.

Watch now as the first bull comes into the arena, notice how high he carries his head, appreciate his strength and his amazing speed, faster from a standing start, they say, than a horse. It would be virtually impossible at this point for a matador to kill such an animal with a sword and a piece of cloth. The animal—which John McCormick calls "an event in nature, one which we know in the pit of the stomach, suddenly and viscerally" (27)— must be slowed down and weakened and his head must be brought lower so the matador can put in the sword from the front, passing over the right horn to place the sword high up in the withers, between the shoulder blade and the spinal column at the proper downward angle to cut the bull's aorta.

The precise spot for the sword to enter—referred to in the colorful, religiously tinged argot of tauromachy as *la cruz,* the cross, or *el hoyo de las agujas,* the eye of the needle—is not large, about the size made by putting together the tips of your index fingers and the tips of your thumbs. Every movement in the *lidia,* as the entire process of dealing with the bull from its moment of entry is called, leads up to and prepares for the uncovering of that spot where the sword must enter. Every aspect of the lidia, which John

Leibold describes as "ringcraft or strategy" (20), then, leads to the killing of the bull by the matador. Once we understand this unified function of all parts of the lidia, each of the three suertes falls into line and makes sense.

Watch now before the suerte de varas, as the matador comes out and gives the bull its initial passes. Sometimes one of his assistants, his *banderilleros*, will call the bull first, but often the matador himself begins in his receiving passes to slow the bull down and to concentrate or fix his charges on the lure. If the bull charges cleanly, the matador may do a series of artistic passes, probably *verónicas* (plate 20a), the basic cape pass named for the way Saint Veronica held the cloth she offered to Jesus (John Fulton reproduces El Greco's painting of Saint Veronica on page 104 of his *Bullfighting*).

When the horns sound, the two *picadores* or pikemen come in on their horses and the suerte de varas begins. This suerte is often misunderstood by the public, especially non-Hispanics, and is frequently abused by unscrupulous or timorous matadors, yet it forms an essential part of the lidia for two reasons.

Do you see the large hump of muscle on the bull's neck? That is the *morrillo*, the lifting muscle that drives the horns and gives them their terrible power. Remember, the bull's head must be lowered in order for the matador to kill him. That lowering process is best accomplished by picking the bull, by citing him to charge the horse and driving the vara into the place where the morrillo joins the shoulders. The picador's lance weakens the muscle, and the bull's effort in driving against the horse and the horse's protective covering, the *peto*, wears him down.

The other reason for the suerte de varas is to judge the bull's bravery. Here under punishment a bull's bravery or lack thereof usually shows. Watch how the bull charges, whether quickly or reluctantly, fixedly or tentatively.

Let's observe this bull. The matador places him properly just within the smaller painted circle on the sand, facing the horse, which is three-quarters facing the bull, beyond the larger painted circle (the picador is not supposed to cross the larger circle). The bull charges at once when the picador shouts and brandishes his lance, coming from the smaller circle, which is to say from some distance, an indication that he is a brave bull. Notice that the bull keeps his head down and pushes straight ahead against the peto, in spite of the damage the picador is inflicting, again the sign of a brave bull. If he bangs the metal stirrup or turns aside or runs away, he is showing various degrees of lack of bravery.

Now the matador is citing the bull away from the horse. This drawing away is called the *quite,* whether it be from the horse or from a comrade, and if the bull is good the matador can do another series of cape passes, also called a quite (pronounced *key*-tay).

Nowadays most bulls receive only one or two picks. A really brave bull ought to have three, but contemporary picadores often give three or four picks in one, a practice to which the public usually reacts with whistles and jeers. Our bull is being taken back for a second pick. Again we should watch how he acts. If he once more charges quickly and from a distance, he is indeed a brave bull, since now he knows what will happen and charges anyway.

This part of the lidia is the one that new aficionados like least, but in time they can learn to appreciate this window on the bull's behavior. When the *presidente,* the legal representative who officiates at the corrida, determines with his advisors, a veterinarian and an ex-matador, that a bull has been sufficiently picked, he shows his white handkerchief on the railing of his box, the horns sound, the picadores and horses exit, and the suerte is over. Frequently a matador will petition the presidente—by removing his *montera,* his headgear—to change the act so the bull will not be excessively slowed down.

The second act, the suerte de banderillas, is much more popular with the average público and seems spectacular since a man without a cape faces the bull. The purpose of this suerte, at least theoretically, is "to provide the bull with a change of pace and a chance to breathe after his encounter with the picadores and to sting him into new strength for the muleta work which is to come" (Liebold 143). Perhaps more important still, it allows us—the spectators and the matador—to judge the bull's behavior, especially his degree of aggressiveness and his ability to recover after the punishment of the horse. You can also see whether the bull charges straight or cuts in on the man and whether he waits or charges at once. All these judgments become possible only if the banderilleros (also called *peones,* peons) perform properly. Frequently they do not.

One day when César Rincón and I were on a training walk near his house outside Madrid, he commented to me that if it were up to him, he would probably abolish the suerte de banderillas because he believes that in general more harm than good comes from the encounter. He said, "If there's any cruelty in the corrida, it's in the banderillas. They don't correct anything. I don't think the bull feels pain in the horse but the banderillas are gratuitous. I would abolish them." I bring this up now partly to dispense with the suerte. It may be one of three, and it can be spectacular when performed by a great technician such as Luis Francisco Esplá or Víctor Mendes, but it is the least important of the three suertes.

The most important is the last, the suerte de matar, with its attendant muleta work, known as the *faena*, that leads up to the kill. To be a figura, a matador must be good with the muleta and he must kill efficiently. In the last suerte the man and the animal face each other alone and for an extended period of time.

Once the matador goes out alone with the muleta, he has a period of fifteen minutes to work and to kill the bull. At ten minutes the presidente signals with his handkerchief for the first *aviso*, or warning, to be sounded by the horns. At thirteen minutes he signals for the second. If at fifteen minutes the bull is not dead, the presidente signals the third and final aviso and the bull is taken out to be killed in the corrals, generally a disgrace to the matador, although it happens sooner or later to anyone who kills a sufficient number of bulls.

In the early days of toreo, the faena (literally it means task or job) consisted of a few *pases* only intended to line up the bull for the kill. Modern toreo, however, has seen the faena—the passes themselves—develop into the main event and the most artistic part of the corrida. It is the artistic emphasis that distinguishes and characterizes modern toreo. This emphasis is essentially a product of the last hundred years of toreo, especially since the "Golden Age of Juan and José," Juan Belmonte and Joselito. (The latter, thought to be invincible, was killed in the ring in Talavera on May 16, 1920, by an old, runty, near-sighted bull). In particular it is due to what has come to be called Belmonte's revolution.[5]

Before Belmonte the reigning dictum of toreo was "te quitas tú o te quita el toro"—either you move or the bull will move you. But Juan Belmonte, who was physically impaired, could not and did not move.

As Antonio Caballero succinctly explains, "Not having the indispensable conditions for the trade, he changed the trade." Belmonte, unable to remove himself from the line of charge, forced the bull to move around him while he remained still, in the process transforming toreo from a kind of Roman circus combat—whence, probably, our anachronistic English word "bullfight"—into an aesthetic endeavor, into one of the fine arts. What had been mostly a matter of legs and movement became, in Belmonte's revolution, a matter of arms and stasis.[6]

As Caballero insightfully remarks, Belmonte "introduced into the fight the dimension of art: of the imaginary"; glossing and citing classic taurine writer José Bergamín, he continues: "without the imaginary, 'the art and play and fiesta of toreo would be nothing more than a barbarous and ritual slaughter.'" But Belmonte—and, through him, Joselito—gave toreo, in Bergamín's words, "a spirituality that it had not had; as though he had given it a soul." Straight-line toreo began to arch into a curve around the man, repose replaced agility, and, as Caballero continues, Belmonte "became an artist because he could not become a gladiator" (100–101). I am reminded of Cervantes, who, unable to succeed at poetry or playwrighting, the preferred genres of his time, had to settle for the creation of the modern novel.

Understanding this basic tenet of Belmonte's revolution—you do not move, you move the bull around you—with its consequent infusion of imagination, inspiration (already a divine concept), and spirituality, is fundamental in understanding how a faena, the heart of the corrida, works. It is also important because César Rincón is as pure a *belmontista* or, to be more accurate, *posbelmontista* as I have ever seen (plate 7).

Watch the matador now as he begins the faena. His first passes should make the bull submit to and follow the lure. Most modern passes are based on the notion of *temple,* of precise smoothness of execution. When a brave bull charges an object, just before he gets to it, he lowers his head to gore, because from a lowered position he can use the powerful leverage of the morrillo to inflict a wound with his horns. He will lower his head to gore in the same way a snake coils to strike most effectively. In a sense he cocks his head by lowering it, readying it to fire.

When the matador cites the bull, he shakes the muleta to attract the bull's attention. The bull charges, lowering his head to gore the challenging object. Just at the moment before the bull reaches the cloth, the matador begins to move the cloth forward in front of the bull, past his own body (plate 10b). If he does it with the right timing, the effect is something like Zeno's paradox: Achilles (the bull) never catches the tortoise (the cloth). But instead of being based on sophistical reasoning, in toreo—more complicated than philosophy—the bull never catches the cloth because the matador moves it at precisely the right speed to keep it in front of the bull as a moving target almost within reach. Temple, the matador's secret weapon, prevents the cocked gun from firing.

If the matador moves the muleta too slowly, Achilles gets the tortoise and discovers it is all a trick, and if he does this a few times he will stop going for the lure and go for the man. If the matador pulls the lure too fast, the bull will lose the lure and discover the man, with the same result. But if the matador tempers the charge, harnessing the animal's instinct, the bull will keep his head "in the muleta" as though trained (plate 24).

A really brave bull has *nobleza,* nobility, meaning he does not have a treacherous or tricky charge, and *fijeza,* fixity, meaning he will continue to charge intently the ever receding muleta. If one of the great matadors gets such a bull on a day when he, the matador, is fit, you will see the rare magic of the art of toreo.

Our generic matador, however, is not doing so well. He is trying to do the main passes, the *derechazo* or right-handed pass and the *natural* or left-handed pass, but notice that he cites from a position in profile to the bull and not frontally. Also he sometimes steps back with his rear leg instead of forward into the pass. Finally, instead of taking the bull around him, he is simply taking advantage of the bull's momentum rather than controlling where the bull goes. All of these maneuvers remove some of the emotion from the passes.

In the "classical" version of the derechazo or the natural (they differ in that in the derechazo the sword spreads the muleta, making it larger, while in the natural the unextended lure is smaller and more fluid), the matador cites from a frontal or near frontal position, especially in the first pass in a series; he steps into the pass (often called *cargando la suerte*);[7] and he takes the bull around his body, forcing the bull to submit to the trajectory the matador designs, making the bull go where the bull does not want to go, as the maestro Domingo Ortega put it (plate 18c).

Our matador has now done the requisite number of passes, four or five series of left- and right-hand passes, the series finished each time with an appropriate *remate* or finishing pass, in this case the *pase de pecho,* the chest pass, the most common today (plate 17a). But he did not manage to ligar, to link up the passes so that the rhythm creates a building tension broken by the remate. Notice the crowd is quiet. No one is even bothering to whistle or jeer or say rude things about his family. The matador has failed to "transmit" emotion.

We can hope that, at the very least, he will kill the animal decorously, but probably he will not. Remember: Our matador has been killing him since that opening cape pass, or trying to kill him. Theoretically killing him softly with silk, wearing him down with the horse, spurring him on with the sticks, dominating him and bringing him to bay with the muleta. If he has not done well up to the kill, it is not likely he will kill well either.

To kill well the matador has to do the most dangerous maneuver in toreo: he has to pass his unprotected body over the right horn of the animal as he pushes the sword in with his right hand, and at the same time he must deflect the animal's charge away from himself with the muleta held furled in his left hand. To make that complex motion, he must cross his right hand (the sword hand) over his left (the muleta hand), and he must cross the muleta low in front of the bull to attract the animal's head down and away from the man's body (plate 21b). Usually the man goes to the bull, killing in the manner called *volapié*, literally flying or moving feet, so called because the man advances toward a stationary or nearly stationary bull, putting in the sword and exiting on foot. Or he may choose to kill *recibiendo*, literally receiving, by citing the bull to charge, remaining stationary as the bull impales himself on the carefully extended sword, while directing the bull's charge away from his body to the right by crossing with the muleta. Killing recibiendo is more difficult and more dangerous because the bull is the aggressor and the man has less control (plate 46d).

Let us watch our matador now. He lines up the bull, profiles in the position from which he will cross, the sword at chest level, the muleta low, furled and pointed toward the bull. Now he moves in on the bull, crossing with the left to draw the bull's head down and away, but leaning his body out to the other side to avoid going over the horn. It is not an elegant posture, and the sword, which did penetrate, has gone in somewhat off to the side and low. He is lucky, though; he's gotten an effective spot and the bull is going down. Not the best performance we could see, to be sure, but one typical of the average work the average spectators will see in their first or four-hundredth corrida.

As we head back to Los Clarines, after five more bulls more or less equally unexciting, you will no doubt wonder why I could not have written us a more interesting corrida for our first time together at los toros. And your objection is a good one. I thought about many possibilities—using more dialogue, describing a great corrida—and even considered resurrecting the old lady Hemingway used to advantage in *Death in the Afternoon* and then threw out of the book. But resurrecting someone Hemingway had thrown out bothered me.

Then there was the lady in the green dress in John McCormick's *The Complete Aficionado*, the one who rooted for the bull, cheered when the animal caught a *novillero* (apprentice torero), and thought that "bullfighting" was barbarous and that Mexicans were cruel and uncivilized. But she was so awful and so real I did not want any part of her either.

So I did it this way, to include as quickly as possible on the inside those readers on the outside, and to refresh the memory of those who have not seen a corrida in five or fifteen years. For novice aficionados to have seen a great corrida their first time out would be unlikely, even with beginner's luck, and would doubtless offend the sensibility of the patient aficionado who sits out countless leaden afternoons awaiting the ephemeral glory of one of the occasionally inspired artistes of the ring. So I have opted for realism. Seasoned aficionados will understand, and the seasoned aficionados who read this section will also realize that I have planted a few theoretical seeds that will sprout in later chapters.

Who Is This Guy?

2

It was one of those moments that changes the direction of your life. I had gone, somewhat perfunctorily, to my usual bar in Narixa to the east of Málaga to watch the corrida from Madrid on television. My own afición had, in fact, waned slightly over the years. When you get hooked on toreo, they say you are bitten by the *gusano*, the worm, of afición. I had been bitten badly in the '60s, but in the '70s and '80s, as the *fiesta* itself seemed at times to wane, I did not keep as current as I had before, largely I think because there was no figura in whom I was passionately interested. (In Spain the corrida is often called collectively the *fiesta*, the *fiesta brava*, or the *fiesta nacional*.)

So on this day I took my usual seat at the first table near the television set, ordered a glass of wine, and proceeded to watch what I expected would be another lackluster corrida from the great Feria de San Isidro, the most important series of corridas of the year from the critically all-important Madrid ring, the premier plaza de toros in the world.

The truth is, I was not paying proper heed. Much of what happened that year from Madrid did not warrant rapt attention. The lack of a critical mass of great figuras such as we had in the '60s, as well as the public's demand for ever larger bulls, which resulted in overweight animals that lacked mobility and could not charge, frequently made for tedious afternoons.

Yet suddenly I am shouting, "That's it! That is toreo! Who is this guy?" No one in the bar seems to know. "Watch how he cites the bull from a distance facing the animal straight on and then takes the bull around him as it charges. That's *it*!"

Figure 3. Before the corrida, Madrid, May 21, 1991. César Rincón, so little known that he was listed as Venezuelan on the program, just before making taurine history. Such unknown foreign matadors had virtually never triumphed in Madrid. No Colombian had. Ever. By permission, Botán.

Afición, like certain viruses, seems not to die. It fades away, sometimes for long periods, only to reappear more virulently than ever. That afternoon, in front of a television set, far from the madding delirium being produced in the Madrid arena, my afición comes rushing back.

His name is César Rincón and his performance that afternoon is the most moving I have seen since May 15, 1966, when I watched Antonio Chenel, Antoñete, in Madrid with the extraordinary "white" bull Atrevido from the ranch of Osborne. I do not know it as I watch him, but that wave of afición and emotion will bring with it a decade-long commitment to tell the story of a virtually unknown young Colombian matador who on that day, May 21, 1991, in the sixth bull turned the Madrid plaza upside down and helped change the course of contemporary toreo. It will be the most intense period in my professional life—the most intense, the most committed, the most dangerous, and the most beautiful.

May 21, 1991

3

Jean Cau once likened a corrida to going out at five in the afternoon to await the arrival of the Reyes Magos—the Wise Men, who in Spain bring children gifts as Santa Claus does in more northern climes—his point being that once in a while they actually showed up, which was to say that, however rarely, the corrida would be a success (*Las orejas* 106). In Madrid in May of 1991, it had been a long time since anyone had seen one of the Reyes Magos, and even longer since anyone had likened a young matador to the messiah come to resurrect the fiesta nacional.

To understand the extraordinary significance of César Rincón's performance that day, seasoned aficionados will want to think back on the taurine scene then, remembering that although there were some excellent matadors—José Mari Manzanares, Espartaco (plate 5c), Niño de la Capea, Roberto Domínguez, Paco Ojeda, Ortega Cano (plate 5d)—none of them had set the public on fire the way the matadors of the previous generation—Antonio Ordóñez, Luis Miguel Dominguín, Paco Camino, Diego Puerta, El Viti, and especially the outrageous and controversial El Cordobés—had done; remembering as well that what may have started as genuine reform, to prevent horn shaving and underaged and undersized animals, had developed a fanatical fringe, especially in Tendido Siete, section 7, of the Madrid ring, the most vocal of whom, armed with inquisitorial fury and green *pañuelos* (handkerchiefs) to signal their demand for the removal of an unworthy animal from the ring, were capable of cowing the presidente or the most self-assured of figuras, such as Espartaco. Although the fiesta nacional was flourishing in the provinces, to say that in Madrid it was in the doldrums would be an understatement.

As Michael Wigram expressed it in a piece entitled "The Rise and Fall of San Isidro," the combination of "very overweight bulls," weak programs, "and the vociferous ignorance of the yobbo claque in Siete have turned San Isidro into the malign fiesta." Wigram ended by citing matador Luis Francisco Esplá's phrase describing San Isidro as the "institutionalization of boredom" and called it "a form of collective masochism."

Antonio Caballero succinctly summed up the situation in Madrid on the day in question when he wrote that he had gone to the plaza resigned ahead of time to seeing "practically nothing [casi nada], because in recent times the aficionado's life was the stuff of resignation and tedium: nothing is more boring than the bulls [the corrida] when they are boring and lately they are always boring" (150–51).

On May 21, 1991, the Madrid ring, usually filled to its 23,000-seat capacity and often completely sold out, was not quite full. Up top on the sunny side there were open spaces. Why? Because the *cartel*—the card, the bill of performers—was not one to inspire the average aficionado to rush out and pay the necessary $100–200 for a couple of decent seats, especially not on a working Tuesday: bulls of Baltasar Ibán to be killed by Curro Vázquez, a torero favored by some Madrid insiders for his artistic purity but never a figura; Miguel Espinosa, called Armillita Chico, a Mexican from a respected taurine dynasty but cold and, of course, a foreigner; and César Rincón, not only a foreigner but virtually unknown and a Colombian, although the handbill that day labeled him Venezuelan. Then too, this corrida was being televised on channel 1 of Televisión Española. Die-hard aficionados could always watch it at home or at the local bar.

As it turned out, not much happened. All but two of the bulls (fourth and sixth) were protested, especially by the loud lads in Seven, for their ungargantuan size. Curro Vázquez and Armillita both had trouble with their bulls, which, even when "small," had too much *casta,* that extraordinary taurine aggressiveness that makes a Spanish fighting bull one of the most formidable animals on earth, for them to handle with style. Neither of them killed well, and they were met with silence and some of the derisive whistling meant to chastise a weak performance.

Nothing much happened, that is, until the sixth bull. In his first bull (the third), César Rincón had drawn some attention and even warm applause, even though he failed to kill well. But the animal was relatively small at 490 kilos, and there were many protests from Seven that obscured most of his work. On the other hand the sixth bull, Santanerito by name, was larger, an impressive animal at 542 kilos, black, high in the shoulders with a massive hump of a morrillo, long-faced, short-necked, with sharp upward-curving horns—not a beautiful bull by taurine standards, nor one to appeal to toreros with that short neck, but one that commanded respect, even in Madrid.

Although Santanerito took three varas, he was not particularly bravo in the horse, waiting, pawing the ground, having to be placed or re-placed close to the picador. Meanwhile César Rincón was showing *ganas,* desire to torear, with his liquid verónicas gaining ground on each pass and, in the quite, a series of rhythmic *delantales*—"aprons," verónicas in which the cape is held tight against the body—that brought the horns of Santanerito, who charged strongly from close up, very near his waist. A crescendo of olés and applause, and the buzz of approbation that hums around the plaza when the afición sits up and takes notice, followed as he put the bull in line for the second pick with an exactly timed *larga,* a one-handed cape pass. When the Madrid ring snaps to attention out of the lethargy of a boring corrida, it is like an immense animal coming suddenly awake.

In the banderillas Santanerito "came up," as the *taurinos* or taurine professionals say, charging aggressively at the peones as they came within range.

César Rincón began the faena by "doubling" the bull, taking command from the start, his low passes forcing the animal back on himself, bending him into position. He finished the series with a *cambio de manos,* taking the bull backhanded with his right hand and switching the muleta seamlessly into his left as the bull passed, and a pase de pecho that drew warm applause. As he set for the next series, the buzzing continued.

At this point César Rincón did something natural to him—but something of a novelty in May of 1991 in Madrid. He approached the bull for a series of right-handed passes but stopped and cited about ten meters away. Santanerito did not charge and Rincón gradually edged forward, crossing in front of the animal, facing him squarely and citing with the muleta extended as far in front of him as he could gracefully reach. Santanerito launched himself now in a gallop, with the charge of a toro bravo. Rincón stood his ground, Santanerito lowered his head and took the lure, all the way through. Rincón turned with one step, leaving the muleta in Santanerito's face and the animal took the engaño again and then again, until he slipped, breaking the series.

The details are important here. The ring was abuzz again and the olés were coming. Why? Because César Rincón had just executed an artistic and coherent series of derechazos in the most classical style. He had done nothing new, but he had done something "old" perfectly, something "old" with a purity of style that was to become his trademark and that seemed to have been missing in Madrid since the glory days of Antoñete.

Santanerito, a bull with great casta, who had begun a bit like a manso and developed his true character of toro bravo as the lidia progressed, was what they call very *enrazado,* meaning that he had a great deal of raza, that he was not docile or facile. Santanerito did not like the current state of affairs and began to rebel against Rincón's domination. The battle of wills that often characterizes great toreo had begun.

In the second series Santanerito took two passes and then hooked upward, trying to take the muleta away from the matador. In the third Santanerito cut in on Rincón in three of four passes, and although Rincón held his ground, it was clear he was losing dominion over the bull. The fourth series was somewhat indecisive, as Santanerito shortened his charge, looking for the truth behind the lure. Rincón switched the muleta to the left hand, but the animal cut back on him after the first pass, nearly catching him.

At this juncture César Rincón took a calculated risk. The normal procedure when an animal shows himself to be difficult is to kill without further artistic work. Instead Rincón fed Santanerito the edge of the muleta and ran him from Tendido Seven straight to the center of the ring where, Rincón reasoned, the bull, being more bravo than manso, would have to charge. Far from his assistants' capes, the matador is more at the animal's mercy, making the center the most dangerous place in the ring. It was also a risk because if he failed here in *los medios* to make the animal charge, he risked looking inept as well as mistaken.

But his strategy worked. Santanerito put his head in the muleta and went all the way through on the first natural. On the second, the olés began. On the third, Rincón drew the animal around beyond his body, behind his left hip, and although the bull hooked at the muleta at the end of the pass, the effect of the pass pulled a voluminous OLE from the crowd. In the fourth, made without ceding an inch of ground, Rincón crossed in front of Santanerito and passed him in another natural. Strategically positioned, Rincón stepped around and into the animal's line of charge. Santanerito was on the muleta instantly, but Rincón drew him past in a three-quarter circle that broke the faena wide open, the matador erect, the muleta unfurling as though it had a mind of its own, the bull lunging after the cloth in a deep circling charge around the fragile axis of the matador's waist, as though entranced by the unfurling muleta constantly receding just out of horn's

Figure 4. Citing, Madrid, May 21, 1991. Rincón, exposing his body completely to the bull, yet offering him the cloth. No tricks here. The bull can freely choose what he will charge. By permission, Botán.

reach. As the muleta reached the end of its trajectory, the tip starting around and away from the bull, the single beast in the stands roared its approval, unanimously invoking the name of God (*olé* derives from Allah). Rincón allowed Santanerito to exit in a high natural, over the horns, and Santanerito rose up after the lure. Without taking a step, Rincón forced the animal to turn to take the muleta in a chest pass that, as it reversed across the matador's chest, drove the bull's charge into a near figure-eight. The effect brought Santanerito to his knees, literally and figuratively—and not because the bull was weak. The battle of wills was over. Rincón turned his back and walked away. The plaza de toros reverberated with murmurs and shouts.

Rincón followed up with a series on the right, citing from a distance and deliberately bending the animal around himself in three-quarter circles. Santanerito was a *toro importante,* a bull aggressive and strong enough to take—even to require—the arching punishment, and Rincón broke him exquisitely, almost delicately, in these derechazos in the purest classical style, purer, in fact, than anything many of us had ever seen. He was lucky to have such a formidable bull, but he knew how to employ the bull's strengths, making the animal's power work against him. And that is the essence of César Rincón's toreo.

Belmonte, they recount (some say it was Guerrita), once said: "Hope to God you never get a truly brave bull," implying that a truly brave bull would eat you alive, at the very least showing all the obvious defects in your toreo. On this day, the unknown *sudamericano* in the apple-green-and-gold suit of lights (the suit the color of hope, according to Rincón) got a brave bull and with it he began working against the tide of contemporary toreo. What he did looked "old" in its grace and art, and indeed it touched an "old" spot in the collective heart of the Madrid afición. But in fact his work was fresh and inventive, advancing a technique of citing from a distance begun in the '50s and '60s by Miguel Báez, Litri, and polished by Antoñete. Santanerito was and is the most important bull of his life, both because he was a great bull and because he led to all the rest.

One more series on the left, intentionally citing from a distance to underscore his domination and classicism, and a series of two-handed passes, *ayudados,* with the muleta in the left and the sword extending (*ayudando*) the muleta, and César Rincón was ready for the kill. The público, on its feet, had capitulated to this unknown soldier.

Now, could he kill in the same style, with the same purity, with the same lack of tricks or stunts or vulgarisms?

Figure 5. Pass on the right, Madrid, May 21, 1991. Rincón making a classic derechazo with Santanerito. Notice how the hard-charging bull has his head down and "in" the muleta, controlled by the matador's wrist. By permission, Botán.

Rincón lined the animal up and with no hesitation cited, pushing forward and lowering the muleta, but his body remained motionless, not stepping forward. He waited for the charge, which came almost at once, crossed with the muleta, pulling the bull just around his body, and guided the sword three-quarters in, high up in the withers. César Rincón had killed recibiendo, in the purest method, crowning the glory of his faena with the glory of his kill.

It was not a perfect kill recibiendo, nor was it far off (slightly low, slightly forward, and he lost the muleta), yet its effect was fulminating. As Santanerito went to the ground in less than twenty-five seconds, the Madrid ring turned upside down, demanding the double trophies of the bull's ears for the matador. Rincón's *vuelta*, his tour of the ring, with Santanerito's ears in his hands was the prelude to an apotheosis. Beyond that, it was graceful, humble, thankful, and respectful, lacking in the vulgar triumphalism too often apparent in recent toreo. And having cut two ears, the most precious of his career, César Rincón went out godlike on the shoulders of the crowd, through the Puerta Grande, the Great Gate, into the now forever unanonymous night of the capital of the world of toreo. And "all Spain," as the Spanish media phrase has it, was watching.

To "cut an ear"—a symbolic trophy once equivalent to a bonus of meat from the animal—in Madrid is a high honor. To cut two in Madrid is the taurine world's maximum triumph, and the news flashed to Colombia and the rest of América Latina. What did it mean for a Colombian to leave on high by the Great Gate of Madrid? No Colombian had ever crossed that threshold. Pepe Cáceres had been the finest hope during his lengthy career, but he had failed, only to die on the horns back in Colombia. What did it mean to a country devastated by civil conflict and defamed by the drug cartel to have such a hero? On May 21, 1927, at the age of twenty-five, a man from the United States landed the first solo flight across the Atlantic in Paris. On May 21, 1991, at the age of twenty-five, a man from Colombia opened the Puerta Grande of Las Ventas del Espíritu Santo in Madrid. After their respective May twenty-firsts, neither César Rincón nor Charles Lindbergh—analogous heroes from different times and from cultures at odds—would know the comfort of obscurity again.

Charles Lindbergh was sometimes called the "last hero," and for the United States perhaps he was. Colombia still needed a hero desperately. Any great torero can be seen as a hero, but César Rincón's case was subtly different, since he would have to shoulder a double burden as the lone hero sent to slay the beast and also as the solitary torchbearer for his unhappy homeland.

Night of May 21, 1991

4

As César Rincón was borne under the high neo-Mudéjar archway of Madrid's Puerta Grande, he passed into taurine eternity, into the company of the select few who have ever achieved that distinction. He passed symbolically, as Madrileños like to say, from Madrid to heaven, and as he did so, tears flowed down his young face, dirty and sweaty only minutes ago, then rinsed off in the *callejón*, the alleyway between the stands and the arena, and now bathed in an uncontainable stream of joy and emotion. Blood from both his bulls stained him from the silver crucifix of his tiepin to his knees. It was the baptism of a young man destined to become a new figura del toreo.

The crowd snatched tassels and pieces of his suit of lights, and the Guardia Civil had to get him a taxi to take him back to the Hotel Foxá 25 where he had dressed, as the van that had brought him to the ring had broken its oil pan in the nervous scramble before the corrida. In the taxi, Rincón and his brother Luis Carlos (plate 4b), who serves as his *mozo de espadas,* his sword handler and dresser, were barely able to speak, and it was not until Rincón reached the Foxá and entered the madhouse of media people, well-wishers, glad-handers, and friends that he began to shake off the emotion and the tears. As soon as humanly possible he ducked into the shower where, he claims, he stayed for nearly an hour. It was the only place he could be alone with what he had done. Later he would comment, many times, "It was the most beautiful day of my life."

Luis Alvarez, described in the next morning's *El País* by taurine critic Joaquín Vidal as levitating in the callejón with the face of a cherub, had as

Figure 6. From Madrid to heaven, Madrid, May 21, 1991. The dream of every matador is to be carried in triumph through that neo-Mudéjar archway, known as the Puerta Grande. The fulfillment of the dream shows on Rincón's face. By permission, Botán.

usual had a busy day. That morning, just a few hours before César Rincón's triumph, Alvarez had heard about the upcoming substitution for injured matador Fernando Lozano (gored in the thigh in Madrid on the seventeenth) for the following day, May 22. As soon as he heard, Alvarez audaciously began to put in motion Rincón's replacing Lozano—just in case Rincón should have a triumph that afternoon, as Alvarez hoped fervently in his soul he would. What Joaquín Vidal had left out in his description of Rincón's manager after the triumph was that when Luis Alvarez levitated in the callejón with the face of a cherub, the cherub had a Havana cigar clamped confidently between his teeth.

While still in the callejón, Alvarez leaned up and spoke to Manolo Chopera in his first-row *barrera* seat. Manolo Chopera, with and for whom Alvarez had worked over the years, is the most important *empresario*, promoter, in the bull world, in control of a number of rings in the north of

Spain, the south of France, and Latin America. "César will torear tomorrow," he told Chopera.

"¿Sí?"

"¡Sí!"

Then Luis Alvarez went out to hail a cab to the Foxá where his torero was trying to make his way into the shower. Four years later Antonio Caballero's wife Cristina would tell me how they had been sitting right behind Chopera in his barrera seat that day. "Chopera was so excited he was leaning out over the wire cables to applaud for Rincón. Afterwards he turned to us and said, 'It's been twenty years since I've applauded a torero.'"

The way César Rincón tells it, he began to become emotional in the middle of the faena. He told Emilio Martínez from *El País:* "It had never happened to me before, but I was so happy and the emotion was so strong when I heard the olés and when I thought about my mother and my sister, helping me from heaven, that I broke into tears in the middle of my faena, and after that I hardly know what happened."

Then he did something very characteristic—he told Martínez he wanted to dedicate his success to two Colombian journalists who had been freed that day from Pablo Escobar's Medellín-based drug cartel that had been holding them hostage for months: "That way it's a great day for me and for my country, which is at a crucial moment in its history and needs any kind of good news it can get" (May 22, 1991).[1] From the very first moment of his triumph, César Rincón was concerned about Colombia's well-being and was identifying himself unselfconsciously with that well-being, becoming a kind of taurine ambassador for his country.

Room 803 of the Foxá is a small suite. With twenty people in the living room it seems crowded. On this chaotic night there were literally hundreds coming and going, mostly trying to get in. Lines backed up into the hallway. Control was difficult. Some of the wrong people got in and good friends were turned away. Others congregated downstairs at the narrow bar on the ground floor. Upstairs the phone rang constantly. People flooded in and out in the hot, tobacco-laden air, and camera flashes lit the room like heat lightning.

When Luis Alvarez arrived the journalists jumped him. More flashes popped as he smiled and lit a new Havana.

In Rincón's mind there was only the triumph. Santanerito had altered his destiny, he thought. "I went out on the shoulders of the crowd, me, the *indito* [little Indian], clutching in my hands the dearest ears of my life," he exclaimed later to French taurine writer Geneviève Fondeviole-Stefanuto. "In front of the television cameras that broadcast live to the farthest corners of the [Iberian] peninsula the live images of the apotheosis of a small anonymous Colombian, the first ever to cross the threshold of the Puerta Grande of the Plaza Monumental of Madrid. Unthinkable!" (34). His brother Luis Carlos ceaselessly repeated the phrase "You did it, César, you did it."

Luis Alvarez, above all, knew who had done it, and now he had to talk his torero into doing it again. Tomorrow.

Espartaco, the current *número uno* or top matador, was on the cartel along with veteran matador Francisco Ruiz Miguel, a longtime favorite in Madrid. Two years later, on one of our walks, César would tell me that Espartaco was the contemporary matador he most admired, because of his integrity as a person and because he had maintained his position as número uno for seven years. If Rincón could triumph again and in that company, argued Alvarez, no one could say that his success today had been just a lucky break. The offer was tempting to the torero, but he also realized it was tantamount to betting double-or-nothing. As Rincón tells it, Alvarez puffed on his enormous cigar and said, "You have to say yes, César" (F-S 35).

Hotel bathrooms are unsuspectedly important places in the lives of toreros. They are the bunkers, the last resort, the ultimate redoubt against the slings and arrows of outrageous public life. There in the bathroom of suite 803 were César Rincón, sitting on the edge of the tub, and Luis Alvarez, cigar enclamped, sitting on the toilet lid. There they made their most crucial decision. Alvarez argued that Madrid was somewhat hostile to Espartaco's status as a figura and that Ruiz Miguel's recent comeback had not been successful. A triumph on the same cartel would mean that César Rincón had risen from anonymity to stardom with *hegemonia,* with clout, in a period of roughly twenty-four *hours.* Such a rise was unprecedented. (The only possible comparison is Mexican matador Carlos Arruza's presentation in Madrid on July 18, 1944.)

While Rincón considered the situation, Alvarez reminded him that the Lozanos, the Madrid empresarios, needed an answer now. As Rincón tells it: "Finally we arrived at the decision that we had to accept. And I was in great shape, with a lot of sitio and plenty of morale. You have to go for it, as a torero you have no choice." But what if the bulls were bad and offered no chance for success? Alvarez promised to wangle another substitution, if necessary, and then left to sign the contract. Rincón says: "If I had bombed with the Murteira bulls the next day, they would have been after Luis Alvarez to strip him of his apoderado's credentials" (JV 247–48).

When Luis Alvarez finished the next day's contract, he joined Manolo Chopera and Chopera's son Pablo—Pablo and his brother Oscar, known by the malas lenguas as *los mastines*, the mastiffs, are the Chopera heirs apparent—in the intimate Basque seafood restaurant Kulixka on the Calle Fuencarral for a late supper, even by Madrid standards. Late but profitable: they arranged nineteen corridas for César Rincón in Chopera's plazas in Spain and France, and toward dawn Luis Alvarez said, "And if we go out the Puerta Grande today, the price doubles. Right?"

"Right!" said Chopera.

May 22, 1991

5

Long before Luis Alvarez headed for a couple of hours of sleep, the morning papers with their reviews of the corrida were on the street. Joaquín Vidal described Rincón as floating "amongst the white clouds of glory," meaning the thousands of handkerchiefs petitioning the two ears. Although, Vidal continued—playing on the Colombian novelist Gabriel García Márquez's style known as magical realism—it must have seemed like a dream to Rincón, "it wasn't a dream, it was reality. Possibly a magical reality." All that remained of a largely boring afternoon, according to Vidal, was that "magical reality of the present moment; the bull dominated, the dominating torero transforming into art his taurine passion. And the ring was an uproar" (*El País*, May 22, 1991).

Vicente Zabala, longtime critic for *ABC*, presciently called Rincón the "new César of toreo," recalling that the Venezuelan torero César Girón, from a previous generation, had also opened wide the doors of Las Ventas on the strength of his own merits. And he remarked that no one had handed Rincón his triumph: "In toreo, as in life, only sacrifice has reward" (May 22, 1991).

A general sense arose among the critics that Rincón's triumph was no fluke. Doubtless part of this sense of surety came from the fact that some of the critics had seen him in a tough corrida of Celestino Cuadri bulls in Madrid on the twenty-eighth of April in which he had acquitted himself well—well enough with difficult bulls to justify the single berth for San Isidro that Luis Alvarez had arranged. Some had seen him in Valencia the summer before when he had cut one ear in his first triumph in an important ring in Spain. And a few, such as Fernando Fernández Román of Televisión Española, had seen on video his triumphs in Colombia, where certain local critics, for example Oscar García Calderón, had been saying for some time that if Rincón could do in Madrid or Sevilla what he did in Cali or in Bogotá, he could own the world (JV 264).

And they were all correct. César Rincón had done it and had deserved it, but today, Wednesday, the question was: Could he do it again? Could anyone do it again? Taking the substitution could only mean that Rincón had unequivocally accepted the double-or-nothing bet.

What were the odds? Had anyone ever done it before? The Madrid afición wondered and tried to remember. Not two days in a row in San Isidro. Were César Rincón and Luis Alvarez crazy? Speculation built through the day like a summer thunderhead. To expect to triumph two days in a row was some kind of hubris; it was an affront to the taurine gods or divine providence. What if the Murteira bulls did not charge—what then? And chauvinism reared its horny taurine head: A Colombian, no matter how good he thought he was, against Francisco Ruiz Miguel, the specialist in difficult bulls, and Espartaco, the número uno? He'd be just like all the other Colombians. Pepe Cáceres never opened the portals of Madrid once. [In fact, he cut one ear, the only ear a Colombian matador had ever cut in a regulation corrida in Las Ventas, on April 29, 1962.] It was just too much to expect (I&B 113–14).

In those days one actually heard it said, categorically, that a mestizo could not become a figura del toreo.

This time the ring was full, and the *reventa*, the scalper's market, had an excellent day, especially with those they call *sudacas*, the derogatory term for South Americans, mostly Colombians who turned out to see their new national hero at any price. The best seats brought "close to a thousand dollars" (Caballero 153).

The bulls from the Portuguese ranch of Murteira came out less than ideal. An old taurine saying goes "Corrida de expectación, corrida de decepción," which means that the corrida you place your hopes on will let you down. The veteran torero Francisco Ruiz Miguel was applauded in his first bull but was unable to shine in his second. Espartaco, long persecuted by the Madrid público for being número uno and for being from the province of Sevilla, had a bad day, receiving whistles in his first and a full-fledged *bronca*—loud, insulting protestations—in his second. César Rincón earned an ovation in his first, a bull that would take only one pass at a time, making it impossible to ligar, but he went on too long and received an aviso from the presidente. With five bulls dead, it had been mostly decepción.

The last bull, Rincón's second, Alentejo by name, weighed 550 kilos, was black, deep in the chest, swaybacked, fat in the neck and morrillo, and had wide but not particularly long horns. In the cape he charged erratically, nearly catching Rincón against the fence. Like his brothers he showed himself to be manso with the horses, but he had a fine, easy gallop and carried himself well. In spite of his buoyancy, the crowd whistled at his *manse-dumbre,* his manso-ness, as he fled from the first several light picks. Rincón clearly did not have much faith in him.

Then in the last pick, Alentejo began to charge the horse more aggressively. And he nearly caught Monaguillo de Colombia, Rincón's longtime friend and banderillero (plate 2c), in the first and third pairs of sticks. Was Alentejo "coming up"?

Being unsure, Rincón did not dedicate the bull's life to the público of Madrid, a natural gesture of gratitude for his triumph the day before. But after the first couple of passes with the muleta he realized how good the now hard-charging bull had become, realized in fact that he might just have heaven's gate at hand again. The crowd, in a foul mood most of the afternoon, was instantly alert, and by the third and fourth passes the olés began to build, reaching a strong choral rhythm as Rincón finished an unbroken series of six derechazos with a right-handed chest pass and then a left-handed chest pass without moving a centimeter.

Now plainly confident, Rincón backed off ten meters to the center of the ring and cited the bull. Alentejo took one hesitant step, then charged the extended muleta at a gallop. Rincón waited until the bull had covered more than half the distance and then began to move the muleta slowly past his body. But Achilles never quite caught the tortoise. Rincón bent Alentejo into a wrenching half circle before releasing him, only to leave the muleta in the bull's face and link three more half circles. He finished with a brilliantly improvised pass that began as a chest pass but ended as an ayudado, smoothly transferring the muleta in mid-pass from his right hand to his left, as he forced Alentejo around his body in yet another, reversed, half-moon.

Pandemonium broke out in the ring as the público began to realize that César Rincón—*their* torero now with his triumphant breakthrough yesterday, a Madrid torero now—was about to do it again. (Had he been bad, his bronca might have equaled Espartaco's.) The olés rocked the ring with each pass. Now people were on their feet and the chant "¡To-re-ro! ¡To-re-ro!" echoed back and forth. To equal the magnitude of this triumph, Joaquín Vidal would write for the next day's *El País,* "you'd have to go back to the

Figure 7. Chest pass, Madrid, May 22, 1991. Classic beauty in the pase de pecho. Rincón's left arm and leg run parallel to Alentejo's rise after the muleta, and the animal has passed his entire length around the man, turning back toward the man's "opposite" shoulder. It was such classicism that rocked the foundations of Las Ventas. By permission, Botán.

distant times of the great maestros of tauromachy." On this second day of triumph "lifelong aficionados and transient spectators united their views" and "irreconcilable enemies hugged each other," according to Vidal, and he was not really exaggerating, merely pointing out the somewhat miraculous nature of Rincón's performance (May 23, 1991).

At this point Rincón cited with his left hand for naturales, the muleta unextended by the sword, the cloth freer, looser, more beautiful in its *vuelo,* its flight—and also smaller and consequently more dangerous. Approaching the bull from a fully frontal position, he extended the muleta as far as he could. Alentejo charged at once, following the vuelo of the muleta past and around the matador, and turned and charged to take three more impeccable naturales. Alentejo was turning quickly at the end of each pass, so Rincón dropped back two steps between passes, allowing the bull to come to the muleta, bury his head in its unfolding mystery, follow it through, and lose it on the other side.

Figure 8. Citing from a distance, Madrid, May 22, 1991. Citing from such a distance is the most striking feature in Rincón's repertoire. Notice, however, how here he is actually leading with his "opposite" leg, showing complete confidence in his ability to control the charge with the lure. By permission, Botán.

The rhythmical effect of these precisely timed passes gave the impression that Rincón was dancing with Alentejo. If there is anything about César Rincón's totally classical, which is to say totally Spanish, repertoire that is South American, it is this rhythmical linking of passes. The sense of dance, less a flourish than innate timing, is one of Rincón's natural gifts—he loves to dance, especially salsa—and in form he surpasses all the toreros I have ever seen at it. It is not simply a matter of linking the passes, but rather with the proper bull—Alentejo was that bull, buoyant and with *alegría*, happiness, in his charge—it is a matter of taurinely inspired choreography. To finish the series, Rincón swung into an exactingly timed chest pass that brought the crowd to its feet applauding while he almost waltzed away, smiling at the crowd, his back to the bull (except for the "tail of his eye," as they say in Spanish), leaving Alentejo bewildered and alone.

While Santanerito was doubtless more "important," Alentejo should not be underestimated, because he allowed the afición of Madrid to glimpse the seldom seen *alegre* or upbeat side of César Rincón's toreo. The next morning in *Diario 16* taurine critic Ignacio Alvarez Vara, Barquerito, would call Alentejo the bull of the feria.

As the cries of "¡To-re-ro, to-re-ro!" continued, Rincón finished the faena with a series of derechazos, citing from a distance, feet together, now deliberately dancing with Alentejo, and then, by contrast, another series of classic naturales that stood out for the way in which the matador approached to cite. Not only did he cite frontally, but he placed his left leg out in front of his right leg, so that he was actually leading with the *pierna contraria* or opposite leg, offering in the process his whole body as an alternative to the lure of the cloth. Alentejo took the lure then, and Rincón wrapped the animal around his waist, turning him in more than a half circle before finishing the pass behind his hip. This way of citing with the inside leg forward and rotating his waist backward in the direction of the pass is difficult to do, but it is characteristic of his toreo. What he lacks in length of arm and leg, Rincón makes up for in suppleness of waist, flexibility of wrist, and the valor to put

Figure 9. On the shoulders of the crowd again, Madrid, May 22, 1991. Not only had this unknown matador crossed the threshold of the "cathedral of toreo," now he had done it twice in twenty-four hours. Rincón was a sensation. The taurine world reeled. Las Ventas would never be the same. By permission, Botán.

himself serenely in that extreme frontal position. Weaving together three more naturales, he finished the series with a chest pass that finished Alentejo. As Rincón walked away to exchange his sword, he did not bother to look back—even with the tail of his eye.

With the killing sword now in hand, Rincón gave Alentejo a series of ayudados, citing again from a distance, lined the bull up, and cited twice to kill recibiendo. But Alentejo began to paw the ground defensively. The plaza held its breath as Rincón put in a virtually flawless volapié. Alentejo, mortally wounded, rose high up in the air on his hind feet, resisted momentarily, began to totter sideways, and then crashed over in a heap, all four legs in the air.

The ring was a delirium. Twenty-three thousand people were on their feet, waving those white clouds of glory, applauding and shouting "¡To-re-ro, to-re-ro!" Before the *alguacil*—the bailiff in eighteenth-century costume who is the presidente's representative in the ring—could give Rincón the ears of Alentejo, the matador was already hoisted on the shoulders of the crowd and had to lean over precariously to receive them. After two triumphal vueltas, accompanied by a rabble threatening to reach Goyaesque proportions, he left the ring on shoulders through the Puerta Grande with Alentejo's ears clutched firmly in his hands. The chants of "¡To-re-ro, to-re-ro!" followed him through the high horseshoe arch toward the Calle Alcalá, floating heavenward into the deepening indigo air.

The first *abrazo* or embrace for Luis Alvarez came from Manolo Chopera: "Hecho," said Chopera. "Done." As agreed in the early hours of that morning, Rincón's double-or-nothing bet had doubled again.

Night of May 22, 1991, and After

Room 803 at the Foxá was a madhouse again, but César Rincón was smiling this time. So was Luis Alvarez. Still, the first thing Rincón told Emilio Martínez of *El País* was that no matter how happy he was with his triumphs, he could not forget the thousands of innocent victims of violence in Colombia, victims of the *narcotráfico* and victims of *terrorismo:*[1] "I would like to dedicate this triumph to them."

When Martínez remarked that Rincón seemed more serene about his second triumphal trip through the Puerta Grande, the matador quipped, "I must be getting used to it, *hermano.*"

Rincón went on to say that he was beginning to believe the dream of his double triumph, but that he owed a lot to support from the público too. Martínez asked him if he had taught Espartaco a lesson and Rincón replied: "Well, maybe I was luckier in the bulls I drew and in my treatment by the afición. They were hard on him." And then, not wishing to appear too modest, he added: "The truth is I did win today, and it wasn't just luck. I was more 'decided' and had more *torería* [taurine comportment, valor], but he's still the maximum figura, the número uno."

Rincón claimed that he did not aspire yet to the position of número uno and that, for the moment, he was happy to be the best of the sudamericanos. Then he added, perhaps jokingly: "But the Spaniards had better watch it, eh?" (*El País*, May 23, 1991). Espartaco, always a gentleman, was more succinct. As Luis Alvarez remembers it, Espartaco told Colombian radio: "From all the evidence, it is César Rincón who holds the scepter of toreo" (F-S 129).

Rincón, it seems, was as capable of walking the tightwire of public opinion as he was adept in handling the bulls. It was just as well, because now César Rincón was a media event, and an international one at that. In Spain the general public knew virtually nothing about him, an ideal situation that only added to his emerging status.

A critic in the taurine weekly *Aplausos* wrote that Rincón had beaten the Chief, and that, not to cast aspersions on anyone, Rincón had earned it, as well as earning a new kind of record for San Isidro. Who, the critic wondered, had gone out the Puerta Grande twice in any single San Isidro? Chicuelo II, he answered, in 1954, Litri and Puerta and El Viti in 1966, Paco Camino in 1967, Angel Teruel in 1969, El Cordobés in 1970, Paco Ojeda in 1983, Manili in 1988, perhaps someone else—but two days *in a row,* "absolutely no one. No torero can take that honor away from Rincón" (I&B 115).

I cite this commentary at length not merely to single out Rincón's feat but also to make another point. The toreros listed above, all Spanish, were already famous figuras or at least very well known to the afición, having had the whole span of their careers well publicized in Spain. César Rincón, on the other hand, was a novelty and a mystery. Like a foreign knight from across the sea who triumphs in the jousts, or an unknown athlete who wins in the games, Rincón had the double-edged attraction and repulsion of alterity, of the *other.* When he was good, he was everyone's champion, especially Madrid's. But later on when he was not as good, or when he was unlucky, he would be—for a sometimes distressingly large segment of the público—that Colombian *hijo de puta,* the Spanish equivalent of "son of a bitch."

César has talked to me about this ambivalence toward him, and what he said bears recording here because it colors much of what follows: "Cuando estoy bien, me gritan, '¡Torero, torero!' Cuando estoy mal, me gritan, '¡Colombiano! ¡Hijo de puta!'" [When I'm good, they shout, '¡Torero, torero!' When I'm bad, they shout, 'Colombian! Son of a bitch!']. It disturbs him, of course, to be called hijo de puta—even though at some point they all get called that—but having the insult attached to his nationality adds another dimension to the affront.

Part of Rincón's triumph was doubtless due to the contrast between his spectacularly honest toreo and the state of affairs in Madrid when he literally burst onto the scene. Barquerito put it this way: "All the rage that the Madrid plaza is capable of voicing . . . suddenly reversed in favor of the torero from Bogotá, shortly after having been vented on Espartaco and Ruiz Miguel, with neither rhyme nor reason" (I&B 116). Perhaps not rhyme or reason that specific day, but there can be little doubt that the general mood at the Madrid ring was and had been one of deep dissatisfaction, and not solely in Seven.

Carlos Abella, another critic for *Diario 16,* phrased the situation somewhat differently. Praising Rincón's impassioned success, he was impressed with his sincerity, his bravery, his clairvoyance, his polished technique, his variety, his *hombría* (manliness), his honesty, and his utter lack of self-importance. Rincón put forward that opposite leg and left it there, in the place where the bulls give *cornadas,* gorings, the place where the *cortijos*—the country estates, the bull ranches—are earned, and where it is so difficult to make the leg stay still. "How unaccustomed we were!" (I&B 116–17).

Vicente Zabala was struck by Rincón's self-assurance and by the combination of guts and humility with which he had accepted the substitution, risking the annulment of the previous day's success. Right then, by not refusing the Madrid ring, Zabala reckoned, Rincón's meteoric rise, scaling the heights of taurine success, had begun. César Rincón was not playing games of strategy simply to position himself well in his own country. He wished to demonstrate that his triumph the afternoon before was not a stroke of luck.

Extolling Rincón's clarity of vision, his serenity in the face of danger, his knowledge and responsibility, Zabala pointed out that Rincón's performance was hardly a matter of temerity, which is "circumstantial, momentary, and irrational." The history of toreo is plagued with men who were brave for a day, "heroes of one afternoon or only one bull." The difficult thing, as in Rincón's case, was "uniformity, keeping a clear head," the ability to "sustain the beautiful battle" of wills (*ABC,* May 23, 1991).

Later in the week, in his column in *Aplausos,* Zabala would write: "I do not know if [Rincón] will maintain himself in this posture [of success], but one thing is very clear. Anyone who wants to rev up the engines, set the público on fire and have a sterling triumph, had better come out like this Colombian does" (I&B 118).

Writing in *El Mundo de los Toros,* another taurine periodical, "Don Quijote" tried to put Rincón's success into perspective. Toreros from the other side of the Atlantic would come, torear one season or two at most, take the *alternativa* for promotion to full matador after having been on the bill in four *pueblos* (villages), and then go home. Where were the Gaonas, Arruzas, Armillitas, Garzas—the Mexican heroes of yesteryear? And so, he wrote, we Spaniards went along needing the torero who could compete with our own until here he came with a Colombian passport. "He's not a dreamer, he's a realist. He's just seduced the whole of Spanish afición. He's had the un-heard-of audacity to exit on shoulders through the Gate of Madrid (which is what the Puerta Grande is called in Madrid) when not twenty-four hours had passed since his previous triumph. His name is César Rincón and he's more than the very Caesar himself. In his hands he carries two ears, when he just put down the two from the day before" (I&B 119).

The night of his second triumph, in an interview with Charo Noguera for *El País*—this time not the taurine section but the back-page celebrity section "Gente" or "People"—Rincón remarked: "Only about twenty-four hours ago I was asking everybody as a favor to put me on in some ring. Now I have to say: 'Wait a minute.' My life has been utterly transformed."

Admitting he could not contain the tears of emotion the afternoon before, Rincón said, "I couldn't believe it was really happening to me. 'Now I won't be a nobody,' I thought. 'The empresarios won't be so reluctant to give me contracts.' Then when I accepted the substitution, the whole thing started to become more real. Those shouts of '¡Torero, torero!' were the most beautiful I've ever heard in my life."

Reflecting, Rincón admitted that fame was "like a bucket of water. It leaves you pretty wet but you want it so much."

He was also very aware that "they'll always want me to be the same, but a torero is an artist and you can't always be equally inspired." And he reiterated his feelings about his country: "I think that with all that is happening to me I can help to change the bad reputation that we Colombians have because of the narcotráfico and the guerrilla warfare." Charo Noguera commented that "it was not in vain that [Rincón] declared himself a pacifist."

There was one slightly somber note in the interview. Reflecting on his sudden fame, the newest celebrity in the *planeta de los toros*[2] demurred that triumph also had its bitter side: "One feels alone in his happiness," he remarked, quite characteristically as I would find (May 23, 1991).

On Sunday, May 26, 1991, another interview with César Rincón hit the back page of *El País*, this time by Feliciano Fidalgo, who began his slick piece by drawing back the curtain of anonymity as "a legend began to walk."

Fidalgo read Rincón a passage from the beginning of Gabriel García Márquez's *One Hundred Years of Solitude* and wondered: Was that the magic of his toreo? And Rincón responded with a candor that belied his interviewer's malice: "Such beautiful words! What more could I wish than that my toreo could be like that!"

When asked why he had not dedicated a bull to his deceased mother, Rincón replied, "Because that is an homage I feel in my heart, always."

Here are some other interesting pieces of the interview:

Q: Would you prefer death or mediocrity?
A: Death is better.
Q: How did the multitude of Las Ventas excite you?
A: My hair stood on end when they shouted "¡Torero!"
Q: How much money did you have the day before the corrida?
A: That's funny. I had to ration everything.
Q: With all the money in the world, would you still torear?
A: I don't know.
Q: Are prayers worthwhile?
A: Very much. I commended myself to God and to my mother.
Q: How many women have tempted you after your success?
A: None, so far.
Q: Would you marry a princess?
A: I already have one [his fiancée, Sandra Briceño, in Bogotá].
Q: Is what you did in Las Ventas like an apparition of the Virgin?
A: Maybe a miracle.
Q: Does fear consume one?
A: If you could weigh it, there would be no scales big enough.
Q: What is Rinconismo?
A: That word whispers in my ear. It's incredible.
Q: What happens to you toreando?
A: I live, I enjoy what I'm doing, I fulfill my dreams, and I am very afraid.
Q: What kind of child were you?
A: I had no childhood, no time to play.
Q: What did your father say when he heard?
A: He cried.
Q: Does your triumph help you sleep?
A: I haven't slept in days.
Q: Been partying these last nights?
A. I haven't had time.
Q: What is a toro?
A: A friend of the torero, the one who can make you great.
Q: Is Spain the mother country or the wicked mother?
A: The mother country. Colombia comes from Colón [Columbus].
Q: Will you become Spanish?
A: No.

Q: Are you more macho now?

A: No, I'm the same.

Q: What do you want most?

A: To be able to retire at the right moment and to enjoy the money I hope to have earned.

Surprise in Granada

On Thursday, May 30, 1991, at the behest of Michael Wigram, I left Narixa and drove the then perilous highway through the spectacular gorge of the Guadalfeo, around the southern and western flanks of the Sierra Nevada, over the pass known as the Moor's Last Sigh—where the mother of weeping Boabdil remarked that he did well to weep like a woman for what he could not defend as a man—and down, now on the new divided highway toward the broad, rich vega of Granada and into the city.

The Feria de Granada has long been one of Michael Wigram's favorites, and this year he was covering it for the new taurine publication 6 Toros 6 (the classic posters for corridas always advertise something such as "6 magníficos toros 6" with the number fore and aft), with which he was associated. Taurine revistas, periodicals, come and go with some frequency, but during the years I followed César Rincón, 6T6, as it is usually abbreviated, would grow under the direction of José Carlos Arévalo and his associates into the dominant taurine publication in the world, first as a monthly, then a biweekly, and finally as a weekly. 6T6 was just beginning as Rincón ascended, so they have documented virtually all of his European career.

From the balcony of the hotel on the Alhambra hill, I could see the entire city below and the green vega beyond, where Federico García Lorca was born and spent his early childhood. To the south rose the white wall of the Sierra Nevada, the highest mountain range in Spain. It was a bright, sunny day and the fireworks for the Corpus Christi celebration made light puffs of smoke in the dazzling clarity over the city. On such a day it was easy to understand why the Muslims had believed Paradise was in the skies above Granada.

I lunched with Michael Wigram, Irene Martínez Capriles, and Charles Patrick Scanlan at a taurine restaurant aptly named the Posada del Duende, a name that could not fail to evoke the spirit of García Lorca, who was the greatest exponent of *duende,* the dark, earthy, Dionysian spirit that lies at the center of Spanish and especially Andalusian art.

In *Totem and Taboo* Freud writes of the gathering of the clan for the ritual meal, and that is precisely what this lunch was. In our clan—*la gente del toro,* the people of the bull (aficionados', critics', and writers' branch)—we gather every season from the far corners of the western world, in this case England and Venezuela and the United States, though many other countries are frequently involved, for a ritual meal preceding or following the sacrificial rites. And the meal is as important as the sacrifice; in fact, as in antiquity, it is sometimes inseparable from it.

After a long lunch and much taurine conversation, we walked across town, had coffee at a bar just below the plaza de toros, and went in early to avoid the inevitable last-minute rush. The cartel seemed reasonably promising: the veterans of Sevilla, Emilio Muñoz and Espartaco, along with Jesulín, the gangly *gaditano* (from the province of Cádiz) who had recently taken his alternativa, with bulls of Peralta. But inside at the small bar we received a surprise. "No torea Jesulín. Torea César Rincón," we were told: Jesulín will not torear. Rincón will.

It was a better afternoon than we could have expected. Emilio Muñoz did little to remember, but Espartaco was excellent with his second bull, a large chestnut-colored animal from which he cut an ear, showing everyone why he had been número uno for so many years.

The público in Granada has plenty of afición, and obviously many of those around me in Tendido Six had seen César Rincón on television. Both of his faenas on Corpus Cristi were reminiscent of his performances in Madrid, crossing to cite, citing *de frente* (frontally), citing from a distance. His classicism was favorably received and he cut a well-deserved ear on his first bull.

His second bull was another *castaño* (chestnut) and Rincón was even better with it, "connecting" with the público, somehow combining with no trace of vulgarity the strictest classicism and the valor of the "gladiators." Michael Wigram would compare him in his "chronicle" in *6T6* to the torero of the '6os, Diego Puerta, who was often called Diego Valor because he was so brave (3:64).

But beyond Rincón's valor, there was his sense of proportion, of art, of doing everything properly yet at the same time withholding nothing. This latter quality is called *entrega,* and in toreo it means selfless and unselfconscious giving of oneself in spite of the danger. Rincón has as much of it as any great torero I have ever seen, and more than most toreros except for the suicidal *tremendistas,* the perennial sensationalists who are almost always vulgar, clownish, or stupid as well, qualities that pollute their entrega.

Seeing Rincón live that first time, but not yet having in mind doing a book on him, I realized that he was one of the greatest toreros I had ever had the pleasure to watch, perhaps, for me, the greatest. He showed the classical aesthetics of Paco Camino. He had the sense of distance and terrain, again classically conceived, of Antoñete. He possessed the valor of Diego Puerta. And he demonstrated the *pundonor,* the honor that comes from self-respect, of El Viti, a quality that Rincón often refers to as *responsabilidad,* responsibility to the público, to his sense of art, and above all to his own sense of taurine and personal integrity. And my favorite toreros had always been Paco Camino, Antoñete, and El Viti, with Diego Puerta close because of his entrega and valor. Rincón also had a natural vibrancy all his own, an indomitable and tenacious presence that would not give in or give up, and a personal way of connecting with the público. In spite of his modesty, honesty, and lack of *fanfarronería* (showing off), he could instantly turn hot, emotionally and physically hot, without looking vulgar. And that heat, that glowing, spontaneous, impassioned vibrancy, has a very direct appeal to the público. His eyes even seem to change color, going from café con leche to a darker, sometimes burning brown, almost black. To put it in the simplest theatrical terms, while never holding back, he does not overact. A taurine critic would say he has charisma, that he is a torero *emocionante,* one that produces emotion in the público.

Now in Granada, as Rincón prepares to kill, I feel some of the unconditional emotions an aficionado feels at such a time: elation, apprehension, awe, the mysterious collective sense of triumph of which you feel a small but integrated part, and the personal sense of victory you feel when "your torero" has done it. When it is your torero, there is no little sense of vicarious accomplishment as well. And he was, I realized that day, my torero. After this corrida Michael Wigram would always speak to me quite naturally of Rincón as your torero.

But it was not as though I had chosen him. It was not a conscious process; it was rather something that I gradually became aware of, more as if he had chosen me, a logical impossibility, I know. Nevertheless that is how it felt and, besides, one does not "adopt" a torero for logical reasons, any more than one chooses a close friend or a mate for logical reasons. In toreo reason has nothing to do with it.

Rincón cites, crosses, and places a flawless volapié high up in between the withers of the brave castaño. Then, in rapid succession, the bull is staggering, the crowd is standing, the matador is facing the bull with his hand up in triumph, the bull is stumbling and going down, and thousands of white doves are taking wing over the stands as Rincón retrieves the sword, taking the slightest bow.

He is awarded an ear but denied the second in spite of an insistent petition. No one can understand why the presidente refuses the second ear, which is as justified as it had been both times in Madrid. Nor is this the last time a presidente will capriciously deny César Rincón the full award. It does not matter much this time: he is on the shoulders of the crowd, having cut the requisite two ears, and he is once again going out the Puerta Grande.

Corrida de la Beneficencia

The 1991 season had begun with the usual jostling for position among the top matadors. Espartaco was reckoned to be the número uno for the seventh or eighth year. Paco Ojeda, the revolutionary sensation of the early '80s, was out of retirement and considered strong again. Niño de la Capea, or Capea as he is often called, was another of the "monsters of toreo." Manzanares, the great artist, was always a factor. The young *ídolo* of Madrid, Joselito (plate 5b), could sweep the season if things went right for him—if, as they say in taurine argot, "the bulls respected him." But a funny thing happened.

In the first important feria of the year, in Castellón, veteran matador José Ortega Cano—who had made news by walking the pilgrimage route of the Camino de Santiago (the Way of Saint James, which stretches across Spain from the Pyrenees to Santiago de Compostela in the far northwest) instead of going to América for the lucrative ferias of Lima and Quito, Cali and Bogotá, Manizales and Cartagena de Indias—had a miraculous (some said) resurgence and "broke through" on his second bull, cutting two ears. He repeated the feat in the next feria, at Las Fallas in Valencia in March—two ears on his second bull—and was *triunfador* (most successful matador) in both ferias. He followed with a succession of triumphs in small towns, culminating in a "magical" faena with the bull Espanto from Juan Pedro Domecq in Sevilla's Feria de Abril. This triumph—the faena of his life, according to critics and matadors alike—was an ironic one because Ortega Cano had not even been contracted for Sevilla, but was substituting for Capea, who had been gored three days before as he went in to kill a difficult Cebada Gago bull.

Only three days before Capea's goring, Emilio Muñoz, Sevilla's eternal hope, had also been gored. So, coming into San Isidro, the picture looked a little bleak. Espartaco could not "find himself." Joselito and Jesulín, the other young star, had both performed poorly in Sevilla. Capea and Muñoz were hurt. The season was something of a shambles.

Ortega Cano had another important triumph in Zaragoza, cutting three ears, and Jesulín was gored. The nearly month-long marathon of corridas began in Madrid and went on and on: Capea, Manzanares, Joselito, Ojeda, Espartaco, and two dozen second-stringers. Of the Spaniards, only Ortega Cano came through strongly, on an afternoon when he could have cut three ears but had to content himself with tours of the ring owing to faulty sword work. When it was all over, Juan Mora, Ortega Cano, Enrique Ponce (plate 5a), the Mexican Eloy Cavazos, and the Portuguese matador Víctor Mendes had each cut one ear.

And César Rincón—with four ears—was unmistakably the triunfador of San Isidro.

So as the Corrida de Beneficencia, frequently the most prestigious corrida of the year, approached, it began to be apparent that the obvious choice for the cartel was a *mano a mano*[1] between two toreros who at the beginning of the season nobody would have given a *duro* (nickel) for, the one a veteran surely on his way down, the other an unknown foreigner. But such is the unpredictable planet of the bulls.

There was only one problem with this cartel. The Centro de Asuntos Taurinos (Taurine Affairs Center) of the Comunidad de Madrid (the Madrid provincial government), which sponsored the Beneficencia—theoretically a benefit corrida for a selected cause—had previously objected to the Lozanos' inclusion of an unknown Colombian matador in San Isidro. And now they had to go, on bended knee, with hat in hand and foot in mouth, to plead with Luis Alvarez to allow his torero to appear.

As Rincón explained it, "The first problems arose with my being included in the Feria of San Isidro. The Comunidad de Madrid criticized the inclusion of my name in the carteles when they went over them with the co-empresarios, the Lozano brothers"—in theory the Comunidad shares the responsibility with the Lozanos, although the Lozanos do all the actual planning of the program—"but finally they respected my name," which means they did not force his exclusion.

Rincón went on to explain that the Comunidad de Madrid had asked him repeatedly to appear in the Beneficencia, that Luis Alvarez had said no several times, and that finally the representatives of the comunidad had offered "la 'plata' más fuerte [the highest price] ever paid to a torero in the most important plaza in the world"—an offer, in essence, he could not refuse (*6T6* 3:17).

Several years later in Bogotá, Luis Alvarez would confirm to me that the price paid including the television rights was 22.5 million pesetas. An article in the *Los Angeles Times* on July 9, 1991, bylined Richard Boudreaux, quoted the price as $175,000, exactly the amount Alvarez had told me. It does not surprise me that Alvarez remembered it, but I think it is interesting that Mr. Boudreaux was able to get the precise figure at the time. At any rate, that was the price: $175,000.[2]

The duel in the sun, as the press sometimes calls it, took place on June 6. The bulls were from the prestigious *ganadería* or bull ranch of Samuel Flores. King Juan Carlos I and his mother, the Condesa de Barcelona, were in the *palco real*, the royal box. On a sunny afternoon, the Madrid afición turned out, elegantly dressed for the gala occasion, and filled the ring to capacity. The flags of Spain and Madrid flew over the plaza, and the flag of Colombia was draped over the railing in the *andanada de sol*, the highest tier of seats on the sunny side. Unfortunately the flags were flapping in the persistent breeze that blew a little too hard all afternoon. As the old taurine proverb has it, the wind is the worst enemy.

An hour into the corrida very little had happened. Ortega Cano's first bull had casta but was weak in the legs and somewhat *soso*, insipid, charging with little conviction. Ortega Cano, bothered by the wind and the bull's persistent swinging of the head, perhaps lacked conviction as well. Rincón's first was sent back as *inválido*,[3] a bull too weak to stay in the ring. So was the *sobrero*, the reserve bull. The fourth bull was then moved up to second position, but this one was worse than Ortega Cano's first, often refusing to charge, despite Rincón's nearly morbid insistence. The wind bothered Rincón as well, making the cape and muleta flap unaesthetically and, had the bull been more aggressive, dangerously. As it was, just before he died, the bull managed to nick Rincón in the left ankle.

In that first hour, the most interesting part had been the gracious *brindis* (dedication) by the two *diestros* (swordsmen) to the King, customary on such an occasion and carried off in both instances with unusual aplomb. Ortega Cano said: "Majesty: I wish to dedicate the death of this bull to the brotherhood that exists this afternoon between Colombia and Spain, of which you are the main representative. Va por usted [a set phrase, similar to 'This one's for you']." César Rincón, in turn, said: "Your Majesty: It is an immense pleasure to dedicate the death of this bull to you for what you represent for our country, Colombia, since the blood we have we owe to all of you. My pleasure."

Each of the dedications was followed with the ritual comic interlude—watched with raptorial attention by 46,000 eyes—of tossing the montera up to the high palco real and into the outstretched hands of His Majesty. Both the King and his mother were aficionados, she more than he. The Condesa, despite being confined to a wheelchair, attended many corridas before her death in 1999, always occupying the palco real. The King can sometimes be seen in the barrera in the company of friends such as today's *ganadero* or breeder, Samuel Flores.

So far, Samuel Flores's bulls had a nearly impeccable presentation. They were *aleonados* (built like lions, long and lean), deep-chested yet low in the shoulders, with huge forward-pointing horns, very typical of their Parladé *encaste*.[4] Up until now, however, their appearance had been deceiving and it had begun to look like the classic afternoon of toreros without toros. Rincón's first two animals, the ones sent back, had been notably weak, the first falling three times like a huge dark sack of potatoes, the second crippled with a broken front hoof. When Ortega Cano's second bull, in third position although in fact the fifth bull to enter the ring, trotted in, however, events took an unexpected turn.

Solitario looked like his brethren, but he took three strong picks, putting up plenty of resistance. Ortega Cano then proceeded to do the best faena out of the hundred or so of his I have seen. He has the ability to be an inspired classic torero but often performs in a self-conscious, overly theatrical way, playing hard to the gallery. On this day, however, and especially in this faena, Ortega Cano abandoned his poses and his overacting, and combined temple and inspiration to achieve a natural and graceful work of art. He killed recibiendo on the first thrust, inching the sword in ever so slowly, even though he sidestepped slightly at the last moment, and he cut both ears from Solitario, earning the unanimous applause of the público.

César Rincón thrives on competition and hates to lose. In the decidedly competitive framework of a mano a mano, he now found himself up against a guaranteed Puerta Grande for Ortega Cano, regardless of what the Spanish matador did with his last bull. Ortega Cano had been lucky to draw Solitario, a bull with great class and a frank charge, but he had also known exactly how to handle it. As he remarked afterwards, "A very good bull. And a very good torero, no?" Toreros are seldom known for their modesty.

Tomillero—number 37, the once-sixth bull now moved up to fourth, black, weighing 505 kilos and sporting a pair of horns so large they gave him the top-heavy ungainliness of a bull elk—lacked the strength of Solitario, but he was going to have to do. Rincón received him with verónicas done in the style of Sevilla, his feet together and his hands low. The olés were thunderous. In his first quite, Rincón gave three *chicuelinas,*[5] each from a distance, his body spinning against the flow of the cape (plate 54). He ended with a sculpted *revolera,*[6] drawing the cape out from under the bull's muzzle and swirling it around his waist. Then as he left the bull at the horse with a perfect larga, someone unfurled a large Colombian flag in Tendido Seven. The happiness of a great taurine afternoon was beginning to settle over Las Ventas. Even the wind seemed to take a break now and then.

Monaguillo de Colombia, whose name is Rodrigo Arias (*monaguillo* means altarboy), put in two pairs of banderillas in stunning style, both times bringing his feet and arms together almost in the bull's face, leaning out over the "terrible balcony" of the horns as from high over his own head he drove home the shafts, spinning away at the last instant. Monaguillo had to remove his montera to acknowledge the applause, but he did so only after Rincón—who had caped the bull into position himself, so intent was he on this bull's being correctly handled—gave him permission.

There was a moment when, if you watched Monaguillo's eyes, you could see that he was pleased by the applause but trying not to show his reaction until he got the sign from the matador. When the sign did come, a great smile washed over Monaguillo's face and he relaxed into the applause. Rincón walked over and gave him a hug and a kiss on the cheek as the applause continued to thunder above them, the público all on their feet now. It was already beginning to smell like a grand triumph.

Rincón dedicated Tomillero's death to the Colombian journalist Francisco Santos. "Pacho" Santos, son of Hernando Santos, the director of Bogotá's most important paper, *El Tiempo,* had just been released from 244 days' captivity by Colombian drug lord Pablo Escobar. Pacho Santos was one of ten journalists held hostage—two of whom had died—to blackmail the Colombian government in a year-long horror described by Gabriel García Márquez in his account of the entire affair, *News of a Kidnapping,* as "only one episode of the Biblical holocaust that has consumed Colombia for more than twenty years" (8). To say that this dedication was poignant—Pacho Santos was one of the two journalists, the last ones freed, to whom Rincón had wished to dedicate his first success on the evening of May 21—would hardly do the moment justice. To the millions of Colombians watching the corrida on television, no words could have surpassed what Rincón said with his characteristic straightforwardness: "Pachito, it's a great pleasure to have you here, after eight months in captivity, enjoying a corrida. It's the most beautiful thing in the world, and I hope we can have you here many times at the bulls. This one's for you." It is hard to imagine what crossed the mind of Hernando Santos, who had never expected to see his son alive.

Rincón began the faena with *estatuarios*—statuary passes, so called because the matador does not move. It is a high pass, done with both hands, taking the bull under the muleta, and with the right bull it looks spectacular. He continued with derechazos, characteristically citing from a distance, and naturales, citing de frente. After several series of four or five passes, Rincón began another series of naturales, the first two of which were smoothly executed, passing the bull close to his body and leading the animal to well behind his hip. At this point the plaza was "like water for chocolate," just about to boil over. In the third pass, as Rincón crossed in front and cited, Tomillero started to put his head down to charge, then stopped, his head now raised, looking directly at the man's body. Rincón kept the muleta exactly where it was with the bull virtually on top of him. Tomillero looked straight at Rincón and Rincón did not move. Then, because the muleta was nearer and because the man did not move, Tomillero lowered his head and continued his charge as Rincón led him past. The público, already in a state of excitement, bellowed its approval, and Rincón turned to give the bull the chest pass, only to have Tomillero stop again and jerk his head up just under Rincón's chest, his right horn coming within inches of the matador's face. Now the crowd literally boiled over, surging to its feet. Once again with his classical passes and stoic valor César Rincón had won them over—had, as the taurine phrase has it, "put them in his pocket."

Rincón lined the bull up and drove straight in over the horn, running the sword in to the hilt. Tomillero caught the muleta crossing in front of him with his right horn and tossed it high in the air. Then, mortally wounded, he turned slowly in circles and settled on his knees. Rincón looked up at the crowd as handkerchiefs began to blossom like sudden jasmine flowers, and a small smile of incredulity passed over his face. In the broad daylight of a June afternoon, in the most important ring in the world, in front of television cameras broadcasting live to Spain and Mexico and South America, César Rincón had cut two ears from a brave bull in his third consecutive appearance.

Rincón was in such a daze as he limped to the barrera, he forgot to retrieve his montera from Pacho Santos. His brother Luis Carlos motioned for him to go get it. Sheepishly, but very pleased with himself, he turned and walked, limpingly but deliberately, across the sand as shouts of "¡Torero!

Figure 10. Stoic valor, Madrid, June 6, 1991. Although Tomillero is crowding him, Rincón cedes nothing. By permission, Botán.

¡Torero!" echoed around the ring, and on the sunny side the crowd clapped in the Gypsy beat of a *bulería*, something the Madrid ring rarely does.

Back at the barrera Rincón told commentator Federico Arnás, "Yes, it was quite a feat, but I don't ever want to back out of a fight [competition with Ortega Cano]. I am very determined and I too am going to be a figura del toreo. The bull was testing me, and I had to wait him out." Not only was he becoming a figura, he was rewriting taurine history in the process.

As Rincón took his triumphal tour of the ring with Tomillero's ears, he carried slung over his shoulder a woman's purse that had been thrown to him. Attached to the purse was a long silk scarf in the colors of the Colombian flag. The mano a mano was tied: Spain, two ears; Colombia, two ears. But the afternoon was not over.

Ortega Cano received his last bull—Flauta by name, heavy in the horn, black like all his brothers, and weighing 536 kilos—with four verónicas and a larga as beautiful as anything I had ever seen him do with the cape. In the third verónica you could actually see him slow the tempo so that the pass seemed to float by in slow motion, and his one-handed remate was rendered in liquid sculpture. Then he took Flauta to the picador with four walking chicuelinas, never missing a step, and left the bull placed for the pick by improvising a half chicuelina, snatching the cape out from under the bull's nose and leaving him targetless in front of the horse. The applause never stopped as Ortega Cano went on to execute a quite of verónicas and a *media verónica*, a half verónica that closes upon itself, doubling the animal around the man, with his feet together in the style of the retired Sevilla artist Pepe Luis Vázquez, not so much showing off as displaying an inspired mastery of styles.

After the second pick, Rincón took his quite and, not to be outdone, performed two rarely seen *tijerillas*—the scissors pass, so called because the arms cross like scissors as the matador inverts the cape, leading with the inside arm—and finished with a revolera, adding an extra turn to it at the end.

The quites had turned into a contest, and out jumped Ortega Cano to do chicuelinas so close that the bull nearly knocked him down on the first pass. When Flauta resisted charging for the second, Ortega Cano took off his montera and gently lobbed it in the bull's direction. Flauta took a swipe at it and charged, allowing Ortega Cano to get off two more chicuelinas and a media verónica, which he followed by going to one knee directly in front of the bull's nose. As Ortega Cano knelt, his head on a level with Flauta's foamy muzzle, Flauta blinked, towering over the matador, twitched, quivered, dripped foam, and regarded Ortega Cano almost quizzically. But the bull stayed in place, and Ortega Cano defiantly remained kneeling and looked up at the tendidos. Then as Ortega Cano walked to the callejón, the entire plaza rose to its feet and Rincón came out to give Ortega Cano an abrazo.

Ortega Cano's faena seemed less spectacular than his cape work, but it earned him another ear in spite of his having to use the *descabello*, the short sword used to sever the spinal cord, twice. And two or three of his passes, done with great temple, approached the sublime, so that even though his kill was not perfect, the público felt in the mood to award the ear, an extravagance the presidente had to accept as the petition clearly exceeded the necessary majority.[7]

Rincón doubtless saw himself as behind again in spite of his triumph in the previous bull. He would cut an ear from the last bull at whatever price. And the last bull came sixth, of course, precisely the numerical position of the bulls from which he had cut two ears in his previous triumphs. In the ultrasuperstitious planet of the bulls, everyone understands such numerological reasoning. No hay quinto malo, they say, for example: No fifth bull is bad.

If César Rincón had cut ears in the sixth two times before, he knew the público would expect him to do it again, or at least to cut one as Ortega Cano had done. In Colombia they would depend on it. And therein lies the greatest yet most natural perversity of the taurine public. A matador, perhaps more than any public figure, is expected always to reach or to surpass his own peaks of achievement. The hero must forever be heroic—and if possible more heroic than ever before—or perish in the process. Not to do so is to fall from grace.

The eighth bull of the afternoon, in sixth position, bore the name Colito. He carried the number 8 and weighed 543 kilos. High in the shoulder, dusty black and streaked in chestnut, with upward-pointing horns, a thick neck, and a long face, he also turned out to be a dangerous manso, although the degree of his mansedumbre would not show until later.

In the first pass the bull pursued the cape with such force that he elicited a collective gasp from the crowd. In two successive passes he lunged upward after the cape. In the third verónica he ripped the cape from Rincón's hands.

In the horse, Colito appeared violent but not brave, banging away at the picador's stirrup and attempting to get away. Neither Rincón nor Ortega Cano could make a pass in the quite and Rincón was nearly gored. After two more picks, Colito remained violent and had a persistent tendency to swing his head in every direction.

As Ortega Cano had dedicated the fifth bull to the público and Rincón had not yet done so, he gallantly marched out to the center of the ring and offered Colito's life to the afición of Madrid. What, wondered seasoned aficionados, could he possibly do with this violent and unpredictable bull?

Colito turned out worse than anyone had expected. But instead of having a rough charge, after two inconclusive series of passes the bull retreated to the barrera and refused to come away. So Rincón, himself refusing defeat, took the battle to the bull and the bull to the wall.

A manso feels protected by the *tablas*, the fence. There he goes on the defensive, not wanting to leave his *querencia*—the territory where he feels least insecure. Rincón, seeing that Colito had become intractably committed to the barrera, daringly chose to try to force the bull to charge the muleta back and forth between himself and the fence. Instead of simply killing the bull, Rincón devised a way to make the animal's refusal to leave the tablas work to his own advantage, intuiting that while Colito would not leave the fence, he might charge along the fence.

First he gave the bull a derechazo. Then, as the animal turned back on him, without changing his position Rincón made a right-handed pase de pecho, followed by another derechazo, still without moving. Finally, changing hands behind his back, he forced Colito into a natural, followed by a pase de pecho with the left. Five passes, five strangely linked passes without moving, back and forth almost in figure eights, through an alleyway he had created himself, knowing that there and only there would Colito charge. The fence played the hard place and his own body the rock. The Madrid ring could not believe its eyes and swept to its feet in applause as the series ended.

I think of that ploy as an example of a man's intelligence, inspiration, bravery, and will triumphing where a triumph seemed impossible. Those five passes partook of the essence of toreo—making the bull go where the bull does not want to go—and especially of César Rincón's toreo: It was his will against Colito's. And Rincón won. That series—remember that Colito was not only an unpredictable manso but also still strong and violent—remains for me one of the high points of César Rincón's career. Out of intransigent animal force and negation, Rincón had created order, pattern, and form. It was not a beautiful faena, but it was the exact faena that this bull required. On that almost perfect June afternoon (it was still windy, although less so along the fence), the taurine gods were well pleased.

Figure 11. Apotheosis, Madrid, June 6, 1991. César Rincón, José Ortega Cano, and the breeder, Samuel Flores, are hoisted on shoulders and paraded in triumph as night falls and the lights come on. No one in the tendidos has moved. By permission, Botán.

Colito meanwhile had had enough. He was on the ropes. He went up against the fence beside the Puerta de Arrastre, where the dead bulls are dragged out by the mules—perhaps he smelled the blood of his brothers on the sand—and like a boxer going to his corner, Colito lay down. He quit. He threw in the towel, surrendering to Rincón. But Rincón forced him up— Colito was not tired, he had simply refused to continue—and proceeded to repeat the series, just in case the público or the taurine gods or the millions watching from América had blinked or doubted their eyes.

First a pase de pecho with the right hand; then when Colito turned, a derechazo, working him along the fence; then when he turned again, a natural. Partway through the natural Colito stopped, and Rincón held his ground, shook the muleta, called to the bull: "¡Jájay! ¡Toro!" Colito, his horns even with Rincón's legs, had only to raise his horns and veer centimeters to the left to gore the matador. Rincón shook the muleta again, a third time, a fourth, and finally Colito, his head still down, followed the cloth past the man's legs, through the space between the legs and the fence. Colito turned and Rincón gave him a pase de pecho, without having moved at all. Once again Rincón had run Colito through the gauntlet, and then it was over. Colito surrendered again. Madrid surrendered again. Millions on television surrendered too.

Colito wandered off and lay down in front of the *toril*, the gate through which he had entered the ring and the natural querencia of a manso. Rincón raised him, but now had to go in to kill in the only place Colito would remain standing, parallel to and almost leaning against the fence.

Allí va a ser, the taurinos say: That's where it will be. Colito stood alongside the fence next to the toril and Rincón drove in on him—the bull having no place to go, his left horn against the fence, no place to be deflected to as Rincón came over the right horn—and buried more than half the sword.

Colito charged away from the fence, strong still, snatched the muleta from Rincón, and threw it back toward the callejón. Then he attempted to return to the fence. Going in a circle and finding he was no longer strong, he weaved, went to his front knees, and toppled over dead.

A blanket of white handkerchiefs fell on the plaza de toros, and César Rincón and José Ortega Cano, having cut three ears each, were paraded in triumph—embracing and holding hands, the conjoined triumph of Spain and Colombia—along with the ganadero Samuel Flores, around the ring in an apotheosis. As they were carried from the ring on their way up to the palco real to pay their respects to His Majesty, the entire public were on their feet, and above the triumphant pasodobles the band was playing came the collective chant "¡Toreros! ¡Toreros!" and then the Spanish national anthem and finally the cries of "¡Viva el rey!" as a warm early summer night, windless, settled over the taurine capital of the world.

Glorious Summer

→ **9**

Every season when I go to Spain at the end of spring semester, I think, retouching Shakespeare: "Now is the winter of our discontent made glorious summer by this sun of Spain." But that should not be taken too literally. It rains frequently in Sevilla during Feria, even when the so-called April Fair, following a late Easter, pushes well into May. It rains in Madrid in May, too. Sometimes it even snows, as on that sixteenth of May in 1926 when one of that year's three San Isidro corridas was snowed out and Ernest Hemingway, holed up in the Pensión Aguilar on San Jerónimo, wrote three short stories, or at least later remembered it that way. Summer does not really arrive until June, especially north of Andalucía. Until the fortieth of May, goes the proverb, don't put your coat away.[1]

The Corrida de Beneficencia in Madrid rather divides the spring and the summer and, coming as it does after the ferias of Sevilla and Madrid, is often touted as the most important corrida of the year, although frequently it turns out to be the classic corrida de decepción. The mano a mano between Ortega Cano and César Rincón in 1991 must be considered truly exceptional, one of those rare corridas that actually met or surpassed expectations.

It even met Joaquín Vidal's expectations: he called it "simply memorable" in his review on June 7 in *El País*, memorable because two toreros of today "recovered from the night of time all that which had elevated the exercise of toreo to the category of art." Never mind that, back in the night of time, toreo was not an art; this was Vidal's way of bestowing high praise.

Coming perhaps more to his point, Vidal went on to say that this corrida's most memorable quality was that it had amounted to a full-scale revo-

Figure 12. Between the horns, Madrid, June 6, 1991. Rincón, citing Tomillero with his body, the muleta behind him. By putting himself in such compromised terrain, Rincón had cut an incredible seven ears in three successive afternoons. In Madrid. Antonio Caballero would call it "a miracle that will serve to illuminate the decade." By permission, Botán.

lution "against the ridiculous tauromachy that the figuras of contemporary toreo had imposed." Certain of Ortega Cano's passes were "pure art, and between the torero-artist and the engrossed público that contemplated his work there was a total identification of emotions and sentiments." If the implicit criticism of other toreros was overdone, the praise for the triunfadores was not.

Rincón, continued Vidal, surprised everyone with his unusual tijerillas, and after finishing the series with a baroque revolera, he had walked from the bull with such grace that he seemed to have "suckled toreo in the heart of Triana," high praise indeed, since Triana is traditionally held to be the most taurine section of Sevilla and Sevilla the most taurine city of all.

Javier Villán wrote an open letter to César Rincón and Ortega Cano in *El Mundo* the same day, calling them insurgents and their work a manifesto against the established taurine order. Rincón was a warrior with the moves of Nureyev; he was aesthetics, passion, brains, harmony of movement, and serene and fierce valor. Villán compared Rincón's toreo to the poetry of his namesake, Peruvian poet César Vallejo, affirming that in the work of both were the "heraldos negros," the black heralds, which were like the "sonidos negros," the black sounds of which García Lorca had so eloquently written.

The black sounds indicate the presence of duende, and duende for García Lorca was the Dionysian essence of the mystery of Spanish art, especially toreo. Rincón, Vallejo, García Lorca: There is no better artistic company.

Rincón had such mastery, José Carlos Arévalo maintained, that instead of giving the bulls the lidia they required, he forced the bulls to accept what he gave them. Pointing out that Rincón crossed into the bull's terrain, offering his own body as bait, and made them charge, Arévalo wrote: "You have to be a hero to convert the exception into the norm." Three times out the Puerta Grande, seven ears in seven bulls: "Does anyone give more?" he wondered (6T6 3:43).

With touches of irony, Antonio Caballero explained how boring, as usual, the first hour of the corrida had been. Two bulls were returned to the corrals behind the ring, the man behind had his knees in your back, the man in front his back jammed into your knees. Then there was the inevitable *entendido,* the man in the know who explained the corrida to everyone around him. When Rincón dedicated his bull to Francisco Santos, just released by the drug lords, the entendido had said, "He's dedicated it to one of the cocaine kings from his own country." And Caballero remarked with a gnostic sniff, "Those in the know never know."

Eventually the corrida came to life. After all, as Caballero wrote, "César Rincón doesn't know how to get out of Las Ventas except through the Puerta Grande." Why was Rincón different from the others? Because, explained Caballero, he had the particular quality—extremely rare in a torero—that he would always torear. Perhaps most important, the unmitigated seriousness of Rincón's toreo "obliged all the others to do as he did or to retire from the ring." Caballero finished his review cumulatively and prophetically: "And Rincón, in three afternoons, in three *salidas en hombros* [being carried out on shoulders] through the Puerta Grande of Madrid, had accomplished a miracle that will serve to illuminate the decade: he had rescued us from tedium" (156–61).

Indeed, César Rincón's three consecutive triumphs in Madrid in less than three weeks not only convulsed the taurine world and catapulted him to instant and enduring fame, they may have set an unreachable goal, a mark that will never be equaled. But the triumphs of that spring were over now, and the summer marathon that begins in June stretched before him. Days and nights in the car, trekking through the heat, up one side of the bull's hide of Spain and down another, with excursions into southern France. Day after day of killing, eating, driving, riding, arriving at a new hotel, trying to rest, dressing, killing, eating, driving.... How would he hold up, having to compete with Spain's best, always with his fame preceding him, lifting expectations? It was not a matter of idle speculation. One thing was clear: none of the Spanish toreros in that competitive sphere was going to cede anything to the Colombian.

What made Rincón an exception among *fenómenos*—latest sensations— was that he was already a maestro in his own country, "forged hammer-blow by hammer-blow, chiseled from the stone of years of experience, step by step, with effort, with sacrifice, taking all the time it took, without pausing but without hurrying" as Pepe Dominguín, Luis Miguel Dominguín's brother, a former matador and current taurine journalist, described him. That was how, continued Dominguín, "from the distant Andes" Rincón had brought back to Spain what the Spanish professionals had exported there but which here in Spain "was in a dangerous state of lethargy." Rincón was a figura del toreo whose "presence revived the truth, drawing flame and fire from the coals—and there were coals—of the true art of toreo" (6T6 3:21).

After San Isidro and the Beneficencia, it took a while for contracts to come in. Except for substitutions, which Luis Alvarez jumped at, no spots had been reserved in the closest ferias for the remote possibility that a César Rincón would come along. When substitutions did come, Rincón triumphed with two ears in Granada, as we have seen, and with two ears in Cáceres on June 1.

Then the contracts did begin to pour in: on the twenty-third in Avila, the twenty-fourth in Badajoz, and the twenty-sixth in Soria, he cut the only ear each day.

I went to the corrida in Soria. I was then acting as site director for the Fifth International Hemingway Conference, to be held in Pamplona in July 1992, and was making frequent trips to the capital of Navarra. It happened that I was just finishing a series of meetings and was able to meet Michael Wigram in Soria for the corrida: Ortega Cano, Espartaco, and César Rincón with bulls from the ganadería of Antonio Ordóñez.

Ortega Cano and Rincón were on the bill together many times that year. Together with Espartaco, who was not about to relinquish the title of número uno, they made up the cartel everyone wanted to see. On this particular afternoon Espartaco "fell from the cartel" with a minor injury, however, leaving us another mano a mano between Ortega Cano and César Rincón. Rincón stole the show, cutting the only ear on a fine, warm afternoon with uncooperative bulls, as the summer season hit full stride with the fiesta of San Juan, which celebrates the summer solstice.

After the corrida I followed Michael back to Madrid, and we watched the sun setting beyond the Guadarrama Mountains on one of the longest days of the year, as the full moon rose over the breadbasket of Castilla. As I drove, I thought back a couple of nights to the young men and boys in the little square of the Virgen de la O in Pamplona, jumping through the bonfire of San Juan. They had burned a straw man at nightfall and danced, and as the fire burned down enough, they began to run and jump through it in one of the oldest rituals in the Mediterranean world. All around Pamplona and in many other towns throughout Spain they were burning such fires, immolating the ancient scapegoats and celebrating the ageless fertility rites of the beginning of summer. Catching the spirit, I leaped gingerly across a corner of the fire—to appease the deus loci and to keep any evil spirits at bay.

On Monday, July 1, I pick up John Ewing, an actor and aficionado, at the Madrid airport for a drive up through Castilla to see Ortega Cano, Espartaco, and César Rincón in Burgos. John's flight does not get in until almost two, so we skip lunch and race north. We arrive in time, buy tickets, and, famished, proceed to find a tapa or two before the corrida while I explain to John why I think Rincón is important. John thinks I am exaggerating about Rincón and being dramatic about getting to Burgos for the corrida.

But the taurine gods are kind to me this day. Maricarmen Camacho's bulls are excellent and all three matadors are in top form. In the fourth bull Ortega Cano has another great faena. Espartaco, who has not been himself all season, "breaks through" brilliantly on the fifth bull—which is good enough to be given a vuelta of the ring for its bravery: no hay quinto malo—and not only shows the afición of Burgos why he has been número uno for seven years but also how he has evolved from a rough-and-tumble tremendista to a maestro of exquisite temple.

Again, however, César Rincón steals the show. The sixth bull tosses him and Rincón, although unhurt, loses one of his *zapatillas*. Kicking off the other, he storms back in stocking feet and reduces his opponent to complete obedience. The *peñas,* the young men's celebratory societies, dance in the stands and cheer on their new hero.

Pepe Dominguín will write of Rincón's performance in Burgos: "César Rincón steps forward every afternoon with the truth out front, with a toreo that alarms us with its closeness and with its obvious danger in citing to the contrary horn, something he then resolves with harmony and the length of his passes. He puts out a great deal, a very great deal. When he torears[2] in those terrains and in that way, let us pray to God that the bulls respect him and that they do not take from us this protagonist who wants to return toreo to what true toreo has always been. Purity and honesty, above and beyond the current fashions—with exceptions—that hold sway today. Rincón is not, clearly, a revolutionary of toreo, but he is, and he is demonstrating it, a regenerator of the forms of eternal toreo" (6T6 4:31).

Each of the matadors cuts two ears and they all go out on shoulders together. Burgos—except for the usual noisy demonstrations against the current city hall by the peñas—is a happy town, and John Ewing is a happy aficionado, a new convert to Rinconismo.

Afterwards Michael Wigram asks John his impressions of the corrida and John says, "Ortega Cano was okay but uninspiring. Espartaco was technically perfect but dispassionate. Rincón is a crowd pleaser, passionate, also technically perfect. If I were to see one again, it would be Rincón."

On July 5 Rincón again cut two ears from a bull of Maricarmen Camacho, this time in Teruel, just as he had cut two ears from a bull of Marcos Núñez on June 27 down in Algeciras. Coming into Pamplona, the next important

Figure 13. The category of hero: Rincón in Pamplona, July 9, 1991. Rincón with the Cebada Gago bull that gored him in the right testicle. When I took this photograph, I had no idea I would end up writing this book. But I did know I was watching a great torero.

feria after Madrid, Rincón has earned an outstanding eight salidas a hombros so far this season. Nor will he disappoint us in Pamplona on July 9.

The bulls are a matched set with evident *trapío*, taurine presence,[3] from the esteemed ranch of Cebada Gago. Portuguese matador Víctor Mendes is splendid with the banderillas as usual, but the real attraction—the second largest ring in Spain is packed to the rafters with the peñas singing, dancing, throwing flour, and squirting champagne as usual over on the sunny side—is César Rincón.

Rincón dedicates his first bull, very *astifino* or sharp of horn, to the dualistic afición of the festival of San Fermín—young, rowdy, and inattentive on the sunny side; older, serious, and attentive in the shade. Opening the faena with estatuarios at the fence, Rincón then goes to the center of the ring and cites with the right hand. The bull charges from the tablas at a gallop and Rincón characteristically puts the muleta as far forward as he can, stepping into the pass with the opposite leg. But the bull cuts in on him at the last second and his right horn rips through the matador's *taleguilla*[4] about navel-high. Rincón holds his ground somehow and, although the front of the taleguilla is ripped open, he continues passing his dangerous opponent. Another centimeter and, as William Lyon will write on July 11 in the newly resuscitated *El Sol*,[5] the bull would have "ripped out his appendix." The rest of the faena is highly emotional, characteristic Rincón, with the torero not ceding the bull a millimeter. Even the peñas pay attention, but he fails to kill well, losing the ears.

The fifth bull—sometimes there is a quinto malo—hooks badly, charges with his head up, and tries to put his horns in Rincón's face. Again Rincón, appearing fearless, does not budge, and the faena is consequently full of emotion and danger, with a very vibrant final series of naturales.

If Rincón has a fault, it is that he sometimes goes on too long—and he is not the only torero guilty of this—in order to give the public its money's worth. Today he does exactly that, and the bull, which is too dangerous and quick-to-learn for such extended play, trips him up and is on him instantly, goring him on the ground. Rincón struggles up, visibly shaken and doubling over in pain. The bull has nailed him, as William Lyon will delicately put it, "in the part of his anatomy where it would hurt the worst."

Rincón somehow withstands the pain and manages to kill the animal—as the peñas go wild, rising, dancing, and shouting their approbation: "¡Torero! ¡Torero!"—and then heads for the *enfermería,* the infirmary located inside the plaza, while his banderilleros take a tour of the ring with the bull's ear. It turns out Rincón has two *puntazos,* small gorings, in the right testicle, which are in need of stitching up.

We all figure the mishap means he'll be off the cartel two days later, and back at the taurine bar of the Hotel Maisonnave that is the general opinion. But we are wrong. Not only does he torear, he adds spectacularly to his growing legend. With his stitches still in place, he lines up for the *paseíllo* or opening parade next to Roberto Domínguez and Rafi Camino, a maestro and the son of the great maestro of the '6os and '7os, Paco Camino. The overcast afternoon feels thick and sultry. The bulls of Osborne are spectacular, astifinos with plenty of trapío. Rincón limps and is visibly in pain the entire time, even though later he will claim that from the moment he began to dress he forgot about the pain.

He is also concerned about the fact that he is getting caught virtually every afternoon. The Cebada Gago bull that nailed him is on his mind. He remembers how the bull chopped at him as he lay on the sand and he remembers thinking that the bull was going to cut him in half. One critic remarked that he had his distances wrong, but Rincón said no, with all due respect, that was not true. What was perhaps true was that he was taking too many chances. It was all a question of centimeters and fractions of a second. That was the reality of toreo. The price of success was high and you paid in blood. Still, that goring had been particularly painful (JV 166–67).

When the unforgettable afternoon is over, Roberto Domínguez has listened to the deafening indifference of Pamplona, and Rafi Camino, having let the bull of the feria "get away from him" with his ears intact, has earned mild applause. The afternoon belongs entirely to Rincón, who cuts an ear from each bull and is carried out on shoulders, to the horror and dismay of those of us who sympathize with his physical situation.

The reviews the next morning are superb. Joaquín Vidal of *El País* titles his piece "Rincón Continues His Ascent" and remarks that his two-handed pass would have turned the Madrid and Sevilla rings upside down. He especially praises Rincón's intelligence in handling his different bulls—the first was reticent with a marked querencia at the fence and the second was a beautiful *burraco,* black with white patches on the belly, with plenty of casta.

Barquerito of *Diario 16* also praises Rincón's intelligence, describing how he "put in his pocket" both the serious public in the shade and the festive public in the sun. The headline reads "Rincón Reaches in Pamplona the Category of Myth or Hero."

In a review titled "The César Rincón Syndrome," Javier Villán of *El Mundo* tops all the competition, claiming that Rincón "has *cojones* of iron." How else could he ride, tranquilly seated, on the sweaty and equally ironlike shoulders of the crowd? Villán ends by proclaiming that César Rincón was in a "state of grace and, even though a goring had lacerated his testicles, he was prepared to convert the Columbus Quincentennial into a discovery and conquest from the other side."

And all of them are correct. The Colombian conquistador was in pain, as everyone could see. But he transformed that pain—ignoring it—into the art of toreo and ascended in a state of grace into the realm of the hero at the center of myth. It is because of afternoons such as this one that toreo exists, because now and again a torero can surpass all expectations, perhaps even his own.

Endless Summer

The record of the rest of the season—especially when measured in ears cut and salidas a hombros—reads like a litany of successes. The number of ears is never an adequate way to evaluate any torero's achievement, but it is a rough gauge of an activity that is difficult to quantify. And no torero cuts ears with regularity in important plazas without having done something of note. César Rincón cut these ears: two from a Carlos Núñez bull on his debut in Barcelona on July 14, two from a Guardiola on July 25 in Mont-de-Marsan, his first triumph across the border in what many later called the faena of the year in France, three from Bohórquez bulls in the Basque town of Azpeitia on the thirty-first, two in Iscar on August 3, two in Berja on the fourth, two in El Escorial on the ninth, two in Pontevedra on the eleventh, two in La Coruña on the thirteenth, two in Bayonne—another triumph in an important French ring—on the seventeenth, and on and on, until at the end of the season César Rincón had gone out on shoulders twenty-eight times in the European season.

No one was prepared for this kind of success, least of all César Rincón and Luis Alvarez. In recent years the two of them and the *cuadrilla*—the quadrille, the group of professionals: brother Luis Carlos as mozo de espadas, Juanito Márquez (plate 4c) as *ayuda* or assistant, the chauffeur, the three banderilleros and two picadores—would usually travel in two large vans. But in 1991 all they had was a used van and a car, and Luis Alvarez and Rincón went in the car, which meant one of them had to drive.

Sometimes their schedule looked as though it had been designed to be as difficult as possible. In reality, it corresponded to a high demand for Rincón's *actuaciones*, his performances, and the widely scattered calendar and geography of taurine events. Consider, however, the following forced marches: on August 9 a corrida in El Escorial, outside Madrid; on August 10 in Antequera, almost on the Mediterranean coast; on August 11 in Pontevedra in far northwestern Galicia, well over a thousand kilometers away; on August 12 in Huesca, over next to France, in the shadow of the Pyrenees; on August 13 back to Galicia for a corrida in La Coruña; on August 14 all the way across Spain and into France for a corrida in Dax; on August 15 back across almost the whole north coast to Gijón; on August 16 the easiest drive, to El Espinar outside Madrid, where they probably arrived sometime before dawn; on August 17 back to France for a corrida at Bayonne; on August 18 down to Málaga on the Mediterranean; on August 19 up to Bilbao on the Atlantic.

When they recall that hectic summer, neither Alvarez nor Rincón can figure out exactly how they did it. The stories are conflicting, as well they might be, and funny, and involve strange anecdotes about charter flights, missed airplanes, hair-raising drives, Rincón's dressing in the car, and other stories not in every case conducive to complete faith in their veracity. The intentions I doubt not, but the "facts" are understandably sometimes out of sync. It surprises me that they can remember as much as they do. (Actually both have excellent memories, and Rincón's memory of the bulls he has killed would put a computer to shame).

The most amazing fact of that summer—after the twenty-eight salidas a hombros, of course—is that Rincón did much of the driving. He enjoys driving and tends not to feel comfortable with other drivers. Once he confided to me that Luis Alvarez had an alarming tendency to nod off, even to go to sleep with his eyes open. Anyone who has made even one thousand-kilometer journey across the nocturnal bull's hide of Spain will immediately sympathize with Luis Alvarez's tendency, but Rincón's insistence on driving also made sense. What made less sense is how César Rincón, even at twenty-five, had the energy to drive and to triumph. Perhaps the latter supplied the former. In any case the summer turned into a kind of interminable grind, punctuated by the sweet sounds of success. To this day César claims he is sleep-deprived.

Among César Rincón's many great corridas that year, a few deserve special attention. One such corrida took place on August 13 in La Coruña: Roberto Domínguez, César Rincón, and Joselito, with bulls of Lamamié de Clairac, a ganadería Rincón had had trouble from before.

The corrida, in which Rincón cut the only ears, stands out in two ways. First, Rincón cut two ears from Fogonero, the fifth (yes, the fifth) bull, with a very strong petition for the tail and a bronca to the presidente for not conceding the award. Rincón himself claims it was the best faena he did that year and one of his best ever.

The other has to do with luck. For a torero, Rincón should not be considered particularly superstitious, but all toreros have their *manías,* their quirks or idiosyncrasies. In a profession in which the luck of the draw determines the bulls you will face every day, these manías are perhaps more understandable than in, say, accounting or teaching Spanish grammar. When I say Rincón is not superstitious, I mean—to take a classic example—that triskaidecaphobia, fear of the number thirteen (rampant among taurinos), does not plague him, not even with a ganadería he does not or did not prefer. In fact, the "unlucky" number seems almost always lucky for him, as it was on this day, *martes trece,* Tuesday the thirteenth, in Hispanic cultures exactly what Friday the thirteenth is in Anglo cultures. He does "make the cross" with his feet before the paseíllo and he touches wood, not because he is superstitious but, as he puts it, just so something bad will not happen. He hides his head in his cape and never watches a bull enter the ring (plate 64a). And he also has an irrational fear of mice.

Furthermore, if you ask Rincón about luck, he will tell you that luck—good and bad—plays an enormous part in what happens in the ring, but that that in itself is no reason not to help your luck along when you can. I believe Rincón's positive attitude actually influenced his luck at times, especially that season—or, to put it the other way around, if thirteens or Clairac bulls crossed his mind that day, any negative thoughts he had were banished by his consuming desire to triumph.

That was his manía, to triumph, and such was his state of grace on that August thirteenth that his art combined with Fogonero's nobility and bravery—Fogonero means fireman, as on a train or steamship—lit up the new covered plaza de toros of La Coruña as surely as they would have lit up the usually darksome skies of Galicia outside. And later at the wheel playing back the "tape" in his head with Fogonero charging gallantly and repeatedly from a distance, with the matador himself receiving the animal's charges immutably, with the plaza chanting in unison "¡Torero, torero!" in response—playing that "tape" surely also lit up the dark night Rincón had to traverse to Dax, two hours beyond the French border.

The twenty-eighth of August in Linares, one of the main feria dates for that town, is enough to give any torero pause—Manolete was killed there on that date in 1947. In 1991 Ortega Cano, César Rincón, and Joselito contracted to torear a corrida of Baltasar Ibán bulls (especially among taurinos "corrida" also refers to a string or set of bulls to be killed). It is always a grave moment as that event begins, even forty-four years after the fact, since they still observe a minute of silence in memory of Manolete. But the Ibán bulls were good, with plenty of casta and with enough nobility to allow for a great afternoon: Ortega Cano cut the ears from his second and Rincón cut one ear and then two, and both toreros, yet again, were hoisted up and paraded out into the hot, white streets of the festooned town. That summer Ortega Cano and César Rincón could have printed up cards saying "Have Apotheosis, Will Travel." For César Rincón it marked the twentieth salida a hombros.

Even when Rincón had an "off" day, which was rare, or bad bulls, he seemed somehow to shine. On September twelfth in Albacete, Joselito cut the only ear in a corrida of Torrealtas only to have Emilio Martínez write two days later in *El País*: "The Madrileño turned into a Colombian with the red bull, to which he gave distance and space, with which he crossed and from which he did not flinch, not moving his feet, finishing off each pass back of the hip and ending up placed for the next."

Martínez called Joselito's performance shooting with borrowed ammunition, a phrase that indicates the kind of effect César Rincón was having on the season. Such an effect did not always go down well, and more than one "dirty trick" was pulled that summer. Only two days before, Rincón had a corrida across the bay from Lisbon in the little Portuguese town of Moita, which was celebrating its Feira de Setembro. When Rincón and the cuadrilla got to the Portuguese border, they met sudden unexpected resistance from the border guards, who insisted on taking the van and the car apart, unpacking all the folded capes and muletas and suits, rifling through the suitcases, setting the drug dogs on them, and checking all the vehicles' nooks and crannies. At first Rincón and the cuadrilla were amused, and Rincón even recalled an anecdote about Juan Belmonte's trouble on the same border, but they soon realized that the guards were seriously searching for drugs and that they—professional toreros under contract—were being treated as probable criminals. When the guards began undoing the muletas and ripping open the capes to check inside, Rincón blew up and shouted at them, "Explode the tires, destroy them! Don't you know that's where the drugs go, inside the tires?" (JV 199, 201).

Rincón wondered at the time whether someone had alerted the border patrol that they might be carrying drugs or whether it was the Colombian passports that did it. In either case he was furious. They barely made it to Moita in time for the corrida, and Rincón has not performed in Portugal since that day.

When we talked about the incident later, both Rincón and Luis Alvarez were convinced that it had been an intentional setup. Curiously enough, a certain torero had been on the bill with them the day before in Albacete and again that day in Portugal, and had arrived ahead of them. Still, there was no way to prove anything and no way to bring a complaint against what may have been nothing more than innuendo—and from whom, the torero, his manager, a disgruntled banderillero, the underpaid chauffeur? Whatever the case, the incident stung.

Even when Rincón did not manage to cut two ears and go out the Puerta Grande, he almost always made an extremely positive impression. And the more important the ring, the more likely he was to succeed, not because he slacked off in smaller or lesser rings, but because he responded so well under extreme pressure and competition.

Bilbao, one of the most important ferias of the north of Spain, which celebrates its weeklong Corridas Generales in August, provides a good example. Enrique Ponce, the splendid young torero from Valencia and Jaén (both claim Ponce, who was born in Valencia but trained in Jaén), emerged clearly as the triunfador, having cut three ears. That same day Rincón cut one ear from a Torrestrella, but Michael Wigram wrote that because the bull had trapío, because it transmitted a sense of danger, because it had a very dangerous right horn, and because Rincón dominated it completely, his faena was "the most important of the Corridas Generales of 1991" (6T6 5:40).

Rincón had bad enough days in Albacete and Murcia (September 9, 12, 16) to make some critics wonder if he was tired. And Joselito, who was already in 1991 the best swordsman in the business, gave him a bath in Valladolid on the nineteenth in a mano a mano, cutting three ears to Rincón's none. But in Salamanca on the fourteenth Rincón cut two ears, and then again in Salamanca, where the very taurine público is tough, on the eighteenth in a mano a mano with Julio Aparicio, the son of the maestro of the same name, he cut another two. On the twenty-first in Talavera, Rincón cut three ears while the great artist Manzanares and Joselito, who now lives in Talavera, cut none. So it is hard to believe he was tired. It was, I think, that both the public and the critics had already come to expect him to "walk on water" every afternoon. Perhaps, too, they were looking for a weak link, a chink in the armor, some fray in the whole cloth.

Nor did Rincón appear tired as he blitzed through the ferias in France, becoming as strong a figura as he was in Spain and beginning a reign in that country as número uno that would last six years. After the two initial triumphs in Mont-de-Marsan and Bayonne, and a fine performance in Dax where he cut an ear despite uncooperative bulls, he went on to be triunfador in the Roman coliseum in Arles on the eighth of September and to have a very important afternoon in the other Roman coliseum at Nîmes, in a mano a mano with Joselito with a difficult corrida of Samuel Flores bulls in which Rincón cut the only ear. José Carlos Arévalo wrote that Rincón's performance reminded us "that toreo is an act of intelligence on the edge of the abyss, that to torear is to put your life into the task at hand." His faena with his first Samuel Flores bull had given us back "the authenticity of the fiesta brava. They gave him an ear but he deserved two" (6T6 5:71–72).

In October 1994, Alain and Brigitte Briscadieu (plate 48b), close friends of Rincón's, invited me to their house in Bordeaux, in part so I could peruse Alain's collection of French newspaper clippings about Rincón. Here is the briefest impression of the headlines only, headlines that give an accurate sense of Rincón's reception in France, where the newer afición is less set in its ways, less traditional but never less critical: "Torerazo Rincón"; "Le sacre [coronation, consecration] de César"; "Le sérieux de César Rincón"; "César-issime!"; "César, roi d'Espagne"; "Rincón s'impose"; "César Rincón: Torero-torero." This was the beginning of what the French aficionados came in short order to call Rincónmanía.

As the temporada, the taurine season, wound down, summer came to its abrupt end and the quick chill of autumn in northern climes set in. But there was one piece of news that would keep aficionados' hearts warm until the early days of October. Against all expectations and beyond any necessities, César Rincón, already the clear triunfador of the season, had decided to come back to Madrid for a corrida in the Feria de Otoño, the short autumn feria that closes the season in Madrid and that most figuras do not even want to think about.

Talking to God

→ 11

Not a few seasoned aficionados figured Rincón must be crazy. Maybe he had received one too many *volteretas,* tossings. To come back seemed a useless risk. And if he had a bad day? On the other hand, the afición of Madrid would be ready to see César Rincón, who by now had created an unparalleled aura of expectation in the capital.

Rincón figured: Madrid has given me everything, I owe everything I am to Madrid, I have a responsibility to the público of Madrid. He had said it a hundred times. Now he would try to prove it once again.

It was Tuesday, October 1, 1991: bulls of Sepúlveda, one of the best ganaderías that year, for José Mari Manzanares, César Rincón, and David Luguillano, who was to confirm his alternativa. (A torero must confirm—repeat—the ceremony of the alternativa in Madrid, unless he has initially taken his alternativa there.) The weather was clear and there was little wind.

Luguillano would have had a good afternoon under normal circumstances, normal meaning if César Rincón's heroics had not overshadowed his artistic faena. When Rincón came into the ring, the applause engulfed him, and from that moment the afternoon was his. The maestro Manzanares did very little except be there—and perform one valuable quite.

Rincón's first bull, a black Sepúlveda, typically high in the shoulder, cut constantly into the torero's terrain, making cape work almost impossible. He approached the horse more as if to dance than to wreak havoc. The crowd whistled and clapped in time at this manifest mansedumbre.

Yet Rincón saw some potential for triumph in the animal and began by taking him straight to the center of the ring and citing from a distance. And the bull charged, and because Rincón dropped away after each pass, not drowning or crowding the animal, he continued to charge. On the second derechazo the olés began, and on the third, fourth, and fifth grew in intensity until Rincón finished the series with a chest pass and walked away to the thunderous applause Madrid was now accustomed to giving him. In successive series his intuitive sense of distance and terrain appeared faultless.

Then as he approached for a final series, the bull flew up from the muleta, suddenly in Rincón's face, and Rincón, with the bull doubling around to gore him, reached out with his left hand and pushed himself away from the bull's morrillo. By this instant reflexive action he saved himself from being gored, but when his hand came away from the morrillo it was red with his own blood.

Rincón had slashed his left thumb on the exposed barb of a banderilla. He quickly sucked the blood off, ignored the pain, and killed the bull in style, cutting a well-deserved ear. But the seemingly insignificant gash on the thumb was a harbinger of painful events.

The manso of Sepúlveda—another bull in Madrid, another ear for Rincón—was only the prelude for the real drama. The fifth bull, Rincón's second, was not a Sepúlveda but a 563-kilo substitute from the Portuguese ranch of João Moura, Ramillete by name, number 175, born in November 1986, making him but a month shy of his fifth birthday. Ramillete—although afterwards few would call the bull by name, referring to him instead in the mysterious way names work in the taurine world as "el toro de Moura"—Ramillete had a dark chestnut hide, going to black around his head and legs, and very sharp black-tipped horns. Deep in the chest, slim in the hindquarters, Ramillete was a magnificent animal possessed of an almost preternatural aggressiveness. What, aficionados began to wonder, had the taurine gods wrought for César Rincón? Afterwards more than one critic would use words such as "demoniacal."

Rincón knew at once he had a hard-charging bull and received Ramillete with six fluid verónicas, a tight media verónica, and a revolera to cap the series. In spite of the torero's temple, the bull seemed to charge progressively harder with each pass, finally catching the cape with a sharp horn point and ripping it out of the matador's hands. Then as the lengthy applause for Rincón grew and subsided, Ramillete stood over the cape, which was spread out on the sand, the way a lion stands over a kill. When Monaguillo took him away in a quite, Ramillete chased him to the barrera.

"El toro de Moura" was more fierce than brave. He had a certain predilection for the fence and an unpredictability in his charge, a clever way of sizing up his target, that precluded classic *bravura*. And he was *bronco*, with a rough charge. After two hard picks by Anderson Murillo, another longtime Colombian friend of Rincón's now in the cuadrilla (plate 2a), Luguillano tried a quite, but when he cited, Ramillete watched him the way a cat watches a mouse. When the bull did charge, he followed the cape, but in the media verónica he snatched Luguillano's cape away from him and stood on it. Murillo's third pick did not seem to affect the animal at all.

The suerte de banderillas became a matter of survival. In the first attempt, Manzanares jumped from the callejón in a split-second quite, saving the banderillero from grave pursuit. The banderilleros managed to get in one stick at a time for a total of three, and Monaguillo, who was handling the cape, had a hard time protecting his colleagues, finally having the cape jerked out of his hands, too. When it was over, Ramillete stood with his head as high as when he had come into the ring, and the ring was very much his dominion.

In the callejón Luis Alvarez told Rincón that he should dedicate the bull to the público. From Rincón's reaction, keen eyes could see that they were having a "discussion." Rincón assented, but he knew the bull was under-picked and that he was "growing," getting stronger, in spite of the punishment they had given him. He told Alvarez to wait for him in the enfermería, as this bull was clearly an assassin. "No," said Alvarez, "I'll wait for you at the Puerta Grande, because that's where you will be."

Rincón marched gallantly out to the center of the ring with a we-who-are-about-to-die-salute-you expression on his face and duly dedicated the death of "el toro de Moura" to the afición of Madrid. Later he would say that he was silently "damning Luis Alvarez and everybody else that had gotten him into this mess" (JV 69). Antonio Caballero commented that Rincón seemed from deep inside to be dedicating his own death. "It was," he continued, "a matter of finding out which one was more potent" (172). And if there existed the remotest doubt about the animal's potency, that doubt was instantly dispelled as Ramillete trapped one of Rincón's banderilleros against the tablas, missing eviscerating him by just a few centimeters.

As Rincón went forward for the faena, Ramillete stood facing him, next to the tablas, his head high, his tail lashing, blood pumping from the wounds in his morrillo and back, literally bloodied but unbowed. If Rincón was afraid of this animal—he would remark afterwards he had felt a sense of desperation (JV 69)—it did not show in the least. But perhaps that is the essence of bravery: not having to be brave, nor performing some unconscious or involuntary or isolated act of bravery, but knowingly, repeatedly choosing to face such an animal in spite of the inescapable fear within. There is an old taurine saying, "El valor no quita el susto"—bravery doesn't get rid of the fright. The toreros call it professionalism or responsabilidad, but there is more to it than that, especially with a bull like Ramillete, a "wild beast" that Rincón later said "tried to rip loose his head or his heart on every charge" (JV 33).

There is a heroism in a torero like César Rincón that is of epic proportions. It is foreign to our time and place, and in spite of having observed it in Spain since 1962, I find it still foreign to me. I have studied it but I do not pretend to be able to explain it. The great torero remains an enigma—even to himself.

Anyone who faces any bull has a certain bravery, even if he subsequently panics, but only a few toreros have that epic quality, and most days you do not see it. Yet on such a day as this, in such a confrontation of wills, for the aficionado there is—categorically—nothing grander, more uplifting, or more terrifyingly beautiful. It is an ur-drama in which everything is real rather than represented, in which a Promethean hero literally wrests the order of humanity from the savagery of nature. That confrontation of wills is what I think lies behind Antonio Caballero's phrase "It was a matter of finding out which one was more potent." It went beyond performance, it was a matter of life and death, or, as Rincón would later describe it from a different perspective, it was "the meeting of two fears" (F-S 93).

Walking lightly, Rincón approached Ramillete and in short order gave him six doubling passes, punishing him as much as a torero can punish an animal. But when the series was finished, Rincón had only begun to break the bull, and so far it did not show in the least.

Now in virtual silence—rare in the quarrelsome Madrid plaza—Rincón took Ramillete to the middle of the ring, and there Ramillete stood with his huge curly head held high. Rincón led him through four derechazos, the olés breaking in on the second, but in the fourth pass the animal jerked free from the cloth dangerously close to the matador.

A second series of four produced more olés, but after the pase de pecho Ramillete whirled and charged straight at the man as he was walking away. Rincón spun, gave the animal a severe doubling pass and, with Ramillete now with his back toward the fence, went to one knee in front of the bull, face to face with him for a full three seconds, then rose and walked away in a theatrical recovery, this time toward the center of the ring, as the crowd surged to its feet in applause.

Ramillete never quite recovered from Rincón's reversal, and the matador, however slightly, swung the balance of power in his own favor. Once again he moved the animal toward the center of the ring where he would charge more freely, producing four more derechazos and a pase de pecho that formed the nucleus of the faena, the derechazos long, smooth, and linked in a building rhythm. The olés on the third and fourth moved beyond choral acclamation to ecstatic shouts. The pase de pecho sprung the coil winding Ramillete ever more tightly around the man's waist as Rincón, changing the muleta to his left hand, guided the animal past his chest and away and up and out, Ramillete rising after the lifting cloth like the bull-god Dionysos bursting the bonds of human prison. Yet the bull was only momentarily free as Rincón walked away, more victorious than at any moment of the faena or perhaps of his life, and the crowd began a chant of "¡Torero! ¡Torero!" that carried on to ten repetitions.

In the next series Ramillete, becoming more defensive as he tired, broke rank in the middle of a pass, but Rincón, clearly now the more potent, subjugated him again and finished the series with another powerful chest pass.

With Ramillete looking now from the matador to the cloth and back, Rincón began a series of seven heart-stopping passes with the left hand, which was the bull's more dangerous side. In the first pass the bull bumped him. Then, as Rincón was setting up, slowly, deliberately, carefully, for the second, in one of those unintentional silences that sometimes fall on an emotion-charged ring, a hoarse Castilian voice boomed through the emptiness: "¡Viva Colombia!" and the crowd roared back, as though at a political rally or a boisterous wedding, "¡Viva!" as Rincón gave Ramillete three naturales, was nearly caught, recovered, improvised with two ayudados, and finished with yet another immense pase de pecho, standing his ground when Ramillete turned on him. In front of Tendido Six, just inside the circles, they stood motionless, the matador and "el toro de Moura," the matador straight and still, the toro finally no longer at eye level with the torero, breathing heavily, his head lowered. The plaza was on its feet cheering as no other crowd cheers, and Colombian flags waved in the waning light.

One final series of right-handed passes close to the fence, which was now the only place Ramillete would charge, to prove his domination, and Rincón again went to one knee, this time for five seconds, and this time the matador's head looked slightly higher than the bull's.

Now came the time to kill. Rincón's first sword thrust hit bone. It was accurately placed, but the luck of other afternoons in Madrid did not hold. The second thrust was flawless, however, eliciting a roar of approval from

Figure 14. Improvisation, Madrid, October 1, 1991. Rincón, improvising his recovery from nearly being caught by Ramillete, "el toro de Moura." The animal, at the end of the faena, is still charging hard and still has his head up. This is the portrait of a battle that would take Rincón once again from Madrid to heaven. By permission, Botán.

the crowd, and Ramillete circled aimlessly at the fence and went to the sand in less than half a minute.

The plaza was on its feet chanting again: "¡Torero! ¡Torero!" Amid the sea of white handkerchiefs, Colombian flags danced, but the presidente—possibly because of the *pinchazo*, the sword prick—awarded only one ear. The crowd demanded the second to no avail. It did not matter: César Rincón was going out the Puerta Grande anyway. For the impossible and unimaginable fourth consecutive time.

The público made him take two vueltas. The first was slow and victorious yet unassuming as always, with a very contented Rincón raising his eyebrows now and then in mute greeting to familiar faces in the ring. The second vuelta was alone and quicker, without the flowers, the articles of clothing and handbags thrown into the ring, without the flags and the fanfare. César Rincón and his público. *His* público: Madrid.

To finish, Rincón went to the center of the ring and crossed his arms over his heart four times, bowing to the four quadrants of the ring, or perhaps to the four winds, or maybe even in thankful recognition to the taurine gods for each of his four triumphs. Then he crossed himself and, as he trotted back to the callejón, raised his montera to thank the presidente. The crowd continued to whistle, to insult and deride the presidente for failing to concede the second ear in one of Rincón's greatest performances ever, anywhere. *6T6* would say that he had resurrected toreo in Las Ventas and that his two great faenas that day had "turned him into the maximum triunfador of the 1991 season" (5:3), while *El Sol* the next day would crown him "César Imperator."

Rincón himself was more succinct: "Risking it all was a new challenge. Either you are or you are not. It was a test of my capacity, which is why I dedicated a bull that I did not like to the público" (*El Mundo*, October 2, 1991). When he returned to the callejón, still in a highly charged emotional state, he exclaimed: "I knew if I 'doubted' him, he would overpower me. So I never 'doubted.' That's why I was successful. In the dedication I was aware that the faena would be the Puerta Grande or the enfermería" (*ABC*, October 2, 1991).

José Carlos Arévalo would go straight to the point about what Rincón had accomplished. True toreo, he would write, is not a repetition but a restoration. "It is as though [toreo] were created for the first time, because it arises as the most exact response to a [bull's] charge, one that is unrepeatable, distinct, differentiated in each instance, different in every bull. That is why people go to the ring, because in between so many repetitions, once in a while toreo is resurrected" (6T6 5:35).

The religious language is not only unavoidable, it is precisely right. True toreo, like myth or belief recreated in rite, carries us back to sacred time, to the enactment itself, to the cathartic purity of something long gone from our "normal," profane world, to original time—*ab origine, in illo tempore*—when the puny, thinking man-god emerges victorious over the hard dark gods of animal nature.

Pepe Dominguín would venture a step farther: "What Rincón did in Madrid is like talking to God and getting an answer," a phrase they would print on the cover of 6T6 with a photo of Rincón lighting a candle at his *altarcito,* the small portable altar toreros take with them (6T6 5:36).

(No one had to explain who those three distinguished and neatly turbaned Near Eastern gentlemen were, sitting together and watching the corrida intently from the barrera seats of Tendido One.)

Later that evening César Rincón dined with the mother of the King.

He would return to the streets of Bogotá, where he had once peddled junk, wrote Rubén Amón the next day in *El Mundo,* "like Armstrong, Aldrin, and Collins returning from the moon."

Debacle in Sevilla

→ **12**

The original cartel for October 4, 1991, created enormous expectation: Ortega Cano, Espartaco, and César Rincón in the Maestranza of Sevilla with bulls of Torrealta. It amounted to a final showdown between Ortega Cano and Rincón, clearly the leading contenders for the season's top spot. And it gave Espartaco, from nearby Espartinas, a chance to redeem himself: in spite of his number one position in the *escalafón*—the numerical ranking of matadors by number of corridas—he had not had the kind of brilliant season that had kept him on top for the last half dozen years.[1]

Sevilla is the most taurine city in the world. Many aficionados believe the Maestranza to have the finest, the most knowledgeable, the most demanding afición anywhere. The site of Ortega Cano's inspired faena in April, it was the one great plaza in Spain César Rincón had yet to conquer. And it was practically Espartaco's hometown. In an analysis titled "The Crime of Sevilla," José Carlos Arévalo wrote: "In Sevilla, at the end of the season, the hierarchy of the fiesta would be resolved in a single afternoon" (*6T6* 6:28).

Yet beyond that, Arévalo quite accurately described the event as universal recognition of the fiesta, since the corrida was to be televised to all of Spain and carried by several European and many Latin American channels. In Colombia the day was declared a holiday. It was also to be the taurine opener for the upcoming Expo 92—the Sevilla World's Fair—held as part of the Columbus Quincentennial the following year. It is hard to say which was greater, the hype or the actual expectation.

What went wrong? Virtually everything.

On September 12 in the little town of Baza in the province of Granada, Ortega Cano was caught by the fourth bull, receiving a twenty-centimeter cornada in the right thigh that fractured the fibula. It was not considered a serious goring, but it would keep Ortega Cano off the cartel in October and cost him another two dozen contracts as well.

A mano a mano between Espartaco and Rincón would have been the logical solution, but the afición of Sevilla does not necessarily respond to logic. It does respond to tradition. Perhaps for that reason Diodoro Canorea, the empresario of the Maestranza, talked the then fifty-seven-year-old Sevilla "artista" Curro Romero into accepting a place on the cartel, in the process offering him more money than he was paying Rincón or Espartaco (20 million pesetas each, more than $150,000, was the number bandied about). Both Rincón and Espartaco reportedly said that if Canorea wanted to cut his own profit by paying Curro more, it was none of their business (6T6 6:29).

Someone, either Canorea or more probably the Expo people or possibly both, decided that this corrida would be off the *abono,* not on the season's subscription ticket, not even for reservations. In other words, the aficionados who had paid for the whole season would not only have to pay extra for this corrida, they would have to stand in line to secure whatever seats were available or pay the reventa, neither one a favorite option of the blueblood afición of Sevilla. To add insult to injury, the Expo people got tickets at half price.

The morning of the corrida there were still three thousand tickets unsold, a sizeable percentage of the gate. A plaza only three-quarters full would not reflect well on the matadors, especially not on worldwide taurine television. The fault clearly belonged to the organizers, but it could look like the toreros had failed to generate enough interest.

Then there was the matter of the bulls. Borja Prado, the contracted ganadero, reportedly asked Canorea at the end of August when he was coming to take a look at the corrida, to which Canorea reportedly replied: "What corrida?" Borja Prado: "The corrida for Sevilla, for October." Canorea: "Ah, sí . . . claro, claro" (6T6 6:29).

Enter the vets. The designated veterinarians must always approve a corrida before it can be released for the ring. Each bull is inspected to see that he is healthy, that his horns have not been tampered with, and that he has the proper size and appearance. This process is designed to protect the público from abuses. But sometimes it merely allows the vets to wag the dog, or in this case the bulls.

In any case, there was plenty of "muddy water" in the corrals the morning of the corrida. Bulls with trapío were thrown out. Others were brought in to "patch up" the corrida, including sobreros from the ganadería of Bohórquez, which may have been the matadors' major objection. What finally got approved was what they call an *escalera,* a ladder—large bulls running down to smaller ones, an unequal, poorly presented, disproportionate, which is to say undesirable, corrida.

Espartaco, as is his right when the bulls are not the ones he contracted to torear, chose not to perform. Rafael Moreno, his apoderado, said no. Rincón did not like the idea of the escalera either, and Luis Alvarez joined with Moreno in saying no. Curro Romero, who had nothing to lose, "heroically" said he would torear, no matter what. Two hours before it was scheduled to take place, the corrida was canceled. There followed a storm of protest, lawsuits, fines, ill will, and general unpleasantness.[2] No one in the planet of the bulls was pleased, and the fact that the toreros claimed to be protecting the public mollified no one.

Why was La Corrida de la Expo canceled? Because of the shortsighted ticket sales policy of the Expo people, because of lack of planning by the empresario, and because of the lack of authority on the part of the Authorities, the inability of the vets or the presidente to deal properly with the toros and the toreros.

I suspect that Espartaco's people somehow convinced Luis Alvarez that to perform would be a mistake—it is not like Luis Alvarez or César Rincón to back down—but I am not at all convinced that what they decided to do, which was not torear, was not a worse mistake, at least for Rincón. Luis Alvarez would claim they did not give in to anyone's wishes. All they wanted were bulls that would not "defraud the public." Everyone, he said, agreed that the bulls that were approved were "unworthy of a corrida of that category" (JV 280).[3] But where, one can only wonder, were the fearless apoderado and torero who had accepted the double-or-nothing substitution in Madrid in May?

Be that as it may, Sevilla is, as we shall see, a nearly impossible nut to crack, and the farther away from Sevilla you were born, the truer that becomes. No one knows this better than Luis Alvarez, who, although his parents were Andalusian, was born in Morocco and who, with the peculiar malice the planet of the bulls sometimes evinces, was not always allowed to forget that he had been born a *forastero,* an outsider—even, according to the "evil tongues," a *moro,* a Moor, which of course he was not. I think César Rincón would have been better served by performing, even with "unworthy" bulls, than by alienating the memorious public of Sevilla, which would never quite forget. In hindsight, Luis Alvarez made a mistake in strategy in choosing the greater of two evils.

Fortunately for Rincón, his historic triumphs in Madrid tended to counter the debacle in Sevilla. In the end those triumphs helped to make it clear that whatever reason César Rincón had for not appearing, it was not because he wished to avoid a challenge or because the bulls were intimidating. When Rincón later maintained it was a great shame the corrida had to be canceled, I agreed, but I had to reflect that it was a particular shame for him, not only because it would prejudice him in Sevilla but also because it was the only flaw in an otherwise magnificent season.

Ave César

Avianca flight 010, proceeding from Paris via Madrid to Santa Fe de Bogotá, arrived many hours late, landing at midnight on October 11–12, 1991, exactly 499 years after Columbus had first gone ashore on the little island he named San Salvador.

The new Salvador of Colombia, the conquistador of the Old World stealing Spain's thunder a year before the celebration of the discovery of the New World, was greeted by a crowd no less impressive than the Roman mobs that thronged to greet the ancient Caesars. Tens of thousands, led by the mayor of Bogotá and the governor of the Department of Cundinamarca, waited at El Dorado Airport for the arrival of Julio César Rincón, and the streets were lined from the airport to the Plaza Bolívar, thirty kilometers away in the old colonial center of the city.

It was the largest crowd César Rincón had ever seen. Everyone was there, he said, his friends, people he had never seen, the high society of Bogotá, the beggars, the young, the old, the beautiful and the not so beautiful, as well as some who were just curious. And they were all acclaiming him, applauding, even dancing. It was, he remarked, crazy. A hoarse voice rent the night: "¡Viva Colombia!" The municipal band of Bogotá played the national anthem and everyone began to sing. You could hear people sobbing. A baby cried. "I cried too," said Rincón, "hot tears" (F-S 37).

The police formed a cordon around Rincón, dapper in a navy suit with white shirt and dark print tie, trying to protect him from the human tide of touchers, kissers, and well-wishers. They finally managed to perch him on a ledge in the airport, above the dangers of the mob, so he could respond to the hundreds of print and media journalists. César Rincón was terrified by this crowd, so different from the público of the plaza de toros. Perhaps because of that, he spoke of the fear and of the *soledad,* the aloneness, of the torero, and he said, "I am happy. But you cannot imagine how much fear I have felt for so many months in order to be back here with you again" (I&B 142).[1]

Then came thirty kilometers of shouting, flag-waving multitudes, thirty kilometers of celebration and music and horn honking, with César Rincón riding high on a fire truck so people could see (but not touch) him. He claimed it was the greatest salida a hombros he had ever had. But he wondered if all this did not somehow transcend the bulls. Colombia, he thought, needed these sudden emotional charges, these grand events, to remove some of the sting from national shame. Something to forget the violence and the conflict. It needed someone—a torero, a soccer player, a cyclist—someone to be proud of, someone in the papers for the right reasons (JV 13). He must have felt as though he were carrying the entire country with him up there on that comically inappropriate but practical fire truck. Later he would remark, "Every time my name appears in the papers . . . it's as though all Colombia were washed clean of so many insulting things" (JV 202).

Rincón, pleased though he was by the extraordinary acclamation—how many flags, how many scarves, how many scraps of paper did he autograph?—wanted to get home, wanted to be home without thirty kilometers of people, wanted to alone with his soledad. Years ago his mother had told him, "Someday you will come back here. . . ." Now that day had come, to wipe away the memory of all the empty-handed homecomings in the interim. But Mamita was not there to share it with him, and he spent a few hours resting in the uptown Hotel Cosmos (F-S 37).

The next morning the parade downtown began at 8:00. Escorted by three helicopters, Rincón spent five hours on the fire truck (fifteen meters long, made in the USA) like a war hero, then received two decorations: the *ayuntamiento* (city hall) of Santa Fe de Bogotá conferred on him the Orden Civil del Mérito and the president of the republic awarded him the Cruz de Boyacá,[2] the highest distinction Colombia confers. Among the many things César Gaviria said to César Rincón while decorating him, what impressed Rincón most was not the praise showered upon him by the president but this remark: "Five hundred years had to pass for a criollo to be carried on shoulders through the great gate of the worldwide cathedral of toreo."

(Technically a *criollo*, a creole, is a Spaniard born in the New World, but by extension it has come to mean a native of the New World and especially, in current usage, a mestizo.)

As Rincón was replying, "That's a lot of years," he remembered the Colombian journalist who had written just a short time before that *mestizaje*, the mixing of Spanish and Indian blood, could not produce great toreros (JV 51). That mind-set, of course, was part of the problem. As Germán Castro Caycedo, a popular Colombian journalist and writer, would explain, taurine writers had always insisted that great toreros practically had to be born in Triana. Then along came this Camilo Pardo Maña, himself a mestizo, claiming that mestizaje could not produce great toreros. "There existed a certain taurine racism," Castro Caycedo continued, "practiced by the indios and the mestizos themselves. César Rincón has broken that evil spell, as it were, that negative attitude" (JV 259–60). Out in the street a banner, recalling Bolívar's dream, proclaimed: "César, Emperador de Colombia."

Rincón also liked Gaviria's phrase "César Rincón's twenty-six years of *vigilia* [watchfulness, perseverance] were mightier than the inertia of half a millennium," and he remembered the president's quotation from Federico García Lorca that the plaza de toros is the only place you can go "with the assurance of seeing death surrounded by the most dazzling beauty." Death as a spectacle. That, mused Rincón, is one of the greatest things about the fiesta, something those who attack the fiesta reject and condemn. It is not a barbarity because it is not gratuitous. It is a creative act aimed at the revelation of art. And every art, he thought, every stellar moment of humanity, has a counterbalance of sacrifice, risk, even of immolation (JV 53).

President Gaviria's last words impressed Rincón as having a significance that went beyond their application to the art of toreo: The fiesta brava, said the president, "beyond the mere spectacle, symbolizes man's capacity for transformation and purification. Courage and intelligence and art, against strength and brutality and fear. Death serves as a pretext so that life can be affirmed." Perhaps, thought Rincón, that is the only way to govern Colombia: intelligence and art against brutality and fear. He wondered if Gaviria were converting a discourse on the nature of the art of toreo into political theory and, remembering another comment of Gaviria's—that man "ought to divest himself of his original animal nature and discipline the force of his intelligence. Both the bull and the tauric elements of the torero die"—believed the president was, indeed, speaking metaphorically (JV 56).

To all of this Rincón replied briefly, trying to unite the past and the present: "Five hundred years after that twelfth of October, on which there was a conquest, a Colombian, on this twelfth of October, has returned triumphant. In the name of Colombia, Spain opened for me the gates of the world. Now we have brought something back here" (JV 56).

Six Miracles

On October 20, 1991, César Rincón cut two ears from the sixth San Martín bull in the Plaza Monumental de México—the world's largest plaza, with a capacity of more than 46,000, twice the size of Las Ventas—and was carried out on shoulders by the sellout crowd, extending his taurine dominions to the vast afición of the high plains of México. In Lima he had bad luck with the bulls but still managed three ears in three corridas. With better luck in the Venezuelan plazas, Rincón totaled nine ears in four corridas. And in Ecuador in two corridas, he cut four ears and was awarded the Premio Jesús del Gran Poder and the Premio Ciudad de Quito. Manuel Molés, the announcer for Radio Caracol and a highly visible taurine journalist in Spain, summed up Rincón's American season, which he followed day by day, by saying that every place Rincón passed through was conquered land. It is possible, he continued, "to be an American torero and run [*mandar en*] the fiesta. César Rincón conquered Spain, and at the same time, he discovered for us the real Latin America" (JV 296).

Yet the climax of the season came on December 15, 1991, in the Plaza Santamaría in Bogotá, when César Rincón "locked himself in" with six bulls for the Corrida de Crotaurinos on a Bogotá afternoon that was, mirabile dictu, without wind and without the violent rains that had been lashing the city for days. (Crotaurinos is short for Cronistas Taurinos, the taurine journalists' association of Colombia. The event is Bogotá's version of Madrid's Corrida de la Prensa.)

"Everyone" in Colombia was there, including the president and Gabriel García Márquez and the entrepreneur Ardila Lulle, to each of whom César dedicated a bull, plus hundreds of aficionados from France, Spain, and other parts of Latinoamérica.

As Rincón made the paseíllo, the public welcomed him with shouts of "¡Torero! ¡Torero!" and with thousands of white handkerchiefs, as though he had already earned ears, or as though a sudden snowfall had blown off Montserrate, the Andean mountain that looms over the Plaza Santamaría. But the icy storm clouds had cleared at noon from around Montserrate, and this was the sunny reception of the afición of the Plaza Santamaría for their hero, home from the wars in Spain (and in France, Portugal, Mexico, Peru, Ecuador, and Venezuela) like Theseus home from Crete (in the evocative opening paragraph of *The Bull from the Sea*, Mary Renault wrote of Theseus's return, "It was dolphin weather, when I sailed into Piraeus with my comrades of the Cretan bull ring. Knossos had fallen, which time out of mind had ruled the seas")—a fitting homecoming and a fitting close to one of the greatest seasons in the history of toreo.

It was also an extraordinary triumph: Rincón cut four ears and took a vuelta in another, and had he had better luck with the sword, he would have cut even more. But the number of ears was the least important part of this historic afternoon. Fernando Fernández Román from Televisión Española, who had journeyed over to be announcer for the corrida, called Rincón's reception impressive and moving and said the broadcasting experience was "priceless." The crowd's reaction "gives us all goosebumps because we [in Spain] are not used to spectacles of this caliber." Very impressed by Rincón's power of concentration, Fernández Román remarked on how easy it would have been, with so much emotion in the plaza, for Rincón to have lost his composure. Instead there were "*muletazos* [passes with the muleta] of incredible fluid beauty" (JV 293).

Fernández Román put his finger on the outstanding artistic merit demonstrated by Rincón—a torero known from the outset more for his dominance and his lidia than for his arte—all afternoon. But the arte was there, just as Rincón and Luis Alvarez had insisted all season long it could be, while Rincón had battled his way through the ferocious Ramilletes and Santaneritos of the Spanish season. If it is true that valor does not get rid of the fright, it is also true that valor does not take away the arte, at least not in César Rincón's case. But for arte you need the proper bulls, which is to say smaller, more mobile, less intractable, and on this December afternoon he had them.

There was the Achury Viejo that came out in first place, with a fat morrillo, a high head, and forward horns, to which Rincón gave six exquisitely designed naturales, the bull perfectly wrapped in the *bamba* or "curtain" of the muleta, and then a full-length pase de pecho, after having just been tossed in a pase de pecho when an erect banderilla had caught in the epaulet of his traje like a third forward horn and jerked him alongside the bull until the bull had hooked his right horn under Rincón's *chaquetilla,* his short jacket, and lifted him two meters off the ground, thrown him, and then rolled him in the sand as he bumped with his horns trying to find a place to sink them. Rincón had risen, waved away his banderilleros, and continued to pass the bull. That bull he killed recibiendo and cut one ear instead of two because the bull was slow to die.

And there was the very noble fifth, a 470-kilo short-horned black bull named Flor de Monte from the ganadería of Antonio García to which Rincón gave six verónicas, each pass seeming to float Flor de Monte on a magic carpet of billowing cape as he moved him from the tablas to the medios where the matador eased the bull's charges to a stop, only to pick him up again and take him to the horse with *cacerinas,* a behind-the-back, butterfly-like walking pass that Rincón flourished as a gesture to the memory of the Colombian maestro Pepe Cáceres.

The crowning moment had come in the third bull, a beautiful 460-kilo *cárdeno* or salt-and-pepper named Paquero, from the ranch of Colombia's distinguished breeder Ernesto González Caicedo, a man we shall meet again.

Rincón received Paquero, who sallied from the toril at a gallop, with five verónicas with his feet together, the first four made without moving his feet at all, the fifth with only a minute adjustment, finishing with a revolera. The olés shook the foundations of the plaza as Paquero charged, fast, frank, brave, and alegre, and the matador stood and withstood the charges by the motion of his arms and waist. Here was the bull César Rincón had been waiting for all season, a bull that put his head down and a bull that put his head into the cloth.

Beginning the faena with ayudados, Rincón took Paquero away from the fence, then ran to the center of the ring and cited. Paquero charged and Rincón passed him behind his back, following with derechazos and more derechazos as Paquero turned into a kind of charging machine. Weighing 460 kilos (instead of 560 or 660) and being brave, Paquero charged every time César Rincón presented the muleta. Soon there was no break in the passes and one derechazo melted into another. As series succeeded series, Paquero continued undiminished, his head lowered every time the lure was presented to him. One sees bulls like this now and then, in Colombia or in Mexico or in the Santa Colomas of Ana Romero in Spain, but the demand for huge bulls in Spain—"elephants" or "mastodons" they are frequently called—usually precludes this kind of collaboration between toro and torero, what Rincón calls that involvement between the animal and the man that produces an indefinable emotion, strong and troubling at the same time, an ecstatic feeling that seems almost sexual (F-S 87).

As Rincón initiated a series with the left, Paquero stepped on his left foot, the leading foot, tripping the torero and nearly catching him as he turned and charged back. But Rincón rose faster than Paquero could turn, presenting the animal with the engaño, which he unhesitatingly followed.

Although the incident was, as Rincón would say when it was over, "not important," it illustrates a problem that has consistently plagued him. Because he is short—1.67 meters, or 5'5¾"—and because he works close to his bulls, he is frequently stepped on. Down the road this kind of incident would take its toll in more ways than one.

After the naturales Rincón did a series that for me was the high point, for beauty and inspiration, of the faena. He started with a *circular*, taking the bull as though in a derechazo but continuing to turn, mostly with his waist, in a complete circle. This pass, perfected by Luis Miguel Dominguín, can be a kind of trick pass, done behind the horns, but done properly, as Rincón did it, without moving in behind the horns, with the horns coming around his legs in a circle, it is no trick. As he finished the circle, Rincón spun around to do a *martinete*, named for the Mexican matador Manolo Martínez, a right-handed pase de pecho done by quickly turning to the opposite side, a maneuver that also changes the bull's charge to that side. He ended the series with a pass that began as a pase de pecho with the left, except that at the point at which the bull would normally exit under the muleta, Rincón pulled the cloth back, spinning into a *molinete*[1] and out of the bull's terrain. It sounds complicated and flashy, but it was neither. It was liquid choreographic inspiration at its taurine finest, the passes linked as seamlessly as though César Rincón and Paquero had rehearsed them.

At this point Rincón began to get drunk on toreo—the only thing he ever gets drunk on—which is to say he was enjoying himself so much he did not want it to stop. Neither did the público, which began to petition the presidente to spare Paquero's life.

Perhaps even Paquero was enjoying their collaboration. Rincón believes a bull can experience the same sense of joy a torero feels. He says he can read it in the bull's eyes, which tear up with pleasure. "And when art is born from such a close and voluptuous compenetration, I believe it can be called love. Yes, it is love, no more, no less." With such a bull, Rincón has confessed he feels "a great sadness" when the time to kill comes (F-S 87).

Even though Rincón continued to torear, performing every type of pass imaginable, going beyond the time for an aviso, which did not sound, the presidente would not grant the pardon, to the chagrin of the matador, the public, and the breeder. So in something of an anticlimax Rincón killed him, as the crowd whistled at the presidente, with a good *estocada* or sword-thrust in to the hilt, and cut both ears from this exceptional animal.

After his victorious vuelta, back at the fence some girls yelled at Rincón to throw them the ears but Rincón looked up, smiled, and, not about to give them away, said "¡Mías!" His pride at bringing out all that Paquero had in him—the worst performance a torero can have is not being "up to" a truly great bull—as well as his friendship with Ernesto González Caicedo precluded, especially on this historic afternoon, his giving away those ears. They were indeed, as Rincón yelled to the girls, "Mine!"

Fernández Román called Rincón's triumph "toreo de cante grande, de cante jondo con un acento colombiano," meaning that his toreo had the grandeur and the depth of the finest flamenco music, but with a Colombian accent. When taurinos want to confer high praise they frequently invoke such comparisons, since both toreo and flamenco, as García Lorca explained so well, can produce the essence of Spanish and Hispanic art, the transformation of duende.

If there was a dissenting voice anywhere, it was the voice of Antonio Caballero, who clearly recognized the genius of César Rincón but somehow felt that the afternoon had lacked something. Perhaps, he wrote, it was that we were expecting too much: "In Colombia, lately, we are not satisfied with anything short of a miracle" (257).

Not all the bulls had permitted Rincón to cut ears, of course, but even with the good ones, Caballero believed, "the torero was always above the level of the bulls." There is more than a little truth in what he says, but my own opinion is that in Paquero, the hard-charging cárdeno of Ernesto González Caicedo, César Rincón had a worthy opponent. In any event, the most telling note of disappointment in Caballero's review came from his admission that "we were all expecting not one but six miracles" (258).

Render unto Caesar

If I were to write that César Rincón's 1991 temporada was the single greatest season any matador ever had—which it clearly was for any number of *Rinconistas incondicionales,* his die-hard fans, staunch admirers, and stalwarts—I would immediately call down the wrath of taurine critics and historians and any number of seasoned aficionados as well, partly because that is the nature of the beast: vehement argumentation and even vehement arguments are all part and parcel of afición. So I will not do that; I will simply say that in 1991 César Rincón had one of the greatest seasons any matador has ever had.

Rincón was, of course, very aware of his success, and one of the first things he would make clear to me was that no one, not even himself—or perhaps especially not himself, given the quotient of luck involved—could ever expect to repeat that season. Of one thing I am certain: no one is likely to break Rincón's 1991 record by going out on shoulders in Madrid five consecutive times in one season. And I, for one, would never wager that anyone will tie his mark of four, a feat made all the more extraordinary by his having begun as an unknown in Spain.

Virtually all the taurine broadcasters and journalists declared César Rincón the triunfador of the entire season. I say "virtually" because the case of *6T6* is a bit unusual. As we shall see shortly, they did and did not declare him triunfador. But everyone else did, except SER radio, which awarded Ortega Cano their prize. The taurine weekly *El Ruedo,* for instance, put a photograph of Rincón being carried on shoulders after his faena-of-the-year-in-France at Mont-de-Marsan on July 25 on its cover, with the caption

"El Gran Triunfador" (39 and 40: cover). And the newspaper *Diario 16* awarded Rincón their Trofeo Diario 16 as triunfador of the season.

The taurine annual *El Taurino Gráficio 1991* pronounced the Colombian Caesar "emperador" of the year (154), and in their opening piece Rafael Campos de España named Rincón "the absolute triunfador of the temporada," praising his brave artistic spirit and the virtue of his humility, which together formed "an authentic beacon for getting to 'the truth'" (5).

Their competitor *Anuario Taurino Internacional 1992: Temporada 1991* was equally acclamatory, calling Rincón "the axis of the season" (8). Juan Posada, who was an active matador from his alternativa in 1952 through 1958 and has since been a taurine writer, thought Rincón had made himself into the "máxima figura" of the season, by applying the basic rule of leaving the bull the required space and by "possessing sincere valor, clear intelligence, the ability to think quickly in the middle of the faena, and personal and professional maturity" (16). In the lead article Vicente Zabala criticized the Spanish toreros for being so style-conscious that they all ended up alike—with no style at all. He extolled Rincón's key virtues and placed him at the center of a renaissance of toreo, comparing him to the previous generation of Ordóñez, El Viti, Puerta, and Camino, all of whom had had their flesh torn open numerous times "because they put themselves in the same sitio[1] as this Colombiano" (7).

At *6T6*, however, the staff evidently could not come to agreement. We have already seen that in issue number five, after his great triumph with "el toro de Moura," *6T6* declared Rincón triunfador for the temporada 1991. But in number six, a resumé of the top thirty matadors of the season in Spain and France, they named Ortega Cano in first place, or perhaps I should say they placed him as number one, since they did not exactly say he was the triunfador except in passing, in fine print on the table-of-contents page. In fact, José Carlos Arévalo called Rincón the "principal figura" in his long editorial piece on the 1991 season (6:37). And in a round-table discussion of the season reported by *6T6* in which the participants were José Luis Suárez-Guanes of *ABC*, Barquerito of *Diario 16*, Fernando Fernández Román of TVE, and Michael Wigram, Pepe Dominguín, and Arévalo from *6T6*—Rincón came out clearly number one. Barquerito began by naming the first three "Rincón, Ortega Cano, and Julio Aparicio. In that order."

Following that comment, Ana Fernández Graciani, in charge of the piece, wrote: "The gold: With no room for doubt, to César Rincón." She reported that his triumphs were reflected everywhere, beginning in the box offices. She asserted that he had done a great deal for the fiesta, "obliging other [matadors] to commit themselves," and cited isolated phrases used to praise him: "The perfect antidote [to the general state of affairs in the fiesta prior to Rincón's breakthrough]" and "El gran triunfador" and "A very clear leader." The silver went to Ortega Cano (6:92).

Elsewhere in the number, precisely in the introduction to the ranking, the staff as a whole remarked that they had "the sensation that they had ranked justly and at the same time the impression that they had been mistaken" (6:45).

Michael Wigram penned a glowing piece defending Ortega Cano's *maestría* or mastery, but he ended by praising both toreros: "I haven't the slightest doubt that José Ortega Cano and César Rincón, in their 1991 versions, are two grand toreros who have arrived at an opportune moment to reveal the truth and to denounce falsehood" (6:42), seeming in the process to "tie" the two matadors, although Ortega Cano was listed first.

Carlos Abella's piece on Rincón came across unequivocally: he discussed Rincón's surprising authenticity, calling him from the first afternoon he had seen him—before the San Isidro breakthrough—"the best torero I have seen in a long time," emphasis on "a long time." He had predicted wrongly that, toreando the way he did in San Isidro, Rincón "would not make it to Pamplona," and now he was glad for the fiesta that he had become "a perfect example of how it is possible to combine artistic purity and dependability, bravery and sincerity, pride and discretion." In effect, to reduce Abella's piece to its essentials, Rincón had rescued the fiesta from the uninspired superficiality of Espartaco and company on the one hand and Paco Ojeda and his school, harmful for their immobility and for always being on top of the bull, stifling the charge, on the other.

Many aficionados, he concluded, will forever remember 1991 as the year of Rincón's "living dangerously," amid shouts of "Ave César," and "many of us will consider it one of the best years of our lives." The "sincerity of the artist" and an "honest conception of art" had made a triumphant return, and the man responsible was "a small Colombian with an enormous heart and a privileged head, one who had come straight into our company by going directly to Glory" (6:43–44).

I find Abella's assessment of Rincón's Spanish and French season accurate, poetic, and representative of the majority of critical opinion. Why then were the staff of *6T6* equivocal in their judgment about who was number one, placing Ortega Cano first but extolling Rincón noticeably more? We may never know, at least not beyond the obvious answer that there simply was no consensus. But why *was* there no consensus, when Rincón's season was so extraordinary? To reverse the question, if Ortega Cano—rather than a Colombian—had gone out on shoulders four consecutive times in Madrid that season instead of once, would there have been any doubt about who was number one?

During the winter, in Colombia and then back in Spain, Javier Villán gathered critical assessments of Rincón's status. Several of them raised interesting points.

In the first place, what did César Rincón mean to Colombia? Guillermo Rodríguez, then president of the Crotaurinos press association, to which Rincón dedicated the last bull on December 15, answered: "Rincón is the great triumph of Colombia, our clamorous vindication. He redeems us from the great frustration of Pepe Cáceres, who was unable to triumph fully in Spain." And what was true of Colombia, said Rodríguez, was equally true of the rest of taurine Latin America (JV 274).

Germán Castro Caycedo voiced a similar opinion, remarking that "As an artist and as a mestizo, César Rincón is the equal in importance to García Márquez or to [the painter Fernando] Botero, to use two examples well known in Spain." Rincón, he said, "gives us confidence as Colombians, something which, historically, we have never had" (JV 260).

Oscar García Calderón, who headed the taurine section of the Bogotá newspaper, *El Espectador,* and had known Rincón since he was a child, added: "We Colombians had a complex that no torero from here could ever open the Puerta Grande of Las Ventas. And now there's Rincón, who did it four consecutive times" (JV 264).

Alberto Lopera, a popular Colombian taurine broadcaster and writer, pointed out that organized cuadrillas of Spanish toreros had been performing in Colombia since 1892. In other words, "it took one hundred years to achieve a perfect maturation of the Fiesta here." He did not say "years of solitude," but the allusion inevitably leaps to mind. He also expanded the horizon by observing that the importance of Rincón for Spain was that he had "given back to the art of toreo the whole Truth, with a capital T" (JV 268).

Camilo Llinás, the president of the Corporation of the Plaza Santamaría—the profits from which help build parks and hospitals in poor sections of Bogotá—thought that 1991 "was a consequence of César's past, which had not been easy and during which he had not been given anything." That toughness of character was behind Rincón's great season. When Camilo Llinás added that Rincón did not want to be just number one, that he "wants to be legend and myth" (JV 270–71), I could only wonder if he were speaking for Rincón, for himself, or for Colombia.

In Spain the reactions lacked the nationalistic tone but were every bit as positive. Andrés Amorós, professor of literature at the Universidad Complutense in Madrid and author of numerous books on toreo, saw in Rincón "an extraordinarily well organized head both in the ring and out." Amorós judged that Rincón had not only surprised the público in Madrid, "he had left them flabbergasted." Rincón, as everyone now knew, had come to restore the lidia, to put himself face to face with the bull (*ponerse de frente*) and withstand the charge (*aguantar*), "withstand while being fully aware of the bull's charge." And the emotion? "The emotion derives from conscious valor. We can see clearly that in citing, and in the *embroque* [coming together in the same terrain] with the bull, Rincón takes risks." Amorós was reminded by Rincón of the maestros Manolo Vázquez and Antoñete: "Just when we are so accustomed to seeing the step back, the citing in profile, and *el encimismo* [being on top of the bull, "drowning" the charge], Rincón comes along, cites from a distance, and faces the bull" (JV 282).

That same Antoñete, Antonio Chenel, who had given César Rincón the alternativa on December 8, 1982, in Bogotá, had one of his greatest days in Madrid on June 3, 1982, with the Garzón bull Danzarín in the pouring rain. On the same cartel was the Colombian matador Jairo Antonio Castro, and in the tendido that afternoon to watch Jairo Antonio's confirmation by Antoñete was an unknown sixteen-year-old Colombian novillero named Julio César Rincón.

Years later when Carlos Abella asked Rincón how he had connected so perfectly with the Madrid público, Rincón told Abella that on that distant afternoon he had discovered that the afición of Madrid loved to watch the bull charge from a distance and to see the torero show "his knowledge of distances and terrains" (6T6 6:44), precisely the speciality of Antoñete, the man who, taurinely at least, out of retirement at age fifty, would become Rincón's most influential model in actual performance. I know Rincón would never forget that afternoon in the rain in 1982. But which did he remember more? The image of Antoñete citing—kicking his zapatillas off first—from a distance, Danzarín charging through puddles after the elusive muleta, the crowd wet, himself wet, yet on fire with Antoñete's liquid sculpture? Or was it Antoñete taking the vuelta with the two ears of Danzarín in his hands, the matador's tears nearly invisible because of the rain, and the sight of Antoñete on soaking shoulders disappearing through the portals of glory and up the Calle Alcalá? Could it have been both?

And what does the maestro Chenel think of Rincón's toreo? What for him was the most significant aspect of Rincón's accomplishments in 1991? "Something very simple, which everyone is now convinced of: César Rincón has come along to put things in their proper place."

Villán wondered if the maestro saw any resemblance, as some had commented, to his own toreo? Antoñete replied that César Rincón was César Rincón, with his own personality and his own very authentic style of art. But what he could tell Villán was that "Rincón does the toreo that I like, the toreo that every great torero and every true aficionado dreams about" (JV 284).

Antoñete went on to say, with his unique authority, that Rincón's "toreo was the toreo of always: distance to the bull; technique, because without technique it's impossible to cite from a distance or to catch the bull in the belly of the muleta and take him around behind you, smoothly, rhythmically. That is *dominio* and when it all comes out right, the beauty shows through and becomes art."

Villán remarked that Antoñete made it sound as if anyone could do it, and the maestro replied that to do it had enormous merit and tested one's valor to the limit. "It looks easy but you have to do it. There's that key moment, decisive, when you have to wait for the bull, to wait for his charge, to wait for his start." Theoretically all the professionals understood this moment very precisely. "But some do it and others don't. All of us, or almost all of us, know what it is; it's how to do it that only a few of us know" (JV 285).

In 1991, César Rincón knew how to do it and did it as no one I had seen since Antoñete himself with the white bull, perhaps even as no one I had ever seen. He made taurine history that year in a single season with accomplishments that could never be taken away from him, regardless of what the future held. As the psychologist, physician, professor, and taurine writer Dr. Fernando Claramunt expressed it at the end of the 1991 season, "By now, Rincón is already a torero of legend," one who possesses a particular charisma: "Rincón is a small man, he doesn't look like a fighter, and yet he has an immense heart. That gets to people" (JV 289). It got to me—it was exactly the toreo that this aficionado had for a long time found only in memory or in dreams.

Yet beyond the torero of legend and beyond the toreo of dreams turned into reality, there was also the hero. Fernando Sánchez Dragó, author of the best-seller *Gárgoris y Habidis: Una historia mágica de España*, which as its title suggests delves into every corner of Spanish arcana, sees Rincón very much as I have from the beginning—mythically, heroically—and explains in words that can serve as my own: "In the taurine world I seek the thread

Figure 15. Distance to the bull. Antoñete would say that "it's how to do it that only a few of us know." Rincón knows. And one of his main "secrets" is giving distance to the bull. In this characteristic photo—the legs open, the head back, the hand low—he is so far away, you can't even see the bull.

that ties us to the ancient world, to the conception of the hero, of the demi-god, of Theseus. I have no difficulty placing César Rincón in that context" (JV 297). Nor do I. In fact that is his context. What was it César said to his presidential namesake? "Five hundred years after that twelfth of October, on which there was a conquest, a Colombian, on this twelfth of October, has returned triumphant." How very much, indeed, like Theseus returning to Athens: "Knossos had fallen, which time out of mind had ruled the seas." The Minotaur was dead.

Obscure Beginnings

↠ 16

Hernando Santos said of César Rincón in November of 1991: "What we never expected, occurred. What for a [Colombian] taurino was the maximum aspiration, happened. The sight of a Colombian torero perched on the pinnacle of world toreo seemed like a dream, like a utopia. That this Colombian—born in our city, an inhabitant of our neighborhoods, nourished by our food—could scale such heights, was not believable" (I&B vii). Yet César Rincón's stature in 1991, however Olympian it may have appeared, had been achieved only by Herculean dedication, and for much of his young life he had rather resembled rock-saddled Sisyphus.

Santos, a lifelong aficionado, was the first to recognize that Colombians had been unjust with Rincón by not realizing that he had, in fact, already done in Bogotá what he later did in Madrid. Perhaps, thought Santos, the "imperial complex" the Spanish toreros occasioned every December by their arrival in Colombian rings had blinded Colombians to the true worth of their own (I&B viii). In any case, Spanish prejudice against Colombians and the Colombians' own taurine inferiority complex were only two of many obstacles César Rincón had needed to surmount in his unprecedented climb to the summit. Rincón would say of himself in retrospect: "The fundamentals of your art were already there and you had expressed them with the same purity on more than one occasion. Yet it's true that nothing had come of it" (JV 84).

When I first became interested in toreo in 1963, I was fascinated by the beauty of the liquid sculpture of the cape and muleta and by the hieratic ballet of the toreros themselves in the face of death. Two things I understood early on: that the sacred ballet represented the essence of the affirmation of life, and that the only way to understand it was to learn to do it.

John Fulton, the matador from Philadelphia, had just taken his alternativa—in Sevilla, on July 18, 1963—when I was introduced to him by our mutual friend Perdita Hordern at the Miramar Hotel in Málaga in August of that year. The Miramar was one of the grand taurine hotels of the '60s and it exuded taurine ambience.

El Cordobés, just then the rage, was there, and Perdita and I remarked on his sitting alone one evening on the terrace eating pasta with his fingers. The ghost of Hemingway, only two years dead, seemed to frequent the bar with Antonio Ordóñez, and I drank wine with John Fulton, who, being a natural teacher, immediately began my taurine training. John told stories about his friendship with Hemingway and with Juan Belmonte—who had shot himself the year before—and with Joselito's brother Rafael el Gallo. When I asked him how he had decided to become a matador, he said: "When I was thirteen, I saw Tyrone Power in *Blood and Sand.*"

"And that did it?"

"That was it. When I came out of the theatre I knew I wanted to be a matador and to live in Sevilla. When I told my parents they said, 'That's nice.'"

Curiously enough, Rincón's father, Gonzalo, says that one Sunday in Bucaramanga in 1952, when he was fourteen, he saw *Sangre y arena* (*Blood and Sand*) and decided to become a matador. He can still remember the film quite well and has described to me in detail how Esther Williams took Ricardo Montalbán's place in the ring and had a great triumph. If a woman can do that, Gonzalo Rincón had reasoned, so can I. (Never mind that the Esther Williams–Ricardo Montalbán film was not—even though Gonzalo insists it was—*Blood and Sand* but an MGM film called *Fiesta,* made in 1947, the year after John Fulton saw *Blood and Sand.*)

At the time Gonzalo Rincón was working in a photo lab, so he got some old negatives of taurine scenes, had a cape and muleta made like the ones in the photos, cut down all the plants in the walled-in backyard of the modest house where his family lived, and began to train himself to be a torero. (As we shall see, his son would also cut down a tree or two when necessary.)

He went to work in a local restaurant, taking pictures of the clients so he would have enough money to see the local corridas, but the job did not last long and the owner refused to pay him. Gonzalo Rincón had a little rum to console himself and, being unused to it, arrived home in a poor state to be told by his father that either he brought him money the next day or he would have to leave home. The next day Gonzalo Rincón managed to get a little money from the restaurant owner, bought himself a new shirt, put his few belongings in a cardboard box, kissed his mother goodbye, and caught the bus for Bogotá.

One of thirteen children, Gonzalo Rincón left school after the third grade. For many thousands of children in Spain and Mexico and Latin America (and now and then Philadelphia, Los Angeles, or Brooklyn), to be a matador was to be famous, rich, and crowned with glory. For most of those it could also mean getting out of grinding, if not starving, poverty. For Gonzalo Rincón it meant a chance to be something other than a photographer's apprentice, a day laborer in construction, a busboy, or a dishwasher.

Too proud to beg and too honest to steal, he quickly found himself broke, lost his few possessions, and ended up sleeping on benches in the Parque Nacional. A friend rescued him from starvation and got him a job—as a restaurant photographer. Eventually he fell in with the local taurine aspirants and began to train again, this time with a real capote and a real muleta. By taking pictures of other toreros in village events, he insinuated himself into the group and eventually faced his own animals.

One of the problems with toreo in Latin America is the lack of *ganado bravo,* "fighting" stock. There simply are not enough toros bravos to go around. As a result, in the local village ferias—inconceivable without a taurine spectacle—they use the *cebú,* the zebu, an animal familiar as the Brahman or Brahma bull used in rodeos. Cebú are dangerous beasts—they regularly maim and occasionally kill rodeo riders—but they lack the "noble" charge of the toro bravo.

The first animal Gonzalo Rincón faced, as they tell the story, was a monster of nearly six hundred kilos. In the family mythology, they say the animal snorted at him and Gonzalo Rincón fell over backward five meters away. The crowd threw shoes, cushions, anything at hand.

Yet Gonzalo Rincón went on trying to torear cebú in the provinces, having one disaster after another, and losing money in the process since, unlike the other toreros, he refused to pass the cape—to beg—before the corrida (I&B 3–7).

María Teresa Ramírez, a light-skinned, light-eyed young lady of seventeen, born in the town of Tenza in the Department of Boyacá, was living in Bogotá and working at a laundry when she noticed that at the local lunch spot there was a young man of twenty who never took his eyes off her. Years later young Luis Carlos and César would often ask María Teresa this favorite question: "Mamá, what did you see in Papá that made you marry him?" And she would answer invariably: "Me enamoré," I fell in love (JV 81).

Their first three children, Luis Carlos, Sonia, and Rocío, were born in Bucaramanga. In Bogotá, César—Julio César Rincón Ramírez—was born at 9:00 A.M. on September 5, 1965, in the maternity hospital of San Juan de Dios in the medical complex of Hortúa. Marta, the youngest, would soon follow. When César was born, the sun was shining and there had been no comets or any unusual occurrences that anyone remembers. There was, in fact, no sign of what was to come, only his name, Julio César, which is not uncommon in Colombia.

Today in Bogotá there are an unconscionable number of kidnappings and murders every day. The statistics are horrific, so unbelievable there is no point in citing any. The south side of Bogotá is the most disadvantaged area of the city. Old cars belch smoke, lurid paint peels from the houses, and many of the people have prematurely aged faces. The streets are full of holes and sometimes full of homeless children who run in packs. Adapting the French word to Spanish, they call them *gamines* in Bogotá. No one knows how many there are.

Santa Fe de Bogotá is a sad city of six million inhabitants, sad because of its present, sad because of its past, sad with a rainy, fog-bound climate, hemmed in at 2,600 meters by the eastern range of the Andes on the east, open to the savanna on the west. The north, where César Rincón would eventually live, is for the rich. The south, where he lived as a child, is for the poor. The center seems to be for whoever has the guts to take it, now the army, now the gamines, now the private armies of the wealthy—the good wealthy and the bad wealthy. When César was growing up it was not as bad as it seems today, but it was bad enough. And yet the Colombian people, in some angelic perversity, some holy flying-in-the-face of their own destiny, are for the most part hospitable, soft spoken, courteous, and refined.

The Rincón family moved around the south side of Bogotá, living in different barrios, first Santander, then Matatigres and El Carmen, then Venecia, and finally Fátima. When César was eleven they rented in Fátima part of a house in Calle 50 Sur, South 50th Street. Three families lived in the house of Hermógenes Martínez and shared a common patio and kitchen. This situation was not misery, but at best it was poverty with dignity and usually something to eat. There were two bare rooms—or one divided into two—plus a small space that Gonzalo used as a darkroom. Sonia, the oldest girl, slept alone, the rest in pairs, Gonzalo and María Teresa, Marta and Rocío, and Luis Carlos and César, head to toe.

César worked when he was not in school, as all his siblings did, from a very early age. He is given to saying somewhat adamantly, "No tuve infancia," I had no childhood. While that may be an overstatement, he did start working around the age of ten, first in a shoe repair shop, then as a scrap collector, hauling a wagon around the streets of Bogotá with his sister Sonia until, as he remembers it, an evil junk dealer ran over their wagon and put them out of business. César also sold bleach door-to-door, and along with his brothers and sisters worked for a time in a fabric warehouse and a glass factory.

His mother labored as a domestic and as a laundress, while Gonzalo Rincón continued as a photographer and served a brief stint at the Treasury. By working together, they managed (JV 56–60).

The poverty César Rincón grew up in has possibly been exaggerated. There was enough money for Gonzalo Rincón to squander some of it in his disastrous taurine ventures. And perhaps more telling still, César grew into a healthy child, short but healthy, the shortness probably more genetic than a matter of diet. Compared to, for example, Antoñete, who grew up in the post–Civil War poverty of the streets of Madrid, César seems robust. Still, nothing was easy.

"I had no childhood," says César Rincón—and also, with some frequency, "I was born a torero." He is sure that his chromosomes were programmed for him to be a torero just as surely as he was programmed for his "coffee eyes" or his short stature. That was the "legacy" of his father. And since "no one can escape his genetic destiny," then it follows in César Rincón's logic that he "would become a torero."

Chromosomes aside, he was certainly raised to be a torero. He remembers, when he was still very small, trying to imitate with a rag the passes he saw his father make, and he remembers his father's joy, his encouragement and his vibrant olés. His first público, from the tenderest age, was his doting father, his loving mother, his sisters, and his brother Luis Carlos, who had somehow escaped the taurine "virus" (F-S 7).

The first animal to which the young César presented the lure was not a bovine but a small white *gosque,* a Colombian dog, named Príncipe. Rincón is fond of saying the dog taught him his first lessons in temple, since he had to keep it from chewing his rag to pieces.

Around age eight César remembers crying with rage at his inability and clumsiness, remembers his father scolding him, remembers María Teresa berating his father for scolding him, remembers that the games were not a

Figure 16. Gonzalo Rincón. The photo was taken in the corrals behind the Santamaría ring in Bogotá in December 1995.

game but a very serious matter. By the time they moved to Fátima, César was training with some regularity under his father and sometimes with a taurine family friend, Alfonso Brillón, in the interior patio of the house of Hermógenes Martínez.

Gonzalo Rincón, a classic "stage father," seems to have projected onto his young son all his own frustrated desires. He failed at every taurine endeavor he ever engaged in, failed in all but one—Gonzalo Rincón made his son into the greatest torero ever to emerge from South America. How he did that is something of a mystery, but his son remembers him as very patient and imperturbably calm, never raising his voice (the scolding at eight doubtless the exception) and, above all, never for an instant doubting that the boy would become a gran figura.

For a number of reasons Gonzalo Rincón was not successful as a torero—he never once made a profit—but in his head he knew what a torero was and how he had to torear. And somehow he conveyed that Platonic toreo, of which he himself was incapable, to young César. No one should underestimate Gonzalo Rincón's importance in his son's career, especially as regards manners, literally and figuratively, in the ring. Many of the great toreros have come from fathers who were less than great toreros—Paquirri, Manzanares, and Espartaco, for example—and Juan Belmonte and El Cordobés, from nontaurine families, are exceptions. What in Gonzalo Rincón was an impossible dream was to transmute in his son into the stuff of a hundred afternoons a year.

Nor should we underestimate María Teresa Ramírez's role. César remembers her every morning before dawn with a song to wake him up and a *tinto,* a Colombian coffee, for her *negro*—the pet name she called him because he was the darkest of the children—remembers her as the one who had confidence in him, remembers her as the one who told him over and again, "You are going to be a great torero, my son." When he thinks of those days he recalls a house and a patio; a patio and his apprenticeship as a torero; his apprenticeship and his mother watching him, leaning on the railing of the passageway. When things go badly, César Rincón usually thinks to himself: "Hay que seguir"—You've got to keep going. That tenacity of purpose came from his mother (JV 26, 76).

From his earliest days of training he wanted to be like the national hero Pepe Cáceres so that one day he could buy his mother a beautiful white villa. It was she who would tell him when he first left for Spain: "One day you will come back here crowned with laurels. And when you return to El Dorado Airport, they will roll out a long red carpet, as for a king. Oh, yes, because you will soon be the great Julio César of toreo" (F-S 8–9, 20). Rincón is fond of saying that he owes his mother everything.

In January 1977, at age eleven and a half, the little César—not yet four feet tall—crossed the Rubicon, as he puts it (F-S 11). Paco Camino, a figura since the early '60s and a matador with enormous "cartel" or popularity in América, and José Antonio Campuzano, a young matador from Sevilla with promise but not yet at peak, were to *tentar*—to test cows for bravery—in the ganadería of Fernando Reyes Neira. Alberto Ruiz el Bogotano alerted Gonzalo Rincón and managed an invitation for César, which was the only way he would be able to stand out from the throng of would-be toreros gathered at the *tienta,* the testing, and be able to torear. It was an important event, and television cameras showed up to film Camino, who was in those days the reigning maestro of maestros.

The hyperbolic taurine mythmakers and yarn spinners make it sound almost like the young Jesus among the rabbis at the Temple. César Rincón says he emerged from that tienta with the reputation of the young Mozart of tauromachy—an interesting twist since Camino, long known as *el niño sabio* or the wise child, has often been called the Mozart of toreo, a phrase

Carlos Abella would eventually use as the title for his 1994 biography of Camino.

Different versions exist of who said what. The most widely disseminated one has Camino, who let César torear one of his *vaquillas* or young cows to his heart's content, saying, "Este va a ser figura del toreo," this kid is going to be a figura del toreo.

During the Feria de Abril in Sevilla in 1995, John Fulton and I had a *copita* of manzanilla with Paco Camino in the taurine bar and restaurant bearing the unlikely name El Donald, and I asked him about what he said that day. Camino remembered it well and said that, yes, he had made a remark to that effect.

"What was it exactly that you saw in him?"

"Hombre, a natural sense of terrain and perfect distances. A very privileged head, something most unusual in a kid his age."

"That sounds like a description of you at the same age."

Camino smiled and said with that rapid and slightly mischievous grin that has characterized him to me since I first met him in Pamplona in 1963: "Yes. Well, yes. Very similar, in fact. I gave him my muleta, I believe. He used mine to torear and then I think I made him a present." Camino is well known for his wit and I knew from his expression that I had narrowly escaped a major ironic broadside with my implication that César was a niño sabio.

"How has your prediction turned out?"

"You know, my son Rafi and I were watching that corrida televised from Madrid on the day he broke through, and I said to Rafi, watch how he's not going to let the ears of this bull get away. He is a true figura."

The child César was such a natural that day of his debut that he became instantly famous. Prodigies are very desirable commodities in the taurine world, and César's prodigiousness was helped along spectacularly when the tienta was shown on television. As he recalls, everyone began yelling and shouting, "Come here! Come here, everybody! 'El negro' is toreando!" He says the neighbors must have figured he was just giving passes to the dog. Luis Carlos and his mother, however, were extremely excited. Rincón remembers that his mother was so impressed that she became instantly certain he would become a great torero and that her early morning coffees had produced "the effect of a miraculous brew" (JV 94–95).

Such was the emotion generated by this tienta that even what was said in the papers is uncertain. One source reports that on January 30, 1977, *El Espectador* asked: "Will Julio César be the Messiah of Colombian toreo?" (I&B 22). Another source claims that on January 30, 1977, *El Espectador* wondered: "Will this César be the new César of toreo?" (JV 301). Same date, same paper, same effect, but different "quotes." Render unto both. The taurine world is never exactly precise. If the wording is in dispute, the fact is not: César Rincón had made an instant name for himself in Colombia, in the process becoming a kind of national mascot and achieving a privileged position in his profession right from the start. From age eleven-and-a-half on, he found that he was what he would always say he had been born to be: a torero.

First Steps

17

That day at the tienta of Fernando Reyes Neira no one believed that the young César Rincón had never faced an animal other than his dog. Such was his fluidity and natural sitio that everyone assumed he had practiced with at least a dozen vaquillas. César was undoubtedly brilliant that afternoon—no less an authority than Paco Camino continues to affirm it—and he was already showing his characteristic style. I have seen very early photographs of him—now mostly missing, unfortunately[1]—that revealed the toreo that shook the foundations of Las Ventas. But little César, as good as he seemed, had also been fortunate to be alternating with Camino, Campuzano, and Alberto Ruiz, and no matter how precocious he had looked, he was still as green as the Andean grass. Now he had to torear as much as possible and to train with professional zeal. At the tienta he had merely taken the first step along that initiatory road that makes the proverbial Chinese journey of a thousand miles seem like a training run.

And so, with his father acting as his mentor and manager, he began to torear at tientas, in festivals, in any event where there was anything with horns and casta. He did manage to avoid performing with cebú, which, aside from the danger caused by their uncertain charges, are thought to interfere with a torero's sense of temple with animals of casta.

He began to train regularly with Juanito and Paco Márquez, two older boys who had already become professional novilleros. Juanito Márquez would eventually abandon his taurine aspirations but he would remain with Rincón as the ayuda to Luis Carlos, although in reality he did much more than an ayuda normally does, sometimes training with Rincón and running the *carretón*—the training cart, made of a bicycle wheel, with bull's horns on

Figure 17. The beginning (January 1977), with Paco Camino. Most of the early photos of César Rincón have been lost. This is a photograph of a photograph I made one day at César's house. He was distressed at having lost others by loaning them for previous books and would not let this cherished memento out of his possession.

the front—for him. Another friend and training partner from those days is Ricardo Chinza, a young locksmith who also once harbored taurine aspirations. Ricardo Chinza built the carretón they used in those early days and would later serve as one of Rincón's chauffeurs.

As Juanito tells it, César used to wake them up around five every morning at their family's house in the Ricaúrte barrio. That was too early for the house of Márquez, so they often made César crawl into bed until a little later, when they would all head for the Parque Nacional to train, jog, and play soccer. Inevitably taurine training began to replace school.

César also went to tientas with the Márquez boys, especially at the Vistahermosa ranch owned by Francisco García. Palomo Linares, the only matador in recent history to cut a tail in Las Ventas (1972), acted as senior matador, and although the ganadero and the matador became irritated sometimes because the boys seemed to show up out of nowhere—the simpático Spanish journalist and announcer Curro Fetén used to alert them—both Palomo Linares and his banderillero Enrique Bojilla were impressed with César's natural talent (perhaps Bojilla, too, alerted the boys). Later on Palomo Linares would give César a suit of lights, orange and silver, which he would wear in his debut as a novillero in Sevilla, and Bojilla would always be one of his believers.

There are many anecdotes about this early time, but one of Gonzalo Rincón's favorites has to do with a certain journalist who ran into the proud father and his miniature torero at the Parque Nacional where the toreros trained. The journalist seemed horrified and told Gonzalo Rincón he was a *sinvergüenza*, a shameless person, for exposing his son to such a world. That same journalist would later proclaim that from the first time he saw him train as a boy in the Parque Nacional with his father, he knew César would become a figura. He even claimed he had told Gonzalo Rincón so at the time.

From the tienta in early 1977 until he went to Spain for the first time in 1981, César appeared in some three dozen public taurine events, some more legitimate than others. On June 29, 1977, for example, he performed for the first time in the Santamaría ring in Bogotá, but the event, organized by Tarzán de Colombia, was what they call a mixed spectacle, made up in this case of a cockfight, a wrestling match, and the lidia of two *becerros* or calves, all accompanied by a band of musicians.

He performed with becerros and novillos in small-town ferias in mixed nocturnal events usually involving comic *enanos,* dwarves, especially two groups called Kalimán Torero and Superlandia Internacional. Then on the first of October, 1977, having just turned twelve, he cut his first ear, from a becerro of Abraham Domínguez in the important Cañaveralejo ring in Cali. He also wore his first traje de luces that day, a blue-and-white suit his mother had made by cutting down a larger suit of uncertain origin.

After two years of becerros, Rincón graduated to novillos with picadores, killing his first in Cali on December 26, 1979. His first *novillada* with picadores in Bogotá took place on January 13, 1980. The small matador was unable to kill his second novillo in the allotted time and received three avisos. He had dedicated the bull to Palomo Linares and, although he did finally kill it in style, technically the animal died too late. No one seemed to care, given the boy's sense of style and his guts, and that day the fourteen-year-old César Rincón became a favored son of the Santamaría ring.

At fourteen César Rincón was not only the youngest novillero in Colombia, he was also the smallest, and his lack of stature turned into a severe impediment when it came time to kill. He was still so small that his father once stuffed him under the seat of the bus on the way to Cali to avoid paying the extra ticket, or at least that is the story they tell.

At this time the young Rincón trained under a Colombian banderillero named Efraín Olano, a man who had been in Spain for a number of years, first as a novillero and then, after a bull damaged his knee, as a banderillero. Olano—who later worked as Rincón's *veedor* or bull spotter in Colombia and as the *mayoral* or foreman on his ranch—became so concerned about César's lack of growth that he took him to see Dr. John Raúl Sabogal, whose treatments may have helped the boy grow, although not yet enough for him to kill his novillo in the allotted fifteen minutes.

Efraín Olano worked with the young torero in intense training and taught him a great deal at tientas, where the tiny prodigy acquired experience in handling the cows: learning how to take them properly to the horses, how to take them away, how to give the animals the correct distance, so the ganadero could judge them properly. Rincón became quite proficient at these tasks at a very early age and was fortunate to have Olano's attention and guidance.

Rincón remembers that it was very early on, while he trained with Efraín Olano at tientas, that his toreo took shape, which is to say that the toreo he had been trying to learn in practice, and which he had so successfully performed that day at the tienta with Camino, became a reality that he could consistently execute with any number of animals.

The secret, he remembered, was "waiting for the bull de frente, advancing the muleta very flatly, catching the bull in the muleta from the beginning and taking it around behind you in a semicircle. This is so difficult to do that at first it seems impossible, but when you get used to it, it becomes the basis for proper toreo." Such toreo was not possible, however, "if you took the bull from up close or if you took it in a straight line." Why didn't everyone do it this way? Because it took a lot of valor and you had to measure the distances exactly. It also took "a sense, or a gift, of perfect temple. And great knowledge of the animals" (JV 128–29).

Not surprisingly, what Rincón remembers and elucidates coincides in virtually every respect with what Antoñete would later say about Rincón's toreo and great toreo in general. César Rincón may have been short in stature but from the beginning he stood very tall in technique. Efraín Olano is responsible for much of that technique, and Olano remembers the minutest details of their sessions, even down to practicing the pase de pecho the way Manzanares performed it, taking the left hand all the way across to the opposite shoulder (I&B 32). Rincón, like virtually all toreros today, greatly admires the style of Manzanares.

At one of those tientas Efraín Olano also persuaded a man known in the bull world as Pedro Domingo to become Rincón's apoderado—a favor that Rincón would later characterize as not the best thing Olano ever did for him. Pedro Domingo's real name was Darío Piedrahíta Cardona. He came from a wealthy family in Medellín and his brother Jaime was a senator. After failing as a torero he spent some time in the United States working as a dental technician. The worm bit him again and he went to Spain, where he took his alternativa from Gregorio Sánchez in the little wine-growing town of Cintruénigo in Navarra. Back in Colombia he became president of the Unión de Toreros de Colombia and tried through his brother to pass a law, which would later haunt him, prohibiting more than one non-Colombian on any cartel. He was an empresario by this time, and for a while he ran the Santamaría ring in association with the Lozano brothers (Lopera 188). It was at this stage that he managed César Rincón.

In May of 1981 Pedro Domingo, having signed a contract with Gonzalo Rincón, took the fifteen-year-old to Spain, where he hooked him up with the comic taurine group known as El Toronto, another troupe of dwarves, managed by the Lozano brothers. César Rincón was scheduled to perform the "serious part" with small but legitimate animals.

Since he had not yet turned sixteen, he was not allowed to perform with picadores in Spain and had to content himself with two novilladas without picadores in small towns. Still, his nocturnal performances with El Toronto—the comic groups usually perform as a lighthearted finale at the many regional ferias—allowed him a chance to work in some of the most important rings in Spain and familiarized him with the important ferias in which he aspired to perform. Contract talks with the Lozanos fizzled, but as he crossed and recrossed the dusty roads of Spain for the first time, the young torero learned many lessons, getting to know the enanos well and being touched by their bravery and by their clowns' sadness.

While in Madrid, he stayed in a pensión called the Hostal Picos de Europa (named for the high mountains in Asturias) on the Calle Silva, just off the Gran Vía in the center of Madrid. A taurine pensión frequented by some of Palomo Linares's cuadrilla, the hostal was run by a warm, motherly woman named Lidia Fernández who instantly adopted César as one of her own.

Back in Colombia, Rincón's career failed to develop the way he wanted. He performed in only five novilladas that season of 1981–82, partly because the empresarios preferred to put on corridas, which made a larger profit. He would do better, he was sure, once he had the alternativa. Pedro Domingo, meanwhile, guaranteed him at least forty novilladas for the next season in Spain, now that he had turned sixteen and could perform with picadores. The plan was for him to torear with the best of the Spanish novilleros and take the alternativa at season's end. As Rincón would say, "Who could ask for more?" (F-S 17).

Into the Abyss

18

The 1982 season in Spain started well for César Rincón. He began with high spirits, determined to conquer the *Madrepatria*—the Motherfatherland, as they sometimes say in Spanish—and to make 1982 the year of the Indito from Colombia. Pedro Domingo secured contracts for Rincón to appear with the top novilleros: Luis Miguel Campano, Curro Durán, Morenito de Jaén, Fernando Lozano (of the same Lozano family), Juan Mora, Emilio Oliva. Rincón performed in the best company, and if his successes far exceeded mediocrity, especially given his age and lack of experience—one ear in Zaragoza, two in Torrijos, three in Jaén, three in Santander—he nevertheless did not manage to "break through," failing to triumph in his debuts in Barcelona on July 4 and in the Maestranza of Sevilla on August 8, where he wore Palomo Linares's orange-and-silver suit of lights.

Then, on August 16, 1982, less than a month before his seventeenth birthday, the bottom dropped out of his world: his mother, María Teresa Ramírez, and his sister Sonia Rincón were asphyxiated by a chemical fire in their rented rooms in the house of Hermógenes Martínez in the barrio of Fátima.

All the details are not clear, and some contradictions exist. Still, what apparently happened is that María Teresa left a candle burning, a candle like countless she had lit to the Virgen de la Macarena, Sevilla's revered patroness of toreros, to protect César in Spain, and also to protect his sister Rocío, who was to make a trip to Pereira, where she had nearly drowned a few months before.

The fire took place during the day. Gonzalo Rincón had gone to work at his job at the Departmental Treasury and was to deliver some photographs to a client. Then he was to have bought a new color television he had promised the family, but a call intercepted him at the Treasury. He was needed at home at once. When he arrived in a car from the Treasury, he found the house destroyed by smoke and his wife and daughter dead on the bathroom floor from asphyxiation. Marta, who had also been home, had escaped into the patio.

Somehow the candle had tipped over and ignited the darkroom chemicals. María Teresa and Sonia had taken refuge in the bathroom, but the poisonous smoke had seeped in. Marta had fled out the inside door into the patio to get water or help and the door had locked behind her. A neighbor called the firemen, but by the time anything could be done, it was too late. The women were dead and the contents of the house were ruined. Gonzalo Rincón had lost his wife, a daughter, and everything the family owned.

In Madrid it was late. César Rincón was at Lidia Fernández's pensión on the Calle Silva. Pedro Domingo was less than forthright about telling him what had happened, perhaps wanting to keep him from returning home. Finally Gonzalo Rincón spoke to his son by telephone. César Rincón and Pedro Domingo evidently had words, but they left the next day for Bogotá. Meanwhile, María Teresa's brother Silvino Ramírez took the family in.

A week later César Rincón returned to Spain to torear in Cuenca, because he was sure that was what his mother would have wanted. But his world was no longer intact.

The young torero managed to get through an additional seven or eight novilladas, cutting ears more times than not. In the last one, on an October afternoon in the old Roman town of Mérida, he cut an ear in his first, but the second novillo caught him in the right thigh, pitching him into the air and then trapping him on the sand, inflicting his first serious cornada, his "baptism of blood." Efraín Olano had told him the bulls could not gore him because he was light, so now Rincón sent him a postcard to the contrary. He remembers that it was not as bad as he had thought it would be, and that he had been reminded of a time when he was six and had been cut badly in the back by some barbed wire, an event that seemed to affect Luis Carlos more than it did César, who was already a stoic.

The goring was clean and the operation seemed to go well. Back in Madrid, Mother Lidia Fernández and some cabaret hostesses staying at the pensión took care of the young torero with great patience and care, but the wound continued to suppurate and would not heal in spite of high doses of antibiotics. Although the operation had gone well, someone—such as the surgeon who had performed the operation—had left a drainage tube inside the wound. In Madrid Dr. Máximo García de la Torre, horrified when he opened the wound, removed the drainage tube, which Rincón's flesh was doing its painful best to incorporate into his body, and re-operated, this time with excellent results and quick healing.

When Rincón returned to Bogotá, the full force of what had happened in August hit him. This inner wound would not close. Now there were two mysteries. Along with the mystery of killing the animal he so admired came this mystery of his mother's and sister's deaths. Thinking about his mother's absence, he would wonder, "I thought about the fact that you were always going to be my protection, because perhaps that was why you had died, to protect 'el negro.' It is absurd and cruelly meaningless. Life is full of absurdities. Then I thought that it would be to you that I would pray most, as I am doing now, and I told myself again that at seventeen I could not give up" (JV 139). From that time on, a photograph of his mother and sister would become the centerpiece of his altar, and the spirit of his mother would be with him always, but most especially in the plaza de toros.

Late one afternoon in Dax in August 1995, after a corrida, César Rincón was reminded of that fatal afternoon. He was explaining it—describing it almost as if he had been there—to Joan Simpson and Tim Bairstow, aficionados from Edinburgh we will meet later, and he said: "There were some cardboard boxes my father had, that he used like a darkroom where he used to develop photographs. It had chemicals in it, and the chemicals were what killed them. Afterwards there was no more darkroom. He took photographs for the taurine and horse racing sections for *El Espectador* and *El Tiempo*. And before that he used to take couples up on Montserrate."

He spoke in an even tone, but I remember thinking there was a family history in that one paragraph.

Young Matador

19

Trying to forget the tragedy, Rincón began intense training. He had not taken the alternativa as Pedro Domingo had planned, and he had appeared in fewer than twenty novilladas. There had been talk of his *doctorado*—his doctorate, the alternativa—in Zaragoza during the Feria del Pilar, the last important fair of the year in Spain, but like many taurine projects, it never progressed beyond the talking stage.

At some point Pedro Domingo must have realized that the alternativa in Spain was virtually impossible, at least without another season for Rincón as a novillero, a price in time and expenses that he doubtless did not choose to bear. Nor could he afford to become the sole empresario for a corrida for the alternativa in Spain. So Pedro Domingo convinced Rincón that the only course of action was to take the alternativa in Bogotá.

Rincón, impatient and enthusiastic, less than experienced but champing at the bit, agreed. On the positive side, for the público of Bogotá it would constitute a taurine event, a piece of history logically following Rincón's career in the Santamaría ring. Better to be a favored son in the capital of Colombia than a nobody in a provincial ring in Spain.

Was he prepared for the alternativa? With only a few dozen novilladas with picadores, he was not even close. Furthermore he was recuperating from a serious goring, without enough time to get his sitio back. Yet with luck, if he could manage to learn with toros as he would have done with more novillos, he could end up well positioned. And there was no doubt that it was less difficult to get contracts for a corrida than for a novillada. Did such considerations amount to a lack of professional responsibility on Pedro Domingo's part, or Gonzalo Rincón's? Of course, but it would hardly be the first time for either of them. They were willing to gamble, and so was César.

Another factor on the positive side: in Bogotá, Rincón could appear on the best cartel. And that is precisely what took place on December 8, 1982—bulls from the excellent ranch of Vistahermosa owned by Francisco García, where Rincón had often trained at tientas, for Antoñete, José Mari Manzanares, and César Rincón.

Antoñete and Manzanares were the perfect *padrino,* godfather, and *testigo,* witness, for Rincón's ceremonial induction. Antoñete was considered a genuine maestro of toreo as well as a specialist in citing from a distance and citing de frente, precisely the salient characteristics of the soon-to-be-matador de toros. Manzanares had long been seen as the artists' artist, the man in recent toreo capable of the greatest sculpted beauty. I always thought of him, from the first time I saw him in Córdoba in 1974, as the direct inheritor of the arte of Paco Camino and Antonio Ordóñez.

As it turned out, the only thing historic that happened was the ceremony itself, for which Rincón wore the traditional white-and-gold suit of lights. No one had a triumph. Both Antoñete and Manzanares offered to let Rincón choose his bull, but he and Efraín Olano thought it was better to take part in the *sorteo,* the drawing of lots, as usual. So Rincón performed with the first animal, "alternating" his usual spot as third in seniority with Antoñete's as first. In the ceremony, just before the faena of the first bull, Antoñete and César Rincón exchanged their trastos, Chenel ceding his muleta and sword for Rincón's cape; they embraced as usual, and Antoñete said: "Muchacho, give yourself to your profession—love it. When you love a profession as hard and as beautiful as this one, when you really want it, the profession will eventually reciprocate. In it you'll find the greatest moments of happiness in your life, if you can only overcome the bad ones" (JV 283). In the same way that truisms become truisms because they are so true, Antoñete's boiler-plate speech was to become a virtual prophecy.

César Rincón walked to the center of the ring and looked upward, evoking the memory of his mother and sister—the tragedy was well known in Bogotá and the entire ring had observed a minute of silence before the corrida—and then proceeded to the callejón, where he dedicated the bull to his father.

The critic at *El Tiempo* thought Rincón "justified the reputation he had earned in Spain," and called the faena "of great quality" and deserving of the petition of the ear. The new matador had hit bone twice and then put in an effective sword, enough for a triumphal tour of the ring but not enough for

an ear. At *El Espectador* the critic judged Rincón's performance more severely, calling the alternativa somewhat lackluster owing to the bull's spirit-
lessness. César Rincón was a willowy youth, barely seventeen, who showed
some valor and knowledge but did not show "the experience necessary to
take the alternativa."

In the braver sixth bull, the order having reverted to the usual seniority,
the young matador—probably less nervous now that the ceremony was
over, now a matador de toros, now for better or for worse a full-fledged professional killer of full-grown bulls—gave a stronger performance, and his
work, according to the more severe critic at *El Espectador,* was "continuously
applauded and his faena had excellent moments, especially in the derechazos." He again killed with two pinchazos and a good thrust and "would
have cut an ear" had he killed more effectively.

When it was all over, Rincón claimed to be satisfied, remarking that he
"took advantage of the good qualities [of the sixth bull] and felt very comfortable with what he did" (I&B 51–53).

No one tried to pretend it had been a fortuitous beginning. Probably the
most positive remarks had been that Rincón seemed to have a promising
career ahead, which was to say he had not had a disaster. Still, he had to be
concerned with his weak killing, and at least one source reports that he
became so demoralized that he considered renouncing the alternativa and
becoming a banderillero (I&B 53).

At year's end, César Rincón had two corridas in the Feria de Cali. In the
first, with Espartaco and El Soro, the newest sensations from Spain, he was
only applauded while his Spanish compañeros cut an ear apiece. On December 31, 1982, he ended his *annus horribilis* well, cutting two ears from a
brave bull of Ernesto González Caicedo.

But the horror was not over. Just when César Rincón was beginning to
make money, Pedro Domingo presented him with a bill for expenses in-
curred in Spain in the amount of 12 million pesos, more than $150,000. It
would take him two years to pay off the debt, and the way Pedro Domingo
demanded payment destroyed their professional and personal relationship
from then on.

The only humorous anecdote to emerge from that relationship came
later when they made a final settlement. Rincón was taking Pedro Domingo
to the airport to go to Argentina and wanted Pedro Domingo to pay him
what he owed him for several recent corridas. Pedro Domingo preferred to
pay when he returned. Rincón told him that he needed the money now.
When Pedro Domingo refused, Rincón, an able and fearless driver, began to

accelerate through one of Bogotá's traffic nightmares, weaving at high speed through the endless stream of rickety trucks and buses, heading at ever increasing velocity toward the airport. Pedro Domingo grew paler and finally screamed for Rincón to stop. Rincón pulled over and Pedro Domingo wrote him a check on the spot. "He was trembling," remembers Rincón, who never did comprehend how he could owe Pedro Domingo so much money. That was the Faustian torero's revenge on the Mephistophelian empresario who always gave Rincón "the sensation that he was toreando for the devil" (JV 179–80).[1]

Limbo

The 1983 season began well for the new matador. In spite of his inexperience, he had triumphs in the ferias of Cali, Manizales, Cartagena, and Medellín, alongside Espartaco, Dámaso González, Paquirri, Tomás Campuzano, and other Spanish figuras. In Cartagena, in a repeat cartel of his alternativa, he outperformed Antoñete and Manzanares, and he had a bull of Vistahermosa *indultado*, pardoned, in Bogotá. (When a bull is judged brave enough, especially in Colombia where new breeding stock is in short supply, he can be "pardoned," spared, in theory to breed. An *indulto* is both a triumph for the matador, who is awarded symbolic ears and tail, and a great honor for the breeder.)

Rincón and Manzanares met in a mano a mano in Bogotá, where Rincón emerged with more trophies, but his greatest day of triumph had to be February 20, 1983, when he and reigning national hero Pepe Cáceres competed in a mano a mano in the Santamaría ring with Vistahermosa bulls. The veteran only managed to take a vuelta in his second bull, while Rincón cut an ear in his second and both ears in his third. The junior matador, who all his professional life had aspired to be like the veteran, had clearly surpassed him. The national press, of course, drooled over the young challenger who had crossed swords with the maestro, clearly winning the first of their frequent duels.

If it had not been for the debt to Pedro Domingo, César Rincón would have been making good money. As it was, by March he managed to rent an apartment for his family and get them out of his uncle's house. The independence of his family had become, and would remain, a primary goal for the young provider.

In 1983 the usual bickering and jealousies caused the taurine agreement between Spain and Colombia to be suspended, prohibiting Colombian toreros from performing in Spain. Rincón went to Mexico instead. Pedro Domingo had made some vague agreements to put Mexican toreros on in Colombia in exchange for Rincón's performing in Mexico. But Rincón's Mexican season, although it did have one stellar moment, can hardly be considered a success.

After two fruitless corridas in Peñitas and Tijuana, he confirmed his alternativa[1] in the Plaza México with bulls of Mariano Ramírez. Rincón, who was caught twice without serious consequences, had bad luck with his bulls, and although he killed well, he appeared nervous or tense. The critic of *El Heraldo* remarked that Rincón could not accommodate himself to his bulls, perhaps because he was "not yet very accustomed to the charge of Mexican bulls" (I&B 62). At best the reviews were mixed.

On September 4, however, in a grand corrida of Jaral de Peñas bulls in Tijuana, Eloy Cavazos, David Silveti, and César Rincón all had resounding triumphs. That afternoon, according to Rincón, with ideal bulls and divine inspiration, he proceeded to torear better than ever in his professional life, better even, he would later tell Efraín Olano, than his great day in La Coruña in 1991. Clearly César Rincón had found at least two Mexican bulls to which he could accommodate himself.

Following a strong season in the winter of 1983–84 in Colombia—where day by day, feria by feria in Palmira and Cali, Manizales and Cartagena, Medellín and Bogotá, the young matador added, triumph by triumph, to his experience and his reputation—César Rincón decided to return to conquer the Madrepatria (the agreement was no longer suspended), where he fully intended to live the dream of all young matadors to be carried in triumph from the Puerta del Príncipe, the Prince's Gate, of La Maestranza de Sevilla, and from the Puerta Grande de Las Ventas de Madrid. *Casi na*—practically nothing—as the Andalusians say. He would begin by confirming his alternativa in Madrid.

Pedro Domingo, now in association with Manolo Cano, continued to manage Rincón, attempting to recoup his investment with little success, although he did manage to set up the *confirmación*. First he arranged four corridas in the provinces. The worst moment came in Tafalla, just south of Pamplona, when on August 19 Rincón nearly sent a bull of Fernández Palacios back alive; the best came on August 26 in Tarragona when he cut two ears from bulls of Cortijoliva and went out on shoulders for the first time as a matador in Spain.

The long-awaited confirmación took place on September 2, 1984, with a *corrida de remiendos,* a patchwork corrida made up from what is left of the breeders' stock. Rincón ended up with two impossible bulls from Lamamié de Clairac, the ganadería with which he would be so triumphant in La Coruña in 1991.

Manili served as padrino, José Luis Vargas as testigo. Manili was known as a gladiator, a torero who will torear anything. He had been called the "ugly duckling" of toreo, but in 1987 and 1988 would turn into a great swan of bravery with the feared Miura bulls. In 1984 he was modest at best, performing in seventeen corridas. Pepe Luis Vargas was already one of the most severely gored of living matadors, although his most spectacular goring, in Sevilla in 1987, was yet to come. It was hardly a deluxe cartel on that Sunday, September 2, three days before Rincón's nineteenth birthday and the very day "all Madrid" would be returning from summer vacation. No one was severely wounded, but all three of them sweated blood, as the taurinos say, perhaps more aptly than in most professions.

Rincón remembers that Manili said to him in the ceremony that it was a tough profession, but that maybe the bulls would respect him—"respect" is a euphemism for not tearing you to pieces—and that maybe he would make it. He also remembers the desolation of his hotel room after the corrida. It seemed to him "like a wake" in which he was both the dead man and the mourner (JV 220).

He returned to Colombia with the objective of his confirmación completed, but the season was to him a Calvary. More than anything he recalls waiting—waiting for the silent telephone to ring, waiting and having to pay everywhere for everything, waiting and paying and crashing again and again into the solid barrier of prejudice of the Spanish bull world: "César Rincón, that sudaca. . . . Never!" (F-S 26).

In the winter of 1984–85, Rincón again alternated in Colombian rings with the Spanish figuras Manzanares, El Soro, José Ortega Cano, Julio Robles, Palomo Linares, Dámaso González—and the young Spanish matador José Cubero, Yiyo, who was only a year older than Rincón. José Cubero and he had appeared together once in a corrida in Cartagena the year before, but this season they performed together three times and quickly cemented their friendship. They seem to have gotten along instantly, in the ring and out, and they soon began to train together and to form a bond of mutual esteem and admiration, in spite of the fact that both were extremely competitive. Their toreo—both in the line of Antoñete—was very similar, and José Cubero would quickly become César Rincón's closest Spanish friend.

Rincón's Colombian season progressed well enough, especially since at this point he emerged from his debt to Pedro Domingo. He had triumphs in Bucaramanga and Cali in December and in Cartagena and Manizales in January. In February in Sogamoso he pardoned a bull of Ernesto González Caicedo named Profesor, although without presidential authority. On March 10 in Bogotá, he triumphed with Huagrahuasi bulls from Ecuador, on the cartel with Palomo Linares and Manzanares, a historic afternoon known as the Corrida del Clamor, the clamor being to celebrate the release of bull breeder Abraham Domínguez from his seven-month captivity by kidnappers. And in his final corrida, in Ibagué, he again bested Pepe Cáceres in a mano a mano.

But Spain was still there, unvanquished.

Tomás Redondo, Yiyo's manager, agreed to help Rincón, now a free agent, when he returned to Spain. And he kept his word: Yiyo and Rincón had corridas together in Tarragona and Benidorm. Then on August 24, 1985, in Tarazona de la Mancha, a small town in Don Quixote country, Yiyo and Rincón both cut ears from bulls of Antonio Pérez. It was the only time they triumphed together.

By now they were the best of friends. Rincón had accompanied Yiyo for his corridas in Pamplona and they had watched the *encierro,* the running of the bulls, together from the Telefónica building with the journalists Antonio Olano and Antonio Carabias. Afterwards they all went to Marceliano's— an old Hemingway haunt, unfortunately no longer there—to eat the local *chistorra* sausage and fried eggs and to drink the rosé of Navarra (the toreros skipped the breakfast wine), after which Yiyo and Rincón went off to train. The young toreros were amused by the "hippies" sleeping in the parks despite the outlandish noise of the celebrating crowds, and the next day they all headed back to Madrid.

The friendship and the camaraderie and everything else came to a halt on August 30 in Colmenar Viejo, just north of Madrid. Yiyo had been called in at the last minute to substitute for Curro Romero, who had "fallen from the cartel." Had it not been so sudden, Rincón would doubtless have gone with him, but Yiyo did not have time to contact his friend.

Antoñete, José Luis Palomar, and Yiyo with bulls of Marcos Núñez comprised the new cartel. Antoñete had been applauded, Palomar had cut an ear. In the sixth bull, Burlero by name, Yiyo gave one of his finest performances, the kind that justified his title as the Prince of Toreo. He was certain to cut ears if he killed well.

After a pinchazo, he went in straight, killing perfectly. But the bull, even as it was dying, turned on him, tripping him, knocking him to the ground. Yiyo rolled away instantly, but Burlero hooked violently with his left horn, catching Yiyo in the back, then standing him up. As Yiyo came off the horn, his banderillero Pali Pirri heard him say, "Me ha matado"—he has killed me—an instant before he fell, dead of a ruptured heart (Olano 33).

José Cubero thus strangely fulfilled his own prophecy. In an interview on Radio Nacional de España after a triumphant afternoon in San Isidro in 1983, he had said: "You ask when I think about death. All toreros have death in our faces. Some express it one way but I express it with sincerity. You ask when I think about it. When I turn out the light on my night table, when I'm finally alone. I think that a horn will rip out my heart, but I always respond to that nightmare by saying, 'What does it matter?' I am a torero and my father passed along the vice in my blood. And it's better to die from a corná [goring] than on the M-30 [beltway around Madrid]. The sad thing is that I wouldn't be able to help my family" (Olano 7). Today all young toreros know those fateful words by heart.

César Rincón saw the images on television, saw the cornada on the sand that went straight to Yiyo's heart, saw Yiyo hanging from the horn as Burlero stood him up, watched Burlero stumble a few steps and collapse, saw Yiyo on the sand, inert and limp. Rincón thought: How could such a young, powerful, physically able torero "have died that way? How could a dying bull have gored so accurately? What strange vengeance had been wreaked here?" (JV 114). Mute and stunned in front of the television, César Rincón got no answers.

His Spanish season—with five corridas and six ears—was over. His best friend in Spain was dead. Tomás Redondo, who would later take his own life, was a broken man and wanted nothing further to do with the bulls. That afternoon, Rincón remembered, he "lost a friend, and the bullrings of Spain once again shut me out." He wondered if there were some mysterious logic at work. Did he need to mature more? Had he taken the alternativa too soon? The one thing he could find no justification for was the death of Yiyo, and he now felt "more alone than ever" (JV 116). He ordered a new suit of lights in jet and burgundy—the colors of the suit of lights Yiyo was buried in—and returned to Colombia.

César Rincón knew all along that his triumphs in América meant nothing in Spain, but now he began to realize that his lack of triumphs in Spain was having a negative effect on his reputation at home. Every year he returned with little or nothing to show. Then in the winter of 1985–86, dispirited, he had a weak temporada in Colombia, without a single solid triumph and with several notable failures, including a bad afternoon in Bogotá when he bought the sobrero and still could not perform well. (In American rings a matador can purchase, with his own money, the substitute bull, thus giving himself a third opportunity.) César Rincón was beginning to earn a reputation as the great promise that had failed to materialize—"*uno más*," just one more, as the taurinos say.

The 1986 season was his worst yet: he calls it a disaster. Returning to Spain under Jerónimo Pimentel, a former Spanish torero who had become an empresario in América, Rincón thought he might at last get to perform. But Pimentel, who had theoretically promised him a minimum of fifteen contracts in Spain, was even less successful than his predecessors. Rincón spent the time waiting endlessly for the telephone to ring and appeared only once the entire season, in a benefit festival in the Costa del Sol tourist town of Mijas, in which he killed one animal. Back in Colombia at season's end, Pimentel claimed César Rincón owed him $15,000, but Rincón took him to court and won, telling himself in the process, "No more Spain, no more Pimentels" (JV 228).

The only gratifying memory of Spain that year came from his friendship with the Spanish matador Julio Vega el Marismeño, who took him into the marshes of the Guadalquivir to torear at night. The friendship would last through the worst of times. Eventually Julio Vega would become César Rincón's veedor in Spain, and in many respects his unofficial trainer.

Back home, too, things were bleak. Rincón, now without a manager and with a declining reputation, could not secure contracts in Colombia. At about this time he began to pray to Saint Jude, called San Judas Tadeo in Spanish, the patron of lost causes and of people in hopeless or desperate situations. You may have seen prayers to him published in the "personals" of the *International Herald Tribune:* "Sacred Heart of Jesus, pray for us. Saint Jude, worker of miracles, pray for us. Saint Jude, helper of the hopeless, pray for us. Amen. Say this prayer nine times a day, by the ninth day your prayer will be answered. It has never been known to fail."

New Year

Ernesto González Caicedo, who had arranged for him to appear in the Feria de Cali, told Rincón he must not lose hope, that Spain was only a setback, that it was not his fault but the fault of the Spaniards who had excluded him. Rincón could overcome it all if he worked at it hard enough, if he could *mentalizarse,* be mentally prepared. As the maestro Pepe Luis Vázquez once said, "The only way to handle a bull is with your head, by getting him inside your head" (Zumbiehl 56).

On New Year's Day 1987, César Rincón broke through—*rompió,* as the taurinos put it, an interesting usage that suggests as much a mental break-through as a physical one—in the prestigious Cañaveralejo ring of Cali, on the cartel with José Ortega Cano and El Soro in a corrida of Guachicono bulls. The third bull, which was given a vuelta for its bravery, bore an auspi-cious name: Añonuevo. César Rincón cut both ears from Añonuevo in one of the most important faenas—both personally and artistically—of his life. That day César Rincón rescued his career, suddenly fulfilling his childhood promise, at once maturing and rising from the ashes of the tragedies of the past five years. His definitive triumph showed a strength of character wor-thy of his name and an ability to come back in the face of adversity that would characterize his career. It was the first real measure of his stature as a torero. At twenty-one he had come of age, heroically.

Rincón has said he was lucky to *cuajar* Añonuevo—to "nail" him, to put his unmistakable personal signature on the faena—but I do not think it was luck. Neither did Ernesto González Caicedo, who always knew in an instinc-tual way—instead of hoping against hope, as Gonzalo Rincón would do— that César Rincón would coalesce into a figura when the time and the torero were ripe. From that New Year's Day and Añonuevo forward, they were. Perhaps Ernesto González Caicedo was an agent of San Judas Tadeo.

They awarded César Rincón the Señor de los Cristales trophy as triunfador of the Feria de Cali that year, and he went on to torear—the phone began to ring and the doors of all the plazas opened as if by magic—nearly thirty corridas in Colombia that season. Apoderados popped up like genies, but Rincón took on none, preferring to continue as his own agent, slowly forging in the solitary ring of his soul the uncreated toreo of his people.

Threshold

During the seasons 1987 through 1990, César Rincón made himself into one of the greatest of American toreros. Without going to Spain, he triumphed repeatedly in every plaza in Colombia, not only in the important ferias but in small country rings too, driving and puddle-jumping over and around the triple Andean backbone of Colombia and occasionally into Venezuela, to places with names like Yumbo or Funza or Ubaté, with names reminiscent of other places such as Aquitania, Armenia, Montelíbano, or Pamplona, with names that evoke paradise, fantasy, or fiction: Floridablanca and Aguazul and Darién, Chinacotá and Popayán, Saravena and Anapoima. The names may frequently have been more poetic than the reality, but little by little Rincón hammered himself into the most solidly capable and artistic torero his country had ever produced.

In 1987 Rincón totaled thirty corridas, in 1988 another thirty, and in 1989 forty. He bought a *finca,* or ranch, and a flat on the north side of Bogotá. His career seemed unstoppable. Only one goal remained beyond his reach: the Madrepatria.

The greatest of American toreros—the Mexicans Gaona, Armillita, and Arruza and the Venezuelan César Girón—had definitive triumphs in Spain, where their status as figuras was equal to their status at home in American rings. Manolo Martínez, the most recently dominant Mexican figura, frequently gets excluded from that short list because he never sustained in Spain a string of triumphs equal to his category in Mexico, where he was the máxima figura up until his death in 1996.

Pepe Cáceres had a number of corridas in Spain, but he never broke through the way the Mexicans and the Venezuelan had. Cáceres maintained himself as a top professional in Colombia, a genuinely revered maestro for more than thirty years, and while he acquitted himself as a thorough and competent professional for a decade in Spain, he did not attain the category of figura. On July 20, 1987, in the plaza de toros of Sogamoso the bull Monín from the ranch of San Esteban de Ovejas gored the fifty-three-year-old matador in the chest as he went in to kill. After a month of agony, Pepe Cáceres died in the hospital in Bogotá on August 16—five years to the day after the Rincón family tragedy. His death was mourned deeply by Colombians and by taurinos abroad.

The only South American torero to achieve true artistic greatness in Spain was named César—César Girón, who from 1954 to 1956 dominated toreo in Spain.[1] If this new Colombian César really wanted to be Caesar— *aut Caesar aut nihil* in Cesare Borgia's words—he would have to return to Spain and he would have to triumph. Julius Caesar himself had wept in Spain at his professional impotence when he saw a statue of Alexander in the Temple of Hercules near Cádiz. César Rincón, with so many triumphs alongside the Spanish figuras in Colombian rings, must have felt a similar sense of professional inadequacy, a sense that may have spurred both Caesars on to greater glory.

The key to the return was clear enough to Rincón: he could forge his own toreo in Colombia, but for the wickedly difficult Madrepatria he would have to find exactly the right apoderado. The word had gotten out among the taurinos: "Watch out for the Indio" (F-S 32). The Spanish figuras who yearly trekked to Colombia were very aware of César Rincón, since they had to compete with him on native ground, often coming out on the losing end, and Gonzalo Rincón's photographs of his son appeared with some frequency in the winter issues of *Aplausos*. As Rincón's stature continued to increase, the hawk eyes of the Lozano and the Chopera clans lit on him too.

César Rincón talked to his old friends the Lozanos. Gonzalo Rincón talked to the Choperas. But the matador was not going to consider returning to Spain without a minimum guarantee of fifteen corridas, the number at which he would actually make money. For that he would need someone dedicated to his career. Then one day—no one seems exactly sure when— Manolo Chopera talked to Gonzalo Rincón about Luis Alvarez, who had worked for and with the Choperas for years and who was already managing the Venezuelan matador José Nelo, Morenito de Maracay. Gonzalo Rincón remembers that Chopera said Luis Alvarez would make a good apoderado for his son, better even, he said, than Chopera himself.

Rincón believes he met Luis Alvarez in 1988. Luis Alvarez is not precisely sure when he first took serious notice of César Rincón, but he remembers seeing him on that difficult afternoon of his confirmación in Madrid in 1984 and then many times later on in Colombia, where it had become impossible to miss him. Luis Alvarez had been Morenito's manager for a number of years, and Morenito was now appearing some forty times a year in Spain, a positive factor in Rincón's eyes, one that he could not fail to take into account.

Rincón and Morenito appeared together in one corrida in Sogamoso in 1986. They performed together again in Medellín in February 1989, and they were on the same cartel at least twice in Cali in January 1990. There were also days when the toreros did not appear together but would turn up at tientas or social events, places and times when Rincón and Luis Alvarez were eyeing each other, getting to know each other, wondering without deciding, beginning to talk. From the first, Luis Alvarez was impressed by Rincón's toreo, especially his ability to get everything possible from each animal, but he also noticed early on that Rincón's killing was not perfect.

By the end of 1989 César Rincón and Luis Alvarez were conversing in earnest, and in 1990 they launched their first campaign, a kind of reconnaissance expedition, a testing of the waters, a carefully planned strategic maneuver designed to prepare the torero, to reacquaint him with the behavior of Spanish bulls, and to prepare and cultivate the critical soil of print and media journalism. In 1991 would come the full assault. They signed a contract in the presence of a well-known taurine notary named Buenaventura, who was an ardent supporter of César Rincón—how could they fail?

Rincón appeared in fourteen corridas in Spain during the 1990 temporada, including the first-class rings in Valencia and Bilbao, in both of which he cut an ear. His "balance" for the fourteen corridas ran quite high: twenty-two ears and two tails. He even made money. The association with Luis Alvarez went smoothly, and although Rincón was not Luis Alvarez's only torero—aside from Morenito, he was also managing the promising young Enrique Ponce—their relationship began to strengthen, and in time Rincón would evolve into Luis Alvarez's prime concern, with Ponce going elsewhere and Morenito becoming secondary.

In 1990, when he arrived in Spain, however, Rincón amounted to Luis Alvarez's third matador. He and his brother Luis Carlos and Monaguillo lived in the summer house of a generous friend, José Luis Lorente, up in the mountains outside Madrid in the pueblo of Cabanillas de la Sierra. Lorente not only lent them his house, he also lent them a car.

It was so cold up in the pueblo that at times they slept with their clothes on. José Luis Lorente took me up to the house in June 1996, now warm, sunny, and in bloom, and showed me the yard where Rincón and Monaguillo had trained, cutting down some of the Lorente family's trees (a walnut and a peach tree) to have more room—as his father had done years before in Bucaramanga—and taking apart the Lorentes' bicycle to make a carretón. Lorente took it philosophically. He knew that Rincón would break through, and that was all that mattered to him or to his daughter Natalia, then a teenager but already a great aficionada and admirer of César Rincón, and later an announcer for Telemadrid, doing the interviews of matadors from the callejón.

The plan worked: Luis Alvarez secured the contracts and César Rincón cut the ears. Things did not always go perfectly, but César Rincón and Luis Alvarez both knew how to make adversity work to their advantage. For example, Alvarez arranged a contract for the northern coastal town of Santoña in the province of Santander, but the representatives in the ayuntamiento, who in this particular case had the last word, turned him down. In the meantime Rincón was scheduled to torear there in another corrida not run by the city-hall types—and he cut three ears and a tail. The city-hall types, in a situation very similar to the one for the Corrida de Beneficencia the following year in Madrid, immediately removed their veto—and Luis Alvarez in turn rejected the contract. One corrida fewer, but a moral victory for the strengthening partnership between torero and apoderado.

Finally César Rincón could return to Colombia having accomplished what he had set out to do. The Madrepatria jinx seemed to be warded off by the good offices of Luis Alvarez. Fourteen corridas, good reviews, plenty of "hair touched," as the taurinos refer to cutting ears—and next year they planned to torear at least twenty-five. Rincón told José Luis Benlloch in *Aplausos,* as though already rehearsing for the upcoming Columbus Quincentennial: "The time when the Spaniards came to Colombia to 'do the Américas' is over. Now we will do Spain" (August 6, 1990).

Luis Alvarez, who sometimes refers to luck as La Divina Providencia, could congratulate himself on his new torero's "first season" in Spain. La Divina Providencia always struck me as a kind of sacred version of Lady Luck. Or perhaps Lady Luck was a profane version of La Divina Providencia: in either case she could be fickle, and if she had intervened positively in the Madrepatria, there was always the plain old patria, Colombia.

On November 4, 1990, the Agustín Barona Pinillos ring at Palmira having just been renovated, César Rincón and Gitanillo de América were to torear mano a mano with bulls of Ambaló. The first bull, Baratero, not large, with a light stripe down his backbone and with forward pointing horns, after an artistic faena by Rincón, was ready to die. Rincón lined him up and threw himself onto the morrillo, sinking the sword in up to the hilt. The kill was superbly executed, as artistically pure as his faena, but Rincón "stayed in the bull's face" an instant too long, or perhaps the bull cut in. Baratero hooked upward with his right horn, even as he began to die, catching Rincón in the right thigh, high up near the groin, burying the horn in his flesh, turning him in a high cartwheel and spinning him off onto his head.

Luis Carlos came running. Gitanillo came running. All the banderilleros came running. There are various versions of what people said: It's like Manolete's goring! It's just like Paquirri! All César Rincón could say—inadvertently echoing Varelito the day he was mortally wounded in Sevilla—was, "Me la ha pegado," he's given it to me. No one remembers what happens in such a moment when panic reigns, but one thing was clear from the geyser of blood jetting from the thigh wound clutched tightly in Rincón's hands: the horn had punctured the matador's femoral artery and his life-blood was disappearing.

Rincón claims he did not suffer, that you do not feel the pain then, just a burning sensation, like a hot iron. What he remembers is his feeling of impotence at not being able to stop the blood. He squeezed as hard as he could, but the blood kept bubbling up and squirting through his fingers. He could feel his strength flowing out with his blood. Then he passed out and was given the last rites.

As he would later recount, in the enfermería there was no scalpel, not even scissors to cut away his taleguilla. Someone got a tourniquet above the wound, and they rushed him across town to the Hospital San Vicente de Paúl, where they dropped him off the stretcher and started him hemorrhaging again. A team of surgeons tried to revive him. Rincón remembers hearing but not being able to move. What was his blood type? Somehow he mouthed: "O positive." Later he would recall hearing them saying, "We're losing him! We're losing him!" He remembers cottony clouds, a bright light, resignation, a sense of peace. "We're losing him!" Then nothing.

On December 18, 1991, a little over a year after the goring, César Rincón told María Fernanda González, Ernesto González Caicedo's daughter, "I felt dead the day of the cornada in Palmira . . . I lost consciousness and I felt that I was going . . . it was a very hard time . . . I was fighting to stay in there . . . to keep from going" (149, her ellipses). María Fernanda, a close friend of César, had been with Jorge Molina at the ring in Palmira, and both of them (whom we will meet again) had rushed from the ring to the hospital in Palmira to give blood.

When Rincón recovered consciousness the following day, he was far from out of danger. Within a short period he went into shock again. They rushed him back to the operating room, reopened him, and discovered a "new" trajectory of the cornada, one leading upward, which they had somehow missed before and which was now hemorrhaging. After opening his abdomen and working on him for six hours, they decided to send him to the hospital in Cali.

In Cali the nightmare began all over. First the staff did not want to admit him. When they did, the doctors decided he had an infection—in fact he was very close to dead again—and they opened him up once more. This time they left the wound open, so it could heal from the inside. (A grisly photograph of the open wound would appear in the December 3, 1990, issue of *Aplausos*.) The "new technique" worked. A week later, after a final operation, the healing proceeded smoothly.

Within two weeks César Rincón was back in Bogotá, in the capable hands of Efraín Olano. He was scheduled to torear on December 8 in Quito in the Feria de Jesús del Gran Poder. Rincón was determined to recuperate and to prove, above all to himself, that mentally and physically he had not been affected by the nearly mortal blow in Palmira.

Rincón remembers circulation problems and a swollen ankle that would not go down. Efraín Olano took him to see two more doctors: both advised him to walk and torear as much as possible, and both indicated his surgery had—eventually—turned out nothing short of miraculous.

For the next two weeks Rincón trained exhaustively, first at a tienta at Chicalá, the ranch of Floro Hernández, followed by some four-to-five-year-old vacas at Antonio García's new finca, Punta Umbría, cows that Rincón remembers were not exactly "appropriate for a matador who three weeks before had been at death's door" (JV 190), but which proved to be an excellent test. Efraín Olano would call one of those vacas the bravest he had ever seen.

In the week before the corrida in Quito, Rincón trained with cows at the ranches of Isabel Reyes (Clara Sierra) and Luis Fernando Castro (Guachicono), all the while obsessively practicing killing with the carretón. On December 4, Ernesto González Caicedo gave him a bull, Azteca by name, to kill *a puerta cerrada*, behind closed doors. Rincón was able to torear to his liking, and he eventually killed the animal recibiendo with a good sword but not without some hesitation. Rincón was nervous, at one point telling

Enrique Calvo el Cali to kill the animal. But Ernesto González Caicedo inter-vened and said, "You kill it, César." Afterwards Rincón felt much better and thought at the time that Quito was within reach. "You have to bury your dead," he would later remark in the aphoristic style of taurinos, "so they won't stink and so they won't rot on your shoulders. I had buried my *cadáver* from Palmira" (JV 190).

Killing had always been César Rincón's problem. His stature was and clearly always would be a handicap in this regard: unlike a tall matador who can reach well over the horns, Rincón has to clear the horn from close in, clear the horn and then clear out before he is caught. In countless perfor-mances prior to his goring in Palmira he had lost ears with faulty sword work, and had returned perhaps more than his share of bulls alive. Then in Palmira—killing well but not getting clear in time—he had almost been killed. Had he, in fact, buried that corpse?

Five weeks after the goring in Palmira, Rincón appeared in Quito on a cartel with Spanish matadors Roberto Domínguez and Fernando Cámara with bulls of Santa Rosa. Ricardo Chinza, who drove the van, remembers that shortly after they crossed the border into Ecuador they heard a taurine radio commentator say that Rincón had only come for the money and that he had no business appearing before he was fully recuperated.

Was he recuperated? His leg was still painful. And how was his head? Would that cadaver from Palmira rear *its* head at an unforeseen moment? Would a zombie from his subconscious—in spite of the good kill recibiendo with Ernesto González Caicedo's bull—suddenly intervene when he had to kill in public? Rincón could not help wondering. A matador never knows until after the fact, and any number of potentially great matadors had lost their "nerve"—some only temporarily, others for good, often with the expla-nation that the bulls had punished them severely or that they had not "re-spected" them—after lesser gorings than Rincón's in Palmira.

At Palmira Rincón had crossed the slippery, agonizingly physical thresh-old of shock and pain and blood and nerve, but he had also begun to float through that clean, well-lighted, metaphysical threshold into death's other kingdom—"miraculously" to return. His spiritual nature made him aware of "where" he had been. What he could not know for certain ahead of time, regardless of that awareness or perhaps because of it, was what his physical reactions would be, back on "this side." So having trained as though exhaus-tion were salvation, he now went on to Quito with a cold fury. He had to make sure he had exorcized the otherwise benign demon of inadvertent self-protection, even the least degree of which, in the ring, could prove disastrous.

After the corrida the radio commentator retracted what he had said about Rincón. After a faena grande in the second bull, Rincón threw himself on the bull as though his life depended on it. In a way, it did: never thinking of Palmira, he threw himself behind the sword "so that the memory of a mishap would not follow me for the rest of my life" (JV 187). Luis Alvarez believes Rincón's killing improved from Quito onward, that after the goring he killed with more authority, more accuracy, and more bravery. A photograph in the December 24, 1990, issue of *Aplausos* leaves no room for doubt about the quality of his kill. "From that point on," Luis Alvarez told María Fernanda González, "I knew César was prepared for the Spanish season" (205).

He was awarded both ears, the triunfador of the afternoon and of the feria. Not surprisingly, Rincón went on to win again the Señor de los Cristales trophy in Cali, and in Bogotá in four consecutive afternoons he became the triunfador of the temporada, cutting eight ears. The Madrepatria was out there, as always, but this time Rincón was coming loaded for bear—specifically the bear eating from the strawberry tree that is the folk symbol of Madrid. He would later remark: "Remember, I had come a very long way, from the night with no tomorrow, and that was why nothing could interfere with my rise, no thing and no one" (F-S 34).

When José Luis Lorente took me up to the house in the sierra he had lent to Rincón, I saw an issue of *Aplausos* dated January 28, 1991. Here was the hand of Luis Alvarez. On the cover was the smiling Caesar of American toreo, flowers in hand as he strolled the Cañaveralejo plaza in Cali while the air filled with Córdoba hats thrown in unison as homage from the Peña Taurina La Sultana, the oldest of the *porras* (as taurine clubs are called in Colombia) in Cali. At the foot of the cover was a description of prizes Rincón had won that season.

Remembering, José Luis Lorente told me of the Sunday afternoon in May 1991 before Rincón's breakthrough the next Tuesday in Madrid. The subject came up as Lorente was telling me about the dismembered bicycle (which Rincón later replaced), the trees they had chopped down, and the former state of the grass, now quite lush but at that time eliminated in the training area. Lorente and his wife, Emi, were up at the house since it was a beautiful Sunday, and Rincón, suddenly distressed at what he had done to their property, promised to replant the *pasto*, which is what they called grass or lawn in Colombia. Emi was on the porch ironing. Hearing Rincón, she said: "Don't you worry about the pasto! What you have to worry about is going out the Puerta Grande on Tuesday!"

"I will," said Rincón. "I will, and then I'll replace the pasto."

José Luis Lorente shook his head and said, as though he were remembering a catastrophe, "My God. He had no idea of what was in store for him."

1992

The moment that led to the writing of this book occurred one June evening in Madrid. Michael Wigram and I were sitting in the Plaza Santa Ana, discussing a recent English-language taurine book that purported to represent "a season," and Michael remarked what a shame it was that many readers would be misled by it, since it did not represent a season at all. Without giving it a thought I say, "Obviously someone should write a real chronicle of a real season."

Michael smiles diabolically and I realize that I have walked into a trap. "I suppose I'll have to do it," I say, realizing dimly how difficult it will be. Michael's smile turns angelic. "I'll follow Rincón," I say, "and weave the book around him. Actually I've been looking for a taurine subject anyway, to do a sequel to *White Wall*."

"Yes," says Michael, "of course. And with your torero."

Michael and I were playing the usual taurine mind games, but the idea appealed to me immensely. I was ready for the commitment but not remotely aware how complex and perilous such an endeavor could be. A season indeed.

Sevilla: April 19 and 26, 1992

César Rincón had come in strong from América in early 1992. After his early-season triumphs in Mexico, Peru, Venezuela, and Ecuador in late 1991 and his smashing afternoon of six bulls in Bogotá, he had gone on to triumphs in the rest of Colombia as well, beginning with three ears in Cali. In Cartagena de Indias he cut another three ears—to Ortega Cano's two—and was declared triunfador. In Manizales he cut seven ears in three afternoons, and in Medellín in three afternoons he totaled another seven ears, with two salidas a hombros with bulls of Ernesto González Caicedo and El Aceituno. In Bogotá he cut ears twice, including the only ear of the afternoon in a mano a mano with Ortega Cano. And finally, in Ibagué on February 29, César Rincón crowned his American season by cutting both ears from the second bull of Ernesto González Caicedo, and then cutting the ears and tail symbolically from the fifth bull, Corredor, which he pardoned.

But in Spain the season did not begin so well. Although he had a significant triumph in Castellón, César Rincón was not contracted for Las Fallas in Valencia, a more important feria. Sevilla, a ring that was waiting for him, especially after the debacle of the previous fall, was next on the seasonal calendar. And in Sevilla Rincón needed to *convencer,* to be convincing, as he knew only too well.

In an interview with Marisa Arcas in the taurine weekly *El Ruedo* on February 6, he spoke of dreaming about opening the Puerta del Príncipe (which requires three ears cut). But he also talked frankly about the competition, what he cheerfully termed *los compañeros,* meaning the Spanish matadors, who were noticeably pressing as hard as they could. Marisa Arcas averred that Rincón had "heated them up," and he replied that that was true and that as a result they were all trying "to give him a bath." He was well aware that all the Spaniards were "on the warpath for the Indio" and he had heard they were all training more intensely than ever "to hunt down Rincón." He finished by affirming his principal desire: "consolidarme," to consolidate and strengthen his position as figura.

Sevilla 1992, taurinely speaking, had little to do with the Columbus Quincentennial. Instead it was marked by the tragedy of the death of banderillero Manolo Montoliú—gored through the heart in the thirteenth corrida of the feria—and polemicized by the new *reglamento taurino* which, among other things, required the bull to take at least two picks in a first-class ring. For César Rincón that new requirement would not bring good luck.

Easter Sunday is a quiet, sedate day after the previous week's street theatre filled with dying Christs and weeping Virgins. But for the taurinos it marks the beginning of Feria in Sevilla, and the Plaza de Toros de la Real Maestranza de Sevilla with its legendary silences becomes, on that day and for the next weeks, the Holy of Holies of the taurine world. To perform on that day carries maximum responsibility, a subject much on Rincón's mind as early as February. As he told Marisa Arcas in the February 6 interview, "My only concern is la responsabilidad, and that my luck not fail."

Domingo 19 de abril was hot and sunny and the Maestranza was filled to overflowing. Corrida de expectación: Ortega Cano and César Rincón, the triunfadores of the 1991 season, appeared with the young and promising, artistic but erratic Julio Aparicio. Corrida de decepción: the bulls of the Marqués de Domecq were weak and low in casta. Rincón got the worst lot in the sorteo. He managed a few passes from his first, but the second had nothing after the picks.

His second chance came on April 26, in the eighth corrida of the feria. On the cartel were Sevilla's aging legendary artist Curro Romero, Espartaco, and César Rincón—a virtual replica of the previous year's debacle—with bulls of Sepúlveda. The weather was again hot and sunny and the Maestranza was full and fanning hard.

The third bull, Judío by name, 546 kilos, with high, upwardly curving horns, was the most serious animal of the afternoon. Anderson Murillo picked him well but strongly. When he desisted, Judío stayed against the horse, "employing himself" to the fullest. In the quite Rincón made one revolera, then he asked the presidente for the *cambio,* the changing of the suerte. But the presidente stuck to the new reglamento and insisted on another pick.

In the muleta, the animal had little left. Rincón persevered as the bull looked him up and down, stopping halfway through the passes, and he made two circular passes from the back that sent a jolt of emotion through the crowd. Had Judío been stronger—or spent less energy in the horse— there would surely have been a trophy. As Rincón said afterwards, "He was very brave and I knew that if I took him to the horse again, he would use himself up. But that's what 'the authority' indicated and the bull exhausted himself."

To make matters worse, in the next bull Curro Romero asked for the act to be changed after the first pick and the presidente granted it with a smile. Pepe Dominguín was so outraged he would ask: "What is this? Favoritism to the countryman, apartheid, discrimination . . . ?" (*6T6* 10:67).

The sixth bull, Carasucia, was also *serio,* serious indeed. In the banderillas he suddenly "came up," pursuing the stickmen like a fury, almost catching Monaguillo. Rincón began a strong faena with the right hand, ligando as many as seven passes in a series. Slowly but surely the hushed house of Sevillanos began to respond with ovations and eventually *música.*

Rincón wove together six derechazos, citing de frente to begin but closing the *compás,* the position of the legs, gradually with each pass until his feet were together and Carasucia was tightening in on him like a top spinning in reverse. Finally Rincón resolved the tension at the breaking point with a cambio de manos and a far-sending pase de pecho. It looked as though the Maestranza were his.

Then as Rincón changed to the left hand, a sudden wind ruffled his muleta and his composure. Carasucia could not be trifled with, nor could Rincón entrust himself to the vagaries of an errant gust. He waited for the wind to subside. And the rhythm slowed, and his tenuous dominion over the animal broke, and the enthusiasm of the crowd waned. The music stopped. Carasucia turned as ugly as his name and Rincón dealt him a not quite mortal sword.

When Rincón struck with the descabello, the animal responded violently, cracking the matador's left hand with his left horn. Rincón jumped back in pain, doubling over and pulling his hand to his gut. Recovering, he hit the bull accurately, then took a triumphant vuelta complete with flowers and the enthusiasm of the Sevillanos. It could have been an important triumph. If the presidente had not forced the extra pick, if the wind had not spoiled the second faena, if the sword had not taken so long—if all these had not occurred, he could have cut one ear in the first and two in the second, opening the Prince's Gate. Instead he ended with a broken finger and the subsequent loss of his final corrida in the feria.

Jerez de la Frontera: May 24, 1992

Driving from Narixa past Gibraltar and the windy headland of Tarifa, I meet Michael and Irene to see a corrida of Alvaro Domecq bulls in Jerez de la Frontera on May 24 for Ortega Cano, César Rincón, and Miguel Báez Spínola, called Litri like his father and others of his forebears.

When we arrive, we find that four of Alvaro Domecq's bulls have been rejected by the veterinarians, that the corrida has been changed to Carlos Núñez, that Ortega Cano has consequently decided not to torear, and that we are about to attend a mano a mano between Rincón and "Miqui" Litri, as his fans and family call him.

The Núñez bulls come out brave, with casta and *picante* (piquancy or spunk), and each of the toreros cuts two ears and rides out on shoulders. Litri puts in an excellent estocada on his first bull and Rincón kills his last bull recibiendo in great style after classic naturales. What could have been a

Figure 18. Killing in Jerez, May 24, 1992. Rincón likes to kill recibiendo when he has the proper animal, one that "helps" by charging readily and with his head down. This Núñez bull does and Rincón makes a fine kill as the bull impales himself with his own bravery. César did not like this photo because his left foot is up in the air. I like it because it shows the crossing with the muleta and the slow and surely placed sword.

disastrous afternoon—it is a cold, blustery day—turns into a triumph for the ganadero, the empresario, the matadors, and the público.

Madrid: May 25 and June 1 and 11, 1992

The following day, May 25, César Rincón needed the same kind of luck for his first performance in Madrid. Journalist Juan Mora asked Rincón the question on everyone's mind: "Is it possible to go out on shoulders in Las Ventas five times in a row?"

Rincón replied circumspectly: "Well, I'm certainly going to try. As the first torero in history to go out four consecutive times, I could make it five."

"It's that easy?"

"Cutting ears is not like making *churros* [fried dough] . . . but if one has his day and arrives at the ring with the proper hope and desire, and if the bull charges as well, then one is ahead of the game." He went on to say that it was his intention to go out the big gate every time he appeared in Madrid, that Madrid was the plaza that put his career into orbit and gave him the confidence last year to have triumphs in eighty percent of his corridas.

"Aren't you afraid this year they will demand more from you?"

"I don't think so. Madrid will always be demanding. It all depends on luck, on how the bull comes out and on which bulls you get in your *lote* [lot]"[1] (*El País,* May 25, 1992).

Rincón's luck did not quite hold. His first bull, a brave and frankly charging Marqués de Domecq named Precipitado, was a bull for a triumph, but after a highly artistic faena—one clearly intended to open the Puerta Grande—Rincón failed to kill well, hitting bone twice and losing both ears with faulty sword work.

His second animal was not "propitious for triumph," as the taurinos say, having quite a lot of casta and developing too much *sentido* or "sense."[2] Demoralized by his lack of success, Rincón chose not to attempt any miracles and "liquidated" the animal in short order.

I watched the corrida on television in Sevilla with John Fulton, hoping that Rincón could make the fifth miracle happen, but the magic circle of Madrid had broken, as sooner or later it had to, having snapped at the weakest—the killingest—link. John and I were disappointed, much of the Madrid afición was disappointed, all Colombia was disappointed, but above all César Rincón was disappointed. He lamely explained to Emilio Martínez after the corrida: "The most important thing for me was that I demonstrated that I am also an artistic torero. That was my fundamental objective in my first afternoon in the feria." He continued that in this seventeenth corrida of the feria he had "loosed the passion [of afición] as no one else had yet done" (*El País,* May 26, 1992). Still, the fact remained: in spite of an important faena, mighty César had struck out.

Intervening corridas in Córdoba, Aranjuez, and Cáceres failed to rally Rincón, and on June 1 he appeared again in Madrid with an overweight corrida of Baltasar Ibán bulls, managing to elicit only applause. The anti-Rincón faction gleefully contemplated the uphill battle the Colombiano had ahead of him as the season swung into summer, and some of his followers began to wonder if 1991 would be just a memory. Absent from Valencia and "earless" in Sevilla and Madrid, César Rincón was going to have his work cut out for him.

The Corrida de Beneficencia was to come on June 11, with an excellent cartel: Samuel Flores bulls for the maestro de maestros José Mari Manzanares, the maestro de Bogotá César Rincón, and the great young hope of Valencia, Enrique Ponce, already considered a maestro at twenty-one.

On June 11, after finishing up meetings for the Hemingway Conference in Pamplona before lunch, I head south, arriving at Las Ventas about five. In Madrid it is windy, cloudy, and cool. The ring has been sold out for days and the scalpers are getting 10,000 pesetas—that year almost exactly $100—for a place over in the sun.

When the fifth bull comes in, at 540 kilos a typically well-proportioned Samuel, big-horned with a deep chest and light hindquarters, you can feel the electric expectation running around the ring. Rincón receives him in the center with three verónicas and two medias in impeccable style. After a good pick, he makes a fine quite *por detrás,* with the cape held from behind his back, finishing with a revolera, each pass drawing gasps from the crowd as the Samuel's wide horns pass the matador's body at ever closer range.

The Madrid ring pulses with applause and the afternoon seems to warm. Can it happen again, we all wonder in unison. Memory and desire converge in that cathartic crackle of expectation unique to the fiesta, and we all wait for the miracle of grace that wipes away gloom and chill and tedium.

Rincón opens with strong doubling passes, working the bull toward the center of the ring. His first two derechazos are perfect, but in the third pass the banderillas, all six of which have remained in place, jostle him stiffly out of position.

In the second series the bull begins to cut in on him and it begins to rain.

Switching to the left hand, Rincón starts a series of naturales but the bull disarms him.

In the fourth series the bull commences to hook and shake his head.

In the fifth the animal hooks at the end of each pass and doubles back on the matador.

In the sixth Rincón makes three derechazos, risking horn wounds on each pass, and finishes with a long chest pass, to deep applause.

Three more passes—the animal will not accept more than three—and another chest pass as someone shouts: "¡Viva el pundonor!"

By the eighth series it is clear that the animal has become unworkable.

Rincón lines the bull up to kill but faces that same bunch of banderillas, all pointing forward, along with the bull's still-high horns. Somehow he gets in half a sword, but it takes him six attempts with the descabello to drop the beast.

Enrique Ponce, cutting an ear from each bull, goes out on shoulders.

The Spanish anthem plays, and the crowd shouts "¡Viva el Rey!" as Juan Carlos stands, regally handsome in a dark green double-breasted suit. I leave the plaza in the rain to drive most of the night back to Narixa.

Granada: June 20, 1992

I met César Rincón on this evening at the second-floor bar of the Luz Palacio Hotel in Granada. He had come down to greet well-wishers and admirers and, as usual, he was sipping on a Coca-Cola. In spite of having been cheated out of a second ear by the presidente, with the consequent loss of the salida a hombros, he seemed remarkably calm.[3] I introduced myself and told him I would like to ask him about the Columbus Quincentennial for a piece I was doing. He answered that for him the celebration was a wonderful coincidence. "In the old days, since 1492, the Spaniards came to 'do the Americas.' Now in 1992, it's the other way around: a lovely irony." Then with his characteristic shy smile he added, as though he were speak-

Figure 19. Meeting in Granada, June 20, 1992. I had met Rincón less than ten minutes before taking this portrait. I was immediately impressed with his relaxed demeanor and his almost shy, disarming honesty.

ing for millions: "I am the first Colombian torero to become a figura in Spain and that makes me feel very proud."

"That's perfect," I said. "Just what I need. I hope to talk to you some more, but first I need to speak to Luis Alvarez. And, by the way, *enhorabuena* [congratulations]; I think you were cheated by the presidente and should have had the ear of your second bull too. Perhaps more so than the first."

"Yes," he said, "that happens a lot, unfortunately." I found his resignation intriguing.

When I introduced myself to Luis Alvarez, I went right to the point: "I'm interested in doing a book on toreo for the U.S. And, if it's acceptable, I'd like to make César Rincón the focal point. I've been watching bulls for thirty years and he's the best I've seen since Paco Camino or Antoñete with the white bull. Maybe better—for me. He's given me my afición back, as never before."

Luis Alvarez raised his bushy gray eyebrows, gave me an appraising look, and said in his underspoken Andalusian accent, "Could I invite you to a whiskey?"

Pamplona: July 13 and 14, 1992

When I met César Rincón that evening in Granada, he found himself in something of a *bache*, a hole that you have to climb out of, regardless of whether the cause is luck or morale or a physical problem. And the malas lenguas were saying there were two Rincóns: the 1991 version and now this other one who could never live up to the former's glory.

Corridas in Bilbao, Toledo, and Alicante continued his flat streak. Then in Soria on June 24 he cut two ears from Carlos Núñez bulls, and in Tolosa on June 28 he had a triumph, cutting three ears and a tail from Marca bulls. In his next seven corridas he cut ten ears and came storming into Pamplona in great shape for the two final corridas of San Fermín on the thirteenth and fourteenth of July. His season had taken wing.

By this time I was back in Pamplona working on the Hemingway Conference, which we had arranged to begin immediately after the fiesta so conference participants could catch the last two days of San Fermín, conveniently a Monday and a Tuesday when the hotels would have more room.

For the thirteenth, Iñigo Sepúlveda sent an interesting if not altogether easy corrida for Pamplona, and all three matadors, Ortega Cano, Espartaco, and César Rincón, cut ears and went out the Puerta Grande. John Fulton and I, at the corrida together, celebrated Rincón's form, his fine morale, and his triumph, accomplished in the lionhearted style of his 1991 season.

John described the first bull as "a puppy dog with no bad ideas at all." Ortega Cano cut two ears from it, but I thought he was "below" the bull.

Espartaco's first animal was a bit bronco, although he charged with no hesitation, and Espartaco dominated him, did some passes on his knees, and killed well, also cutting two ears. John pointed out, however, that the matador positioned himself frequently *fuera de cacho,* advantageously just out of the line of the bull's charge.

The peñas in the sun are singing "Induráin, Induráin, Induráin," their usual paean to the local cyclist (to the tune of John Phillip Sousa's "Stars and Stripes Forever"), as Rincón's first bull, a high-shouldered 601-kilo black animal named Charrascón, enters. Rincón receives him with two kneeling largas, swinging the cape over his head and out to one side, instantly letting the crowd know he is not going to be outdone, then takes Charrascón to the center of the ring with five verónicas, never moving his feet back and not once allowing the bull to touch the cape. The ovation makes the plaza tremble.

He starts his faena holding on to the barerra with his left hand, but the animal shows a reluctance to charge. When it does charge, it goes furiously, a typical "dangerous manso." Even so, by remaining still and waiting out the charges, Rincón manages two series of passes with each hand. In the fifth series, after five derechazos, he works the muleta back and forth like a pendulum, with his body in the middle of the swing, allowing the bull to breathe. On the ninth derechazo of that series, Charrascón cuts in, catching Rincón sideways and flipping him backward onto the sand. Still holding the muleta, he tries to get up, trips, and falls to his left hand and knee. As he rises, the bull catches him in the right hip, running the horn under his right leg, tripping him again. On his hands and knees, now without the muleta, he tries to roll away as a cape finally arrives to distract the bull.

Limping, Rincón retrieves the muleta and returns to the fray as the peñas shout: "¡Torero! ¡Torero! ¡Torero!" He passes the animal five more times, back and forth next to the barrera of Tendido Six, alternating naturales and high passes, finishing with a deep pase de pecho. John says, "A terrible bull, but he's making it work!"

Rincón lines the animal up and puts in a sword that kills him quickly. John roars, "What will they give him now—the whole plaza?"

In spite of the continuous petition, the presidente awards him one ear.

The peñas are shouting "¡Torero! ¡Torero!" again as Rincón makes two vueltas. When he is through, the chant changes to "¡Hijo-puta! ¡Hijo-puta!" for the presidente, and John comments with an acidity born of many similar experiences: "That is a perfect example of highway robbery of a foreign torero." After Ortega Cano's prancing and stepping backward on virtually each pass and Espartaco's frequently being fuera de cacho, it looks worse than chauvinism. Only the crowd's reaction and Rincón's stoicism keep it from being a travesty.

Rincón still needs to cut another ear to accompany the other matadors out the Puerta Grande. His second bull, a swaybacked manso, proves dangerous in the banderillas. Toward the center of the ring, his charge is short; given the fence, the animal charges better. So Rincón works him along the barrera as best he can. John remarks that he should just kill it, but Rincón continues to work the animal back and forth along the fence. A good sword drops the bull quickly, and the peñas petition the ear for him—an ear for bravery, for entrega, and for the one he failed to receive before. All's well that ends well, and on this afternoon the peñas demand and get poetic justice.

On July 14, Roberto Domínguez, César Rincón, and Enrique Ponce appeared with a corrida of the Marqués de Domecq. The bulls turned out to be difficult, in general refusing to charge. Domínguez and Ponce left frustrated and empty-handed, but in the fifth bull a kind of miracle occurred.

Because for the most part Hemingway is venerated in Pamplona, I was able to secure fifty-five seats for the last corrida, something that would have been completely impossible under normal circumstances. But thanks to the generosity of the Casa de Misericordia, the charitable entity that serves as the empresario in Pamplona, all of the Hemingway Conference participants who wanted tickets were able to attend the last corrida of the feria without the usual scalping (in fact, they paid only $23 each).

Murphy's Law works overtime in the bulls, and for visiting firemen with only one chance to see a corrida, Murphy seldom fails. (After all, Rincón had cut ears the day before.) Also by this time, many of the conferees had heard about César Rincón. Some of them had heard a lot about Rincón. So naturally the corrida was a disaster. The normally splendid bulls of the Marqués de Domecq—the previous San Fermín's prize winner—looked fine but had too little casta. The maestro Roberto Domínguez spent most of his time chasing his first animal, and he killed the second poorly. Ponce was uninspired.

By the time the fifth bull comes in, I am thinking there is no hope. My Hemingway colleagues are going to feel cheated out of their money and are going to be convinced that their on-site director has lost his mind. Those without much of a taurine bent anyway are going to say, well, it was just like I thought it would be, only worse. And boring. And twenty-three dollars!

But the fifth bull, which looks like the others when he comes in, has a secret, and César Rincón figures out quickly what the secret is: the animal will charge at a gallop from a distance, though up close, like his brothers, he is reluctant to move.

The bull is named Manijero and, at 535 kilos, he is not overweight. His charge, when it comes, is frank, and he displays more of the bravery of the House of Domecq than his siblings. Rincón dedicates the bull to the público, and John Fulton does a mock announcer's version of the corrida to the amusement of those around him: "This is going to be the faena of the feria!"

Rincón begins his faena on the fence, completing three spectacular high passes without letting go, then does a fourth off the fence and two chest passes to warm applause, as John comments: "That's how bullfighting should be done, ladies and gentlemen. This is the real McCoy, none of that namby-pamby bullshit we've seen by everybody else!"

In the first series of derechazos Rincón already begins to "lose" four steps or so between passes, knowing from the start what provokes Manijero to charge.

For the second series he backs at least ten meters away and cites. As Manijero breaks into a gallop, John announces: "Ladies and gentlemen, the cyclone of Colombia seems to be hitting his stride. He's got the bull under control and now he's going to mesmerize him." Manijero takes the muleta, going all the way through, and Rincón drops back four steps, taking him again, dropping, passing him again, to finish with a change of hands and a chest pass with the left that has Manijero lunging for the sky. "Yes, sir, ladies and gentlemen, *this* is what it's all about!"

From ten meters Manijero again comes at a gallop, and Rincón spins a molinete, then follows with four derechazos and a chest pass on each side. As in many of his best faenas, a sense of rhythm emerges as he passes and drops back and passes without losing a beat.

Next come two series of naturales, first from ten meters, then dropping back to take the bull past again and again, as though the animal were a trained performer. How did Rincón know what would make this bull charge? Intuition, the ability to think in the bull's face—or ten meters away from it—then to stand still, moving only the muleta as the bull comes, rhythmically guiding the animal past and around him, never letting the horns touch the lure. Intelligence, bravery, timing, liquid sculpture: Rincón's genius.

For the next series, he backs off fifteen meters, as if to see from what distance he can take the bull. Rincón cites, feet together; Manijero gallops. Ten meters: Rincón cites, Manijero charges. Eight meters: Rincón cites, Manijero comes. Five meters: change of hands, Rincón cites, Manijero obeys.

These *unipases*—isolated passes, usually done to allow an overweight animal to rest between charges, but done here to show off Manijero's repeated long charges—heighten the emotion and the beauty of the spectacle. John shouts with the (mock) hysteria of an announcer on the edge of a nervous breakdown: "There's no doubt about it, ladies and gentlemen, no question in anyone's mind why this is the number one bullfighter in the world today, César Rincón!"

"How did you know this was going to be the faena of the feria?" I ask, and John yells back, "I could feel it in my cojones!"

Rincón takes the animal behind his back in a perfect *pase de las flores,* citing in profile and taking the animal around and behind him with the right hand, to continue with more derechazos, finishing with a *pase del desdén,* the pass of disdain, done by snatching the muleta from under the bull's nose, bringing him up short, then turning his back on the animal and walking away.

"Do you think he'll kill recibiendo? He's got the bull for it."

Before John can answer, it becomes apparent Rincón is going to try. John says, "The bull's going to help him," meaning the bull will charge. Twice, as Rincón tries to line him up, the animal charges. Then when Manijero refuses to move, Rincón edges forward for a volapié. As soon as the matator begins to move, the bull charges and Rincón puts in a perfect sword, high up in the withers, *a un tiempo,* so called because the man and the animal move on each other simultaneously. It is a spectacular end to one of Rincón's most spectacular faenas. John announces: "In to the hilt! The best faena of the entire Feria de San Fermín!" Two ears, two vueltas, flowers, music, delirium. It is, in fact, what you go to the bulls for—and everything you hope for when you send someone else.

Guadalajara: September 20, 1992

The first half of 1992 belonged to the young maestro of Valencia, Enrique Ponce. Looking back from year's end, José Carlos Arévalo and Michael Wigram called the 1992 season "the war of the generations," finding that the young phalanx led by Ponce and Joselito, backed up by Litri and Jesulín and aided occasionally by Manuel Caballero and Julio Aparacio, was declaring war on the older generation of established figuras, Espartaco, Ojeda, Manzanares, Emilio Muñoz, and Ortega Cano with help now and then from Dámaso González, Roberto Domínguez, and Capea. In the first half of the season, the young turks held sway with Ponce as captain. But starting in July the veterans made a strong comeback, led by the youngest among them, César Rincón: "The veteran who picked up the gauntlet was César Rincón. . . . Dueling place? Pamplona, Mont-de-Marsan, Santander, and Valencia: Triunfador of the Feria de San Fermín, where he went out on shoulders two afternoons; steamrolling to the point of exaggeration in Mont-de-Marsan, with definitive performances in which the least important thing was the number of trophies; in Santander he lost the tail of a Sepúlveda on his first afternoon and cut three ears from the noble Buendías; and he went out on shoulders, as well, in Valencia" (*6T6* 15:20).

How did César Rincón perform such feats? In the singular prose of taurine critics: "Rincón wrenches lucid faenas from bulls impossible to ligar, citing them from a distance with single passes of gallant vitality and startling truth; he tricks rebellious, violent, or unwilling animals into charging by invading their space, very closely, embarking them in the muleta and subjecting them until they show canine obedience; he can ligar the longest pass to another pass with the purest truth if the animal is enrazado and aggressive, or he can weave together half passes when there is nowhere left to go, working up the crowd if the animal is low on casta." Arévalo and Wigram conclude: "He is without a doubt a *figurón* [grand figura] of toreo" (*6T6* 15:20–21). Rincón in July seemed clearly headed for a duel for the number one position with Enrique Ponce.

On September 19, I return to Spain to finish covering the Columbus Quincentennial and to catch as many of Rincón's late-season corridas as possible before making a full-scale effort with him in the 1993 season. On September 20, I drive out to Guadalajara to see him in a corrida of Torrealta bulls. He does not seem himself, and even though he cuts an ear, I wonder if the hectic pace of August and September—thirty-six corridas in fifty days with fifteen important triumphs—has worn him down. When I talk with him at the Hotel Pax afterwards, he seems in good spirits, so I dismiss the idea, say goodbye, and drive up to Logroño, capital of the Rioja wine country, where I am to meet Michael Wigram, Charles Patrick Scanlan, and others of the far-flung "cuadrilla" for the Feria de San Mateo, and where I will see César Rincón perform twice.

Or so I thought. Rincón failed to appear for his first corrida in Logroño. Some of the local afición, who consider themselves very *torista* or bull-centered,[4] believed he was afraid to torear in their plaza. But something much more serious was at stake: his health.

On the twenty-fourth he performed in a corrida in Valladolid and then, without coming to Logroño for his second corrida, he cut short his temporada, canceling the rest of his contracts, including a vitally important corrida in Madrid on October 2. Luis Alvarez announced: "Rincón has made an enormous effort to continue toreando in spite of not feeling well physically, but the time finally came when he could no longer continue and had to cancel his season for good" (*El Mundo*, September 27, 1992). César Rincón had hepatitis, and the doctors had ordered several months of complete rest.

The symptoms, I would learn, had been bothering him off and on for some time. After consulting a number of specialists in Spain, César had finally been diagnosed with hepatitis C—barely known at the time—by a clinic in Los Angeles. Although there was no way to prove it and nothing to do about it except try to get well, it seemed reasonably clear that one of the many transfusions he had gotten in Palmira after his goring in 1990 was the culpable agent. Rincón headed straight home to Colombia (and to his favorite doctors) where he followed a strict treatment for several months. There were times during the late summer of 1992, he would tell me later, when after a corrida he did not have the strength to get into the shower.

That was the frustrating and inconclusive end of César Rincón's 1992 season. I could not help reflecting that luck had been a major factor in this season—especially bad luck. *6T6* rated Ponce número uno, and they gave second spot to Joselito. Rincón, who finished his unfinished season with eighty-two corridas, eighty ears, and one tail, came in third. They called it quite accurately a season of consolidation as a gran figura: "Contrary to what some 'sages' opined—that he had slept on his laurels—Rincón in fact had gone all out, had given quarter to no one, and had come out like a lion in practically all his performances" (*6T6* 15:70). Like a seriously ill lion: what would Rincón have done, I could only wonder, had he been competing at one hundred percent?

Luis Alvarez outlined the 1993 season's plan for me: "Two afternoons in Sevilla, two in Madrid, the Beneficencia, one in Granada, one in Algeciras, one in Córdoba, all the important ferias and not too many corridas. Maybe sixty or sixty-five." But that was not the way it would happen.

1993

→ **24**

Rincón missed the fall ferias in Venezuela, Perú, Ecuador, and Colombia while he recuperated from hepatitis, following Dr. Sabogal's treatment of acupuncture, serums and supplements, fresh air and rest. His first important appearance took place in the Crotaurinos corrida in Bogotá on December 13, with Manzanares and Joselito. Each of the Spaniards had a good afternoon, cutting an ear apiece. Rincón cut three and went out on high.

In Cali Rincón was, "never better said, a prophet in his own land" (*6T6* 16:29). In general the feria was a disappointment until the last corrida on January 4, when pandemonium broke out in the Cañaveralejo ring: Ortega Cano, César Rincón, and Enrique Ponce with bulls of Guachicono. As the taurinos say, "a corrida for the history books." Ponce cut an ear and was cheated out of the second (chauvinism and favoritism are not solely Spanish). Ortega Cano pardoned the bull Vencedor in yet another of the greatest faenas of his life. Rincón cut two ears from Cazador and one from Lisonjero, a bull that had every intention of killing him, "more dangerous than a box full of bombs" as the reviewer described him. "The technique and valor of the Colombian star literally ate up the ferocity of the bull" (*6T6* 16:34). Everyone, including the ganadero, went out on shoulders. Rincón once again won the Señor de los Cristales trophy.

More triumphs followed in Manizales and Cartagena. In Bogotá on February 13, Rincón cut four ears to Ponce's two in a mano a mano with a great corrida of Ernesto González Caicedo's bulls, thus closing another extraordinary season at home. Could his Spanish season develop the same momentum? Was the hepatitis gone?

Sevilla: April 29, 1993

Rain was pouring down when César Rincón profiled to kill Fugitivo, just as it had done when Fugitivo, branded with the number 13, the third Núñez del Cuvillo bull of the afternoon, entered the normally golden but now leaden and puddle-covered sands of the Maestranza. The corrida had begun late and perhaps should not have begun at all. Umbrellas sprouted in the tendidos like mushrooms of mourning. Rincón profiled at some distance from Fugitivo and cited to kill recibiendo.

He had opened with a long, cadenced series of seven verónicas and a media, taking Fugitivo from a distance on each pass and working him outward toward the center of the ring. Applause was impeded by the umbrellas and deadened by the rain, but Sevilla's reverent olés were very audible. Fugitivo pawed the ground like a manso, then charged the horse at a gallop. Rincón made two verónicas—citing again from a distance and floating the cape out as Fugitivo came to it on the run—finishing with a larga and a revolera.

Anderson Murillo, under Rincón's orders, picked lightly. Manzanares made three elegant chicuelinas, his hands brushing by his body below hip level, to finish with a media. Rincón answered with *gaoneras*—a pass similar to the verónica but with the cape held behind the back—and a revolera without moving his feet, taking the bull from a distance and letting the horns come close to his waist. The rain had let up and the ovation for both matadors resounded as they embraced.

Rincón dedicated the animal to the público of Sevilla, and the forceful silence of that ring spread like an audible shadow. And the rain began again.

Rincón started with two doubling passes, with one knee bent, the first from a distance of fifteen meters. Then citing again from a distance, he linked four derechazos, changed hands, and finished with a straight chest pass, showing the animal's long charges.

In spite of the rain, the band fired up a pasodoble as Rincón initiated a series on the right: four deliberate derechazos, the muleta flat, the matador as tall and straight as his physiognomy allowed, making as elegantly executed a series of passes as he had ever done, to finish with a right-handed chest pass and a *trinchera*, similar to a chest pass but done low instead of over the horns.

Then Rincón tried to take the bull back toward the center of the ring, but the animal was reluctant to go. A sign, like his pawing, that he was somewhat manso? Perhaps the defensiveness of fatigue? In any case, Rincón desisted and began another series in the same terrain. A mistake, or a calculated risk, not wanting to break the rhythm of the faena by insisting?

In the third series on the right, the animal's charge begins to shorten, showing the effects of his repeatedly bouyant charges, and in the finishing trinchera, on the *right* horn, Fugitivo stopped, looked at Rincón, and hooked for him, clearly warning him and nearly catching him.

Rincón switched to the left and linked two naturales, but in the third Fugitivo stopped, looked, and hooked.

Back on the right Rincón made four stylish derechazos, switching sides to finish with a martinete when he realized the bull would not go through again on the same side.

Fugitivo began to paw the sand again. The rain increased. Rincón must then have wondered how he could get two ears out of this faena, which was going "from greater to lesser." Kill recibiendo? Did the bull have enough charge left?

Now he gave the animal two ayudados and a trinchera, to finish the faena but also to test in the first ayudado (on the right horn) and the trinchera (again on the right) whether the bull would go through if he cited recibiendo.

Rincón profiled as the rain came down harder. No one moved in the tendidos. He profiled first in the *suerte contraria,* giving the bull the fence—this animal's preferred exit, as he had shown when Rincón had tried to take him further out—but Fugitivo charged before the matador was ready.

Now he profiled, at a distance, in the *suerte natural,* giving the animal the open ring, which was not his preference, so Fugitivo remained in place. Rincón cited, moving forward only his left leg and the muleta, but the bull did not charge.

He inched closer to the animal, profiled and cited again, thrusting the muleta toward the bull. Fugitivo charged this time, lowering his head and following the tip of the muleta. Rincón leaned in with his right arm, putting the sword straight into the eye of the needle as Fugitivo came forward and impaled himself. Just as Rincón's sword hand reached the bull's withers, with the sword now buried, Fugitivo turned his head to the right, toward the fence, toward Rincón, lifting and hooking as he had done during the faena with that same horn.

Fugitivo lifted and hooked, catching Rincón between the legs, goring him and raising him high in the air. Rincón, impaled on the horn, swung head downward and then, coming off the horn, landed on his back. Fugitivo was distracted by the muleta, which fell in front of his face. Rincón rolled and struggled to his feet, holding his groin and backing away in a hunch, trying to stop the hemorrhaging from a deep place where there was nothing to hold. Finally he collapsed into the arms of the toreros carrying him as fast as they could to the enfermería.

The consternation of a cornada swept the tendidos of the Maestranza, as Rincón's cuadrilla stood watching Fugitivo die the slow death of a toro bravo. Afterwards they bore Fugitivo's ears around the ring in a vicarious and Pyrrhic triumph, while in the enfermería the surgeons under Dr. Ramón Vila began to operate.

Had Rincón made a mistake? Perhaps he had not crossed sufficiently with the muleta, using his left hand to divert the animal's charge around his body. Maybe he had pushed too hard with the right shoulder, the sword shoulder, preventing a proper cross. Or perhaps he had cited from too far away. Was it so far that the charge was finished, causing the bull to rear his head? Fugitivo had warned Rincón several times with the right horn. And he had a slight tendency to go to the fence. Add those factors together and a cornada seems almost unavoidable. As José Carlos Arévalo wrote, César Rincón had offered himself on a life-or-death basis: "The torero fell as a hero, converting truth into something impossible." He went on to say that heroism has no shades of meaning. "It is possible that Sevilla has yet to see fully the toreo of Rincón. But they have understood, better than anyone, his deeply moving hombría" (6T6 18:14).

The horn wound was clean. It penetrated the scrotum, herniating the right testicle and entering the groin with an upward trajectory of thirty centimeters, destroying abdominal muscle tissue but without penetrating the abdominal cavity. The reconstructive surgery was successful, but Luis Alvarez told me—much later—that at one point he thought César might die on the operating table. Rincón was glib, describing cornadas as not having transcendence in his life, as being an occupational hazard. Besides, he had accomplished one of his main goals, to triumph in Sevilla (*Aplausos*, June 1, 1993). Some months later he would explain to French critic A. Dubos that he had "cited from a distance, and at the moment of encounter the bull did not follow the muleta, and there was the cornada. Those are the risks of the métier. That's all" (*Tendido* 60:10). Eventually he admitted it was "a technical error," telling José Carlos Arévalo that when the bull refused to charge, he should have shortened the distance between them. He did not do that, and the bull ended his charge and hooked upward: "As I said, a technical error" (6T6 24:28). But shortly after the operation, in the Sagrado Corazón Clinic,

Figure 20. Goring in Sevilla, April 29, 1993. In this remarkable photograph, we see the instant that Fugitivo thrusts upward with Rincón impaled on the right horn. Rincón has just released the sword, which is exactly placed. He seems to be pushing down with the muleta to protect himself, and his face shows the awareness of his predicament. The umbrellas give a slightly surreal quality to the picture. By permission, Fredrik Hagblom.

he had told José Luis Lorente: "I had to show them my balls so the hijos de puta would believe me, so they would see what I am."

Algeciras: June 25, 1993

It took a month for Rincón to recuperate from the goring, and he was not able to reappear until May 29 in Vic-Fézensac. During his convalescence he missed his corridas for San Isidro in Madrid, scheduled for May 20 and May 25, and was hurt again, suffering cracked ribs, while training with a bull at Victoriano del Río's ranch. Then in Vic-Fézensac, on the day he returned, he reinjured a previously dislocated left shoulder.

A goring such as the one César Rincón had in Sevilla always has consequences. Although a matador may recover his physical capacity quickly—sometimes with a speed that seems almost superhuman—the recuperation of morale, of timing, and of sitio may take much longer. Four months later, looking back, César would tell me that such cornadas do indeed affect you, regardless of what the matador says at the time.

On June 25, I drive down the coast to Algeciras to see César Rincón, Enrique Ponce, and Jesulín with bulls of Marcos Núñez. Rincón has performed in three corridas in the interim, including a triumph with two ears in Aire-sur-l'Adour.

His first faena looks good, but I write in my notebook, "Not the old Rincón yet." He does perform some excellent naturales but the bull is "a rat," as the taurinos say, small and unpleasant. Neither Ponce nor Jesulín have much success, as the ganado is weak.

Rincón's second bull charges well once he gets rid of a cramp that makes him drag his right rear hoof. Rincón does a splendid faena with both hands, citing de frente and firing the crowd up. Then he kills *too* well: the bull lifts his head and catches Rincón under his chaquetilla, carrying him for five or six seconds across the ring, shaking him all the while. Finally Rincón gets loose and waves everybody away. The bull goes down and Rincón cuts an ear. He deserves two, but the presidente does not concede the second trophy.

At any rate Rincón seems unhurt. What looked like many seconds with the horn under his rib cage turned out to be a horn caught in his *fajín*—the long sash wrapped several times around his waist—tangled there, which is why it took him so long to get loose. In the callejón Luis Alvarez looks shaken up. Rincón afterwards says it only proved that the cornada in Sevilla had had no effect on him, but he says that to the press (*El Ruedo*, June 6, 1993).

Ponce is exquisite with his small bull and cuts an ear, which would have been two except for a pinchazo before killing well. Jesulín does his usual "number," very close to the bull, in the style perfected by Paco Ojeda, suffocating the animal's charge. But he is brave—although anti-aesthetic, too fast, gawky, and gangly—fun, and almost endearing, although he kills poorly.

Afterwards at the bar of the Hotel Alborán, where everyone agrees Rincón is taking too many chances, I recall an image from just before the corrida: As I was walking up the stairs to the ring, the Rincón Chevy van passed, circling the high plaza de toros in front of me, and César looked down and waved. Then they were swallowed by the crowd as the van moved slowly around toward the *patio de caballos*—the horse patio or "back door" where the matadors wait, in the realm of fear, for the corrida to start. He had worn a strange look of concern. Was it premonitory? Clearly he is getting hit too often: the goring in Sevilla, the ribs at Victoriano del Río's, the separated shoulder in Vic, now this catching today, of little consequence but, had the horn penetrated a few more centimeters. . . . Is he pushing his luck beyond the "normal" danger of the profession?

Entering the dining room to speak to Rincón, I inadvertently catch the end of a "discussion" between him and Luis Alvarez. It has to do with a substitution that Luis Alvarez wants him to take and that Rincón at that moment decidedly does not wish to consider. The cuadrilla sit in silence as the matador fulminates. Such "discussions" between matador and apoderado are common enough, but this is the first time I have seen his well-known temper (he calls it his *mal carácter*) in action. Luis Alvarez, on the other hand, appears the soul of equanimity.

In all fairness to Rincón, it turns out that besides the new pain in his chest he also has a case of tonsilitis and a very high uric acid level, the latter, according to him, because of the pressure and the fear associated with his work (*El Ruedo*, June 6, 1993).

Pamplona: July 9, 1993

At noon on July 9 in Pamplona I went to the *apartado*, the separating of the bulls after the sorteo, to inspect the Marqués de Domecq bulls for the veteran Dámaso González, César Rincón, and Juan Mora.

The animal Rincón would kill in the second slot was a castaño, weighing 629 kilos, the bull for fifth slot a black bull of 625. If they did not fall down, they looked as though they could be very good.

Rincón dedicates the castaño to the rowdiest taurine público in Spain, then proceeds to rivet their attention. The bull charges from a distance, as the best of the Marqués frequently do, and Rincón waits for him, citing de frente, his outside leg forward, with that buoyancy of spirit, almost impishness, that has caused many taurine writers to call him a small torero with the heart of a giant. César Rincón is unmistakably "back." Cutting two ears from the big castaño, whose name is Fresón, he takes the long, slow vuelta of triumph, draped in the sashes and pañuelos of San Fermín, becoming one of the triunfadores of the feria (on July 13 Jesulín will cut four ears from the Torrealta bulls) and going out once again on the shoulders of the rowdy crowd.

The following night, at the Mauleón, one of the old Pamplona eateries I have frequented since 1963, I have dinner with Javier Villán and Salvador

Figure 21. Domecq bull, Pamplona, July 9, 1993. Fresón, the fine castaño of the Marqués de Domecq from which Rincón would cut two ears. Just before the apartado, the separating of the bulls into individual pens.

Figure 22. Colombian flag over Pamplona, July 9, 1993. Rincón, bearing the Colombian flag, is carried in triumph by the peñas of Pamplona, after cutting two ears from Fresón, the kind of repetitive animal that Rincón likes best. Rincón was "back" after the goring in Sevilla.

Távora, who is to my mind the most exciting theatre director in Spain and the only real heir to García Lorca's poetic and theatrical legacy, as well as having been a novillero in his youth and having cut two ears and a tail in a festival in the Maestranza of Sevilla. We have a fine discussion about the corrida as theatre, as "showbiz," as entertainment, and Távora confirms something I have always suspected but am glad to hear from no less an authority—writer, director, scene designer, actor, flamenco performer, and torero. The subject is the nature of fear and Salvador is adamant: It is not the fear of what the bull can or will do to you, it is stage fright that is the worst. Toreo has elements of theatre—or pretheatre, but theatre nonetheless—and the worst fear is the fear of looking ridiculous. Javier Villán, who was a theatre critic first and became a taurine critic later, agrees completely.

Some months later César would confirm that, for him at least, *miedo al ridículo,* the fear of looking ridiculous, of failing, the opposite side of the coin of responsabilidad, was what preoccupied him. But, he said, it was not that simple. "There is fear of the bull, but more than that there is a conjugation of different fears that affects you. The público, of course, the animal itself, the whole responsabilidad. But there's no doubt that toreo is also different in some ways from theatre. You don't have a written script. You may have an idealized concept of toreo in your head, but once the actual animal comes out, everything you've thought about is finished, no? And at that moment the bull makes you suffer more fear or less fear, no? He makes you feel very proud or very disillusioned, no?"

I told him: "I like that phrase about the conjugation of different fears because it catches the variable nature of both fears, the physical fear of the bull and the fear of looking ridiculous."

"Responsabilidad," said César, "responsabilidad."

"Responsabilidad to the público?"

"Yes. To the público. And to yourself."

Well, I thought, so it is not so cut and dried after all. I remembered the other side of the argument, presented in the realistic taurine novel *Juncal* by Jaime de Armiñán. Juncal, retired, is talking to his son, who is a novillero, about fear, and he says: "You have to call things by their name, and fear is called fear; not responsabilidad, not stage fright or fear of the public: fear of old blackfoot, of the one that yanks your feet off the ground" (245). No, it was not simple, but César's "conjugation of different fears" encompassed it all or all of them. The possibilities struck me as infinite, César's phrase as enlightened.

After Pamplona I returned home to Pensacola for two days to pay bills and make sure my house was still there, and then left for Guilin, China, where I was to give the address at a Hemingway conference. Over Hot Springs and Little Rock and the flood-swollen Mississippi, I could hear the songs of San Fermín lurking within the jet's purring roar. San Fermín gets into your head, into your blood, into your heart. This year had been my best "fiesta" yet, and I took it all the way to China with me. On the sweltering Western Hill over Guilin, down the archetypal Li River, through the landscape of Chinese art, for three weeks through mainland China—those songs stayed with me and sustained me. Spain, especially taurine Spain, the Spain of the twentieth chapter of *Death in the Afternoon* but in our own time, is as memorable as it is ineradicable.

Linares: August 30, 1993

When I return to Spain on Sunday, August 29, with the ghosts of China and the effects of a bout of Shanghai flu mostly gone, I feel glad to be back on sacred taurine ground and soon I am motoring swiftly south through La Mancha. A cool front has turned the sky Velázquez blue, and the windmills above Consuegra, often lost in the summer haze, stand in relief against the dark sky with the brightness of a knight errant's vision (plate 39a).

Down in Linares, where it still feels like summer, I lunch on clams and crab and fried anchovies with manzanilla (normally things I like very much but after the chicken feet, the endless carp, and the unidentifiables soaked in MSG in much of inland China, it seems food fit for the gods), and then go to watch Palomo Linares, out of retirement, and Espartaco and Chamaco with Los Guateles bulls.

Juan Antonio Ruiz Román, to give Espartaco his full name, performs with his first bull in a style that can only be called maestro-maestro. After a majestic faena, he puts in a good sword but finishes the animal with six descabellos.

The rest is boring because the animals will not charge and the matadors can do nothing. Boredom: the enemy of the corrida. What we want—I fresh from China and the States, the people of Linares in feria—is glory, not boredom. Not blood and sand, but glory. Not blood sport, but glory, the vicarious vanquishing of our own fears. We want a hero. In the last bull Chamaco cuts an ear with his elegant tremendismo, his hair askew, his tie undone, yet nonetheless quite the *caballero*. It is after nine when we leave the plaza and a full moon is rising in the fading light of late summer. I have a wonderful dinner in a Chinese restaurant called the Ciudad Feliz, the Happy City.

In the interim since Pamplona, César Rincón had drawn a high percentage of difficult or bad bulls. Even so he had cut at least one ear in thirteen out of twenty-eight appearances. And he had triumphed on several occasions: on August 7 in La Coruña, Manzanares and Espartaco and Rincón all went out the Puerta Grande, along with the mayoral of Victoriano del Río; the next day down in Puerto de Santa María, Rincón cut an ear from a Los Guateles bull and another from a Núñez del Cuvillo, and Filiberto Mira of *Aplausos* wrote that it was "one of the best afternoons of [Rincón's] life" (August 9, 1993); on August 15 he had another important triumph, cutting two ears from his second Samuel Flores in Dax, further cementing his reputation as número uno in France; and in Saint-Sever on the twenty-second he earned three ears from the Lamamié de Clairac bulls (perhaps idol is the proper description in France). Nor did sharp-eyed critics miss an important afternoon on August 17 in Bilbao with the Sepúlvedas, when Manzanares cut two ears and Espartaco three to Rincón's one but everyone agreed that Rincón had, once again, been cheated out of the Puerta Grande by the presidente. Still and all, his record was not as perfect as he would have liked. A top matador needs to cut—although there is nothing carved in stone—an average of one ear per corrida. Rincón was above that average since Pamplona, but I knew from talking to him and to Luis Alvarez that they were not happy. They kept speaking of a *mala racha,* a bad streak, of bulls.

At one point I asked César point-blank: "Do you think that somehow you are paying with this mala racha for the great luck you had in '91?"

He looked at me and replied as though it were a mathematical certainty, "Sí, claro." Beginning with the corrida in Linares, I would see each one of his performances for the rest of the season, and I would have a chance to judge for myself.

August 30 in Linares was the first day in my intensive "campaign" with César Rincón—sixteen afternoons that I thought, along with the Feria de Cali in Colombia in December and January, would be the heart of my project. It all begins very optimistically on my part. I collect my gear—cameras and pocket recorder—and head off to the ring, to my seat in row 4 of Tendido Three. I have a group of simpáticos around me in the cramped old Santa Margarita ring who are amused at my efforts to take photographs and record my impressions simultaneously. The corrida is a mishmash of Luis Algarras, Pérez-Taberneros, and one Mari Carmen Camacho. Rincón, wearing the "hope green" suit of lights he had worn in his first triumph in Madrid (I always think of it as lime-sherbet green), draws a fair Algarra and a Pérez-Tabernero that Luis Alvarez did not like at the sorteo. He should have an ear, without question, in the first, but the presidente refuses in spite of a majority petition. Prejudice, stupidity, bullheadedness?

At the Hotel Aníbal afterwards I meet César's cousin Armando Ramírez and his old childhood training companion Ricardo Chinza, who drive the vans. By this time Rincón is using two vans, one for himself and Luis Alvarez and the other for the cuadrilla. He is the only matador using two vans, and when I ask him about it, he explains that he needs the rest that the second van of his own—a capacious Chevy diesel he ordered from Miami—allows. Plenty of rest helps prevent a recurrence of the hepatitis. Antonio

Ordóñez once said, "If you can't learn to sleep in a car, you can't be a figura del toreo." Rincón evidently has found a partial solution to the problem. As he explains it, he is able to rest significantly better in the full-sized bed in the back of his van, although he sometimes drives the van himself, especially until he becomes sleepy. He also likes the privacy of his own van.

I have a copa with Luis Alvarez at the hotel bar and give him a letter in which I propose that, if they treat me as much as possible as another member of the cuadrilla and get me whenever possible into the callejón to get better photographs, I in turn will bother them as little as possible (*joderles lo menos posible*). Luis Alvarez reads it, laughs, and says, "De acuerdo," agreed. But when I see César after the *tertulia*—the public discussion for aficionados to analyze the corrida—he seems rather removed, and I wonder if he is changing, if the pressure is, in fact, getting to him, the mala racha. Will I have to rethink my plan? I am suddenly beset with some of the difficulties and uncertainties that never cease to plague the toreros.

Rincón's next corrida is not until September 2, so I go to Sevilla to visit John Fulton, who tells me a peripheral anecdote about Rincón. As John was watching, at a neighborhood bar in Sevilla, Rincón's breakthrough corrida with the Baltasar Ibán bulls on May 21, 1991, another matador, now retired and embittered by the profession, likened Rincón's performance to "el burro que tocó la flauta," the burro who played the flute, meaning that it was just a fluke. He went on to say condescendingly, "Hombre, this will be good for him back in his country." John merely replied that Rincón was already a figura del toreo in his own country. Then in October, when Rincón had his triumph with the toro de Moura, John ran into the same matador and said: "¡Hombre! The burro is playing Beethoven!"

Palencia: September 2 and 3, 1993

On the first of September I leave Sevilla, going past the hills at El Carambolo and Itálica that have produced interesting artifacts from Roman and Tartessian times, onto the old Roman Vía de la Plata (now N-630), which runs up the west side of Spain all the way to the Roman legionnaires' town of León, driving through the hills of the Sierra de Aracena with its cork oaks and eucalyptus, through the pig country that produces the finest hams— from the *pata negra,* the Iberian blackfoot—in the world, into the country of the conquistadors in Extremadura, where many towns have counterparts—

Almadén, Albuquerque, Mérida, Guadalupe—in the Americas. Much of the road is two lanes and some of it is mountainous. It reminds me of driving in Spain in the '60s before there were any divided highways.

I am having a fine drive until the Guardia Civil waves me over, for what I can only assume is a random check. I have been watching a big hawk circle as I drive. I pull over—wondering if the hawk is an omen—and we exchange pleasantries. They want to see my papers, which after some searching I manage to produce.

They go through my suitcases and camera bag, paying some attention to the spare tire, looking I suppose for drugs. Where was I coming from? Sevilla. Where was I going? Palencia. What for? To see a corrida. From Sevilla to Palencia to see a corrida? Now they are curious. Why would a foreigner be going all the way to Palencia to see a corrida? I explain to them and they listen politely, as usual, showing mild surprise, and then bid me *buen viaje,* good journey, with that detached and indifferent formality that has always characterized them.

As I drive away I remember a similar incident in 1964. Glenn Lipskey and I, on a break from our graduate studies at the NYU-in-Spain program at the University of Madrid, had taken a bus from Alicante to a youth hostel some kilometers up the beach from the city. We missed the last bus back, and quite late began to walk in. As Glenn was a lieutenant in the Marine Reserves, he thought it might be amusing to teach me how to march.

Not long thereafter we marched—somewhat noisily as Glenn called out his tight-lipped and barely intelligible commands—around a curve on the deserted two-lane coast road and ran into *la pareja,* the pair, as Guardias are often called, because they work in twos. We marched straight up to them— what else could we do?—and Glenn, more restrained now but still militarily unintelligible, called, "Company halt!"

"Documentation."

"It's in the hotel in Alicante," I said.

"You know it's a law that you must carry your national identity card at all times."

Evidently he did not realize yet that we were foreigners. So I explained.

"What are you doing?"

"Do you have a cigarette by any chance?" I asked as a diversionary tactic. They gave us cigarettes, as Spanish etiquette requires, and we lit up.

"We're studying in Madrid," I said, taking the question in its largest sense.

"Studying what? You're down here disturbing the peace."

In the old days of the Franco regime we all knew not to trifle with the Guardia Civil, but I also figured we had better not retreat. "Literature," I replied. "And Spanish culture. And toreo."

As soon as the word came out their whole demeanor changed. "Toreo?" the interrogator repeated, somewhat incredulously. "What do you know about toreo?"

"If you lend me your cape, I'll show you," I said, as politely as possible.

My request caused the other Guardia some amusement, and he nudged Incredulous and said, "Go ahead. Give him your cape." Incredulous turned his back to Amused and asked him to unsnap it.

There was a full moon going down behind him, and with his cape spread and his tricornered patent leather hat backlit in silhouette against the moonlight, he reminded me of a vampire or a storm trooper. I stepped on my cigarette.

Incredulous handed me the cape and I proceeded to do five or six of the best verónicas I could muster—complete with proper body language and sound effects—in the middle of the highway, finishing off with a media verónica and a revolera, which made the Guardia's cape spin around me nicely. As I handed it back to him, he said, "That's not bad at all. Who taught you how to do that?"

"John Fulton, the North American matador de toros who lives in Sevilla."

The Guardias gave us more cigarettes, told us to hold down the noise (why, I can't imagine, since there was no one to hear us), said "buen viaje" in their detached way, and watched us march off quietly—but marching—toward Alicante as the eastern sky began to lighten behind them.

About four in the afternoon I cross the Sierra Candelaria at the western end of the Gredos range into the province of Salamanca at the mountain town of Béjar, which lies along the Río Riofrío, the Coldriver River. From there the road plunges down into the Castilian heartland. Just past the village of Mozárbez (one of the hundreds of historically evocative names that dot wide Castilla), you come over a hill and there lies Salamanca, low along the Río Tormes except for the spire of the cathedral.

Between Salamanca and Valladolid the world turns green and golden, and I eat up the delicious road, lined with fields of mown and baled hay, wheat, sheep, groves of trees, and vegetable gardens, a relief after the austerity of Extremadura. Crossing the great wine river, the Douro/Duero, and the La Coruña road at Tordesillas, I pick up the Autovía de Castilla heading toward Burgos and coast up into Palencia on the Río Carrión at about six-thirty, some six hundred kilometers north of Sevilla. Palencia: "Buena tierra," good country, one of the Guardias had remarked.

The next morning I notice the Rincón vans out in the side parking lot beside the Hotel Rey Sancho. César's big 6.2-liter beige-brown-and-white Chevy diesel, the only American van on the circuit (the van conversion done by Wheel-Master out of New Paris, Indiana), bears the unintentionally ironic license number M-OK 0020. The white (European) Ford Transit turbo-diesel van the cuadrilla rides in—three seats to a row, three rows of seats—sports a Colombian flag, lettering that reads Cuadrilla César Rincón, and on the back door and on the hood an advertisement for Postobón Zumos, the Colombian juice and soft drink company owned by entrepreneur Ardila Lulle, who supplied the van several years before. Behind the hotel in the grassy area next to the pool, two fuchsia-and-gold capotes hang drying in the sun on the children's jungle gym.

Outside the ring on this sunny feast day of San Antolín, the patron of Palencia, I run into Michael and Irene with Tom Weitzner, a dedicated aficionado I first met in Torremolinos in 1963, now El Presidente of the Club Taurino of New York. Inside, the plaza is warm and windless and gradually filling to its capacity of almost ten thousand. Built in 1976 and inaugurated on San Antolín's Day that year, the ring is one of the most comfortable in Spain. The Chopera organization has put together an interesting opening cartel: Espartaco, César Rincón, and the new local matador from nearby Valladolid, Manolo Sánchez, with bulls of Felipe Lafita's ranch, El Torreón, televised by Televisión Española.

Before the second bull enters, I watch Rincón standing, his hands on the *burladero*, the toreros' shield, looking out at nothing. It is not the first time I have noticed his trancelike stare before he begins, and I will see that look many times in the coming days. When Maestrito, a black Torreón weighing 510 kilos, comes into the plaza, the look disappears, replaced with the concentration that characterizes Rincón's scrutiny of each animal.

Maestrito rams into two burladeros, splintering his left horn and breaking a bit off the right, but Rincón picks him up at the fence and starts a series of impressive verónicas, moving the bull step by step out into los medios. He makes the final verónica with his feet together and finishes the series with two revoleras, the cape spinning around his waist like a flamenco dancer's train, to a grand ovation.

Figure 23. Flamenco dancer's train, Palencia, September 2, 1993. Rincón giving a revolera to Maestrito from Felipe Lafita's ranch, El Torreón.

Anderson Murillo "shoots the stick" into Maestrito's morrillo, hitting him while the bull is still more than a meter from the horse, then releasing him. I can hear but not quite understand what Rincón is telling him and Mona-guillo (doubtless to "take care" of this bull, because Rincón can "smell" a triumph).

Curro Cruz, a fine banderillero now in Rincón's cuadrilla (plate 3a) but coming off a goring in Bilbao, puts in a bad pair of sticks, one of which is too low. Manolo Gil (plate 3b), the middle banderillero or *tercero*,[1] does no better. Rincón watches, attentive and visibly annoyed, as Curro Cruz tries and fails to put in a final pair.

As Rincón goes out to dedicate Maestrito's death to the public, he receives enthusiastic applause. Turning slowly, he gravely repeats the stock phrase "muchas gracias, muchas gracias, muchas gracias" and, bending, carefully places his montera right side up on the sand, not risking its falling upside down and incurring bad luck.

Rincón's faena is vibrant, as the animal continues to show his casta. Starting with high passes, *por alto,* he moves into two series of derechazos, taking the bull from a distance in the second set and following with four passes *en redondo,* bringing the charge into a near circle each time. After two naturales, Maestrito balks and Rincón flips the muleta around behind himself, reversing the terrain and taking the animal in a complete backhanded circular. At his improvised recourse, the plaza breaks out in strong applause.

As Maestrito tires, Rincón employs an arsenal of decorative passes: the pase de las flores, passing the bull behind his back, *pendulares,* passes switching the muleta from one side to the other with his body in the middle, derechazos with one knee on the ground, derechazos looking up into the stands, all followed by a smile beatific enough to turn the hardest heart, and ending with a delicate *abaniqueo,* fanning the bull with the furling and unfurling cloth. After his last pass Rincón loses the muleta but, without flinching or moving back, he drops to one knee in the animal's face and retrieves it, his inspiration turning a difficult situation into his crowning *desplante* or gesture of domination.

After an accurate sword thrust, Rincón waves his cuadrilla away and stands facing the immobile animal, which shortly begins to wobble, then takes two steps backward, turns, and falls to the ground. The actuación has been *torerísima,* worthy of the highest taurine praise. But the presidente awards one ear.

César comments afterwards that the bull "transmitted a lot [of emotion]," that unfortunately "he had given up slightly at the end, because I would have liked to give him ten or fifteen more passes." Nevertheless he seems quite content with his performance, if not with the single ear.

A year after his alternativa, Manolo Sánchez seems green and nervous. His bull, somewhat soso, lacks the casta of Rincón's, and Sánchez kills him poorly, receiving an ovation from his many sympathizers in the crowd for his artistic work with the muleta.

The fourth bull has little inclination to charge and Espartaco, writing off a gray afternoon, kills him, complaining about his string of bad luck with the bulls.

The fifth does not look any better, but Rincón, in no mood to let the afternoon go without a complete triumph, imposes himself with great taurine savvy on an animal that is very nearly sent back for defects of vision. But this bull, Desterrado by name and a fine-looking animal at 553 kilos, is the classic *engañabobos* or fool-fooler. The crowd protests. Some say he cannot see. But the fact is, in spite of his appearance, he simply refuses to enter into combat. Desterrado is manso.

The crowd continues to protest, shouting, "¡Fuera, fuera!"—out, out! Some sing the Pamplona song of disappointment "Todos queremos más"

(We all want more). Others shout at the presidente, "¡Sinvergüenza! ¡Sinver-güenza!" Rincón does not look happy.

But regardless of how he looks, he knows exactly what to do. He knows that he has to *mimar* Desterrado and not try to *someter* him—to spoil him with kindness instead of subjecting him to punishment—which is precisely what he does, taking him in smooth series of passes, never allowing Desterrado to touch the muleta, always leaving the cloth in his face, constantly giving him a target to charge. Desterrado tries to escape to the fence, but Rincón is there with the flowing muleta to intercept him. It is a masterful job of not allowing the animal's mansedumbre to come through.

After a particularly good series of naturales crowned by a *molinete in-vertido* (a reverse molinete)[2] and a pase de pecho, the crowd surges to its feet in applause. Two more series and the público is again on its feet, applauding Rincón's work with an animal they had wanted to send back. César Rincón has stirred up a *lío*, a commotion, and all at once the music is playing, the crowd is on its feet applauding and chanting "¡Torero! ¡Torero!" inter-spersed with olés, as Rincón continues passing the bull with lower and longer derechazos. There is jubilation in the tendidos, the kind of jubilation you do not see in Madrid or Sevilla but that sometimes happens at peak moments in the ferias of the north, when the feria crowd and the peñas and the serious aficionados come together as one in a raucous choral catharsis that must be seen and felt to be believed.

Rincón squares the bull off, facing him. Desterrado looks the size of a bison. Rincón goes in, hitting bone up high, receiving an ovation for his effort. He prepares the bull again, facing him, the animal seemingly too high to kill. He calls to him "¡Aja, aja!" and again "¡ajajajaja!" and drives in the sword to the hilt, up on top in the withers where it seemed he could not reach. Rincón falls from the impetus of his thrust and loses the mu-leta, but Desterrado is mortally wounded and heading for the tablas to col-lapse.

Rincón goes to the center of the ring, raising his sword to the torrent of handkerchiefs petitioning the ears. Once again the presidente turns frugal, awarding one. But the crowd in ecstasy chants "¡Torero, torero!" as one of the peñas' representatives ties the purple pañuelo of San Antolín around Rincón's neck in his triumphant tour of the ring. For César Rincón it is a grand afternoon, and "all Spain" is watching, although afterwards we would talk about how it should have been four ears instead of two. I remark to him, "If Manolo Sánchez had done it, you know it would have been four." César just nods.

Did Rincón have the best bulls? Was his luck changing? Not really. His bulls were better than Espartaco's, but Manolo Sánchez drew the best lot, especially the sixth, with which he did a long faena, killing poorly. Rincón worked harder, took more chances, got more from his bulls, and killed better. He had earned his triumph. Tom Weitzner remarked afterwards, "Rincón should get a prize for pundonor."

The great cartel of the Feria de Palencia came the following day: a mano a mano between César Rincón and José Miguel Arroyo, Joselito, with bulls of Victorino Martín, one of the most successful bull breeders in the world. Originally the cartel had been a mano a mano between Joselito and Enrique Ponce, but Ponce's goring in Cieza on August 25 had occasioned the substitution of César Rincón. Rincón had been scheduled to fight a mano a mano with Ponce in Bayonne on September 4, but with Ponce hurt, that cartel changed, as we shall see shortly, into a regular corrida. Finally, on September 12, Rincón and Joselito were to have a mano a mano in Dax. The competition among Ponce, Joselito, and Rincón had become the heart of the temporada.

José Carlos Arévalo began talking in August about a duel between Enrique Ponce and Joselito, a duel at the summit, a competition he believed would determine the future of toreo for the rest of the century. He characterized Ponce as very competitive and prodigiously talented, unfairly accused of superficiality, expert in techniques perfected by Espartaco but with his own aesthetic language. Joselito was more intense and more irregular, a classical and brave torero with a vast repertoire, whose work could be very profound. It was going to be hard for Joselito to confront a torero who triumphed so regularly, and hard for Enrique Ponce to confront a torero who could remain calm as the bull brushed past his vitals (6T6 23:24). Only it would now be César Rincón instead of Enrique Ponce. Some would be disappointed, others thrilled.

And what did Rincón think? In an interview with Arévalo he expressed his preference for performing with Manzanares and Espartaco because, he said, he learned something from the maestros every day. To compete with Joselito and Ponce, however, was a "fight in every sense of the word" and "an all-out war in the ring" (6T6 24:30).

In the tertulia after the corrida, Victorino Martín opined that his bulls permit no mistakes, that they have much to torear, that they are fierce. The first one needed another pick. Turning to César Rincón, he said, "They come up." He told Joselito he was "enormous." Rincón, he said, had been

Figure 24. Victorino Martín, Palencia, September 3, 1993. Martín, with his characteristic grin, just before the corrida of his bulls.

very good, especially for the first time he had ever faced these bulls: "To be capable as you were capable!" All figuras ought to face these animals once in a while, "so we can see their credentials." His final judgment was: "When there are toros and there are toreros, that is the fiesta. And when they are good, that is *la leche*."[3]

Rincón, not altogether happy about his performance, was quiet. Joselito managed to confess that, beforehand, "my hands were sweating and my heart was coming out of my chaquetilla," but that soon enough he had felt comfortable. In the shy way he has of addressing an audience without looking at them, yet obviously moved, he summed up the experience: "It was *la hostia*."[4]

It had been a hot afternoon, in every sense of the word, after a morning of chilly rain. The ring was jammed to the rafters, and aficionados had come from all over Spain and France to attend the mano a mano of the season.

The Victorinos are known for having great casta and bravery. They are not impossible to torear, but they are never easy either (plate 6b). The first bull is a case in point. His name is Madroño and he weighs 552 kilos. Like all his brothers he is cárdeno and short-horned, not because he has been "shaved" but because that conformation is not uncommon in the Santa Coloma strain. (In the tertulia the attending vet will assure us the horns had not been touched.) Madroño is a fine specimen with the shiny, alert eyes that characterize the Victorinos, a quick charge, and a readiness to slam into the burladeros. Rincón takes him to the horse with the rarely seen *mariposa*—the butterfly pass invented by Marcial Lalanda, in which the cape flicks from side to side behind the matador's back like a butterfly's wings— and leaves him in position with a media verónica.

After one pick, Rincón does two chicuelinas and a revolera, all to re- sounding olés, and asks the presidente to change the act. Is this a mistake? Victorino Martín will certainly think so. In the faena, Rincón takes Madroño to the center of the ring, where he gives him two powerful series of dere- chazos, lowering his hand and forcing the bull to follow (plate 6a). On the left Madroño cuts in, forcing Rincón to use the right. But he goes immedi- ately back to the left and, as the bull looks him up and down, again obliges him to charge. Finally Madroño catches him on the lower right calf without goring him. Rincón takes the sword, hits bone once, profiles again, and sinks a perfect thrust. Madroño goes down, but there is almost no petition for the ear.

Joselito does a vibrant faena with the second bull, a 458-kilo cárdeno named Playero, but the animal is nothing like Rincón's, showing less dan- ger, transmitting little emotion, and not going all the way through on his charge. Joselito handles him masterfully (plate 6c) and puts in the kind of perfect slow sword only he can do. Playero wobbles a bit and falls over side- ways. Handkerchiefs fly, and Joselito takes a tour with both Playero's ears. He has been very good, but I know that behind the burladero there is a Colombian whose blood is boiling.

Mediaonza, a dark cárdeno, almost charcoal, weighs 550 kilos and has thick curls on his forehead. He is *precioso*, a stunning animal, but he has a defect from the torero's point of view—he cuts in badly, looking for the body.

Mediaonza takes three picks, and in the quite after the last pick Joselito does a good series of verónicas, but the bull takes the cape away from him in the revolera. When Rincón comes out for the faena, I can see from his pos- ture he is uncomfortable. The bull continues going for the body, but Rincón withstands the animal's charges and little by little begins to "put him into the muleta."

The faena becomes a classic battle of wills, with Mediaonza looking straight at Rincón and Rincón forcing him to take the muleta. He does passes of every description, including circulares, four naturales de frente, making the animal go around him, derechazos looking at the tendido, and one pase de pecho (while I am changing film, of course) that is a monument to the pass.

In the war of wills, César Rincón outwills Mediaonza. Finally he puts in a sword right up on top, *en todo lo alto*. But the bull takes time to die, and Rincón misses once with the descabello, gets an aviso from the presidente, and then hits with the descabello. He receives a well-deserved ear, but he must be hurting, knowing that if he had hit the first time or, better yet, if the animal had gone down from the first sword, he would have both ears.

The fourth bull, a wanderer in the ring, is not to Joselito's liking and, true to his uncompromising fashion, he kills him quickly.

In the fifth, Hermosito at 556 kilos, Rincón does another, which is to say a third, complete faena with a difficult bull. The animal crowds him on the left, but Rincón pulls passes out where there are no passes. On the right he links series after series of derechazos, lowering and "running" his hand as far as he can reach, "breaking himself" in each pass, extending himself to his corporeal limits.

The crowd is completely with him this time, and the ring falls silent as he prepares to kill. He profiles, but Hermosito backs out of position. Rincón lines him up again, and again the animal backs away. Hermosito backs away eight times until Rincón finally gets a sword in. Then the animal begins a spectacular death, going in seven slow circles before he collapses. Rincón, who would have cut two ears, or at least one, even from this frugal presidente, receives a grand ovation.

Later Paco Aguado, who was covering the feria for *6T6,* would tell me the animal had a "cloud" in his right eye. Rincón managed to overcome that by taking the bull on the right (with the cloth to the left, the outside, the good, eye), but when it came time to kill, the bull kept backing away, backing out of position and turning his head in order to see. Bad luck, the worst kind: *el mal de ojo,* the evil eye.

Bordador, the sixth bull, rips one of the burladeros apart as soon as he comes into the ring. He is the bull of the afternoon and Joselito is equal to him. He starts by doing largas on his knees when the bull comes in, takes him to the horse with walking chicuelinas, does a complete faena, and finishes with yet another superb sword thrust. Joselito cuts two more ears—this time completely deserved—with a petition for the tail, and Bordador is given a vuelta for his bravery. Joselito makes Rincón come out to salute, and the crowd grabs him and tries to hoist him up. Rincón refuses, struggling, until Joselito insists, and then Joselito and César Rincón and Victorino

Martín's mayoral all ride out on shoulders as the público—no one has left the plaza—applauds.

It was a *gran tarde de toros,* a great and complete afternoon of the bulls. Joselito proved himself yet again to be, when he is up, the most explosive combination of art, inspiration, technique, and valor performing in the '90s. When he is at the top of his form, the enigmatic bad boy of Madrid— he has said he would have been a delinquent if he had not become a torero—is almost impossible to best. Rincón proved himself yet again to be an extraordinarily brave, emotionally moving, committed, and competitive torero.

Rincón had perhaps stirred me more because of his heroic efforts with more difficult animals. But Joselito had moved me too—as well as everyone else in the ring. The afternoon had been, as Victorino Martín said, la leche. Or was it la hostia?

Bayonne: September 4, 1993

When I leave Palencia the next morning, the air is clear and chilly, there is a heavy dew, and in low places a light mist rises from the fertile *campo* or countryside of Castilla. The landscape is painted in shades of green, broken now and then by late crops of sunflowers and fields of hay, harvested and baled for the winter that will soon descend. Nine months of winter and three months of hell, the proverb goes, but the proverb neglects to mention the few days in the early fall that are the sweetest in the world.

Along the valley of the Pisuerga droplets from the irrigation fountains trace lacy arabesques, backlit by the newly risen sun. The once tortuous highways of Spain that were such a challenge in former days have given way along the main routes to fast *autovías* (divided highways) and *autopistas* (expressways, usually toll roads), and now I follow their parallel lines, which are rushing me toward France. The legal speed limit on most of these roads is 120 kilometers per hour (approximately 75 mph), but no one observes the limits willingly, and most of the traffic flows along upward of 140 kph.

The taurinos try to run at 150 kph or more when conditions permit, and some matadors with fast cars, usually Mercedes, cruise at 200 kph and over. They get speeding tickets, although the Guardia Civil often sympathizes with their need to cross the country, and they have their share of accidents, but neither seems to slow them down. Everyone understands the risk, but after the immediate physical presence of the bulls, the dangers of speed seem remote.

Driving, I think back and make notes. I recall Pepe Domínguín in the colloquium remarking: "Between the bull and the torero, I'll take the torero. You can always have a coffee afterwards with the torero." Naturally, having been a matador himself and coming from one of the most famous taurine families of all time, he was a *torerista*. What former matador could be a torista? In any case, we go to the bulls to see the triumph of the man over the beast, the tragedy of the bull's death. I am remembering how Bordador, the sixth Victorino yesterday, tore the burladero to pieces, how he would have torn anything to pieces, anything except Joselito (or Rincón, had he gotten that bull). Before he dies, the bull is the beast. Then he must die, killed by the man. That is the story the corrida tells, the myth it enacts and ritualizes. Had the bull gored Joselito, Victorino Martín would not have been happy. But Joselito triumphed and killed Bordador splendidly and Victorino Martín, happy with the grand death of his fine animal, of all six of his animals, had proclaimed it nothing short of la leche.

North of Burgos I plunge through the three tunnels bored into the ragged blue Montes Obarenes at the *desfiladero,* the rocky defile, that separates Castilla from the far north of the Basque country. A few kilometers beyond, I cross the Ebro into Alava, the southernmost of the three Basque provinces, and the shift is as dramatic as when you go from La Mancha through the desfiladero of Despeñaperros into Andalucía. When you cross into Alava the landscape goes from brown and gray to evergreen. Even the language changes. Hemingway once wrote on an unpublished scrap of paper that Spain was not a country but a continent (Stanton xvi). Gradually you climb into dark forests rife with fat, long-haired sheep and blond cows, dotted with Basque cottages more reminiscent of Austria than of Spain. And the signs announce a service area: *zervitzugunea*. I stop for gas, a café con leche and a slice of *tortilla española,* the ubiquitous Spanish omelette made with potatoes and eaten hot, cold, or room temperature at all hours of the day and night by everyone in the continent of Spain.

At eleven I have the North Atlantic—the Bay of Biscay or the Golfo de Vizcaya, to be precise—on my left, and shortly after noon I pass through San Sebastián and cross into France. Coming into Bayonne, I see the emblematic sign with the twin towers of the cathedral and a toro bravo on it, a sign that always quickens my blood. Another sign says "Première ville taurine de France: 21 août 1853." Over in the Camargue where the Rhône runs into the sea, they would tell you they have been toreando in one form or another for several thousand years, but the first formal corrida in the Spanish style took place in Bayonne a century and a half ago.

At the Hotel Mercure I discover that a virulent strain of Rincónmanía has broken out and that there is not a ticket to be had at any price. Luis Carlos is running all over town trying to get tickets for César's sister Marta and others who have come from Madrid. Luis Alvarez tells me not to worry: "Meet me at the entrance to the patio de caballos."

It is with some trepidation that, ticketless, I join the orderly crowd moving along the Avenue de la Légion Tchèque toward the venerable Arènes de Lachepaillet, exactly a century old, the ring having celebrated its centennial on August 8, 1993. I get around to the door of the patio de caballos in back of the ring ahead of time to wait for Luis (if he were to go in without me, I could not get in at all). The afternoon is perfect for the bulls, sunny, warm, windless, and crowded.

When the Chevy van arrives, I jump in and ride through the gate into the patio de caballos with the cuadrilla. Inside the patio I stay with Luis until he secures an *invitacíon*, a pass, for me. Somehow he then talks the keeper of the callejón gate into letting me in, and once I get inside the alleyway nobody bothers me. The omnipotent hand of Manolo Chopera—this is another of his plazas—is no doubt involved somewhere. This scene, always difficult or uncertain, will repeat itself with variations, but it never fails to make me nervous. Still, I am inside and free to shoot away.

Being in the callejón for a corrida is comparable to sitting in the orchestra pit for a musical, except that in the musical there is no physical danger as there is in the callejón, especially if the bull jumps the barrera. (Occasionally someone is killed that way.)

You can sit in the barrera seats and have an accurate sense of what is going on below, but move just the few feet forward and downward into the callejón, into that no man's land between the safety of the spectators' seats and the danger of the bull's territory, from which the toreros and their cuadrillas operate, and everything becomes radically more real: the wind from a fresh bull when he comes by like a truck; the grunts and snorts of the horses and the bulls; the hooves beating on the packed sand; the clods of sand slung into or over the fence; the heavy swishing sound of the capes; the spittle from the animal's muzzle flying through the air; the thuds of the horns into the wood of the burladero; the clanging of the stirrup as the bull bangs into it; the metallic clatter of the picador's *mona* or iron legging; the shouted or whispered directions from manager to matador and back, from matador to banderillo or picador and back, from sword handler to ayuda and back in a cacophonous and sometimes unintelligible discourse; even the sucking sound the sword makes going in—all these elements are magnified in the callejón.

To take photographs and notes in such a setting presents interesting problems. Since you are part of the action, sometimes you are too close to shoot what is happening. Often the fence is in the way. You must constantly be on guard not to make a movement that might distract the bull, and you must stay out of the way, especially as the banderilleros come past, bent over so the bull will not see them and running with their capes to position themselves where the matador needs them.

This corrida is my first in France. I have heard about the famous silences of the French public, quieter even than Sevilla, they say, and it is true. The French taurine public comes more as a theatre public does, serious, polite, observant, curious—and quiet. They applaud properly as in the theatre. They do whistle when they do not like something, and they are particularly fond of abusing the picadores. But the unnerving thing is the pin-drop silence that descends as a matador begins his faena. My shutter seems terribly loud in such a silence where the only sounds now come from the hooves of the bull on the arena floor or, almost as if disembodied in the quietude, the matador's voice.

The Salamanca bulls of Los Bayones disappoint all of us that day. They are fine-looking animals, "well presented," but they turn out to be dangerous mansos, low in casta. Rincón's first has to be returned to the corrals after it cramps during the picking. No one likes the looks of the sobrero— oversized, lumbering, short in the neck—but Rincón manages a quite of chicuelinas with two revoleras that nearly brings the house down. Because the bull is clearly manso, Rincón has him picked lightly, and he comes to the muleta with a bad right horn and a deadly left. "He's an assassin on that side," Luis Alvarez yells. Rincón takes him on the right, coaxing dangerous passes from his "enemy" by forcing the charge with his body and his position in the bull's terrain. José Carlos Arévalo will compare it to "solving a mathematical problem while walking on the edge of an abyss" (6T6 25:46). What no one in the attentive house fails to appreciate, least of all the Condesa de Barcelona, to whom he has dedicated the bull, is Rincón's extraordinary professionalism. Were the kill not marred by two pinchazos, he would cut an ear. As it is, he receives a long ovation, reminiscent of the applause you might hear at the opera.

Juan Mora, a brave and artistic torero from Plasencia, draws another manso, one that takes up a strong querencia at the fence. Mora works the bull as hard as he can but, like Rincón, has trouble with the kill and fails to cut an ear.

Manolo Sánchez does the least with the best animal so far and kills it poorly.

Rincón's second bull, violent and flighty, turns out to be even worse than his first. A bull without a single good pass in him, he comes to the muleta *gazapón,* with a tendency to walk with his head up (rather than to charge with his head down), looking for the matador behind the muleta. Rincón "withstands horrors" from the animal, managing to "steal" a few passes from him, but he plays him too long and the bull tries to cut him off in the sword, making for a difficult and dangerous kill. At one point Rincón looks up in exasperation and grumbles to us in the callejón, "It's just like the one yesterday," meaning the fifth Victorino that backed repeatedly out of line.

Back at the Hotel Mercure, César is in a fine humor despite the animals. "Which one," I ask him up in the room, "did you like least?"

"¡Ay, ay!" he yells, laughing. "Now you've said it! Now you've said it!" We are laughing because he has turned in a fine performance in spite of the bulls.

As they are leaving, Luis Alvarez says to me: "Come on to Mérida. We'll get you something." Mérida is across Spain, almost in Portugal, and well to the south. I hate to leave one of my favorite areas of France, but Mérida is where I need to be. So I climb into the cockpit of my trusty rental Opel and leave Bayonne about nine-thirty.

Mérida: September 5, 1993

As I drive I think about the danger of the bulls of Los Bayones today and I wonder how César deals with the fear, especially now after the goring in Sevilla. He told José Carlos Arévalo recently that the goring was bad, but that the goring in Palmira in 1990 had been worse. Still, Luis Alvarez has just confirmed to me that they thought César was dying or dead—clinically dead—four or five times in Sevilla. Exaggeration? Perhaps. Maybe it was only two or three times.

Arévalo said to Rincón: "Are you telling me you didn't lose—not even a little bit—your sitio this year, that you didn't have a little bache back in June?"

"I'm saying it and I'll sign it. You're talking about sitio? Yes, sitio. You know, toreros—I suppose writers too—have some strange things happen to us. But the word isn't sitio. The word is morale. Because then [in June] I had valor and will; and why was I going to lose my technical capacity? Morale, the word is morale. Something that can take away your luck. It's when you get a string of bad bulls and then, when you do manage to cuajar a bull, you don't kill it well. Or like when you make a huge effort with a bull that had seemed impossible and then you hit bone or have bad luck with the descabello. And all the while you see that for other compañeros everything is easier and they cut ears like it was nothing. That's when you get that mixture of melancholy and uncertainty. You know it doesn't have anything to do with you, with what you are, but it makes you more tense when you go out to torear" (6T6 24:30).

That interview came out in the latest issue of 6T6 and those questions are much on my mind. One thing: César Rincón is honest about himself and understands how he functions in the ring. I will never hear him express his doubts or his uncertainties more succinctly, and I will never hear him contradict anything he told Arévalo. Everything he will tell me in the months to come, in fact, will only confirm what he said.

About sixty kilometers north of Madrid, sleepy, I pull into the parking lot of a roadside hotel, roll down the seat back, lock the doors, and take a forty-five-minute nap. When I awake, I feel refreshed. It is a clear night with a gibbous moon and you can see the glow of Madrid, shining away in the distance like a new Jerusalem. Luis said Mérida will be good. "Búscame en el Tryp." Look for me at the Tryp hotel.

I slip around Madrid on the new outer beltway, the M-40, and pick up the Extremadura road. At five-thirty I cross the Río Tajo and, knowing that dawn and Mérida are not too far away, I decide to stop for a café con leche. I pull into the first available place, a brightly lit truckstop on the right, and there are the two vans, the Postobón van of the cuadrilla and César's Chevy. Everyone is asleep except for the drivers and Luis Carlos, whom I find inside at the bar having coffee.

Luis Carlos seems surprised to see me, not because of the coincidence—the taurine world is small and the routes well defined, so coincidences happen—but because he has not expected me to come on to Mérida. We talk about yesterday's corrida and he tells me that in his opinion Juan Mora is a fighter, a *valiente,* and that Manolo Sánchez did not come up to the level of his second bull.

He says he has seen so many bulls that he can tell from a bull's eyes how it will turn out.

"Like people?" I ask.

"Sí, sí. Like people, just like people. When you've seen enough of them, they're just like people. Maybe easier."

We caravan on to Mérida, running 150–60 kilometers an hour. Venus rises, bright in the southern sky, Lady Love and maybe Lady Luck for today in the old retired Roman soldiers' town of Mérida. Dawn cracks the edges of the horizon at six-thirty and the sun rises as we are coming into town. It is windy and people are wandering around looking slightly lost from being up all night at the feria.

After an hour or two of sleep, we are up and ready to go to the sorteo by eleven, all except the matador himself. Mérida has spectacular Roman ruins, including one of the best-preserved Roman theatres in the world, which still functions every summer. The dark-red-and-cream-colored Plaza de Toros de San Albín also has visible ruins nearby, and when the ring was built, the workers uncovered an underground Mithraic sanctuary, a shrine to the Persian hero-god who had slain the white bull-of-heaven from whom all gifts came, wine from his blood and grain from his body. Mithra's cult— including the sacrifice of a bull and baptism in the animal's blood for initiates standing below, ensuring immortality—was Christianity's most tenacious rival in the late days of the Empire and, as James A. Michener pointed out in *Iberia*, it was no small coincidence that the plaza de toros should have been constructed in the same place (65). Since this is my first time at the plaza in Mérida, I cannot help recalling that coincidence, but I can discern no obvious reason why the place had been chosen two thousand years ago.

At the sorteo, the usual social groups form up at once, the picadores here, the banderilleros there, the managers and business people in the far corner. Luis Alvarez tells them I am Rincón's photographer, so they let me in. But not until I have been properly challenged first. I walk through the entrance with Manolo Gil, Rincón's banderillero, and one of the doorkeepers asks charmingly: "Y éste, ¿quién es?" And this one, who's he?

Manolo says: "No, he's with us."

Doorkeep: "But they said three."

Manolo: "What difference does it make? You've already got a hundred."

Then Luis Alvarez intervenes and I am allowed to enter the sanctum sanctorum.

At the sorteo all kinds of last-minute negotiations take place, but the main order of business is the intricate matching-up of the six bulls into three theoretically equal pairs (a seventh and eighth bull will be kept in reserve, the sobreros). Thus the representatives of each of the matadors must inspect the bulls and then they must all reach agreement on the pairings before the lots can be drawn. It is never an easy process and sometimes becomes fractious or even contentious. It is the only part of the luck of the draw that anyone can control.

The corrida—that is, the set of bulls, from the nearby ganadería of La Cardenilla, mostly Juan Pedro Domecq stock—looks better than it turns out to be. There are seven blacks and one castaño and as usual everyone likes the chestnut.

At one point we all get rather officiously herded together and Anderson Murillo says: "Here they treat us like *maricas* [derogatory term for homosexuals]. They're all a bunch of *mamones* [suckers]."

Manolo says: "Looks fat to me. Fat and coarse." He is talking about the corrida.

After the pairings are finally agreed on, the numbers of the two bulls in each pair are written on an individual piece of paper (traditionally cigarette paper), the three papers are balled up and put into a covered hat, and then they are drawn by one of each matador's representatives.

After Monaguillo extracts the paper ball, I ask Luis, "Which ones?" and he replies, "It doesn't matter. It's all the same. I'm so tired of falling in love with our lote and then they all come out bad." It turns out Rincón has drawn number 27 (508 kilos), which inside the corrals looks a bit fat, and number 65 (538 kilos). Number 27 will go first, in the second slot, and 65 will be his second bull in fifth place. It is pushing one-thirty by the time we finish and head back to the hotel for lunch and rest before the corrida.

Lunch—the first real meal I have eaten since the day before yesterday in Palencia—turns out to be wonderful: *ajo blanco,* the thick white soup of the region, served cold, rich with ground almonds, redolent of fresh garlic, followed by *merluza a la romana,* hake done in the Roman style, which is to say, lightly battered and fried in olive oil. The merluza—the favorite fish of Spain—comes out tender, juicy, and whiter inside than the snow that fell in Mérida on that long-ago tenth of December when the Roman legionnaires martyred the young Christian girl Olalla.

We are sitting at a large round table: Luis Alvarez; César, with three women whose identities I never get straight; Juan Márquez, the ayuda; Luis Carlos Rincón; Curro Cruz, banderillero and former matador, born in Osuna in the province of Sevilla, age thirty-five, separated from his wife; Manolo Gil, banderillero, from the Cuatro Caminos neighborhood of Madrid, married twenty-three years, four children, a grandfather twice, born in 1945;

Anderson Murillo, Muri, picador (his brother Emerson is a matador), also born in 1945, in Montería, a cattle town in the department of Córdoba in coastal Colombia, married, with a boy of thirteen and a girl of nine, resident of Bogotá for the last twenty-five years; and Rodrigo Arias, Monaguillo de Colombia, Mono, banderillero, age thirty-two, an *ancianito* or little old man, as he says, a bachelor who lives on the road but who was born in Manizales, where he met César when they were still children.

As we are starting lunch, Juan Antonio Ruiz Román, Espartaco, makes his entrance into the dining room, looking more like an emperor than a rebellious slave (except for the horn scar next to his mouth). He is smiling, joking, shaking everyone's hand, very much the maestro. It strikes me that Juan Antonio in street clothes looks smaller and slimmer than Espartaco does in a suit of lights. But all of them, Juan Antonio and César, Curro Cruz and Rodrigo, even Muri, who unlike many picadores is not heavy, are lean enough to model jeans.

During lunch a constant banter takes place. Spirits have risen somewhat and Mono and Muri tease everyone, sometimes hilariously, but they are merciless to each other.

Luis Alvarez, always benignly paternalistic as befits an apoderado (today in the sorteo he called me *hijo*, son, a term of endearment, to be sure, yet he is only four years older than I am), stays serenely out of the line of fire until he has a story to tell, and then all eyes center on him, as he is a gifted story-teller, with true Andalusian wit or *gracia*. Luis Carlos sits quietly. Curro Cruz appears the most visibly high-strung member of the cuadrilla. César, loung-ing in jeans and a striped shirt and moccasins, clearly possesses the fiercest temperament of the lot, yet now, true to his somewhat feline character, in repose seems almost languid. Today is César's twenty-eighth birthday and today Enrique Ponce, who has just turned twenty-two, will reappear in Requena, cutting three ears from Atanasio Fernández bulls.

By corrida time at 6:30, the weather has cleared and the afternoon is warm and windy. Luis Alvarez has secured me a true callejón pass, so I ride from the hotel in the Chevy van with him and César and the banderilleros. (The picadores, who have to warm up their horses, normally go earlier in a car.) There is the usual nervousness before a corrida, but César is in good spirits and his compañeros de cartel, Espartaco and Finito de Córdoba, a somewhat uneven but artistic young matador with two years of alternativa, are toreros with whom he feels relaxed.

Espartaco's bad luck continues and he is able to do nothing with his first. Rincón's first Cardenilla, a negro *bragado*, with a white belly, is named

Oprimido. But there is nothing "oppressed" about the way this animal charges. Rincón dedicates the bull to the público of Mérida and begins his faena with five passes sitting on the *estribo*—the narrow ledge that runs around the inside of the barrera, used to vault the fence—following with derechazos, circulares, molinetes, and pases de pecho, running the hand, linking the passes, and making it immediately apparent that he is going to cuajar this bull (plate 7). The crowd is with him from the beginning, and when he changes hands and does naturales in a full circle, one after another, the tendidos explode with the alegría that Rincón's sense of rhythm produces when he has an animal that repeats.

His sword thrust is well executed but the bull, brave to the end, resists going down (plate 8). After a spectacular death, the crowd petitions and gets—finally! I think—both well-deserved ears. While Rincón takes his vuelta, Luis Alvarez lights an impressive Havana cigar.

Back at the Tryp hotel, which is new and somewhat removed from town, where everything should have been fine, something strange happens to alter the general mood. I have gone to my room, dumped my camera gear, and rested for half an hour. As I head shortly thereafter for César's room, I hear a loud voice coming from his open doorway: "Where is everybody?" It is César, alone, and not in a pleasant frame of mind. At exactly that juncture, a large family of Colombians on vacation surge into César's room to congratulate him and ask him for autographs, and the loneliness of the figura del toreo is mitigated by these ingenuous hounders after fame. Luis Alvarez shows up soon, but the matador is not about to be assuaged. Luis leaves César fuming and I leave as well, thinking to discuss travel plans with Luis. But he has calls to make, so, again realizing my opportunity, I retreat to the bar and have a copa with Curro Cruz, thankful that I do not have to drive again tonight.

"Where are you going?" asks Curro. "Y salud." And health.

"I'm staying here tonight," I reply. "Salud."

"So am I," says Curro, "if I can ride with you."

"Sure," I say, "but I'm going to Sevilla for a couple of days."

"Sevilla's fine," he says. "As long as we get to San Martín for the corrida on the ninth."

"Done," I say. "We'll go up from Sevilla the eighth."

Shortly the rest of the cuadrilla leave for Madrid—César likes to sleep at home when he can, even if it means driving most of the night. Curro and I remain in Mérida to celebrate his triumph.

San Martín de Valdeiglesias: September 9, 1993

Curro Cruz and I arrive in the late afternoon at the Hotel Los Toros de Gui-sando, named for the stone bulls that have pastured in a field nearby for the last several millennia, at the little town of El Tiemblo, not far from San Martín de Valdeiglesias where tomorrow's corrida will take place. The rain we have driven through all day—so strong that at times we had to stop—is over, and the sunset over the mountains promises a perfect day tomorrow.

Next afternoon in the van on the way to the plaza, we realize we are too early and pull off on the side of the road to wait for the other toreros to catch up. The ceaseless banter picks up speed. Mono does an imitation of the female burro that we see in a nearby field, calling out: ¡Ajá—ajá—ajá—ajá—ajandersón!" Puerile perhaps, but such is taurine humor. At any rate, we all laugh. Even Anderson Murillo laughs, although he also delivers a hail of insults to Monaguillo and his family.

By the time we get into the plaza, the afternoon has begun to scowl a bit and the feria banners are agitated. César, however, continues in a good mood, even though we are on the edge of what the toreros call the Valle del Terror—a geographically inexact location, generally west of Madrid, some-thing like the taurine Valley of the Shadow of Death, which is famous for its rough crowds and sometimes outsized bulls. But so far nothing seems out of the ordinary, and the bulls of Fernando Peña are nothing out of the ordi-nary.

The veteran torero from Albacete, Dámaso González, draws an uncoop-erative bull and kills it quickly.

Rincón's bull is protested energetically by the crowd. It does, in fact, look like a novillo, but the crowd overreacts with shouts of "¡Fuera! ¡Fuera!"

Rincón manages to turn around what has begun poorly. Fortunately the animal has a good left horn, and Rincón does textbook naturales to musical accompaniment and olés. After putting in a good sword, he takes a vuelta with the ear of his opponent.

His second bull is a good-looking cárdeno, but it hooks badly on the right, then stops charging altogether. Rincón works with it diligently, trying to coax a charge from it, holding the muleta high so as not to damage or subject the bull, but all to no avail. Finally, amid protests that get out of hand, he kills it as best he can. Some applaud but most whistle loudly. When the bull finally goes down, they give Rincón an undeserved bronca.

When Finito cuts an ear from the last bull with virtually no petition from the crowd, it is almost dark and we hurry to get into the van and back to the hotel. As we try to leave, the crowd swarms around the van. Ricardo Chinza is driving and I am in the other front seat. Ricardo edges the van forward. The crowd is still angry with Rincón, and people are leering in and shouting insults through the windows. Whether Ricardo was at fault in any way I cannot say for certain. I think not, but suddenly as we are easing forward, one old brute pulls back his heavy cane and smashes it into the windshield directly in front of my face. The windshield spiderwebs, but the blow does not break through.

Another drunk is banging on the hood as hard as his ancient arms and hands will allow. People all around are shouting insults. César in the middle seat is very calm. "Call the police, hombre," he says to Ricardo, although how Ricardo is supposed to accomplish that and drive at the same time is unclear. We ease forward and then suddenly we are free of the crowd and on the way back to the hotel. I feel the windshield and realize that the glass is broken all the way through, but the shatterproof material has somehow held together. As we ride back, César recounts how one time in the little town of Lebrija, in the department of Santander in central Colombia, they had to flee on foot: "Some fool jumped into the ring and grabbed my sword, then hit Mono in the face. Mono hit him back, and the whole plaza came after us. We fled and hid out in a garage and finally escaped, but it was tough for a while." By the time we get to the hotel we are all laughing, but no one minds heading out that night for Albacete.

Albacete: September 10, 1993

It is hot in Albacete, with small clouds barely moving across the huge sky of La Mancha. Lunch with Michael, Tomás Weitzner, and Harlan Blake, a retired law professor from Columbia University and longtime aficionado, at the Mesón Las Rejas, the regional specialties restaurant, where we are served vegetable pie and baby goat, is very pleasant, but I limit myself to one glass of the fine local *tinto* or red wine, only enough to taste, since after the corrida I have to drive to Arles in the Rhône delta.

My impending trip becomes the center of the conversation. "My God," says Michael. "My God, do you know how far that is?"

"About a thousand kilometers, I think." It turns out to be 960.

"And you're going to do it alone?"

"I don't have any choice. I tried to get a ride in one of the vans, but they're all full. Rincón's entourage never gets any smaller."

"My God. You'll work at the corrida, taking photographs and notes, then jump into your car and speed a thousand kilometers to the Camargue, arrive at—what? nine or ten in the morning?—and then go straight to the sorteo, have lunch, maybe a half-hour siesta, and then stand in the callejón—I assume Luis Alvarez has enough pull in France to get you in—and shoot photographs for another two and a half hours. And then what?"

"Then I can sleep some, but I have to be up early to drive to Dax for the next day's corrida."

"My God," says Michael. The reason Michael is muttering repetitively to himself is that he has done such drives many times. It is one of the prices of afición, especially of following one torero, and no one knows it better than Michael, who has been doing it since he followed Antonio Ordóñez thirty years ago. "My God," he says. "I don't envy you that one. Of course, you have no choice. You must go. You must see them all."

At 6:00 the ring is *abarrotado*, jammed full, to see Dámaso González, César Rincón, and Enrique Ponce with Núñez del Cuvillo bulls. It is the maximum cartel for Albacete, and Dámaso González cuts an ear from a weak bull that could barely keep its feet until it was hypnotized into charging by the maestro. They love the old warrior in his hometown.

Rincón, who has yet to go out the Puerta Grande in Albacete, dedicates the first bull's life (his name is Mostachón and he weighs 485 kilos) to the Albacete crowd and begins with grand style next to the fence. Mostachón charges from a distance and Rincón works up the público with long, low derechazos. He switches to the left, cites from a distance and Mostachón charges again. But the bull crowds him on the left, catching him, shaking him up, and stepping on him. Rincón rises, furious and unpunctured but limping from the *pisotón*, the flesh-rending, bone-crunching walking-on by a cloven-hoofed animal weighing in excess of a thousand pounds.

On the left Mostachón once again cuts in, then stops and begins to *escarbar*, to dig his hoof into the sand, usually a sign of lack of bravery. Rincón insists, but it is over, and after four pinchazos he gets enough of a sword in to drop the animal. The crowd applauds as he limps out to retrieve his montera.

Ponce also kills poorly, losing an ear, and Dámaso González does a long, vulgar faena to his second bull, missing by only fifteen or twenty seconds sending it back alive. But in Albacete the old gladiator cannot fail and he cuts another ear, ensuring his triumphal exit at corrida's end.

Rincón's second bull, Carachica at 500 kilos, is a manso. But Rincón takes him to the sunny side and—because the bull does not have a clean pass in him—does a Dámaso González–like faena complete with pendular passes, half passes, quarter passes changing hands, and molinetes, all the while looking at the crowd. It is a clever strategy which, coupled with a decent sword, earns him an ear. To Dámaso González's fans it must look like an homage to the maestro instead of subtle parody.

Ponce improvises brilliantly, doing double cambios de mano, changing the muleta from right hand to left and then back on the following pass, but all so seamlessly linked, it almost seems like one long fourfold pass. He finishes with a fanning abaniqueo that approaches ballet. Unfortunately he hits bone twice—in between which he literally leaps with rage—before he gets in a decent sword, cutting one ear and watching with Rincón as the local maestro goes out on the shoulders of his adoring countrymen.

Driving toward Valencia, I rerun the tape of the corrida in my mind, thinking of the three completely different styles we saw: Dámaso González with his in-the-bull's-face style, making bulls charge (even if only half a meter at a time) that had no intention of charging; César Rincón, quite the opposite, advancing the muleta in his first bull as far as he could, the muleta flat, to bring the bull's charge through the longest possible arc around his body; and Enrique Ponce with his unusual combination of dominion over the bull and fluid beauty, weaving fantasies from the charge of an animal trying to kill him.

At 10:45 I stop for a sandwich, 525 kilometers from the French border.

Arles: September 11, 1993

Coming into Arles, I see the emblematic sign: a pair of high-arching horns and a rosette, connecting this ancient part of France directly to the hieratic taurine rites of Crete and pre-Homeric Greece. These people, I think, take their bulls seriously. I hope so, after that trip. I remember coming past the castle at Sagunto, spectacularly illuminated even in the wee hours, and the Catalan towns lit up as though they were full of Christmas trees; then across the border coming along the bay as flat as Florida at Perpignan, and passing the hill castle at Narbonne, glowing pinkly in the light of dawn. Then I had driven along the Via Domitia, the Way of Domitian, the Roman emperor whose winter carnivals were won by the dancing girls of Cádiz, or Gades as they called it then, and I wondered if the girls, the *puellae gaditanae*, had come this way or if in Gades they had loaded their dancing costumes and bronze castanets onto a ship bound directly for Rome. Such reveries occupied my time, along with the odd catnap at rest stations and the plaintive songs of Camarón de la Isla that I played at times loud enough to rouse

Domitian's ghost, until Arles, Tête de la Camargue, finally hove into view at eight-thirty.

After the sorteo I accompany Luis Alvarez and Luis Carlos to empresario Hubert Yonnet's office across from the Coliseum. Gaining admittance is like getting into a fort or a bank vault. After being scrutinized, we are allowed to ascend narrow marble stairs and enter the taurine domain, decorated with local posters and photos. I inspect the photos while Luis Alvarez collects the expense money in cash, stacks and stacks of 500-franc notes (about $100) counted out with the patience of a saint by Luis Carlos. When the counting is done, Yonnet hands me a sticker to wear for the callejón that reads ARENES D'ARLES / CORRIDA du 11 Septembre 93 / CALLEJÓN / M. César Rincón / La Direction. It is initialed HY. As we leave, Luis Alvarez remarks, "They pay César more than they have ever paid anyone in France, and, as you know, in France they pay very well. That's why the corridas here are always so good. They buy the best bulls and they pay the best toreros well. The French know how to organize. We love to torear here."

The afternoon is warm and sunny but with a cool breeze. We leave the hotel at 4:40 and wend our way through the narrow streets toward the coliseum. Inside the van it is quiet and I can sense the edginess about getting there. César breaks the silence to ask the time: "¿Qué horas son?" And Luis Alvarez replies, "Menos cuarto." A quarter of. César leans forward to Ricardo Chinza, who is driving, and says, "'Ta bien, Ricardo"—it's okay.

As the big van eases through the thronged streets that approach the coliseum, people stare in at us, the men with open admiration, the older men with lightly veiled envy. The women appear more circumspect, less revealing, but show no less fascination or curiosity, some smiling, some waving, some merely looking. Aside from his reputation as a matador, César Rincón has a special draw, a personal magnetism in France. He is a hero in the way that any figura is, but perhaps because he is not Spanish, he is seen in a slightly different, somewhat more flattering, more mysterious, light. He is *indien*, exotic and foreign, unlike the fraternal Spaniard who has lived next door forever. In taurine France they idolize César Rincón and you can feel the Rincónmanía as we pass through the crowd. César feels it too, and it feeds him, strengthens him, and makes him aware of his responsabilidad.

To reach the arena, we enter the tunnel of the gladiators—horses, picadores, banderilleros, matadors, managers, sword handlers, photographers, anyone who wishes access to the callejón. This entrance is the only way in, and we proceed through the dark silence of the stones and out into the glare of the afternoon light. The oval amphitheatre has been rebuilt just enough to seat the spectators, and the Roman beauty of the arena imbues everything.

When the paseíllo begins and the band breaks into Bizet's "March of the Toreadors" from *Carmen* as the crowd applauds and cheers, it is easy to understand why César, while never failing to name Madrid as the most important plaza in the world, says, "C'est l'afición française que je préfère"—it is the French afición that I prefer (F-S 109). Hearing the "March of the Toreadors," however clichéd the idea may sound, and seeing the toreros march the length of the Roman oval for the first time makes my hair stand on end. Arles, and the larger Roman amphitheatre in nearby Nîmes, are extraordinary archeological sites and very serious bullrings.

Emilio Muñoz, substituting for the injured Chamaco, does little to justify his presence in the gladiatorial arena. Neither does his "enemy," the first of a complicated and difficult string of bulls sent from Salamanca by Javier Pérez-Tabernero.

Rincón's first, number 49 at 522 kilos, comes into the ring, takes one look, and heads back where he came from. Second time out, Rincón calls to him, and in the almost complete silence you can hear his voice perfectly: "¡Toro, toro!" After dedicating the bull to the afición of Arles, Rincón constructs a faena in spite of the animal's uneven charge, aggressive at first, then reluctant as the matador subjugates him. The band strikes up Herb Alpert's "Lonely Bull" as Rincón forces the manso to charge next to the tablas. The bull wants to quit, but Rincón breaks him the same way he did with Colito, the manso of Samuel Flores, in the Beneficencia in 1991. The crowd is with him, but after an imperfect half estocada and three descabellos, he loses the ear.

The fourth animal is formidable and aggressive. Emilio Muñoz panics, throws the cape in front of the bull, and "dives into the pool," going headfirst over the barrera. With the muleta he seems paralyzed by fear and assassinates the bull with an unprofessional stab in the side. The well-behaved French public replies with a bronca worthy of Madrid.

The fifth bull, number 37 at 525 kilos, another aggressive animal, tries to tear the burladeros apart and flings boards in every direction. Rincón begins at the tablas and makes five passes without moving an inch. Suddenly I am aware that all the professionals of the press, critics and mostly photographers, are cheering for César Rincón, who is taking the bull in long, low derechazos. He performs a grand faena as full of art as of valor, finishing with three chest passes on his knees.

The sword thrust, all the way across the ring from me, looks good, but the animal does not go down. Time passes. Silence reigns. He misses with the descabello (plate 9) and the bull lunges forward, hooks, and picks Rincón up, spinning him in the air.

It is immediately apparent that he is hurt. His right hand appears injured and he is limping badly. Is it the knee? In spite of obvious pain, Rincón strikes a perfect descabello. The bull falls instantly, his spinal cord cut, and the crowd reacts with a mistral of handkerchiefs. The président is tough, granting one ear despite an insistent petition for two. Rincón limps half a vuelta and heads for the infirmary, in pain. As I walk through the crowd back to the hotel—the van is long gone with the cuadrilla—I can hear the ambulance with César Rincón aboard, heading for the hospital.

At the hotel afterwards, César descends the stairs on the arms of Edgar Heyn (plate 4d), his Colombian-born business manager, and Luis Alvarez. He limps but also radiates charisma as he is besieged by the media, by what the media call the glitterati, and by his fans. He nods, greets, answers, signs, acknowledges, poses, smiles, handling it all as if he felt no pain whatsoever. Perhaps he does not at that moment. He is happy to have found that his shin is not broken. It is swollen, however, and he cannot walk. If he cannot walk, we are all wondering, how will he get through a mano a mano with Joselito tomorrow? Luis Alvarez shrugs, as I see them off to Dax, and comments: "Tomorrow."

Murcia: September 13, 1993

On a clear morning I drive back across Domitian's highway, headed for the turn onto the Autoroute des Deux-Mers that connects the Mediterranean to the Atlantic. At Narbonne, where I make the turn to the west, I can see the mountains rising like a wall, the Great Wall of Iberia, behind which developed this extraordinary art that we call toreo, an art that has spilled over the Pyrenees in the last hundred years and that now has its share of devotees in *omnia Gallia,* even recently among Parisian intellectuals and politicians.

As always on a drive, I think about the day before, reflecting, remembering, making notes, attempting to sort out my own feelings as well as what is going on around me, finding this world of toreo, which I have so long admired and so long thought myself a part of, to be both familiar and unfamiliar. One thing has become quite clear: I had never been a part of the *mundillo taurino*[5] except as a foreign aficionado in the tendido. Los toros had been part of my world, to be sure, but I had in almost no way been a part of that world. I had thought I knew a reasonable amount about one of the most complex subjects in the world, but now the material I have to deal with—especially the peculiar taurine physics made up of human personalities, animal behavior, and aesthetics—seems magnified exponentially. Once again I am struck with the sheer difficulty and simultaneously with the raw excitement of what I am involved in, not unlike some Connecticut Yankee in King Arthur's court.

Yet much is familiar because it is so human. Yesterday in the van as we approached the arena in Arles, Luis Alvarez began lecturing Luis Carlos on how not to drive the van, how not to "come roaring up and crunch it to a stop and everything goes bump, bump, bump and you use up tires and brakes. Let it come coasting to a stop; don't be in such a hurry. Conserve. You have to take care of the machine. Conserve. Conserve." It was like a replay in Spanish of my father's teaching me to drive.

Then, in the hotel after the corrida, there were the two young women who had just graduated from the University of North Carolina. In France for ten days, they had gone to the corrida out of curiosity, seen César Rincón, and now wanted to meet him. How did they like the corrida? "We loved it! We didn't think we would, but we loved it. We had no idea what it would really be like, that it would be so *beautiful!*" Now they wanted to come to Spain to see more, to see César Rincón again. They were bitten.

The gusano affects some people that way: instantly and unequivocally. When I told them I had come from Chapel Hill in 1962, seen my first corrida, and had my life thereafter radically altered, they liked the coincidence and understood. It sometimes surprises me how many young people with no previous exposure to the corrida become immediately entranced by its savagery and beauty. Often their reaction comes as a surprise to them and, like the señoritas from Carolina, they feel that something has been misrepresented to them. And it has, because, as García Lorca said in his last interview, toreo is "the most cultured fiesta in the world today; it is pure drama . . . the only place you can go with the assurance of seeing death surrounded by the most dazzling beauty" (3:685).

At Villefranche-de-Lauragais I cut through the country and drive closer to the mountains. Here the woods and fields alternate between picturesque and manicured and the villages have names such as Saint-Sulpice and Grâce-Dieu that conjure up the religious strife of their past.

Before long I pick up the main road to Saint-Gaudens and the wall of mountains stretches parallel to the road—the wall cutting Spain off from the rest of Europe. Jagged and peaked, it looms dark blue against the sky. Near Tarbes you can almost reach out and touch the mountains. Closer, now they are dark green below and treeless at the top and there are thick banks of white cloud held in place by the slopes. At times you can see through to the second and third ranges, and the high peak of Bigorri has a sheer face of rock, rounded at the top.

Beyond Bigorri stretch mountains ever more rugged. Some of them are so steep that they bring the Chinese mountains around the Li River to mind, especially when their horns lose themselves in the clouds. By one o'clock I am coming past Pau and the mountains look like the Sawtooths above Ketchum. When I turn to the northwest at Orthez, a heavy sea wind begins to buffet the car.

In Dax I catch the vans just leaving the Hotel Splendid. César's leg is too swollen for him to perform, and we adjourn to La Chaumière outside Dax for a luncheon of the local specialties, mostly made of duck. One of César's favorite dishes is foie gras, and the fatted liver of the local *canard* is superb. Between mouthfuls of rare liver and sips of Bordeaux, Luis Alvarez, watching the trees bowing in the wind off the Atlantic, avers that God writes straight with crooked lines. Manolo Gil adds: "No hay mal que por bien no venga," the Spanish equivalent of "Every cloud has a silver lining." The wind is blowing at a steady twenty-five to thirty knots.

César, in pain, talks little, but Luis, opening up with the wine, tells me with the apoderado's special finality: "In order to be a figura you have to torear every afternoon prepared to go out on shoulders. Joselito wants to hog César's money since César is the máxima figura in France and they pay him what they have never paid anyone. José wants in on it. So César has to defend himself and not take a bath because he's limping around so badly he cannot torear. That's how the history of toreo is written. César is the número uno and he's going to stay that way."

After lunch Luis says, "Tomorrow in Murcia does not look very probable. Seeing how swollen his leg is, I doubt he can make it, but call in the morning, just in case." After coffee we head for Madrid, while Joselito, who will kill the six bulls, doubtless frets in his hotel.

At San Sebastián the winds shriek in from the sea, and I can see a storm moving swiftly toward the coast. In the high pass at Subijana the wind nearly blows the car off the road. When I stop for dinner at 10:30 outside Burgos, the wind has turned wintry, and leaves fly past me like startled coveys of birds. When I arrive in Madrid, it is 2:00 A.M., but I have left the aberrant weather behind.

At 10:45 the next morning Luis Alvarez says to me on the telephone: "¡Sí, sí! He's better! ¡Vamos a torear!"

"How long to Murcia?"

"Three and a half hours." I doubt this to myself, expecting it to be nearer to five.

Forty-five minutes later I am headed fast along the M-30 ring road toward the Valencia highway exit that will eventually lead to Murcia, that odd, isolated, autonomous province sandwiched between Valencia and Andalucía. I am wondering as I drive how César can torear. Yesterday he could barely walk with a severe limp, and his shin was inflamed and swollen. The power of recuperation in young, healthy toreros is legendary, but still I am left to marvel at the speed of his recovery.

At exactly 3:00, I pull into Murcia, a prosperous and thriving city in the valley of the Segura, with its back snuggled against the mountains to the south. Just fifty kilometers away, on the other side of the mountains, lies the Mediterranean. The temperature feels almost hot and no wind is blowing. I have made it in exactly three and a half hours.

A little before five, in the lobby of the Meliá Siete Coronas waiting with my gear for the cuadrilla to come down, I hear tires skidding and brakes screeching and look up to see a young man in the street. The braking car slams into him like a bull, and he rolls up on the hood, breaking the windshield with his head. As the car stops, he is slung forward into the street in front of the car. A crowd gathers instantly and I cannot tell whether he is paralyzed or previously handicapped, but he seems in critical shape. Curro Cruz steps out of the elevator and asks what happened. When I tell him, he remarks, "Today is the thirteenth," as if that explained everything.

"You guess it was just his day?"

"His or the driver's. Don't tell the matador about it. He might think it's a gafe [jinx], like a funeral procession or a one-eyed man."

I never do find out how badly the man was hurt or even whether he survived, but the sound of the car hitting him will stay with me for a long time. In the van on the way to the plaza Curro and I exchange looks and say nothing. César flexes his leg, stretching the shin, and says, "It's better today. A little stiff still, but the inflammation has gone down." Twenty-seven hours ago in France he could barely hobble. "In any case, as soon as I'm out there with the toro, I won't remember a thing about it. Now if the bull will just charge. . . ."

The Plaza de la Condomina, the fourth largest in Spain, fills; the sun beats down warmly; and the top matadors—César Rincón, Joselito, and Enrique Ponce—prepare to kill a corrida of Jandilla bulls. To make matters potentially more exciting, the year before on the fourteenth with a corrida of

Jandilla bulls, César Rincón cut two ears and Enrique Ponce cut two ears and a tail—symbolically—from a bull named Bienvenido, which he pardoned.

The first Jandilla enters the ring and Curro Cruz "runs" him. Rincón, seeing that the animal sheers away from the fence, drops to his knees beside the barrera and spins his capote out in front of the charging animal's face, over his own head and toward the center of the ring as the bull veers for the cape and charges past him in a *larga cambiada de rodillas,* which electrifies the crowd. Since I am in the callejón, the fence blocks my shot, and that is virtually the last pass César Rincón will make all afternoon.

After the corrida, people crowd around the van, shoving and yelling, "¡Foto! ¡Foto!"

Luis Carlos hands out the few signed photographs he can find, and then yells, "There aren't any more!"

The crowd bangs on the windows anyway, and I observe to César: "Hey, César, not even in ancient Rome."

He smiles through his pain and his disappointment and his fatigue, and as he waves to the crowd that we are beginning slowly to escape from, he says out of the side of his mouth, "Hope is the last thing we ever want to lose, hermano."

Mono ends the discussion with the eternal optimism of the torero, greater perhaps than the wishful thinking of the angler: "Let's hope to God they charge in Salamanca."

We have a subdued dinner in the Siete Coronas with Borja Domecq, the ganadero of Jandilla. He sums up the afternoon to someone on his cell phone: "The corrida came out with very little life." Borja, perhaps nervous or embarrassed at his animals' behavior, talks animatedly and nonstop.

Luis Alvarez—who takes a bad corrida hard, worse than César—stays quiet, listening to Borja Domecq saying: "All the greats of toreo have had their apoderados out in front. The apoderado has to be there—with his torero. None of that señor in Bilbao or Madrid who says on the phone, 'Hey, how were you today, how'd it go?'" Luis, while listening carefully to the limitless clichés that taurinos resort to in difficult moments, remains crestfallen.

Antonio Pinilla (plate 2b), César's other picador, whispers to me: "I've known Luis for more than twenty years and I can tell you, he's made it by himself. Alone. No empresario helped him out. Nobody did. Alone. And that's why he's here, taking care of his torero. He takes care of him and he's here, here with the bad and here with the good, here with everything."

I am watching Luis, whose eyes have turned into opaque half-moons, giving him an owlish look. He pays attention to Borja Domecq but his spirit seems somewhere far away.

César patiently listens to my description of the accident before the corrida. Curro Cruz, silent up to now, interrupts: "Monday the thirteenth. Good thing it wasn't Tuesday."

"No, hombre," says César, "the thirteenth can bring good luck too. For me it's lucky."

"How about today?" I ask.

"Who knows?" answers César, getting up as a sign to the group that he wishes to depart for Madrid now. "Who knows?"

The kid hit by the car knows, I think. At least I hope he does.

Salamanca: September 15 and 16, 1993

Salamanca, the venerable old university town and the bull breeding center of the north, has a unique ambiente centering around the Gran Hotel (plate 10a). It is one of the few places on the taurine circuit where virtually everyone congregates in one place—only the Hotel Colón in the other great tau-

Figure 25. Michael Wigram in the lobby of the Gran, September 16, 1993. The Gran Hotel of Salamanca is one of the great taurine hotels of our time. Here the whole "planet of the bulls" congregates. Luis Alvarez is behind Michael.

rine city of Sevilla can match it. All the action and the interaction—among ganaderos, apoderados, toreros, would-be toreros, journalists, aficionados, hangers-on, would-be hangers-on, both local and from all points of the taurine sphere—take place in the bar and lobby of the Gran. From there, Mono and Muri and I walk the twenty minutes or so up to La Glorieta, as the ring in Salamanca is called, for the sorteo.

It feels hot in the sun and cold in the shade, typical for mid-September, and the wind is blowing from the southwest as a long discussion about the matchups begins. The bulls of María Lourdes Martín Pérez-Tabernero all look about the same, high in the shoulder and long in the face, true to their Atanasio type, and no single bull stands out as good or bad. Luis Carlos does not like the two burracos but we draw one of them anyway. The burraco will be Rincón's lead bull—he usually saves the "good" one—and the black will follow. As we leave, everyone acts pleased because "on paper" we have drawn the best lot.

I arrive late for lunch across the river at the parador, thanks to the infernal traffic jams of Salamanca. Michael and Irene have brought along a Venezuelan friend, Gustavo Trujillo, and his daughter, Menelly. Gustavo served as presidente in the plaza of Mérida, Venezuela, for years and turns out to be a great conversationalist, all the more so since he is a self-described Rincónmaniac. He uses the word *brujo,* sorcerer, to describe Rincón and I tell him: "I couldn't agree more. I've used the same word myself."

"He seems at times to cast a spell on the animal, bewitching it," says Gustavo, "Don't you agree, Michael?"

Michael, who thinks Enrique Ponce the monstruo, does not agree.

"Rincón has a talisman, Michael," Gustavo continues, "an *embrujo* [spell]."

"No, Michael," I interrupt. "Enrique Ponce is a genius but the monstruo is César Rincón!"

Michael is shaking his head.

Undeterred, Gustavo continues: "I've never seen anyone someter a difficult bull like César does. He's so small but he summons a power no one else has. That embrujo."

"He breaks them. When he's on, he breaks their wills. You can see it in his eyes," I contend.

"Yes," agrees Gustavo, seeing in his mind's eye the dark brilliance in the eyes of César Rincón, "you can see it in his eyes."

Michael is looking as though he may have stopped listening.

Rincón would need more than a talisman for these Pérez-Tabernero bulls: they all come out falling down, distracted, with no interest in charging, dispirited, and mansos. The first is sent back to be replaced with a Carlos Núñez that Emilio Muñoz dispatches almost without notice.

The burraco—number 20, Contador, at 560 kilos—proves Luis Carlos to be right. It falls down in Rincón's opening verónicas but then knocks over both horses, and Anderson Murillo has to get away fast, hobbling as best he can with the mona strapped around his leg. The bull cuts in on both sides, looking for the matador's body. After trying repeatedly to straighten out the charge and failing, Rincón kills the only way he can without a certain goring, by going around and putting the sword into the neck from the side. It is the first low sword thrust I have seen him make, but there is a reason for the poor sword of which we are unaware.

In the faena, no one is sure when, Rincón has cut his left thumb with the sword. While working the point into the muleta for a derechazo, he has somehow cut the tip of his thumb—the whole hammy underside of the tip from the last joint to the nail—virtually off. It hangs by a thread, bleeding copiously. Luis Carlos wraps it in gauze and tapes it in place. The talisman seems to have failed: César Rincón has sliced deeply into his Achilles' thumb.

The black—number 2, Cigarrero, at 495 kilos—enters looking for a way out. Rincón, wounded, gives Cigarerro four verónicas, his feet planted, the cape flowing smoothly without the horns touching it, and a media verónica that leaves the bull wondering where the cape went.

After ordering careful picking, Rincón takes his "patient" to the center of the ring to begin the faena. His handicap, rather too literally, is huge. Both hands are bandaged—the right is taped for killing because of a blood blister in his palm, a frequent injury to matadors—yet he cites from a distance, going through a series of derechazos and finishing with a change of hands and a faultless pase de pecho with the left, using only his fingers, not his thumb, to hold the muleta.

After another emotionally charged series on the right, Rincón switches hands and begins to give Cigarrero naturales (plate 10b) in spite of his injured hand, insisting, forcing the bull to charge. Time to kill comes and goes and Rincón continues to oblige the bull to charge. Little by little he forces Cigarrero to swallow ten naturales, one after the other. "El embrujo," Gustavo whispers to me, "¡el embrujo!"

Finally Rincón fetches the killing sword, but instead of killing he does more naturales, citing de frente. "Just what we said," murmurs Gustavo, "just what we said." The naturales are flawless but finally he goes on too long. The bull begins backing away and the presidente sends him an aviso. But the crowd is with him so completely that they whistle at the palco.

Gustavo and I are happy with Rincón's performance, but he has made a tactical error and the bull backs away from him continually. Gustavo says, "He's cowed that animal! He's intimidated it!" It is true, but now Rincón cannot kill because the bull will not hold still long enough. After a pinchazo he gets in a sword, and the animal finally goes down. Once again he has been superb—with bravery, with skill, with desire, with art, even with his special "power"—but he has again been unable to "round out" the triumph. Had he killed well, and sooner, he would have cut two ears from the fifth bull.

Tomás Weitzner and Herby Kretzmer, who wrote the lyrics for *Les Misérables* and who is another longtime aficionado, and I have lunch upstairs at Casa Félix, where the fare is Salamanca's specialty, *tostón,* roast suckling pig. Between bites of pig, Tomás reminisces about Vietnam and Turkey, Herby recounts the old days with Charles Aznavour and Frank Sinatra, and I, unsuccessfully, try to talk about César's thumb.

Up in suite 106 at the Gran, Luis Carlos prepares to dress the matador. Outside a serious rain is falling. Camilo Llinás, the empresario of the Bogotá ring, is talking to César.

Dr. Sabogal arrives, back from a lightning trip to Madrid to obtain propolis (bee glue) to treat César's thumb. "It makes it dry and scar faster," he explains as he administers it. "And it kills bacteria."

I do not see how he can torear today. The thumb looks . . . bad. The tip has been sewn on with seven tiny stitches to hold the flesh in place, but it has not adhered.

César is pulling on his pink stockings. He adjusts the garter above the knee, then rolls the garter and stocking down to just below the knee, awkwardly because he cannot use his left thumb. He eases into the taleguilla and Luis Carlos pulls up as César, adjusting himself, bounces down into the tight legs (plate 10c). Next comes the shirt, frilled and lacy like a tuxedo shirt, and the narrow tie (César always wears black, for his mother and sister). He has to go into the bathroom to use the mirror to tie the tie properly. Camilo Llinás and I laugh, admitting that we too need a mirror.

When César returns, Luis Carlos begins tightening the *machos,* the knee strings of the taleguilla. César tucks in his shirt, pulling up the front of the taleguilla, and Luis Carlos attaches the suspenders. Then comes the *fajín,* the *chaleco* or vest, and the zapatillas. Finally Luis Carlos helps him on with the chaquetilla, and César bends forward, easing the montera onto his head from just above the eyebrows. "What time is it?" he asks.

It is minutes past 5:30 when we get into the van. César, in pain despite the analgesic Dr. Sabogal has administered, looks worried. Rain pours from the darkened sky, and he knows the thumb is useless.

We pull away from the hotel, César waving with his good hand to the fans and the groupies gathered in the rain, and Luis Carlos absentmindedly beats out the rhythm of the Latin music coming from the cassette player, drumming with his hands on the leather sword case. When the music stops, the silence is broken by the noise of the rain. Traffic snarls worse than usually in this weather.

The corrida does not start on time, and the apoderados, the toreros, and the empresarios go into war council. After thirty minutes, they announce that the corrida will start.

It is also turning cold, and because I packed this morning and checked out, putting my gear in the car ready to strike out for Nîmes, some 1,200 kilometers away, immediately after the corrida, I am wearing only a cotton shirt and a cotton photographer's vest. To make matters worse, in the crush going into the ring, someone has lifted my umbrella.

When I get to my seat, it is covered in water, and the vendor is out of rental cushions. There are Michael, Tomás, Herby, Gustavo and Menelly, Ivan and Mary Mosely from the Club Taurino of London, and Harlan Blake, sitting in the last row of Tendido One, in the rain, as if they all had good sense. At least they have rain gear and umbrellas. I sit down in the water beside Harlan, who valiantly tries to protect me by sharing his small umbrella. It is better than nothing at all, but I am concerned about getting the cameras wet.

César Rincón, Joselito, and Enrique Ponce make the paseíllo in the corrida of the feria, sold out for days. But the plaza, somber with umbrellas, looks more like a funeral than a feria.

Rincón cannot hold the cape properly, and his attempts to jam it between the fingers of his left hand do not work. With the muleta he has more success, taking number 12, Inspirado, 505 kilos, to the center of the ring, where he cites from a distance, making those all-the-way-from-out-here-to-back-there linked derechazos that evoke the fervent olés of the afición of Salamanca. The rain comes down but the music begins, and on the other side of Harlan, Gustavo is saying, "Bien. Bien, torero. Bien. ¡Olé!"

Now Rincón switches to the left and the injury seems to vanish. Then to the right, to Inspirado's better horn, for more long, low, linked derechazos to olés and applause. Harlan comments, "If everyone wasn't holding an umbrella, the applause would be thunderous."

As Rincón profiles to kill, I hear a whirring noise. To my horror the film is not advancing. I open the camera and yank out the roll but cannot get the next roll to work either. I hear crowd noise, look up to see Rincón trying to kill, slipping, falling beside the bull, pulling the sword free, the bull almost catching him. There is rain and ruined film everywhere, but I am laughing. Rincón kills the bull on the third attempt. Once again, and in spite of the injury, he would have cut an ear if he had killed well. Still, I know he should not be out there.

The rain falls harder. People are swearing and some are starting to leave. Gustavo is laughing and imitating the swearing—Latin Americans are frequently appalled or amused (or both) by the prodigious public swearing in Spain. Herby breaks into a fine rendition of "Raindrops Keep Fallin' on My Knees." "Might as well laugh," he says, "nothing else to do."

Rincón somehow gives number 80, Malahierba, 565 kilos, verónicas with no hands. The light is almost gone and neither of my cameras is working right. The only thing I can see clearly is that we are not going to Nîmes tomorrow. Rincón's left hand has become virtually useless and he can do nothing with the bull. The crowd whistles. My recorder has stopped too, and Harlan cannot keep the umbrella over me.

Rincón is having a difficult time with Malahierba, a bull that goes for the body. He has not made one clean pass. I say to Gustavo, "That's enough pundonor, hombre. Stop, for God's sake. Kill it!" He kills it and receives whistles that drown in the rain.

In suite 106 of the Gran the mood is somber. The thumb looks rotten, red and black and edged with pus. César says it hurts like the devil. It is clear that he will miss corridas on the seventeenth and eighteenth in Nîmes. What is less clear is how many more he will miss. Dr. Sabogal says, "Seven or eight days, at least."

César, in pain, is talking to Camilo Llinás. "Do you see me married, Camilo?" I think César may be in need of some mothering.

Joselito and his apoderado Enrique Martín Arranz come in to see how César is. Arranz, shaking his head gravely, says, "You can't torear by jamming the cape between your fingers." Arranz is upset that the corrida took place, in spite of Joselito's going out on shoulders. "They should have suspended. They should respect the figuras."

As they leave, José says to César: "Get well, eh? Don't leave me alone out there."

"Gracias, hermano," answers César, smiling but visibly hurting. "The bad part is I can't seem to cuajar a bull with you."

"But you haven't drawn one, either," José says collegially. I can see the scar on the left side of his neck from a bull in Madrid that nearly killed him. "What's fucked up is when they're good and you can't cuajar," he says.

When they are gone, Dr. Sabogal intervenes: "Look, if you don't keep that hand immobile—and I mean immobile—you're going to lose that piece of finger. It's got to have blood, hermano." He wraps the thumb after putting a metal support around the top side of the thumb from the big joint to the nail.

As César prepares to go home to Madrid, I find Michael and Gustavo downstairs in the crowded bar. Gustavo, still wet, as we all are, and still chuckling, says, "Let's go have dinner!"

Talavera de la Reina: September 22, 1993

On the twenty-first César is back in light training and I drive to his house, off the Escorial road in Las Rozas. That area of Madrid, out to the north-west—a few years ago pueblos and campo—has become fashionable and overdeveloped. Whole cities are sprouting up, thirty minutes from down-town.

César's house is beyond the congested development. The terrain is gulch land with scrubby vegetation but a splendid view of the Sierra de Guadarrama to the north. The house is a "chalet," a large freestanding structure with a fenced yard, a pool, and a small plaza for training. There is thick grass from sodding and sprinklers, and Luis Alvarez lives nearby.

A weather front approaches from the north and the day turns breezy and drizzly. As soon as I arrive I begin to meet new people: Diego González, a novillero from Cali whom César has taken under his wing, and Jorge Molina, an aficionado *práctico*, one who likes to torear himself, also from Cali, a would-be ganadero, and an old friend of César, who donated blood for him in Palmira in 1990. Open, friendly, and instantly hospitable, even though this is not his country, he is intrigued with the idea of a gringo doing a taurine book. We become friends at once.

I say hello to Gonzalo, César's father, whom I have met before. "Are you going to Talavera?" I ask.

Figure 26. The house outside Las Rozas. This view is taken from the back, from the mountain side. The training area is just to the left of the house.

"Yes," he says, "si Dios quiere." Gonzalo, like many taurinos, uses the phrase "God willing" frequently.

A large group of people has congregated at the house, as usual: Rincón's drivers Armando Ramírez "Primo" and Ricardo Chinza "Maestro Ricardo," Luis Carlos, the ayuda Juanito Márquez who runs the carretón so well for Rincón. And the maestro himself, very much at home, presently working on Natalia Lorente's car with Maestro Ricardo. A warm ambiente holds sway at the house, a strong clan feeling.

Late in the afternoon we take an hour training walk: Jorge and I, César and Luis, Dieguito and Muri. We walk out through the open campo toward a small chapel dedicated to Nuestra Señora de Retamar, a chapel that César and Juan Mora and Morenito de Maracay helped build by performing in a (charity) *festival* with novillos of Victoriano del Río on April 1, 1993. As Luis tells the story, I sense that César and he are very proud of this little chapel. The late afternoon has an autumnal feel and the gray sky is streaked through now with transcendent light, the kind used in biblical films to signify divine presence (plate 11a).

The corrida in Madrid on October first weighs heavily on everyone's mind—the responsabilidad, all the more evident after several newspapers reported rumors that César Rincón would "cut" his temporada. The corridas in the interim will serve as preludes, as training, for the Madrid corrida ten days away. The impending responsibilidad and the celestial glory of the waning light put us in a pensive mood. Again I am reminded of Jaime de Armiñán's character Juncal, who declares: "Death is at the service of toreros, to give them glory and eternal life" (247).

"How do you see Madrid on the first?"

"A triumph," says Luis, always the apoderado.

"Claro," echoes the matador.

"Puerta Grande, no?"

"Oh, yes," they say in unison. "It has to be," says César.

"And the hand?" I ask. César is picking at his thumb.

"Leave the stiches alone," says Luis.

"It's been a week already. I don't want them to grow into the flesh."

I agree with Luis but do not say anything. I also notice that the big blood blister on the base of his right thumb is still there, the killing blister. No wonder he could not get the sword in.

"You can torear tomorrow in Talavera with your thumbs like that?"

"I have to. I have to train. I have to be ready for Madrid."

"But to be able to rest is good, no?"

"The rest is good—except for the pain. It's hard to sleep. The pain was tremendous the first few days. I'd raise my arm and it would hurt more. I'd lower it and it was worse yet. So it was hard to sleep. The first two nights I didn't sleep at all."

"You couldn't take anything?"

"I took pills like an *hijueputa* but it didn't he'p."

Jorge Molina asks me, "Is the book well along?"

"I have a lot of photographs and notes," I answer, "but I can't even think about writing yet. Things change so much from day to day—right, maestro?"

César looks at me and nods, rolling his eyes in mock terror. "First there was the cornada in Sevilla. Then the tossing at Victoriano del Río's, which was a real *paliza* [thrashing]. Three broken ribs that kept me from sleeping with the pain. Then there was a festival and I fractured a finger and couldn't torear for a week. I've lost about thirty corridas this season. Then that day in Vic when I dislocated my shoulder again."

Luis Alvarez stops the litany: "But that's all finished now."

"How did you get that blood blister on your killing hand?"

"Killing, killing, killing. First it was a little blister. Then it got worse and worse."

"And the hepatitis? That's all over now?"

"I think so. They say it is. They don't seem to know much about this type C."

"That's all over," interjects Luis, perhaps too quickly, making me wonder. "And now to train—"

"And to go out the Puerta Grande," I say.

And at the same time Luis says: "And to triumph in Madrid on the first."

"How's the morale?"

"Bien, hombre. The only thing that bothers me is that the toro has not charged well this season. I've been very unlucky in the sorteos. What José said the other night in Salamanca about not getting good bulls is true. But in spite of all of that, the cornada, everything, I've maintained my season. And that was fundamental. Because since I'm Colombian, every year they want to see you quit, no?"

"Yeah. You're not a novelty anymore. You're just a Colombian."

"Right. They all want to see how you're going to—"

Luis Alvarez interrupts: "They don't like it when an outsider comes in to mandar."

"They say why does a Colombian think he can come here and tell us how it's done," explains César. "That's how it is. Unfortunately. I wish this *extranjerismo* [prejudice against foreigners]. . . ."

"Xenophobia, no?"

"Precisely."

"Let's see when a Spaniard, when anyone, can go out the Puerta Grande four consecutive times in one season in Madrid," I say, catching the spirit of indignation. "It's not that a Spaniard couldn't do it, it's not an ethnic issue, it's just that nobody ever has."

"Yes. For the time being that's there. A record."

"And a very big record it is."

"Big," agrees Luis. "Even after we are dead and gone, no one will repeat it."

"Not even you guys," I say illogically.

"No, not even us," agrees Luis, equally illogically. "Listen, Jósef, there was a series of circumstances that overtook us and allowed us to do what we did. But we had to know how to take advantage of those circumstances. And we knew. And we did. It was not just an isolated event. It was a continuation of many events that began back in América."

"The important thing for me last year and especially this year is that with all that's gone on, I've been able to come out ahead. Thank God for that. And I have a great desire to continue the triumphs. To keep putting the muleta out as far as I can get it, cargando la suerte, bringing him past closely, behind the hip, sending him away, linking him again and again."

"True toreo."

"True toreo. Those ten naturales in Salamanca. They say I went on too long, but if I hadn't, I'd never have gotten those passes. What many aficionados and many critics don't realize is that one needs, many times, not just to put in a good sword. No. But to demonstrate that you're there until the end. I gave that bull ten naturales and they were perfect. At first the animal cut in on me but by the end I was able to thread together ten passes with the left hand. That's what gets to the public, that's what transmits the emotion. Afterwards there are certain aficionados who don't talk about the bull or anything else. Just that: those ten naturales. I like to squeeze everything I can from an animal. Everything."

I realize César is giving me the heart of his toreo: to get the best, to get the ungettable from the bull, like the poet who wants to put the ineffable into language. "You know Gustavo Trujillo, don't you?"

"Claro."

"He was beside me when you did those naturales, and he went crazy. Talking about the embrujo, talking about how you bewitch a bull like that."

I think I see César smile, but the light is going fast as we make the final turn back toward the house.

César would have done better staying home. Talavera de la Reina, an important ceramic manufacturing town for centuries, became famous, or infamous, in the taurine world, when on May 16, 1920, a runty, shortsighted, old Viuda de Ortega bull named Bailador ripped Joselito el Gallo's guts out, ending the Golden Age competition of Belmonte and Joselito.

Gabriel Rojas has sent a good string of bulls, for the most part, to Talavera. Ortega Cano shows off with his, and Manolo Sánchez wastes two fine animals.

Rincón's first bull, on the other hand, is weak and refuses to charge. Yet he kills it well. I cannot help reflecting on how well he is killing the bulls that do not matter, and what bad luck he has with the animals that could produce a triumph. Is it psychological, I wonder, or just luck?

The fifth bull never does come out—they disable it in the corrals. Finally a horrid animal from Sánchez Arjona replaces it. The public demands the bull be changed because it keeps falling down. When they do not get their way, they throw everything at hand into the ring, including beer cans. Rincón and Monaguillo have to clean the ring before the pointless faena.

The afternoon is lovely, the sky blue, the plaza festive. The outline of the town, with the big church in the background, is reminiscent of a Goya tapestry (plate 11b), but the crowd on the sunny side, many of them drunk, remind me more of one of Goya's "black paintings." The público of Talavera normally has a fine reputation, but there is little evidence of it today. In a black mood myself, I reflect that Joselito el Gallo picked a choice pueblo in which to die.

Ecija: September 24, 1993

On the twenty-third Jorge Molina rides with me to Logroño but the weather is cold and nasty and the bulls are worthless. On the way back we stop at the Hotel Landa for coffee and Jorge quips, "At least he's killing well."

The next morning I drive down to Ecija, the town between Córdoba and Sevilla known as the frying pan of Spain. After Dax and Salamanca and Logroño, the heat feels like heaven. I meet John Fulton and Barnaby Conrad at the outdoor café across from the plaza de toros. I am curious to hear what the Dean of American Taurine Letters will say about Rincón.

We sit in the shade of the café awning out of the heat of the sun and drink cold beer with beads of perspiration on the pitcher and glasses, and amid tales from John and maestro Bernabé—two of the supreme raconteurs of the taurine world—I tell them about Logroño, commingling two old taurine proverbs, "The sun *is* the best torero, and the wind (and the rain) *is* the worst enemy. ¡Viva Andalucía!"

The cartel could hardly be better: César Rincón, Enrique Ponce, and Jesulín de Ubrique. The latter has never made it into my preferred category, but he is a massive draw this year, especially in the south. Yet for some reason—probably the financial crisis in Spain in late 1992 and throughout 1993—the ring fills only partially. The bulls of Javier Osborne, except the fifth, turn out to be difficult for the toreros, long on *genio*—the bad, nervous opposite side of the coin of casta—and short on bravery. As a result, the artistic quality of the afternoon is considerably less brilliant than the sun and the cartel have promised.

Neither Rincón nor Jesulín is able to shine with the recalcitrant animals, and although Enrique Ponce cuts two ears from the weak but noble fifth, his performance excites no one in our group. The camaraderie continues well

Figure 27. Barnaby Conrad, Sevilla, September 25, 1993. Barnaby is the dean of English-language taurine writers. His many books on toreo have educated generations of aficionados. I took this portrait the day after the corrida in Ecija, in the Maestranza of Sevilla.

into the evening in Sevilla at the Bodegón Torre del Oro, next to the Guadalquivir River and just down the street from the Maestranza, but I am left wondering what maestro Bernabé thinks of César Rincón. And while we were basking in the comfortable sun of Ecija, Joselito—shedding all vestiges of his reclusive, Hamletian nature—stirred up a lío in the north, melting the ice palace at Logroño with a grand faena as he continued his unstoppable march to the summit of toreo.

Lorca: September 26, 1993

I drive John Fulton and Jorge Molina four hundred kilometers from Sevilla to Lorca to watch Espartaco, César Rincón, and Litri with bulls of Sánchez-Ybargüen.

The bulls, pure Domecq, came out charging and the matadors all cut ears in the kind of afternoon that you might call "apotheosis, small-town-feria style." There, in one of the poorest parts of Spain, as Andalucía runs out and Murcia begins, in a lunar landscape where some people live in caves even today, Rincón finally draws bulls that charge.

The plaza itself has great ambiente with a local marching band, lots of alegría, the señoritas dressed in mantillas, and very friendly aficionados in the tendidos. Lorca strikes me as an old-fashioned and traditional agricultural town, poor and honest, and Espartaco, who ten years before electrified such towns, still knows exactly how to turn them on. He goes to his knees grinning, his hair in his face, and performs an old-time faena for an old-time crowd, cutting two ears.

Rincón, with his more formal style, does not excite quite the interest in this crowd that he would in a more sophisticated place, cutting only one ear in spite of a fine performance.

Litri, in his usual foot-stomping, nervous but brave manner, looking frequently up into the tendido as the bull goes by (as his father used to do), also cuts two ears, although he is not as good as either of the others.

Rincón, his competitive nature fully engaged, comes out prepared to eat his second bull, but the animal crashes into a burladero, damaging his spine, and has to be put out of his misery. Here we go again with the bad luck, I am thinking, and thinking he must be thinking it too.

But the sobrero also charges, after some coaxing and training, and Rincón proceeds to do the same molinetes on his knees that Espartaco has done and the same naturales looking into the tendido that Litri has done—only with more class—until he has the crowd in the palm of his hand. It is high satire by a taurine master. Then, not content with tying them, he backs off and cites from a distance to make several series in his own style. This time around, the crowd is completely his.

The sword goes in well and the handkerchiefs flail wildly in the dying light. The presidente balks but finally concedes the second ear.

Litri cuts another ear and the ecstatic crowd swarms into the ring, hoists all three musketeers on shoulders, and parades them around the town for half an hour. As we leave the plaza John Fulton catches my arm and says, "You know, if César had been born in Triana, they'd have to take down the statue of Belmonte and put up his."

We start the long drive back to Sevilla in the dark, and when we cross into the province of Almería, in the distance we can see, high up on the ridge of a mountain, a remote castle, brightly lit against the blackness of the sky. There is no moon and the castle seems to float in the sky, reminding me of the opening line of García Lorca's poem "Muerto de amor" ("Dead of Love"):

¿Qué es aquello que reluce
por los altos corredores?

What is it shining yonder
up in the high corridors?

Madrid: October 1, 1993

José Carlos Arévalo asked César Rincón: "The life of the torero is a strange one. How can a man turn an animal, in this case the bull, into an intellectual problem? How can the life of a man, both privately and publicly, be influenced by the bull?"

And Rincón answered: "Because el toro is something more than an animal. El toro is luck, good or bad. El toro defines your limits, of valor and of intelligence. El toro makes you triumph in life and at the same time he is the very real presence of death. El toro is like life; he encompasses everything" (6T6 24:31).

In the days before the corrida in Madrid, I spend my time with César, training, walking and talking with him, taking pictures. It will turn out to be the most concentrated time we spend together, with every effort building toward the corrida on October 1.

It is a year and a half since Rincón has performed in Madrid and "things," especially this season, have not gone so well. Madrid could be the place to recover lost ground. On the hallowed sands of Las Ventas del Espíritu Santo, any season could turn triumphant. Or not.

Rincón makes the usual remarks to the press: The '93 season has been very hard—insert litany of injuries and mishaps—perhaps his toughest Spanish season of all. He has talked it over with some of his compañeros and they agree he has had little luck. There have been some fine afternoons, others ruined by bad luck with the sword. In that sense, particularly, the season has been negative. The worst part has been the bad luck in the sorteos. And finally: "I miss that sensation of going out on shoulders from this most important ring. . . . I'm going to give it my all on Friday" (*El Mundo*, September 29, 1993).

Arévalo would sum up Rincón's situation succinctly: "In the difficult and dramatic '93 season, the afición had begun not to believe in his genius as a figura. The young lions of late were now the chiefs of the clan. But Rincón had one trump left: to lay on the line in Madrid his place at the top" (6T6 27:41).

The days leading up to the corrida are the finest weather of that fall. Every day dawns brilliantly clear, crisply chilly in the morning and warm enough to work up a healthy sweat training during the day. From César's house the individual peaks of the Guadarrama range stand etched against the northern sky, especially in the late afternoon: Siete Picos, La Mujer Muerta, and La Bola del Mundo turn indigo against the deep Castilian blue.

September 27, 28, 29, and 30 pass by like falling leaves. César Rincón trains hard, concentrating above all on the sword, practicing killing with Juanito Márquez and Diego González on the carretón for hours at a time (plates 12a and 12b). And we walk, talking as we walk, and I find that César talks more walking than at any other time. We discuss everything from real estate and antiques (Luis Alvarez is a collector and César is beginning to become interested) to women and fame, but the discussion—even about sex—always returns to the bulls.

For example, I am asking: "You hear a lot—maybe too much—about the pleasure you feel toreando being like sexual pleasure. How do you see it?"

"Well. Well. That's not easy. To torear well *is* a pleasure—when you can really cuajar a bull, it's beautiful—but I wouldn't ever compare it to making love with a woman. In both cases there is an entrega, but there are other aspects that are not comparable. Both are matters of passion, but there comes a point when they are completely different."

"It's always seemed something of a cliché to me."

"Yes, it is a cliché, because the 'trend' [he uses the English word] is to compare them, and there are some things you can compare. El toro, like a woman, is different every day. Some are pretty, some are ugly, some are nice, some have *mala leche* [evil intentions]. Some bulls start out great, like a chica you think you're going to fall in love with. Then their real nature comes out. Or some are like a chica you think at first you don't like but in time you get along with and even end up liking, no? All of them are different, just like el toro. But naturally you don't ever feel that tremendous passion that you feel for a woman, and . . . and when you make love with her and try to compare that with el toro, there comes a moment when it's just not the same, the comparison doesn't work. In both cases there is tremendous pleasure, yes, but the pleasures are physically completely different. Perhaps mentally there are points of comparison, no? But physically—physiologically—there is none."

"What would you have been if you had not become a matador?"

"Look, the truth is I wanted to torear since I was very little and what started as a childhood game became my profession. Almost without realizing it. I didn't have any toys—just a little muleta. So that's what I played with. I went to school until I was fourteen, but only because I had to. I never thought about a profession, and it never entered my head that school would ever solve any of the problems of my life. By the time I should have been thinking about a profession, I was already training and toreando, so I only went to school to fulfill a requirement."

"So if you had not been a matador, you would have done something else in the bulls?"

"I think so. That's what I was a part of. That's where I belonged."

"Like a medieval guild?"

"Yes. It was almost by necessity. I suppose I could have always been a taurine photographer like my father or a banderillero—how do I know? The only thing I know is that I have always had this grand ambition. I have set myself very difficult goals. Some took longer than others, but I have achieved them. It has made me very proud and given me a great sense of satisfaction as a man. Because in this world it's hard to survive, as it is in any profession, but in the bulls it's almost impossible to make it. You take your alternativa—like getting your degree—and you find that thousands have done that but only a very few ever get anywhere. There are a lot of muchachos who want to be a torero. But very few make it. Very few."

"But you're not just one of the few—you're also the first Colombian, and one of the very few Americanos, to become a figura."

"Yes, I think that's right. And it makes one very . . . very proud. There is this enormous feeling to think . . . first that I'm the first Colombian, which is very important, and that . . . I don't believe it, you know? Every day I . . . you see how I am, I, I don't go around thinking, 'Hey, look what I did.' It's not easy to express it. Sometimes I feel that . . . that it's very difficult for a Colombian to come to Spain and to do what I have done. It's very important to me that my name has passed into the history of toreo, like Gaona or like Arruza."

"You can count the American figuras on the fingers of one hand."

"Exactly. And how many toreros are there?"

"Thousands," I answer.

"Thousands of toreros. But only a handful make it."

The impending corrida has made César pensive, but he never seems to avoid issues or to skirt the truth. The subject of his cornada in Sevilla comes up again—he brings it up, in fact—and he speaks frankly about it. The two of us are walking through an extended pine grove, where they fought from tree to tree during the Civil War, and he says: "This season has been difficult because the bulls have hurt me a lot. Other years I've gotten my share of volteretas but this year it started with the cornada in Sevilla. It was tough; it was very tough. And you try to tell yourself, this is nothing. Nothing happened. But you don't believe it. Bit by bit you begin to realize that something did happen. That cornadas do leave their mark. No matter how much you try to wish it away, or talk it away, or tell the press it's nothing, there are still the scars, on your legs, in your testicles, wherever, and mentally you have to overcome it, little by little. That's fundamental. You must overcome it. Especially when you don't draw good bulls, when you're unlucky in the sorteo, and things don't work out the way they should. It's very hard to overcome those moments, especially when what you need is for the bull to slide on through the muleta and let you enjoy what you're doing so you can forget. . . . But if they always come out complicated . . . and then when you do get a, good one, he ruins himself. Those are the malas rachas and we all have them. And we're all human, we're flesh and blood. You're not a machine, you're not a watch. And you can break down. Even a computer gets damaged when it gets a virus, and a computer is programmed. We're not programmed."

"I like that. You mean you have to do it all yourself. The *mentalización?*"

"Right. And there's no program for it. You do it alone. Or not."

The wind picks up as we near the house (plate 12c) and César sighs, saying, "Let's hope this wind dies down by tomorrow."

"Will you train at all tomorrow?"

"I don't think so."

"Rest?"

"I don't know. Depends on how I feel when I get up. If I don't sleep well, I won't do much of anything."

"You don't have a fixed system?"

"No."

"Your thumb looks a lot better today." Yesterday it still looked wet and oozy but today it is beginning to resemble a thumb again (plate 12d). "How does it feel?"

César merely shrugs.

"Can we do some more photos tomorrow, before the corrida?"

"No, hombre, I'm sorry. Not tomorrow. Tomorrow I have to be alone. I don't want to see anybody before the corrida."

"Right. Suerte, then, matador."

"Gracias, hombre," he says, but I can tell he is already somewhere else. He is looking at something in the middle distance of his mind as I take a final shot. Responsabilidad, I think, that is where he is, up to his neck in responsabilidad (plate 13).

We need two miracles, I am thinking the next morning at eleven as I head for the sorteo at Las Ventas: the weather needs to clear with a drop in the wind, and the bulls need to charge without falling down. Rincón, I am confident, will do the rest. Still, I have never been so nervous before a corrida in my life. Jorge Molina has told me that he always has an "attack of nerves" when Rincón performs in an important corrida. I am beginning to understand why.

At the plaza it is cold, windy, and drizzly. The ice trucks are unloading, people are coming to see the apartado, scalpers are hawking tickets, and the drably dressed, stubble-faced old men who congregate around bullrings have appeared in spite of the weather.

The bulls—serious, large but not fat, and astifinos—have come from the Puerto de San Lorenzo ranch in Salamanca. César draws number 113, Mariposito, 547 kilos, to come out in second position, and number 50, Campanero, 543 kilos, to come out fifth. Will 113 be lucky for him? I wonder. The other matadors are Curro Vázquez and Oscar Higares, a young matador from Madrid who took the alternativa the year before in this same Feria de Otoño.

At one o'clock I get off the metro at the Sevilla stop in the center of town. Workers from the newspaper *Ya* are striking and shredding newspapers as a protest. The wind whips up little whirlwinds of oversized confetti and spreads it through the streets as if in mock celebration of something grand.

When I come out through the swinging door of the Café Gijón after lunch, it is blowing a gale. Later I can feel the wind inside the Plaza de Toros at the bar of Tendido Ten as it sucks through the doorways. When I take my seat in the barrera of Tendido Ten, the sprinklers wetting down the sand seem to rain on us as the wind picks up the droplets and blows them intermittently onto our heads. I put my pen down on the ledge in front of me and the wind picks it up, twirls it, and blows it back in my lap. Yet the ring has almost filled; only a few seats in Tendido Five, on the "sunny" side up top, are vacant. Today anything anyone does will be against all odds, but more than twenty thousand aficionados have come, just in case. Where, I wonder, are the Reyes Magos when we need them?

Pablo Chopera sits down next to me, and because we have never met formally, although I have known his father Manolo Chopera for many years, he introduces himself. "I know who you are," I say.

Pablo Chopera slyly reverses the game: "And I know who you are—you're the Norteamericano who's doing the book on Rincón."

"Yes," I say. "How did you know?"

"Hombre! Luis Alvarez. Luis Alvarez. Have a whiskey?" He stops the vendor and orders two, giving me one. I start to protest that I do not drink when I am shooting pictures, but he intervenes: "Otherwise you're going to freeze to death. Here's to César, a gran figura del toreo, and to your success. It'll keep your hands from shaking."

I thank him for the toast, take a sip, and put my tall plastic glass on the ledge in front of me to write something in my notebook. As I do, a gust of wind rattles the glass and I reach up to catch it. It does not spill over, but a malevolent whirlwind flips sand from the arena all over us and into our drinks. Laughing and wiping sand off our faces, we order replacements.

I am wondering how the corrida can start. And, in fact, Curro Vázquez, as senior matador, wants to suspend, and so does Rincón, but the empresario complains they have no clear dates for a postponement. Rincón will say afterwards that the matadors had not come to Madrid simply to kill another corrida (*El Mundo*, October 2, 1993), but kill it they would, in spite of the hurricane blasts creating havoc out in the ring.

The main item of note in the first bull concerns Curro Vázquez's peón Antonio Briceño, who missteps and takes twenty centimeters of horn in his left leg. When he comes off the horn, his taleguilla is ripped and you can see the bloody "mouth" gaping on the inside of his thigh.

Mariposito's name—little butterfly—misrepresents the second bull altogether. Antonio Caballero will write: "A frivolous and deceitful name for a war criminal, muscular, black, uncertain and treacherous, one who sought out the thighs of the matador with the sharpened hook of his left horn, intent on killing him" (*Diario 16*, October 5, 1993).

Rincón receives Mariposito with five verónicas and a media, along the fence to stay out of the wind, and the crowd, ready for "their torero," roars approval with increasing olés as he makes it plain from the outset he has not come to trifle. Mariposito turns quickly after each pass and charges back, but Rincón, unperturbed, his feet firmly planted, swings the cape just ahead of the horns, advancing a step with each pass. When he twists Mariposito around in the media verónica, he is directly in front of us, and through the

Figure 28. Pablo Chopera. Pablo and his brother Oscar are the Chopera heirs. Along with their father, Manolo, they are the most powerful empresarios in the taurine world, controlling rings in Latin America, Spain, and France. It is pure coincidence that I sit next to him.

lens I watch the animal trying to hook his left horn back at the torero (plate 14a).

The wind rises as Anderson Murillo picks, shooting the stick and earning a resounding ovation (he will win picador of the year from *El Ruedo*), and Rincón can do nothing now but defend himself. Choosing a lull after the second pick, Oscar Higares attempts a quite, but Mariposito has spent himself bravely in the horse and falls down. Monaguillo grabs the animal by the tail and lifts, bringing him up again. (I mention this because it will have a bearing on the second half of the corrida. For now, suffice it to say that the animal falls but the presidente does not send him back to the corrals). The bull recovers in banderillas and Curro Cruz puts in two stylish pairs to much applause.

Rincón trots out, dedicates the life of Mariposito to the público of Madrid, and begins one of the most emotional faenas I have ever seen. It is another classic battle of wills: clever David with his secret sling of cloth against the awesome force of the double-axed Goliath. But there is one difference this time: the dark Philistine has an unpredictable and treacherous ally in the gale-force wind that, without warning, strips the cloth of all its power.

Rincón begins near the fence in Tendido Nine, the place in the plaza with the least wind. Mariposito, his head held high, permits four derechazos (plate 15a), putting his head down and charging through, but in the pase de pecho he hooks out with the left horn, catching Rincón's sleeve, nearly pulling him over. The olés and the applause drown out the noise of the wind. Never have I felt the entire plaza in Madrid so on the edge of its collective seat with emotion and with support for a torero. The double danger of the wind and the animal escapes no one. On Rincón's face no sign of fear shows and his eyes have darkened in their concentration: *You do it alone.*

Rincón cites de frente, nailing his axis leg in the sand, and Mariposito follows the cloth through but begins to turn on Rincón even before his back legs have completed the trajectory of the pass, seeking out the man behind the cloth. Normally such a quadruped's momentum takes him beyond the man, but Mariposito so avidly seeks the body that he cuts himself short, twisting in less than his own length, ending up out of position for the next pass.

Rincón crosses in front of the bull to correct, forcing the horns to turn toward the lure. When Mariposito charges the second time, he twists himself around Rincón, again pushing him out of position. In between the passes silence falls on the ring, turning each pass into a single heroic gesture.

In the pase de pecho, the left horn again strikes the matador's arm, pulling the muleta away. The bull whirls back toward the man, grazing the top of his right hip and propelling him to the ground. Before Rincón lands he is already spinning away from the horns. As he makes the second roll with Mariposito in pursuit, somone flashes a cape from the burladero, distracting the animal's attention. The screams of the crowd in the face of a cornada turn into a collective gasp of relief as Rincón continues rolling out of harm's way.

The ring hums with tension and commentary as the matador returns with the muleta held behind him, showing only his body to the bull. Just as he eases the cloth into position, the wind picks up, fluttering the muleta toward the bull's snout. Rincón waits and Mariposito looks at the flapping cloth, then at the man. Rincón remains motionless until it appears the animal must charge him; then as the wind begins to slacken, he shakes the muleta and calls the bull.

Mariposito takes the cloth, going through, and Rincón steps into position, linking a second pass and eliciting from the crowd a fervent olé. But on the third attempt Mariposito again crowds in, hooking for the man's leg. Applause breaks out as Rincón again waits out the wind. As he brings the muleta forward toward the bull, small pieces of newspaper—used by the sword handlers to determine wind direction—wing their way over the sand between the matador and the fence like harbingers of winter. Rincón cites, bringing his leg forward in classical form, and Mariposito charges as another olé bursts over the plaza like a bubble of sound, the faena reaching a level of condensed emotion unequaled in my experience. Each pass is worth a series, each series a faena, the faena a season (plate 15b).

Rincón eases toward the animal, the muleta behind him waiting out the wind, and again the plaza erupts with applause for the matador's entrega. This time he links two right-handed passes and finishes with a backhanded *trincherazo* on that treacherous left horn, striding away from the bull with an impeccability of spirit that baffles the animal and brings the ring to its feet, awash in the peculiar cathartic elation that can only occur in the plaza de toros. Once again César Rincón is everyman and everyone is with Rincón, in celebration of the spirit's triumph over adversity. Over in Tendido Eight, I spot that ubiquitous aficionado and eternal promoter of toreros Diamante Rubio—dressed, in spite of the cold, in his usual white guayabera shirt and checkered cap—waving his cane in the air and singing hosannas to César Rincón.

Another trincherazo linked to a derechazo brings forth the joyful olés of a público that has already assured itself of its champion's triumph, but Mariposito will not allow that third pass in succession. So Rincón crosses, bringing his groin past the animal's face in a true *alarde de valor* or display of bravery (plate 15c), and forces the bull to swallow separate pairs of passes. The second time he crosses in the animal's face, with the wind flapping the muleta wildly behind him, the público begins chanting: "¡Torero! ¡Torero! ¡Torero!" Battling the wind more than ever, Rincón continues with a final pair and an abaniqueo, fanning the muleta under the bull's nose. Once more the shouts of "¡Torero!" echo through Las Ventas del Espíritu Santo. Pablo Chopera turns to me and says: "He has this *tranquilidad* that transmits to the público so well—because he knows exactly what he is doing." Tranquillity, yes, I think; tranquillity and fire (plate 15d).

Rincón changes swords and decides on a final remate, a low backhanded ayudado, one of his favorite finishing passes. He steps forward citing, the sword extending the muleta, going to his left knee, all in one motion. Mariposito charges the cloth, but halfway through the pass he swings his right horn out of the muleta and hooks, catching the man on the inside of his right knee, inverting him, spinning him in a back flip and a half, lunging upward with the horn thrust (plate 14b). As Mariposito rises in the air—glancing off his target—Rincón falls to the ground, landing on his head and neck, turning a somersault and spinning away. But Mariposito is on him instantly and the crowd watches in open-mouthed horror.

As Rincón rolls, Mariposito hooks forward with his left horn, but as the sickle-shaped horn hooks toward the middle of Rincón's back—like Yiyo's goring—the bull steps on the matador's left leg, halting his momentum. The horn tip rips across the *hombrera,* the shoulder pad, and drives into the sand just beyond Rincón's body, pinning him under the animal's snout. As the bull works his front feet and horns to pry the man from beneath him, Monaguillo's cape arrives from one side, Curro Cruz's from the other, and Rincón, arching his spine and backpedaling as hard as he can, escapes from under the driving hooves.

Battered, bruised, and shaken—but not daunted—Rincón snatches up the muleta and sword and waves off his cuadrilla. His side is obviously paining him, neither of his hands seems to work properly, he cannot stand straight, and he is having trouble breathing: *You're not a machine, you're not a watch. And you can break down.*

Then he focuses—breathing deeply, trying to get his wind back—forces himself to stand straight, and puts a nearly mortal three-quarter sword into the withers of Mariposito. His first attempt with the descabello appears to miss, and Rincón turns in a half circle in disbelief, fearing he has lost the ear. Mariposito goes in a half circle in the other direction, then seizes up as the spinal cord parts, and drops to the ground. Rincón retrieves his montera and salutes the público, his público more than ever. The gale in the ring turns to a blizzard of handkerchiefs. A river of chills runs through me as he takes his triumphal vuelta with the ear. The wind flattens his hair down and blows sand in his eyes, but he is smiling. In spite of the pain, he is smiling and the público is chanting: "¡Torero! ¡Torero! ¡Torero!" *But only a handful make it.*

The rest of the corrida turns into a long anticlimax. As José Antonio del Moral will comment the next day in *Sur* regarding Curro Vázquez and Oscar Higares: "The veteran of Linares and the youngster from Madrid looked like cardboard cutouts next to the Colombian."

When the fifth bull, Campanero—a beautiful bull, aleonado and astifino, who carries his head high—comes into the ring, everyone fully expects Rincón to cut another ear, if it is humanly possible, and to ride out once more through the Puerta de Alcalá. Rincón drops to his knees by the fence in Tendido Nine and gives the galloping animal an over-the-head larga cambiada, followed by one of the best sets of verónicas—the hands low, the pace slow and cadenced—anyone has seen all season. People take to their feet, literally screaming olés at the top of their lungs.

Campanero charges straight and with the least provocation, so Rincón takes him to the horse with four walking chicuelinas and places him with a larga. Has the wind slackened again?

When Campanero charges Pinilla's horse, he stumbles and the rowdies in Tendido Seven begin to "tango-clap" for the bull's removal. He does have a hint of a limp in his right foreleg, but he takes two picks well, without falling, and continues to charge at a gallop. (Remember: Rincón's first bull, which for some reason was not protested, fell down and had to be "jacked up" by the tail. Remember too that the animal recovered and went on to charge and nearly gore Rincón.) Almost certainly Campanero would have been an excellent bull.

Pablo Chopera looks at me and says, "This presidente is quick," meaning with the handkerchief signaling the bull's removal. Not ten seconds later the presidente, Luis Espada, flashes the green pañuelo over the railing, pleasing no one but the fanatics in Tendido Seven. I can only guess what Rincón is thinking as he watches an almost certain triumph return with the steers, now limp-free, to the corrals. And I can only wonder why Luis Espada, a police officer of the correct rank, is so cowed.

The first sobrero is a Julio Puerta bull, number 34, named Corredor, 510 kilos. Corredor does not run much because he falls down. The green flag goes out even before he is picked. In come the steers once more.

The second sobrero, number 72, is an overweight, dusty-colored Concha Navarro bull named Santito, 605 kilos, about which there is nothing saintly. Santito falls the first time in the opening verónicas. He falls again, or collapses, in the horse. Then he falls again and barely regains his feet. Out comes the green handkerchief. In come the steers yet again to guide Santito out, all of which takes forever. The wind picks up, night falls, the lights come on, and Pablo Chopera orders us another whiskey, "So we can survive." But no one even thinks of leaving.

The third sobrero, number 20, is another Julio Puerta animal named Cubito, 537 kilos. Cubito is a manso but he charges the cape. Rincón gives him six verónicas and two medias that again have the ring on their feet, shouting out the olés. A vast majority of the público fervently wants a triumph for "their" torero as much as their torero does.

But Cubito, being manso, barely touches the horses and wears himself out trying to escape. Resignation begins to show on Rincón's face. And fatigue. Monaguillo puts in a stylish pair to applause. Manolo Gil puts in his usual effective pair, spins, and heads for the fence. Cubito lumbers after him, then charges hard to get him. Curro Cruz intervenes with the cape to make the quite, but Cubito shuns the lure and nails Manolo Gil's leg to the fence as he tries to scramble over. The horn thunks loudly into the wood, even though Manolo Gil's leg is in between. Everyone grimaces and Manolo Gil collapses into the arms of comrades who run with him to the enfermería.

Rincón begins by sitting on the estribo and continues on his knees, determined to rip an ear loose from this turgid beast. But is no use: Cubito begins to paw the sand and ceases charging. Rincón takes him out to the center, in spite of the wind, and manages a few heroic derechazos until Cubito refuses to accept more. All the valor of Colombia will not make this animal charge. There is nothing to do but kill.

The day's long journey into night is over. The Spanish season of César Rincón is over. The wind picks up and it is very cold in Las Ventas. Yet as Joaquín Vidal will write the next morning in El País, "People left the plaza toreando, still moved by the impressive torería they had just witnessed." Diamante Rubio stops me in the passageway inside the ring: "¡Hasta el aire se paró!" Even the wind stopped!

In suite 803 of the Foxá, Jorge Molina and our friend Andrés Holguín and I wait with the others for César to emerge from the shower. When he does finally come out to the intimate applause of those present, he is limping from a *cornada envainada,* a dry cornada that has penetrated the abductor muscles in his left leg without breaking the skin, probably from Mariposito's glancing upward thrust. His left thumb has also reopened, and he has contusions all over his body. In spite of the physical discomfort, he comes out in a genial mood, smiling broadly. And while he is very pleased with his own performance, he tells Fernando Bermejo for quotation the next day in El Mundo: "If the presidente, Luis Espada, had not sent back the fifth bull, I believe I would have opened the Puerta Grande." Luis Alvarez reiterates that sentiment to Emilio Martínez for El País, adding that, in spite of a season full of mishaps, Rincón had "at the end become once more the current maximum figura." Most of the critics will agree with Rincón that

Figure 29. Antonio Caballero with César Rincón, Hotel Foxá, October 1, 1993. César finally makes an appearance, coming into the living room of suite 803 of the Foxá. Among those who greet him—and perhaps have some advice for him—is Antonio Caballero, Colombian novelist, political satirist, and taurine critic.

the bull should not have been returned; Espada will even write a letter, published in *El Ruedo* on the fifth, trying to justify his decision.

Before long, however, Rincón must leave for the clinic to be treated for his multiple wounds, so Jorge Molina, Andrés Holguín, and I head downtown to celebrate our torero's triumph without him. This night and the next, everywhere we go we will run into Colombians celebrating the same thing.

The reviews were spectacular. In *El País* the next day Vidal judged that Rincón had proclaimed "his indisputable hegemony over the taurine ranking of matadors [escalafón]."

On the fifth Norberto Carrasco wrote in *El Ruedo*: "On an afternoon wild with cigar smoke and hurricane winds, Rincón . . . once again occupied his throne in Las Ventas as emperor of toreo."

At *El Mundo* the day after the corrida Rubén Amón said that the afición of Madrid "once again proclaimed him the Caesar of toreo and the number one figura of the plaza of Las Ventas." Javier Villán, in the same paper, talked about Rincón's heroism: "The tauromachy displayed yesterday by the Colombian belongs to another dimension from what we customarily see in the rings." The performance was worth "an ear of precolombian gold."

Barquerito's review that day in *Diario 16* was titled "The Passion of Las Ventas for César Rincón." He described the impressive spectacle of a "frenetic captive attention" and "a constant contagious clamor: Rincón was toreando at home. No doubt about it, after his long absence, Rincón was confirmed as a torero of Madrid. And at a great distance from anyone else who is or ever has been. Not even the Antoñete of the two reappearances from retirement could have felt so swept up by the splendid mass of Las Ventas on a day of passion."

Vicente Zabala in *Aplausos* on the eleventh called him simply "the most important matador de toros to have arrived from Hispanoamérica . . . in the last forty years."

Antonio Caballero, in *Diario 16* on the fifth, invoked "the ancient spirit of heroism," comparing Rincón to Hercules precisely because toreo, like one of Hercules' trials, is unnecessary, even superfluous or gratuitous, "prompted only by the intention of being heroic. Rincón carried the heroic spirit, which is what justifies toreo, in his pocket, along with his handkerchief." He concluded: "Toreo can be more beautiful, more artistic, more et cetera. But not more heroic. And heroism is the profound truth of toreo."

José Carlos Arévalo also wrote in praise of Rincón's heroism: "It was not enough for fear to filter into the tendidos, it was necessary to prove the veracity of that hallucinatory and cathartic heroism. And so as it is written, the matador dealt death to the promise of death incarnate in the bull. Once more the inverse tragedy of toreo was consummated in all its purity, the tragedy in which man conquers death to affirm life, his life as well as the lives of the chorus, whose cathartic release flowed through those white pañuelos calling for the most important ear of the temporada" (6T6 27:41).

All season long there had been talk of *los dos Rincones,* the two Rincóns, presumably the Rincón of '91 and the post-'91 Rincón, the former a figurón, the latter somehow lesser, almost as if there were two distinct people at issue. How many times had I heard the naysayers complain, "This is not the same torero." After Madrid no one could doubt it: there was only one Rincón.

After Madrid, in fact, the two Rincones became a joke. A television commentator had quipped something that night that Luis Alvarez would repeat in an apoderado's litany: "¡Para torear así hay que tener dos Rincones!" To torear like that you've got to have two Rincones!

Figure 30. Enrique Ponce, Pamplona, July 12, 1995. This is my favorite photograph of Ponce. Although this Cebado Gago bull is uncharacteristically close to him, crowding him, Enrique retains his elegant, aesthetic style.

The way it seemed to me that season of 1993, Enrique Ponce was ice, Joselito was water, and César Rincón was fire. Enrique Ponce kept himself intentionally aloof or superior, consciously demonstrating an extraordinary technique and a calculatedly elegant, even exquisite, aesthetic style—brilliant and cold. The Valencian was falsely accused of superficiality because he valued elegance above all.

Joselito attempted to erase himself, becoming neither emotionally removed from nor emotionally involved in his best faenas, being instead deep, tranquil, complete, and impartially perfect—transparent and neutral. Joselito, Madrid's own orphan, was criticized as occasionally truant and as volatile with the crowd, but his real battle took place inside.

César Rincón, within the purest and most authentic canons of tauromachy, engaged in a duel of wills with the bull, passionately giving himself to the Promethean struggle—radiant and hot. When his horned opponents

Figure 31. Joselito, Valladolid, September 18, 1996. José with a Torrealta bull, giving the animal an impeccable natural. Note the neutrality of his stance, the tranquillity of his posture.

were unworthy, César Rincón sometimes appeared lackluster, giving rise to the two-Rincóns hypothesis, yet no one was more fiercely competitive.

Theory aside, I knew that these were three of the most accomplished toreros I had ever seen. Enrique Ponce's technical skills and inspired improvisation, Joselito's profound sense of art, including his magnificent ability to kill, and César Rincón's passionate and heroic classicism made for three very different toreros, each extraordinary in his own personal way. Yet I also recognized that it was César Rincón who had stirred the dormant worm of afición in me, that worm that had retreated to the distantmost chambers of my blood, as García Lorca would have said, but that now roared back to life like an awakened dragon. Without Rincón's gift, I would have had no theory about him or about the others.

When the *6T6* rankings for the season came out at the end of November, Joselito took first place. Enrique Ponce came in second with the prediction that he would—if the bulls "respected him"—pass into taurine history with the same rank as Joselito el Gallo, Luis Miguel Dominguín, Paco Camino, and Espartaco. Manzanares—with only forty corridas and twenty-five ears —was third, Espartaco fourth, Jesulín fifth, and César Rincón, with sixty-nine corridas and fifty-two ears, sixth. Never would I feel more at odds with their ranking than this year. They did call Rincón a "figurón del toreo," an "authentic idol in France," and heroic in Madrid (28:16–21), but I still felt they had gravely underestimated him.

Vejer de la Frontera: October 8, 1993

The end of my season with César Rincón comes with a tienta at Borja Domecq's ranch near Vejer de la Frontera. I leave Sevilla early in the morning and drive out through Medina Sidonia, heading south toward the Río Barbate, into the richest pasturage of toros bravos in the world. Eventually I find the gate marked "Jandilla," and the name—from the ancient Laguna de la Janda—conjures up by association the oldest civilization in the Western world, Tartessos, which existed some three thousand years ago, quite possibly near the edge of the now dried-up lake bed just upstream from the ranch on the Barbate.

This country is the epicenter of the taurine world, famous since the days of Greek myth when Hercules came to rustle Geryon's herd of Tartessian castaños, and since Plato's thirdhand assertion in the *Critias* that the kings of Atlantis, which he said lay beyond the Pillars of Hercules, near Cádiz, practiced bull sacrifices and drank the blood of the victims.

At the tienta I meet two visiting Colombian ganaderos, Felipe Rocha, from one of the pioneering families of ganaderos in Colombia, and Lucas Caballero, married to María Emma Mejía, then Colombian ambassador to Spain. Luis Alvarez is there to celebrate his birthday, Julio Vega el Marismeño to train César (plate 16a), Mono to cape, Muri to pick, Maestro Ricardo to drive, and el maestro de Bogotá himself, of course, to test the cows and one semental. After the torrential rain we all drove through yesterday on the road from Madrid, the bright cool day, bathed in slanting light, seems perfect for the testing, and the Atlantic winds are at ease.

What most impresses me about the tienta is the extent to which César works (plate 16b), giving each vaquilla as many passes as he can, exhausting himself and the vacas,[6] while Julio Vega coaches him: "Good, torero, good. Longer, longer—until you break! All the way around! ¡Bien! ¡Bien! ¡Bien, torero!" He is as intense alone as he is with other matadors. "¡Vamos, bonita!" he calls. Let's go, pretty girl! If she balks, he yells insults: "¡Puta! ¡Vamos!"

"¡Vamos, bonita!" yells Muri to a castaña from across the little ring. She hits the horse hard, breaking off one of her horns at the base. The shell of the horn slides off, leaving only the bloody nerve. Yet she never stops charging, even on the side with the missing horn, pursuing Rincón's muleta time after time. Borja Domecq seems to like her spirit. Finally they take her down, clip the nerve, and bandage her horn stump, making me think he wants to try to breed her. The image of that little red vaca, hornless on one side, charging after the muleta with only her limp, bloody nerve will stay with me.

As the wine flows at lunch, the talk turns from bulls and the care, feeding, and raising of them—about which César, himself an incipient ganadero in Colombia, is as passionate as the established ganaderos—to other subjects: the taurine poets Benítez Carrasco, Rafael de León, Fernando Villalón, and of course Federico García Lorca and Rafael Alberti; then to artists of all types ranging from Liza Minnelli to the Colombian painter Fernando Botero; and eventually to antiques, one of Luis's favorite subjects (he tells us Domingo Ortega was his mentor). At one point Monaguillo, inspired by the locale, even sings flamenco to raucous applause.

All of the working toreros beg off in favor of a siesta, and I go outside for a walk. Through the clarity of the afternoon you can see Vejer in the distance. The house itself is a classic Spanish country house, a bull breeder's cortijo, decorated with famous bulls' heads, tiles, and copperware, the kind of house—with grass around it and gravel in the drive and the extensive pastures beyond—and social situation and profession that most toreros aspire to in their retirements. In the planet of the bulls the heros are the matadors, but the social lions are the ganaderos. And among ganaderos, the Domecq clan reigns supreme.

Rincón has come here, among other reasons, to buy stock for his ganadería back home, that costly investment he has made partly out of "responsibility" to the fiesta in Colombia, where good casta is in short supply. At one point during the tienta when we are discussing his ranch, he confesses, "If I'd known what it was going to cost me, I don't think I'd have bought it. But there it is. And now I want to get the best stock I can from Spain."

Today's tienta is a fitting way, I am thinking, looking out to where the Atlantic lies on the other side of Vejer, to spend my last day with César, who will leave for Bogotá in a few days. I will see him next in Colombia, perhaps with Felipe Rocha's bulls. Jorge Molina has invited me to come to the Feria de Cali, the Sevilla of South America, and I am already looking forward to the trip. I know very well there is only one Rincón, one Rincón in Spain, in France, and in América. That little *rincón*, that corner or spot, of taurine truth is named Julio César, and I am very interested in seeing him in his own dominion.

Cali: December 28 and 30, 1993; January 2 and 4, 1994

Cali's feria, from Christmas to Epiphany, has become one of the premiere taurine events in the Americas. On December 27, I fly to the land of eternal springtime, known to the locals as "the branch office of heaven." Santiago de Cali, less than five hundred kilometers north of the equator, lies at a thousand meters on the eastern flank of the Cordillera Occidental of the Andes, just above the juncture of the Río Cali and the larger Cauca, the north-flowing river that gives its name to the region. When you approach for a landing as the tropical night is falling, Cali looks like a tiara of diamonds draped around the neck of the sierra.

Julio César, the Molina family's driver (proud to be a namesake of the national hero), takes me to the Residencia Stein, a mustard-colored colonial house crowning a steep hill in the residential area, high up near the source of the Cali. The air is soft, and a large ceiba tree watches over the locked wrought-iron gate (so does an armed guard).

Jorge Molina serves on the Junta Técnica, the group that approves the bulls for each corrida, so I am able, through him, to spend time "backstage" at the Cañaveralejo ring. Corridas in Cali begin at 3:00 in the afternoon and the temperature is usually warm. On the twenty-eighth it is 33° and humid as José Ortega Cano, César Rincón, and Joselillo de Colombia II (Edgar Zúñiga) line up for the paseo. The Cañaveralejo, which looks from the outside something like a concrete version of an old-fashioned wide-mouthed champagne glass, has filled to overflowing with eighteen thousand aficionados, as it will every day, the seats sold out since they went on sale the previous March. Caleños are proud of their feria, and the profits from the corridas, overseen by the municipal government, are used to construct hospitals and parks.

Abraham Domínguez's bulls do not turn out to be as good as they looked in the corrals this morning. The first one catches Ortega Cano but fails to gore him. The second, number 110, Arenillo, 489 kilos, takes only one pick, yet the ring claps along with the band's stirring rendition of "España Cañí," perhaps the best-known pasodoble of all, as César Rincón begins his faena. All at once, with the collective alegría that characterizes Cali, the whole ring has joined Rincón in an act of unanimous solidarity and support. Rincón follows the luckless manso to the fence and extracts more faena than the animal deserves, but a triumph is not possible (plate 17).

Number 140 looks and acts like his brother, only worse. Rincón can but dispatch him. The crowd whistles loudly as the carcass plows out behind the mules, and you can feel the disappointment settle on the ring—Rincón's and the público's—as the animal disappears. But as César Rincón and his eighteen thousand incondicionales know, he still has three more afternoons, and nobody can be that unlucky in the sorteos.

After the corrida, at a reception at the Casona del Peñón, I meet many people important in the taurine world of Colombia, as well as others from Spain and Venezuela: matadors, managers, breeders, critics, the entire spectrum of the taurine world. Yet the two I remember most are the daughters of Ernesto González Caicedo, María Fernanda, called Nanda, and María del Mar, called Mares. I met them this morning in the corrals with their younger sister, Jimena, and I am pleased to get to know them better now. Nanda is not only a friend of César—along with Jorge Molina she rushed to the hospital in Palmira in 1990 to offer blood—she wrote her master's thesis in psychology for the Universidad Javeriana in Bogotá on tauromachy, often using César Rincón as her prime example.

On December 30 the cartel promises more than it delivers: Ortega Cano, César Rincón, and Enrique Ponce with Ambaló bulls. Unfortunately the Ambaló bulls have little casta, which produces rumblings in the crowd since Eduardo Estela, the president of the Junta Directiva or board of directors of the Cañaveralejo, is the son of the ganadero, José María Estela.

The planet of the bulls is always small, and in a country such as Colombia it is even smaller than usual. As long as things run smoothly no one objects, but as soon as anything goes wrong—and the bulls are and have been below the acceptable level—words such as "oligarchy" and "incest" begin to crop up. This afternoon the crowd becomes at times enraged and protests throughout the entire corrida, especially with the chant "¡Ganadero, pícaro!" implying there has been some crooked "picaresque" complicity.

Ortega Cano's first bull butts up against the fence and refuses to move. Rincón's first, an *ensabanado* or grayish-white bull that looks interesting and exotic the way all such unusually colored animals do (plate 18a), turns out to be blind and manso and has to be removed from the ring by ropes. The substitute, number 206, Rumbero, 494 kilos, also turns out to be manso. Rincón works hard but the animal refuses to take the cloth. Ponce draws another impossible manso, and Ortega Cano's bull likewise proves useless. So far the main item of interest is the crowd's reaction.

The fifth bull, number 223, 460 kilos, named auspiciously Colombiano, we think may be a little "less bad." Rincón dedicates the animal to his padrino Antonio Chenel, Antoñete: "Maestro, I'm dedicating this bull to you because of the great affection I feel for you, because of the admiration I have for you, and because it is a pleasure to have you here in my country, where you gave me the alternativa. I hope I will never let you down. Va por usted."

The bull Rincón originally wanted to dedicate to him was the white bull—which looked rather like the white bull that Antoñete "immortalized" in 1966—but he has had to adjust his plans. Colombiano will have to do.

Rincón begins by finding Colombiano's distance, then giving him a series of "made-in-Rincón" derechazos, the hand low and smooth, the velocity of the cloth exactly right (plate 18b). Spontaneous combustion breaks out in the tendidos and the applause "smokes." Then comes a series on the left, the passes linked together and finished impeccably, and Antoñete exclaims: "Look how he places himself! Such truth, such feeling in his toreo!" When Rincón remains in place, scant centimeters from the horn, as the bull balks halfway through a pass, Antoñete shouts: "¡Cuidado!" Careful! When Colombiano goes through, Chenel says, "No doubt about it, he is the best. What an emotional faena!"

After a long and varied faena, Rincón kills slightly off center and has to use the descabello twice, reducing the prize to one ear. When he comes to the fence to retrieve his montera, he tells Antoñete: "Maestro, pardon me, the sword went in a little contrary on me."

Antoñete replies: "I admire you greatly. You have become a grand torero. The sword is not important; you went in with your heart." César's eyes water as he turns away and Chenel confides to the journalist Luis Noé Ochoa: "I consider him my son."

Before the corrida Maestro Chenel has remarked to Ochoa, "Rincón has raised the bar very high, not just for Colombian toreros but for some Spaniards as well. And it is very good for the fiesta that there be a torero, from Colombia or Mexico, from whatever country, to put things in their proper place and to say: 'Señores, this is how you torear and you are going to have your work cut out.' And César has that virtue of being able to fire up everybody, the public and his compañeros, and that is fundamental, to have rivalry in the plaza" (*El Tiempo,* December 31, 1993).

Today, however, little rivalry surfaces as Enrique Ponce fails to persuade the final manso to charge, and the next morning the papers proclaim Rincón número uno in the world.

On New Year's Eve, Jorge Molina takes me to a fiesta out at Mares's house. I spend much of my time with her father, Ernesto González Caicedo, and her mother, Halma Valencia, daughter of the former president of Colombia, Guillermo León Valencia, who ended the civil wars of his period, and granddaughter of the Colombian poet Guillermo Valencia. This night we become friends—especially through our mutual admiration for César Rincón.

Many matadors also attend and spend the evening dancing with the Panamerican Sugar Festival beauty queens from numerous countries. The evening on the ample terrace under gigantic Andean trees is sweet with tropical fragrances, and, as a salsa band approaches ecstacy, an equatorial moon rises over the Cordillera Central to see in the New Year.

On the afternoon of January 2, up in César's room in the Hotel Torre de Cali, I tell him about ganadero Juan Fermín Rocha's prediction that, in number 100, he has drawn the bull of the corrida. He looks up at me, shaking his head, and says, "I don't want to hear about it. It's always the same thing. What a great lote I've drawn. And then they come out falling down or jam their *culos* [butts] into the fence or they knock themselves out or they don't charge at all. I haven't had a really good bull in so long, I probably wouldn't know what to do with it."

No one says anything.

"What's the cartel today, Ortega Cano and who?" asks César.

"Joselito," says Luis Carlos.

"¡Me cago en la leche!⁷ I never get a good bull with him! The problem is, there aren't any bulls in this country. They're always the same, the same bulls over and over and they're never any good."

More silence. For some time.

I notice Luis Carlos is distraught. He seems to be looking for something. Meanwhile a French photographer takes pictures of César dressing, and César, who has not put on his suspenders yet, does not want his picture taken with the front of his taleguilla hanging down like a bib. "Tell him no," he instructs me. "Tell him I don't want him to take my picture like this."

Then the real problem surfaces. Luis Carlos cannot find the *tirantas* (in

Figure 32. Drawing of lots, Cali, January 2, 1994. The matadors dread sorteos. They seldom, if ever, attend. Federico García Lorca's friend Ignacio Sánchez Mejías was killed by the only bull he drew himself, in Manzanares on August 13, 1934. The rolled cigarette papers with the lots written inside control the destinies of each matador.

Spain, *tirantes*). It seems that somehow there are no suspenders. "It's always the same thing," says César, quietly. "It's always the same." We wait in silence. "It's the same thing that always happens, Don Luis. Always the same."

The suspenders have vanished. Or have been overlooked somewhere. Luis Carlos, frantic, sends out to round up a pair. Anywhere. One of the banderilleros offers a pair but they are too big, and César says, "Or am I just pissing everybody off? How am I supposed to stay calm? Luis Carlos can't get any tirantas because the hotel people haven't got a fucking clue." Eventually another pair appears. I do not know how or from where, nor am I about to ask.

Waiting finally in front of the elevator, Luis Alvarez says to César: "Well, I'm glad."

"Why?"

"Because every time we have a problem like this, it's Puerta Grande."

"¡Hombre! Don Luis, don't fuck with me. They're only coincidences."

"Yes, but they're coincidences that happen."

I say nothing. Luis Carlos is quiet.

On the radio on the way to the ring, I hear Antoñete talking about César's brindis to him: "It's one of the best of my life. I felt it very deeply and it was very moving, what he said." While I listen, I am wondering if Luis is right about the temperament and the success. Can it not just as well happen the other way around? Is it not the pressure that drives him on? Is not the show of temper a natural escape valve, a by-product of nerves caused by the pressure? Is Luis engaging in a strange superstition of his own? Or being the best apoderado he can be?

The Achury Viejo bulls disappoint us for the most part. Ortega Cano stirs mild applause from the crowd in the first bull, but his kill precludes any ears. The tone of mediocrity seems destined to continue yet another day.

But Rincón receives the second—number 98, Buñalero, 500 kilos—on his knees, with two spectacular renditions of the larga cambiada, followed by loudly celebrated verónicas. Unfortunately Buñalero looks to be what they call *justito de fuerzas*, with just enough strength to sustain his charge.

Rincón has the animal picked gingerly and begins the faena with four pases por alto while sitting on the estribo. The Cali crowd hums, claps in time, cheers, yells, roars, and seems on the edge of breaking into song. When he takes Buñalero to los medios and begins his long, rhythmic derechazos, we find ourselves suddenly in the presence of *toreo grande,* the great and sentient toreo that immediately eclipses all the lesser efforts we have been seeing all week (plate 18c). As Spanish critic Manuel Molés will say in tomorrow's *El País* (de Colombia), "Rincón came to blow the place to pieces."[8] Naturales and derechazos, some citing from as far away as ten meters, succeed each other as flags fly, music plays, the crowd claps. "The best thing about the faena," Molés will write, "was the mixture of passion and talent. His fire in no way blurred the mental coolness necessary to handle this bull, a good enough bull that he made even better."

Rincón lines Buñalero up and drives in, but hits something, managing less than a *media estocada*. As he must use the descabello, he loses the second ear.

Joselito remains absently withdrawn and, in spite of getting a decent animal, cannot coax more than a faint petition for an ear from the crowd. Ortega Cano, after elegant naturales but a weak kill, takes one of his interminable, preening vueltas but without an ear.

Number 100, Barrentino, weighs 464 kilos and takes only one pick. He proves to be a toro *quedón,* a noncharger, and a manso who turns defensive and tricky. How, I wonder, can an animal look so regal, so splendid, so beautiful in the corrals, and then act as though he had a dairy cow's blood in the ring? Rincón does the best he can, but no blood comes from this taurine turnip. As he kills, Barrentino hooks up and catches Rincón's left elbow, causing him obvious pain. So much for Luis's theory, I think to myself, although it was close.

Joselito dislikes his formidable opponent, a prehistoric-looking burraco with high curving horns. But the animal is strong and charges hard, putting his head as far into the cloth as his imposing, upswept horns will allow. Joselito—still playing Hamlet—wants nothing to do with him and kills him quickly. What a shame, I am thinking, that Rincón did not get this animal instead of the feckless manso he drew. The wild bronca Joselito receives creates a tropical storm of voices and gestures around him as he leaves the plaza, in stark contrast to the warm applause and shouts of "¡Torero! ¡Torero!" César Rincón elicits.

At 10:15 Jorge Molina and Andrés Holguín and I are having dinner at the Bistro de París when Nanda and Mares enter unexpectedly with news: "César's elbow is dislocated and they have immobilized it in a cast." The good news is, "he should be able to torear day after tomorrow," in the scheduled mano a mano with Enrique Ponce.

The next night I realize I am getting sick. Jorge Molina and Andrés Holguín tell me I have dengue fever, a tropical virus they say everyone gets during Feria in Cali. Jorge has been sick for several days already but I find that little consolation. Nor does my biblical visitation about this book (mentioned in the prologue) in the early hours of the next morning alleviate my symptoms. I try to ignore it, but the fever, chills, sweats, and aches will not go away.

Before lunch I take a taxi to Ernesto González Caicedo's house for a talk about Rincón's career. The open patio inside his house in the Santa Rita section contains tropical plants, live birds, and a huge Christmas tree. In the study where I wait, drawings by Antonio Casero and Roberto Domínguez, photos of Guillermo León Valencia with John F. Kennedy, de Gaulle, and Franco, and a self-portrait by María Caicedo Méndez (1908–1988) catch my eye. Oriental rugs cover the tile floors, and dark wood and leather furniture give the room an elegant warmth.

Ernesto hobbles in, another victim of the dengue, and we sit across his desk from each other trying not to show the extent of our suffering. Between coughs and silences, Ernesto tells me about the great bulls of his that César Rincón has killed: Paquero in the Crotaurinos corrida in Bogotá in 1991; Ebanista in a mano a mano with Ponce in Bogotá last year; Corredor, the bull he pardoned in Ibagué in 1992; Profesor, another indulto, in Sogamosa in 1985; and Azteca, the bull he gave Rincón to kill after his goring in Palmira in 1990. Then he gives me a sheaf of five handwritten pages listing all his corridas in which César Rincón has performed, as well as all the tientas. I am surprised that he has taken the time to look up all this material and copy it out. He lists a total of twenty corridas between December 31, 1982, and December 12, 1993, in which César Rincón cut thirty-two ears and one tail, with two indultos. Finally Ernesto, who is suffering more than I, excuses himself, telling me, "I hope I'll see you this afternoon in the Cañaveralejo. I don't want to miss César and Enrique's mano a mano."

The noise in the ring throbs through my head as though my skull were a drum submerged in a swimming pool and beaten on by eighteen thousand homicidal maniacs. I review my notes and replay snatches of the mental tape of my conversation with Ernesto, hearing him say, in that weird way in which fever distorts everything: "Two or three years before he broke through in Spain he was doing *toreo de verdad* [true toreo] here in Colombia. The toreo of Paco Camino and Antoñete. It's incredible that somehow that toreo of Antoñete and Camino had gotten lost in Spain."

The Guachicono bulls of Luis Fernando Castro figure among the best in Colombia. Castro has had excellent luck with two imported sementales of Torrestrella, Alvaro Domecq's premier ganadería. Will these bulls follow the lamentable lead of most of the animals we have seen in this cycle, or will they charge and give us, finally, in this last corrida, what we have all come hoping to see? Remembering that Añonuevo—the bull with which Rincón had rescued his career on January 1, 1987, in this ring—came from the ganadería of Guachicono, I wonder if there will be any such animal today.

Rincón receives the first animal, number 211, Sabanero, 488 kilos, with some deference, as it is immediately clear the animal has evil intentions. In the faena Sabanero grows worse, turning into an assassin and a quedón, a killer who waits rather than charging. Rincón forces the animal to charge against his will. The público is shouting "¡Mátalo!"—kill him!—but Rincón pushes the bull instead, invading his terrain repeatedly, finding the proper distance to oblige him to charge. Eventually the bull complies, completely against his will, and Rincón breaks the animal's spirit (plates 19a and 19b). After a pinchazo, he gets in a good sword, cutting an ear and setting a heated tone for the corrida.

Ponce replies with number 230, Vengador, 484 kilos, making smooth derechazos and naturales with a sweet animal. Elegant as a Nordic prince, with never a wrinkle nor a drop of blood on his suit of lights (plate 19c), Enrique Ponce finishes his faena with *adornos*, flourishes, and an abaniqueo that, in his rendition, looks like choreography. After a fine sword, delivered straight in, he cuts a well-deserved ear.

The third bull, number 238, Dije, 436 kilos, looks too much like a gnu. He has an odd, short charge and does not follow the cape well. Rincón begins por alto, going into derechazos, but the ugly toro cuts in on him. Rincón willfully subjects the wildebeesty animal, commanding, "¡Coge! ¡Coge! ¡Coge!" When Dije does take it, Rincón snarls, none too quietly, "¡Hijueputa!" and the crowd celebrates with olés.

On the left Dije cuts in as well but Rincón dominates him with a combination of distance, cloth, and voice. Dije gives up, obeying, and Rincón links a long series of derechazos, clearly enjoying himself now. In the tendidos, people scream with fear as he drops to his knees, driving the animal before him with the rabid afición of a novillero. Then the shout starts and I count the repetitions: "¡Torero! ¡Torero! ¡Torero! ¡Torero! ¡Torero!" When Rincón plunges the sword to the hilt and Dije staggers backward and falls dead from the single stroke, the ring seems to go insane. Cali has waited through ten corridas for someone to bring them to catharsis, and now the prince of tropical heat has accomplished the long-awaited miracle. "Their" prince.

Colombian flags from the Peña Taurina Santiago de Cali, Córdoba hats from the Peña La Sultana, and red berets from the Peña de Cañaveralejo fly into the arena as César Rincón takes a slow vuelta with both ears, his face a quiet portrait that shows he has done precisely what he intended to do.

Barba Azul, number 234, at 528 kilos, takes up a querencia at the fence and will not budge. The animal simply quits, and when a bull quits there is nothing to do but kill it, which Enrique Ponce does, right up against the fence and with great decorum, to a fine ovation.

Tapabocas, number 228, at 452 kilos, does not like the cape. Can César Rincón subject this toro bronco as well? The animal slings *tornillazos*, great corkscrewing swipes, at Rincón's neck and head, and no distance or technique works. Finally he kills the animal as best he can, and I reflect in my notebook that some animals cannot be subjected under any circumstances, meaning not even by César Rincón or Enrique Ponce on their best days. Rincón's face registers an expression of resignation, ma non troppo, with three ears already cut.

Ponce has one more opportunity. Rayo de Luna, number 209, at 512 kilos, a burraco, charges bravely into the horse but refuses to go through with the muleta. Does Ponce "drown" him, staying too close? After many half derechazos, interspersed with molinetes, he goes to his knees, then throws away the sword and muleta in a last-ditch alarde, something I have never seen him resort to before. Then Ponce gets in a deep pinchazo. The bull goes down, and his banderillero gives Rayo de Luna the coup de grâce with the *puntilla,* or dagger. The crowd, in a generous mood, demands the ear.

Both of them go up on shoulders—after César Rincón insists that Enrique Ponce accompany him—but Ponce, not having cut the requisite two ears from one animal, will forgo the Puerta Grande.[9] Meanwhile they parade around the ring in a slow vuelta to ecstatic shouts of "¡Torero! ¡Torero!" (plate 19d).

Up in César's room at the Torre de Cali the usual chaos of a huge triumph ensues. César has clearly shown himself to be the triunfador of the feria with five ears, as well as the winner of the Señor de los Cristales trophy for the best faena. Most important, he has emerged clearly as the greatest torero of any nationality in Las Américas. As a result, everyone in Cali is trying to get into his room to congratulate him.

After the usual abrazo and congratulations, I notice that his left thumb is bandaged. "What happened? You didn't cut it again, did you?"

He looks at the thumb as though it belonged to someone else, shakes his head as if he had no control over the thumb's destiny, then looks up at me and says: "Sí, hombre. Can you believe that?"

"Your Achilles' thumb."

"My Achilles' thumb." But nothing can take the look of triumph, which he is trying unsuccessfully to hide, off his face.

The next day in Manizales, in a corrida of La Carolina bulls we could not get to, César Rincón cut four ears, Enrique Ponce cut two symbolic ears from the sixth bull, named Bolero, a bull he pardoned, and the aficionados of Manizales carried Rincón, Ponce, and the ganaderos through the streets of the city for hours.

As I flew home, I perused the papers and another phrase of Molés, in *El País* (de Colombia) on the fifth, caught my attention: "The Spaniards who came to Cali are going to end up becoming Colombian ambassadors to Spain. Such is the strength of this land and its people. There is no other truth."

1994

When I left Colombia I knew, in spite of my biblical dream, that I did not have the book finished. I would join César Rincón in Sevilla at the end of spring semester and follow him for as much of the temporada of 1994 as I could. Then I would have plenty of experience and more than enough material. That was how I reasoned, but as usual it did not prove to be exactly the way things turned out.

Sevilla: April 19 and 22, 1994

The ambiente in Sevilla during Feria, especially the taurine ambiente, has no equal anywhere. Aside from the Maestranza itself, two places become the center of attention: the lobby of the Hotel Colón and, particularly for the foreign aficionados who gather each year for the rites of spring, the Bodegón Torre del Oro. My first night at the Bodegón, Juanito, son-in-law of the owner, shows me a photograph of Yiyo and Lucio Sandín in the patio de caballos in Pamplona, taken on July 13, 1985.

Yiyo, in street clothes, shakes Sandín's hand, obviously wishing him suerte, as Sandín in his *traje de luces,* his suit of lights, waits for the paseo to form. Behind the two young stars stands the unknown César Rincón, also in street clothes, trying unsuccessfully to shake Sandín's hand as well. In the photo he looks hungry and he is saying with his eyes: "I want to be one of you; I can do this too. Yo. Yo también." Juanito shows me the photo and says nothing, merely wagging his head in the style of Sevilla, not having to remark that Sandín would go on to lose an eye and retire, that Yiyo would be dead within two months, and that the unknown skinny Colombian would become a figurón.

At 6:30 the next afternoon, the nineteenth, the flags flap over the Maestranza and the wind feels chilly. Víctor Mendes, César Rincón, and Joselito make the paseo under a partly cloudy sky, but the bulls of the Marqués de Domecq lack class and "run out of gasoline," prohibiting any brilliance whatsoever.

The ambiente of Feria never lets down, but the bulls—the animals themselves—continue to disappoint everyone. In the Hotel Colón the taurine world agglomerates as nowhere else. One midday I look around the lobby and write down the names of the people I see: José Luis Lozano, in charge of the Madrid ring; Pepe Luis Segura, Ortega Cano's manager; the taurine painter Loren and his wife Lucía; Curro Fetén, the journalist (one of the funniest men in the world); the Marqués de Albaserrada and his wife with the American aficionada Kitty Witwer, who wrote *Divine Addiction* about her passion for the fiesta; Juan Antonio Ruiz Román, Espartaco, matador de toros; Juan Serrano, Finito, matador de toros; Emilio Muñoz, matador de toros—who this very afternoon will have the only important triumph of the feria, cutting three ears from the Torrestrella bulls of Alvaro Domecq and going out on shoulders through the coveted Puerta del Príncipe—with his father and his cuadrilla; Juan Ruiz Palomares, the apoderado of Enrique Ponce; Victoriano Valencia—whose daughter Paloma is Enrique Ponce's fiancée—former matador de toros and currently the apoderado of Pedrito de Portugal; José Luis Cazalla, the apoderado of Luis de Pauloba; Manolo Chopera's sons, Oscar and Pablo; Alberto Borda and Edgardo Pallarés, empresarios from Colombia; the Conde de la Maza, whose bulls on April 11 were better than the average for this feria; ganadero and friend Manuel Fernández Palacios, at whose ranch I will spend several fine afternoons; Ignacio Usechi Goñi, president of the Club Taurino de Pamplona; Patxi Alemán, who runs the Hotel Maisonnave, home away from home in Pamplona; Carlos Balañá, of the Barcelona family of empresarios; Vicente Salamanca, matador de toros; John Fulton, matador de toros; and Luis Alvarez—and these are only those in evidence at the moment I make the list and only the ones I know. Everyone who is anyone in the planet of the bulls eventually shows up at the Colón.

Luis looks rather down, I think, and when we speak I ask him what is wrong. "Nada, hombre, nada. Just the usual weak bulls and the usual injustice from the *palco* [the president's box]. Nada."

I nod in sympathy. "Maybe," I say, "the Núñez del Cuvillos will charge tomorrow. Have you seen them?"

"Yes. They look fine. Perhaps they will charge," he says, giving me a look. It was a Núñez del Cuvillo that gored Rincón the year before.

The corrida on the twenty-second—rescheduled from the fifteenth when it rained—takes place at noon and is a disaster, especially for César Rincón, who does not seem to have taken charge of his temporada. Up in room 518 in the Colón, I notice immediately that Luis Alvarez continues to appear crestfallen. César describes himself to me as *cabreado*, pissed off, adding, "I came to Sevilla with great *ilusión* [hope] to triumph and all I did was 'crash head on' into the 'raw material.'" Luis adds nothing to this declaration, and the fact that César had been given several prizes for his performance last year—including one the night before, presented to him here in the Colón by the head surgeon of the Maestranza, Dr. Ramón Vila, the man who had operated on him—does not seem to ameliorate the gloom now.

Luis Carlos and Juanito are quickly packing up everything around them for a corrida tomorrow in Zaragoza with Joselito and Enrique Ponce. Given César's foul mood and the foul weather prediction, I decide not to leave Sevilla.

At lunch upstairs at the tiny taurine restaurant El Donald, with Antonio Caballero and Cristina, ganadero Felipe Rocha and his wife María Francisca, the ganadero (and Antonio's cousin) Lucas Caballero, and the Colombian critic Carlos Ilián and his wife Marlo, I hear many stories about César Rincón, but we all agree that at this moment he does not seem himself. Morale? His health? No one has a convincing answer.

In Zaragoza the Diego Puerta bulls were mansos and dangerous. Joselito cut an ear. César Rincón and Enrique Ponce heard only silence. I was glad I had not gone.

Back in Madrid the day after the corrida in Zaragoza, Dr. Pedro Guillén operated on Rincón's left shoulder for acute bursitis and tendonitis. The condition had been bothering him for several years and had, as he told Emilio Martínez, kept him "from being at a hundred percent" (*El País,* May 2, 1994). He and Luis Alvarez had decided now was the time, with San Isidro coming soon, to remedy a condition for which he had had to be *infiltrado,* injected, with cortisone on many afternoons in order to be able to perform, and which had flared up alarmingly after his second appearance in

Sevilla. Their plan revolved around a reappearance in the Roman coliseum in Nîmes on May 20, after extensive training in the campo. He would miss several corridas, but the real question was, would he be ready for Madrid in late May—ready mentally and physically?

Dr. Guillén deemed the operation a success. In an interview in *Aplausos* on May 2, Rincón said he did not want to talk about Sevilla: "I'm not looking for excuses for my performances, but all the commentators have pointed out it was one of the worst ferias in recent years, due to the very poor *juego* [play or charge] of the bulls. Mine and those of my compañeros."

The interviewer remarked that many had commented that César Rincón was not having his "best moment."

Rincón replied: "I know that and I would like to take this opportunity to express my disagreement. It so happens that everybody expects to see César Rincón as a triunfador every day and that is impossible if the bulls do not charge. I cannot create emotion with a stationary bull. I need bulls that come from a distance, that repeat. In a word, brave bulls, with fierceness, with their problems, which I will take responsibility to solve. I did not have such bulls in Sevilla." He ended by noting that his spirits were good, in spite of Sevilla, that he was prepared for Madrid, but that he "needed bulls with thrust."

I had heard César and others say the same thing and knew it was true: he did need bulls that charged hard. Unlike Jesulín, working in turn from the style of Paco Ojeda, working from the style of Dámaso González, working from aspects of the style of the original El Cordobés, right on back to Manolete—all of whom, in reverse succession, had mastered the technique of creating a faena from a short- or non-charging animal—César Rincón needed a bull that charged, even a fierce bull with problems, as he admitted, certainly a bull with thrust. Looking back on it all, I am reminded of two things: the old piece of wisdom "Be careful what you pray for," and Belmonte's (or was it El Guerra's?) dictum about praying you never drew a truly brave bull.

I called César the day the interview appeared.

"I'm fine. I feel good. My shoulder hurts but that's normal. Now we'll see if they've really cured me. I have ten more days of therapy. Gradually I'll do toreo de salón and after that work in the campo with vaquillas. It's not really planned yet. You know how it is, a day at a time. But I will make Nîmes on the twentieth, one way or another."

"Did your shoulder affect you in Sevilla?"

"The truth is, it didn't. I was infiltrado. It only hurt afterwards. What happened was that none of the bulls charged. And they only understand ears. The press jumps on anything it can, your shoulder, whatever it is at the time."

"And the público was rather cold to you, no?"

"Ah, yes. As usual in Sevilla if one is not from Sevilla. Never mind that last year I had given them everything. Almost my life." He sounded good, firm, upbeat. "Yes, everyone here is fine. Gracias a Dios."

Not just upbeat, totally believable, completely sincere, as usual.

"I'll see you in Nîmes," I said.

Nîmes: May 20, 1994

I leave for Nîmes on the morning of May 19, driving up through Granada, past Víznar where García Lorca was executed and dumped into a common grave on August 19, 1936. I look back at the Sierra Nevada, still thickly covered in snow, behind the city. You can see the city of Granada and the snow-covered peaks above, but in between the mountains are obscured by heavy clouds, making the snowy peaks seem to float in the sky like that Muslim vision of Paradise. Driving hard, I wind through the badlands of Almería, past towns with the landscape of nightmares, finally emerging into the rich huerta country at Murcia, ochre and low, huddled in its groves against the sierra. Pushing on past prosperous Alicante and the high-rise sprawl on the beach at Benidorm, I circle around Valencia and into the delta lowlands of the Ebro where the last battles of the Civil War were fought.

As the light begins to slant, I skirt the mountains of the moon, the perch of La Moreneta, the little black Virgin of Montserrat, the sawtooth mountain where Wagner set *Parsifal*. At eight-thirty I swing out around Barcelona and make the border just as night falls.

Around eleven the Rincón Chevy van passes me doing better than 150 kph, with Juanito at the wheel, and I tuck in behind, slipstreaming, just like our convoys of the year before. At Montpellier, after midnight, I peel off, seeking shelter in a road hotel (the hotels in Nîmes have been booked for weeks).

The following day I put up in Arles and head back to Nîmes for the corrida. After lunch I locate Luis Carlos, secure my entrada, and stroll through the feria atmosphere of giant outdoor paellas and instant wine bars. Nîmes converts itself into a French version of Sevilla for Pentecost, with details borrowed from the San Fermines of Pamplona.

I find my seat in Les Arènes de Nîmes in the upper Seconde section at an excellent angle for shooting into the lambent light of the late afternoon. The magnificent oval, finished around the year 80 A.D. during the reign of Domitian, holds eighteen thousand *spectateurs* who have come to see Ortega Cano, César Rincón, and Finito de Córdoba with a corrida of Samuel Flores bulls. As the toreros make the long paseo from one end of the oval to the other, the band strikes a stirring rendition of the "March of the Toreadors" and thirty-six thousand hands clap in time.

This is the afternoon I meet Alain Briscadieu, once a novillero, now an art auctioneer and appraiser in Bordeaux, and a close friend of César. (It is not accidental our seats are together, since Luis Carlos handled his ticket as well.)

Ortega Cano's first bull, at 510 kilos, possesses the trapío and the presentation of a toro bravo but exhibits classic characteristics of a manso. Ortega Cano, leery of him, does nothing of merit, and the crowd gives him a sonorous bronca. Alain and I exchange glances, hoping that all the animals do not come out like this one.

The second bull, Lapiceto, number 3, at 500 kilos, acts much like the first: he looks before he charges and his charge has a certain indecision. But Rincón begins a series of verónicas that sets the ring on fire (plates 20a and 20b). When he comes out to dedicate the bull to the público, Alain and I look at each other and say simultaneously: "¿Al público?" (We almost always speak in Spanish, his English not being significantly better than my French.)

Lapiceto cuts in, hooking, cutting in more, but Rincón holds his ground, positioning himself so that the animal can see only the muleta, guiding him, teaching him, encouraging him. On the left hand, series succeeds series, growing in emotional intensity as the animal capitulates to the artful technique that convinces him, that diminishes his fear, that enlightens his charge. When Rincón profiles up close and puts a deep sword straight in, the ring explodes with the chant "¡To-hre-hro! ¡To-hre-hro! ¡To-hre-hro!" All the spectators in the amphitheatre have risen to their feet and the Roman stones reverberate with old glories. As César Rincón tours the oval with both ears, Alain and I are hugging and the Colombiana behind us is jumping up and down. As I sit, I can only wonder how he has done it. Lapiceto was a manso, but he did charge the cloth. Evidently that was all Rincón needed.

Neither Finito nor Ortega Cano, the latter having a bad day, can handle their bulls with much style.

The fifth bull, number 49, weighs 550 kilos and bears the name Conquito. He appears to be mildly lame or at least cramped in his right foreleg, but Rincón teaches and "spoils" him, easing him through a set of smooth verónicas. Antonio Pinilla picks him almost gently and Vicente Yesteras (plate 3c), a former matador turned banderillero who has replaced Curro Cruz this season, puts in two splendid pairs of "sticks" to much acclaim.

In the faena Rincón does passes of every description, starting easy and working up to a grand finale. He cites from a distance so Conquito's charge will take him through, and goes gradually from teaching him to dominating him altogether. Each series builds upon the last, the music plays, and Rincón does a long faena ending with completely frontal passes. The président's aviso only adds to the music, and although Rincón hits bone the first time in, with the second thrust he fells the animal like a tree.

As Rincón takes two vueltas, again with both ears, the amphitheatre becomes a tumult. Alain, close to tears, mumbles, "¡Qué emoción! ¡Qué emoción!" And I am scribbling frantically: "He is better than ever! ¡Qué gran torero!" Once again I have the feeling that I did not choose him, that he chose me. Emotionally we are dragged in his wake, as if he had a team of horses pulling us.

After an excellent faena by Finito, spoiled by the sword, César Rincón is hoisted aloft by the crowd and, as Marc Lavie is to write, "César, the emperor, deserved to cross the Rubicon that is the Puerta de los Cónsules of the Amphitheatre of Nîmes to the shouts of '¡Torero! ¡Torero!' roared by the devoted mob" (6T6 39:31).

In room 112 of the aptly named Hotel Imperator, César glows with his triumph. You can eat the alegría in his room with a spoon. He is talking on the telephone to a friend in Colombia and I hear him say: "¡Te lo perdiste, hermano!"—you missed it, brother! He hangs up and greets everyone with great cheer.

By the time Rincón comes downstairs, the large, ornately decorated lobby has people overflowing into the street one way and into the gardens the other. Cameras flash by the hundreds; people are cheering. There is a divine chaos abroad and champagne flows in celebration.

Eventually we make our way into the dining room. César looks more at ease than I have ever seen him. He teases Alain about French telephones, then turns to an English aficionada and inquires discreetly, enunciating perfectly, "Do you speak English?" It is the first time I have heard him speak English.

She replies amid much laughter, and César shakes his head, saying at once mockingly and gravely in English: "Oh, my God! Oh, my God!"

Suddenly the loneliness of the torero has lifted and César sits, floating, tired, elated, and with a mischievous nimbus about him, as pleased with his two sentences in English as with his four ears in the most important ring in France.

The cuadrilla comes in and everyone is up and hugging again. When we sit back down, Luis Alvarez, nearly as radiant as César, orders Châteauneuf-du-Pape Vieux Télégraphe 1989. César takes a small sip from his glass and nods his approval (plate 20c). Aside from one sip of beer when he was thirsty after a training session at his house, this regal wine he drinks in celebration is the only taste of anything alcoholic I will ever see him take. Drinking Châteauneuf, speaking English: four ears in Nîmes have made a new man out of him. I notice that his thumb looks perfect, as though it had never been cut. But I also see that his left shoulder is suppurating through his shirt.

Madrid: May 27, 1994

Although César cuts an ear in each, corridas in Vic-Fézensac on the twenty-first and back in Nîmes on the twenty-third seem anticlimactic after the great triumph of May 20. A fine fiesta at Alain and Brigitte's country house and his winning prizes at Nîmes cheer him substantially, but we all know what is coming.

On May 27, Madrid is once again waiting for Rincón, so much so that *6T6* has put him on the cover on May 24 (*6T6*, unlike other taurine revistas, does not accept payment for its cover) and featured him in an interview, titled "The Price of Triumph." The interview took place on May 10, when Rincón was training with vacas at Victoriano del Río's ranch outside Madrid. In the interview he continued to assert that he had been drawing bad bulls. Now, after six ears in three corridas in France, aficionados are wondering if perhaps César Rincón was not right.

At the sorteo the bulls of the Marqués de Domecq look splendid in the corrals, but in Madrid you see them from high up and they are difficult to judge. I greet everyone in the cuadrilla and speak at some length with Monaguillo.

"How do you like the lote?"

"I'll tell you after the corrida," he says with his usual grin, then turns serious. "You know—you know, it's all night tossing and turning. Madrid is a great público but if they knew how scared everyone was coming to Madrid—you don't sleep for two weeks—they wouldn't say anything, they wouldn't yell at us, they would be quiet. But between Madrid and Sevilla, where they are too quiet, I'll take Madrid. Look what happened to César last year in Sevilla, and we go this year and they're just waiting to jump him. They don't realize how regionalistic they are. And they are tough *cabrones*.[1] Madrid is better. But only a little. . . ."

At the plaza just after 6:30—it is sold out and scalpers are asking 30,000 pesetas a seat—I wonder: What is César thinking now? But I know what he is thinking about: nothing. He is blanking his mind, going into a sort of trance, having absently watched television, and having prayed before he left the Foxá, having prayed through San Judas Tadeo and his mother for guidance and for luck. Now it will depend, as César sees it—and more and more I am beginning to agree with him—on how the bulls come out. He is a complete and thoroughgoing professional. What is there to think about?

The deep sky of Spain is, as the novelist Alfonso Grosso once phrased it, "difficultly blue," so deep it is hard to believe. The air feels hot and there is only a light breeze. Perfect—if the bulls charge. Sitting in Tendido Ten, row 4, I watch as an old man comes by hawking the *6T6* with César on the cover.

Rincón's first, a black bull named Querellante, number 43, at 558 kilos, knocks down Pinilla's horse and Muri comes up to pick him. Then Querellante falls before the second pick and the crowd wants him sent back. But the presidente changes the tercio.

Rincón begins a classical faena, taking the bull from a distance on the right, crossing to cite, firing up the crowd explosively in the opening series for what does not follow (plate 21a). Querellante, turning defensive, will not take the cloth on the left, even though Rincón insists, and his charge on the right begins to falter. Powerful, but overweight in order to meet Madrid's self-defeating standards, the bull runs out of oxygen. Rincón kills him so well that a huge collective gasp ensues from the público (plate 21b). But Querellante takes a long time to die, and Rincón, wishing to allow the animal's brave death, does nothing to hurry his fall, garnering only a well-celebrated vuelta.

The fifth bull—an enormous dark-headed red bull with "partridge eyes," number 27, weighing in at 602 kilos, Malquerido by name—shoves the horse backward and over and unseats Anderson Murillo, then pursues him around the horse, catching him as he tries to scramble away, hobbled by the protective metal mona on his right leg. When the bull tosses him, hooking him under the rump with the left horn, Murillo flies awkwardly upward, arms and legs akimbo, and as he comes down, Malquerido thrusts up again, sinking his right horn into the man's groin.

Anderson Murillo tries to stand, as the capes whisk the animal away, and falters. The *monosabios* or ring attendants help him to the fence, then pick him up to take him to the infirmary. But Murillo shakes them off, his knees buckling and straightening. His chamois-cloth *calzona* (pants) has gaped open and Murillo, noticing his genitals are in view, tucks himself back in and with a wiggle of his left leg heads back for the horse. Somehow he remounts and administers two more strong picks, even though his right testicle has been eviscerated. (It will be replaced and the torn scrotum will be stitched up in the infirmary.)

Too fat to charge, the big red turns defensive, nearly catching a too-valiant Rincón on several occasions. But when Rincón puts in the sword, he chases the matador across the ring.

Madrid will have to keep waiting for Rincón, but for now at least the pundits have stopped saying he is having a bad temporada.

Córdoba: May 28, 1994

Cordoban señoritas, dressed in fiesta garb for the Feria de la Virgen de Salud, have come to see César Rincón, Finito, the local hero, and Chiquilín, also from Córdoba. The corrida of Gabriel Rojas has been partially replaced with Cayetano Muñoz bulls. Rincón draws a 580-kilo "mule" of Cayetano Muñoz, a white bull weak in the knees that refuses to charge.

His second bull, another Cayetano Muñoz (his Gabriel Rojas, crippled, was returned to the corrals) is not much better and, although he gets a few passes from it, he is not able to link any of them together and can create no emotion.

Finito can do no wrong is his own land. And the taurine gods smile on him. His second animal, Tabernero, number 167, a 546-kilo Gabriel Rojas bull, dull black, low in the shoulder and not too long in the horn, one of those nobly charging bulls that all toreros dream of, trots into the bullring of the caliphs to make taurine history.

Tabernero charges from a distance on the slightest provocation, coming over and over from halfway across the ring. And he behaves with complete nobleza, pulling no tricks on either horn, charging absolutely straight and with great fijeza every time he takes the cloth. Tabernero charges and charges and charges, and the more he does it, the nobler and braver and finer he becomes. Juan Serrano, Finito, has perhaps the greatest moment of

Figure 33. Anderson Murillo, Madrid, May 27, 1994. Although it sounds impossible, Muri is picking Malquerido, the big Marqués de Domecq bull that has just eviscerated one of his testicles. You can see the calzona gaping open.

his taurine career with this nearly flawless animal, creating a faena at the level that such perfection in a bull requires.

Frenzy breaks out in the tendidos: shouts of "¡Torero! ¡Torero!" come on top of hand clapping in the flamenco style of bulerías; handkerchiefs wave, petitioning the indulto for Tabernero. At last the orange pañuelo shows from the presidente's box and Tabernero, after suffering a symbolic killing with a banderilla instead of a sword, trots out under his own steam, seemingly stronger and braver than when the faena began twenty-six minutes and some eighty passes before. (He will be given immediate intensive care by the veterinarians from the Universidad de Córdoba.)

One of the miracles of the taurine world has just occurred. Finito cuts a symbolic tail and the crowd pulls Gabriel Rojas out of the tendido and takes a vuelta with him and the matador both on shoulders.

Back at the hotel we sit in the cafetería with César, who seems laconically philosophical: "There were four good bulls and my two. For variety."

Brigitte Briscadieu peels him an orange, which pleases him no end, and César tells us: "I like the gracia of the people here in Córdoba. A boy about ten yelled to me from the barrera: 'Don't you worry, César, you're the best torero ever born in these parts.'"

Sanlúcar de Barrameda: June 4, 1994

Early June in Andalucía may have the finest weather in the world, I am thinking, as I leave John Fulton's house in the cool morning to drive to Sanlúcar, perched on the south bank of the Guadalquivir where the big, muddy river empties into the Atlantic. César Rincón draws number 2 and number 29 of a corrida of El Torero—a ranch owned by Santiago Domecq, another member of the dynastic taurine family of nearby Jerez de la Frontera—but as we can only see the animals from above, I cannot tell much about them. Following established tradition, after the sorteo the whole cuadrilla heads to the waterfront district along the river known as the Bajo de Guía to eat *tigres,* tiger-striped prawns, and accompany them with manzanilla, the local ultra-dry sherry.

His first bull is returned for a weak leg but the sobrero, number 12, charges well and Rincón cuts an ear in his debut in Sanlúcar, lighting up the feria crowd with his palpable entrega (plates 22a and 22b).

Jesulín, the would-be clown prince of toreo in the early '90s, uses his irrepressible charm on the crowd and cuts an ear as well. When a lovely señorita in feria dress throws him a flower, he looks up, smiles, and yells as though he knew her, "¡Gracias, guapa!" As he hails from not far away, the Sanlúcar público loves him and claps in the rhythm of bulerías as he takes his vuelta.

The fifth bull, number 29, also charges hard but not with the same nobility. The animal watches Rincón and then goes straight for him. But Rincón does a skillful faena, as if the bull were on rails instead of trying to gore him on every charge (plate 22c). When the animal is fully dominated, Rincón drives in an *estoconazo,* a grand sword thrust, that produces a spectacular death, the bull crashing over, all four legs in the air, his dramatic agony framed in the soft yellow afternoon. The early summer light, the silky sea air, the excellent juego of the bulls and the entrega of the matadors—Ortega Cano had trouble killing—build toward an unforgettable feria climax as César Rincón tours the ring with the ears of number 29, smiling as beguilingly as Jesulín but with the dignity and seriousness of purpose that characterize him and his art.

As César rushes past me in the callejón with his cape, staying low to position himself for Jesulín's second bull, I say to his back, "¡Bien, torero!" He swivels around, still running, and winks with a grin. This moment of triumph makes every wait, every disappointment, every frustration disappear. The mood, caught in that winking fraternal instant, has turned as golden as the summer evening and as buoyant as the salty Atlantic air.

Jesulín cuts two ears from yet another fine animal, and the Feria de Manzanilla reaches its collective apogee as César Rincón and Jesulín ride triumphantly on shoulders through the Puerta Grande into the infinite blue evening of Andalucía in June (plate 22d).

Driving from the ring to the hotel, I get lost down near the river, bound in by one-way streets, and I suddenly remember a dream from the night before in which I was lost down by this river and there was some impending danger. Is this precognition or oneiromancy, I wonder, or some déjà-vu-like coincidence? When I finally make my way back to the hotel in Sanlúcar, everyone's mood, especially César's, continues in the clouds. But later, all the way to Sevilla, I have an inexplicable sense of dread.

Madrid: June 7, 1994

Madrid still waits for Rincón. No tickets remain, and the sellout can hardly be ascribed to Emilio Muñoz, who in the fifteen years since his alternativa has yet to cut an ear in Madrid, nor to Juan Mora, who after eleven years of alternativa has had no great triumph in Madrid either. The sellout—and the responsabilidad—belongs to César Rincón. And to the bulls of Baltasar Ibán, the ganadería with which Rincón had his first big triumph in 1991. This time the público will not be disappointed.

At the sorteo I learn that three of the original Ibanes have been rejected by the veterinarians, that one has been replaced by another Ibán, and that the other two slots will be filled by bulls of Victoriano del Río. It is not clear why the animals have been rejected, but the usual reason given, especially by the veterinarians in Madrid, centers around a lack of that difficult-to-define quality known as trapío. In Madrid, lack of trapío boils down to insufficiently gargantuan. We are not yet aware at the sorteo that we are about to receive an object lesson in trapío, proving once and for all that an animal's size in no way indicates its condition as a toro bravo.

As I greet the cuadrilla, I notice that Manolo Gil looks somewhat "serious." He explains: "I couldn't sleep because of the fear. This is a profession that you never get used to. Here I am nearly fifty, and what happens if they let two 'lions' loose on us today and one of them breaks me in half? How do I support my family then?"

Vicente Yesteras has a noticeable limp. I ask, "How will you manage today?"

"It's just a big hematoma. There's some swelling but cortisone should take care of it."

After the pairing up of the lots I ask Manolo: "And the bulls—what do you think?"

"Descarados de cara," he replies in the inscrutable argot of the taurine world, meaning that they are barefacedly long and sharp of horn. The general mood, as always before an afternoon in Madrid, strikes me as a peculiar mixture of glum, serious, wry, and fatalistic, but above all charged with responsabilidad. Tension oozes from everyone.

Rincón has drawn Bastonito, a black Ibán with a white belly, number 25, weighing 501 kilos, born in August 1989, making him very close to five years old, to come out in second place (plate 23a), and Espléndido, a black Victoriano del Río, also white-bellied, number 33, at 558 kilos, born in March 1990, to appear in fifth place. As Rincón knows the Victoriano del Río bulls well and likes them, they have put the Ibán first, reasoning that if he can cut one ear from the Ibán, he will have an excellent chance at the Puerta Grande.

After the sorteo, I go down to the Calle Victoria to pick up my reserved ticket (Tendido Ten, row 2), buy film, and walk up the Paseo de Recoletos, admiring the outdoor exposition of gigantic sculptures by Colombian artist Fernando Botero, especially the "rapture" of the Phoenician princess Europa by Zeus as a bull. Both the subject and the artist strike me as good auguries.[2]

When I arrive at Las Ventas at 6:15, for the twenty-fifth corrida of this San Isidro, a gentle breeze blows beneath a clear hot sky and the threat of a thunderstorm charges the air. Inside, the men take off their coats and the women begin to fan, even in the shade. In the patio de caballos, César Rincón has appeared clear-eyed and calm, speaking to the television cameras in a low, measured voice. As the toreros line up for the paseo, the silhouettes of the picadores loom above the three men dressed in gold. When they emerge into the light, Emilio Muñoz appears tight-lipped and stiff, Juan Mora looks slightly less unrelaxed, and César Rincón seems somewhat introspective or withdrawn, with what I have come to think of as the quasi-beatific smile he puts on to mask his real feeling.

As they approach the presidente's box, nearly in front of me, I can see the vacant look of dread in Emilio Muñoz's deep-set eyes. His performance with the first animal has that same vacancy, although the bull does go quickly on the defensive, becoming quite dangerous. Muñoz in Madrid remains a mystery to me: I do not understand why he bothers to come, so fatalistically does he seem to accept from the outset the inevitablity of his failure.

Bastonito enters the ring at a gallop, stops, turns in a circle, and gallops toward the first movement he sees. Short in length, muscular, wide-horned and astifino, with a high morrillo, his tail extended and his head thrust forward, Bastonito personifies taurine aggression. Will this be the bull that Rincón has been waiting for, that Madrid has been waiting to see him torear, the bull with problems that César Rincón will solve, the bull with fierceness and thrust?

Bastonito, although he lowers his head well, seems almost uninterested in the cape until the second media verónica, when he suddenly whips around, turning in less than his own length and nearly catching it. If nothing else, Bastonito seems strong and fast, and his movements, although quicker, remind me of Santanerito in 1991.

In the horse, Bastonito gradually reveals two qualities: bravery and a fixed, obsessive aggression unlike any I have seen before. The first vara goes on for three or four minutes and, although Pinilla stops picking him, the bull refuses to quit pushing the horse, refuses to take the capes thrust under his nose, the capes of Vicente Yesteras, of Monaguillo, of César Rincón himself, refuses to do anything but try to penetrate the heavy peto protecting the horse. It appears that the bull will exhaust himself here, breaking himself in the horse. The picking begins up in Tendido Eight and continues along to Tendido One. As Bastonito comes by me, working steadily against the horse, I can see one eye, dark and shining like molten glass.

Finally, when the horse angles away from the line of charge, Monaguillo thrusts his cape in Bastonito's face and the bull follows it out and away from the horse. By all rights the bull should be near exhaustion, yet he takes Rincón's cape twice without a pause. Clearly appreciating the animal's bravery, Rincón directs Pinilla back to Tendido Eight, for it is here, at the other end of the plaza from the bull's natural querencia at the toril, that Bastonito can show his mettle. For the second pick Rincón artfully places him with a larga. In the meantime Bastonito seems to have recuperated completely.

As soon as Pinilla works the horse into position, Bastonito rockets into the peto. When Monaguillo again takes him out from the horse, Bastonito snaps around on him, nearly catching him.

Juan Mora makes three smooth verónicas and a revolera in the quite, but in the revolera Bastonito, who has put his head down well in each pass, bends tightly back, trying to catch Mora. The bull takes the cape but also looks for what he "leaves behind him." As Mora finishes, the presidente, Amado Jorge Estéllez, changes the tercio, preventing us from seeing the important third vara that, if the animal continues to charge well, stands as ironclad proof of bravery. Then too, Bastonito appears to need another pick to smooth out the still rough edges of his charge, especially his tendency to *rebañar*, to wash back on the torero at the end of the pass.

In the first pair of banderillas, Bastonito waits without charging until Vicente Yesteras gets almost to him, then charges hard and pursues Yesteras all the way to the tablas, ignoring an intervening cape and forcing Yesteras to jump the fence. At this point Rincón comes out to assume the responsibility of the lidia himself. Manolo Gil suffers a similar pursuit after placing his pair but manages to slip behind a burladero without having to jump. After the third pair, Bastonito chases Yesteras to the fence again, forcing him to jump once more. Yesteras's left foot slips on the edge of the fence and, losing balance, he falls awkwardly into the callejón head first. Unhurt but embarrassed, he must nevertheless come out to acknowledge the warm ovation the público gives him for his spectacular placing of the banderillas.

After asking the presidente's permission (plate 23b), César Rincón carefully drops his montera mouth-down in the center of the ring, having dedicated his faena to the público of Las Ventas del Espíritu Santo. In taurine parlance, "it smells of something grand." But what? A grand triumph? A grand defeat? A grand tragedy? Be careful what you pray for. As Antonio Caballero will write in *Diario 16* on the fourteenth, "'Pray to God you never get a brave bull,' advised Domingo Ortega." Or was it Juan Belmonte? Or Guerrita?

Is Bastonito truly brave or is he wild and fierce? The one thing I know is that he transmits a palpable sense of danger. Even before the faena begins I notice that my hands, loading the camera, are trembling with the taurine equivalent of buck fever, something I do not recall happening before or since. Rincón's face looks pale as he approaches the bull to begin, but his demeanor shows determination. Inconceivable determination.

Yesteras holds Bastonito at the burladero of Tendido Nine. As Rincón approaches, calling to the animal, Bastonito pays no heed. The animal is fixed on Yesteras, who, as motionless as a man on the edge of a cliff, cuts his eyes toward Rincón, then ducks down behind the burladero so Bastonito can no longer see him. It is as though Yesteras had flipped a switch releasing the bull, and Bastonito turns at once toward Rincón's voice and muleta.

Rincón begins with low doubling passes, designed to dominate the animal's charge, but on the second pass, and again on the fourth—both on the right horn with the animal moving toward the fence—Bastonito "washes back," nearly catching Rincón. Out of six passes, the bull has aggressively pursued the man three times. At that point almost any matador but Rincón would decide to use the sword.

Instead he takes the bull to the center of the ring with four more doubling passes, including two on the right, without the slightest doubt or hesitation, and a pase de pecho to finish, dominating and containing the animal's aggression.

Now in the center and from a slight distance, in a rapt silence, Rincón starts a series of four derechazos, each lower and longer than the last, winding the bull around himself, linking the passes by harnessing Bastonito's wild driving force with the supple reins of his cloth, only to release the tightly wound coil in a pase de pecho. But the bull, halfway through the chest pass, curls his neck around, slices his horns upward, and bumps Rincón's elbow, forcing the man to retreat.

Until the pase de pecho Rincón has been in control, but now an open battle begins and seesaws back and forth. There follow two exemplary derechazos in Rincón style, the first made crossing and cargando la suerte, taking Bastonito around the axis leg, the second done with the hand lower, positioned in profile to link up at once with the first. (Antoñete has commented several times that Rincón's second muletazo is the key to his technique and style.) But Bastonito rebels in the third pass and charges back onto Rincón, again forcing him to retreat.

He recovers instantly and, crossing, makes two derechazos and a pase de pecho, this time without difficulty and to grand applause. Switching to the left, he searches for the proper distance to make Bastonito—ever more defensive—charge. By the second series Rincón has found that he must cease trying to link and instead make individual passes, but in the pase de pecho Bastonito again strikes back around on him and chases him, hooking for him three separate times. Yesteras starts out from the burladero and Rincón shouts in frustration, his face distorted and pale: "¡Quieto! ¡Tápate!" Hold it! Get back!

On the right now, Rincón makes two derechazos, but in the third pass Bastonito is chasing him backward again. Rincón insists—and I begin to wonder which of the two is the more obsessive—making one derechazo, then changing hands for a half pase de pecho with Bastonito all over him. In every pass now he puts his life at extreme risk, yet he will not admit defeat, and as he comes out of the chest pass, he nods his head up and down, looking at the crowd. Has he done it?

With his left hand he completes a clean natural without the horn touching the muleta. All around me, even as I shoot, I can feel the tension of people sitting literally on the edge of their seats and on the edge of tragedy. Another natural. Three. Four. Color begins to return to Rincón's face.

He crosses again, citing from a slight distance on the left. Bastonito lowers his head and follows the muleta all the way through, coming out on the far side of the pass where he should come out, instead of in Rincón's face. Crossing, Rincón cites again, de frente, and pulls Bastonito around him behind the hip—classically and cleanly executed. Dropping back, Rincón takes him again, cleanly, and again. Then another and a high pass. The tension just begins to ease, and I realize he has indeed done it! Ten naturales, one by one, finding the distance, obliging the animal to charge, making Bastonito go where Bastonito does not want to go (plate 24). He has defeated this beast of a bull, pass by pass, in the hardest-fought taurine battle of wills I have ever witnessed.

Now comes the crowning pase de pecho. Bastonito lowers his head and follows the cloth. But as he come past Rincón's left leg, the bull's right hind leg catches the man's foot and drags him under the animal's hindquarters. Rincón goes over backward, the muleta and sword fly loose, and Bastonito wheels around searching for the body. Just when the bull would have had him, the muleta, which has snagged on one of the banderillas, flaps in Bastonito's face and he hooks up at it as Rincón tries to roll away. Bastonito's momentum carries him over Rincón and the muleta continues to flop in the bull's face. Bastonito balls up, hunching, trying to find the body beneath him, missing Rincón's face by centimeters, but the animal's impatience to gore frustrates him, and the muleta, now hanging between his horns, blinds him. Then Monaguillo has the bull in his cape and the danger is over. In the tendido we begin to breathe again. Rincón, bruised and shaken, rises to his feet and retrieves his sword and muleta.

As Rincón begins another series of naturales, Presidente Estéllez sends him an aviso. Rincón gives Bastonito a natural de frente, cargando la suerte with classic purity, and then sends him far away in a pase de pecho that brings the length of the animal under his shoulder. When Bastonito does turn, Rincón dismisses him with a pase del desdén and walks away without looking back. He almost smiles as he acknowledges the crowd's applause.

With two ayudados he lines up Bastonito and, going in hard and straight, hits bone. The second time he sinks the sword en todo lo alto, but as he comes out along the animal's side, Bastonito flicks out that lethal right horn, hooking the man's trailing right leg above the ankle and upending him, flipping him onto his back (plate 25a). Rincón is rolling away as he hits, and Bastonito is turning after him (plate 25b). Rincón rolls and Bastonito, in spite of the mortal sword lodged in his life line, pursues the rolling body. This time the muleta falls clear.

When Bastonito catches Rincón, his impatience again betrays him. The right horn flicks across Rincón's back—just above Yiyo's spot—catching in the epaulet of his suit, then sliding past, beyond the man's body, while the left horn, digging down, catches on the inside of Rincón's left upper leg, in the most vulnerable area, the tip of the horn gouging along the flesh where the upper thigh becomes the hip, then popping loose without penetrating.

Bastonito's snout plows into Rincón's chest, rolling him forward, and Rincón, now on his back, curls his upper body as closely around the muzzle of the beast as he can, staying beneath the horns. Bastonito lunges forward, kicking Rincón in the head with his right forefoot and shaking him almost free, but Rincón reaches up with both hands and pulls himself into the animal's face in an extraordinary embrace. For a flickering moment César Rincón looks into that dark shining eye, then sinks his teeth into the coarse curly hair below the eye. The man's face and the bull's face join—the man's face crowned with the terrible curve of Bastonito's right horn—in the passionate and instinctive kiss of the minotaur that saves Rincón's life, just before the capes begin to arrive.

Monaguillo comes first with Vicente Yesteras, Emilio Muñoz and Juan Mora (without a cape) immediately behind (plate 25c). Yesteras tries to grab Bastonito by the horn, and they all distract him long enough for Rincón to roll away from the now faltering beast. Monaguillo takes the animal away with his cape and Bastonito charges in pursuit, then crashes in a dead heap. Rincón has risen, bloody, battered, and injured, but triumphant. The bull is dead, the man stands over his carcass, and the crowd looses the white doves of glory in the tendido. In living ritual, Theseus has slain the monster.

Painfully Rincón retrieves his montera, saluting with his left hand. He clutches the right to his groin where his white suit is turning red with blood (plate 26a). What at first seems a horn wound in the groin turns out to be a deep cut in his right thumb—the blood comes from the cut, and he holds the hand against his groin because he cannot make it function properly. At the fence he suffers intense pain, nearly collapsing (plate 26b). The presidente grants the ear and then a vuelta for the carcass of Bastonito. Summoning some inner reserve, Rincón wraps a towel around his right hand and begins the vuelta of triumph with the ear in his left (plate 26c). Then he removes the towel and places the ear in the right, taking the vuelta as he should, ignoring the pain, ignoring the blood, trying to savor the crowd's acclamation before going finally to the enfermería, from which he will not return (plate 26d). I can see from the way he is walking that he is in extreme pain.

The corrida might as well be over. I order a whiskey—nothing more to shoot today—knowing it will not help anything. I order it anyway, then proceed nearly to ruin the roll of film inside the camera.

At the bar of Tendido Seven afterwards, Arévalo tells me: "There is not and there never has been—that I have seen or that I know of—a torero like him."

Michael Wigram adds: "But he's got to stop killing like that." We laugh because we are all still very much on edge. As I leave the plaza I think: There are toreros technically as good. And there may be one or two as brave. But there is no one with that character. No one. Suddenly I feel myself letting go and the emotion drains away like water flowing down a pipe.

Later at the Foxá, Luis Carlos and Juanito tell me César has a longitudinal incision in the extensor tendon of his right thumb, caused by the harpoon of a banderilla when he put the sword in so forcefully. The surgeon in the enfermería, Dr. Máximo García Padrós, has opened it up, cleaned it out, and put about forty little stitches in the tendon. "He couldn't make a grip with his thumb," Luis Carlos says, gesturing like a lobster. "That's why he couldn't come out for his second bull."

"It was a good bull," I say pointlessly.

"Claro," says Luis Carlos.

"Claro," says Juanito.

We know what we mean.

César has already gone home, but the little lobby and bar of the Foxá will not hold any more Rinconistas. Matador David Luguillano tells me: "I wouldn't recommend that bull to anybody. Not even somebody I didn't like."

Matador César Camacho chimes in (they are still excited and upset): "Rincón's lidia was so good he made the bull look better than it actually was. That bull was deceiving. He wanted to eat up the muleta."

Everyone agrees that Rincón's performance was utterly heroic. What people will not agree on is whether the bull was truly brave and whether he deserved the vuelta or not.

In the first vara he was extraordinary. In the second, he hesitated until challenged directly by the horse's position but then charged very well. In banderillas he waited—not a sign of bravery—and then aggressively pursued. In the muleta he was dangerous from the outset and looking for the matador. He lacked nobility and he charged harder to the inside (toward the fence) than to the outside. He did not, in my judgment, deserve the vuelta. He was brave, fierce, aggressive, and very difficult. He was a killer but not a bull for a vuelta.

Later on, down at the Hotel Victoria's large and very taurine lobby, this topic keeps people buzzing for hours. Arévalo explains: "No, he did not deserve the vuelta. The presidente was wrong to change the tercio. With another vara, he would have been, at least, slower. And probably better in the muleta. But he did not deserve a vuelta."

Then ganadero Victorino Martín, resplendent in an olive green suit and matching tie, declares quietly around the cigar holder clamped in the right side of his mouth: "He was not a bull for a vuelta."

But no one would disagree that Bastonito was an extraordinary bull.

The next morning the comments in the papers about the toro and the torero would not all agree either. Rincón himself was quoted from the enfermería, telling *El País* that the bull was "brave and fierce," but that he "stayed under" the muleta. The vuelta was "a subjective question," he said, "but I don't believe [the bull] brought together the necessary qualities for it."

From his house, in spite of his pain, Rincón reflected, for *El Mundo* at greater length: "No doubt about it, he was very brave. But for the torero he was very complicated, nothing easy about him." Rincón had realized in the banderillas how the bull was, "by the way he chased the toreros without paying any attention to the capes." He thought the animal lacked the nobility to follow the muleta through the pass and that you had to torear exactly right or he would eat you alive. "When he caught me in the kill and tried to tear me to pieces, I remembered Yiyo, may he rest in peace. There were some dramatic moments." In that tossing, he said, "I was very afraid. Time seemed to stand still. I grabbed onto the bull's head because I was beneath his *garras* [claws; that is, horns] and I knew he wanted to rip me apart." But, he concluded, "the important thing is that the plaza of Madrid resounded again with my performance." About biting the bull, César would tell me, as if speaking of someone else: "Yes, I did bite him! You can see it on the video!"

Later Rincón would recall Bastonito's look, which had impressed him greatly: "There are brave bulls that look at you with kindness, and some that you even see cry, but this Baltasar Ibán looked at me saying: 'If I catch you, you are not going to escape'" (6T6 40:24).

For *Diario 16* Antoñete, in his double role as maestro and commentator, described Rincón on June 14 as a "monstruo." He thought that the bull might be the bull of the feria, because of his "fierceness and speed," but said that he lacked "quality." In the same issue Antonio Caballero, with the simplicity and directness that characterizes his writing, called Rincón "one of the bravest toreros ever to set foot on the sands of a plaza de toros."

In *El Ruedo* that same day taurine critic Norberto Carrasco called Rincón's toreo "epic," comparing it to Pablo Neruda's poetry, and remarked that this bull would have "won the battle against any other diestro." His colleague Emilio Martínez called Rincón a "hero, the only one of the escalafón capable of standing up to Bastoncito,[3] the bull of the feria."

José Carlos Arévalo quoted the maestro Pedro Moya, Niño de la Capea, on Bastonito: "It was not a dangerous offensive bravery, but a deadly defensive bravery. The bull had more violence than entrega." Arévalo himself characterized Rincón's response to the bull as moving: It had "the awareness of one who knows where he is going and the heroism of one who, in spite of that knowledge, goes anyway." By crossing and citing and keeping the muleta hand very low, embarking the bull in the cloth over long distances and taking the bull always around behind his own body, Rincón "ended up breaking" the animal. "The last series of naturales, tragically slow, was the culmination, the palpable demonstration that the man had finally triumphed." When man and bull went down together, the bull with the sword in him up to the hilt, epic poetry and tragedy fused in Rincón's message that "toreo is the office of the hero" (*6T6* 40:7).

It seems the further away the critics got from the moment and the more they reflected on it, the more heroic Rincón's performance became. There was one critic, however, Andrés de Miguel, who put himself on the line the morning after the events in a review in *Diario 16* that begins like the Koran and ends like *The Epic of Gilgamesh:* "There is no toreo but toreo and Rincón is its prophet. The prophet that takes us to the promised land of authentic toreo, by risking his life in exchange for the life of the bull, after making the bull submit to his own dominating will." Fate had put together the authentic bull and the prophet of toreo "to produce the revelation." Andrés de Miguel vowed that he had never witnessed "such an emotional moment, when a true torero was enacting the myth of toreo with a mythic bull. He enacted it as it must have been in the original encounter, with blood and fire."

Almería: August 23 and 24, 1994

Rincón had reappeared in León, in the official reopening of the newly renovated plaza, on June 24, cutting two ears from his second Victoriano del Río bull and going out on shoulders with Ortega Cano and Espartaco. He cut two more from another Victoriano del Río in Béziers on July 17, after his first trophyless San Fermín, two from another "important" Baltasar Ibán in Bayonne on August 15, and four ears and a tail from Jódar y Ruchena bulls in Quintanar de la Orden two days later. He also had fine performances in Burgos (July 2), Mont-de-Marsan (July 18), Barcelona (July 24), Santander (July 28), and Dax (August 16) without "rounding out" a triumph. But his bad luck in the draw continued to haunt him. And in the Santander corrida a Buendía bull cracked one of his ribs, putting him out for nine days.

When asked in an interview for *El Ruedo* on August 23 how he was, Rincón replied: "I'm fine, my bulls are bad. It's been a horrible year for bulls. Call it bad luck or whatever you want, but I always get the worst ones."

"Is it always the bulls?" asked the interviewer.

"When things don't go right, I try to analyze them to figure out what I did wrong. Maybe it's not the bull and I just don't see it, but I wish somebody would explain it to me. I'm not a machine and I can make mistakes. One thing that's clear is that it's impossible for this season to be another '91. Everything has to go exactly right and that's not happening. Sometimes I have a great faena, as in Mont-de-Marsan or in Barcelona, and then I kill badly; other times it's just the opposite and I get an ear after a moderate faena and a good kill." ˙

"What do you fall back on at these times?"

"As Manzanares said to me recently, the main thing is to have maturity and incentives. And not to get stale."

Rincón went on to say that it took a long time to reach the top, but only "tenths of a second" to come down. It was hard to maintain and not every year could be the same. He continued to be rightfully proud of his performance with Bastonito, which he called "a feat in which I gave my all."

As I read his comments, I began to wonder whether César Rincón was beginning to develop a certain "broken record" of responses or whether he was caught in a double bind. In 1991 he had one of the most significant seasons in the history of toreo. Everyone, including himself sometimes, expected him to maintain that level: a clear impossibility. His incredible success had doomed him to a relative failure in the future. The only positive way out of it was to open the Puerta Grande in Madrid again.

I return to Spain the morning of August 22, take the Talgo to Málaga, where I pick up the same red Renault I had in the spring, and drive the Mediterranean corniche eastward to Almería, which is in feria. The next morning I find there is no reventa in Almería—at least none I can locate. After the sorteo I end up with an invitación, so I can get in, but with no seat. And the ring is sold out. I spend the first half of the corrida in the entranceway up on the second level, trying to shoot pictures among the jostling mob of other freeloaders. César Rincón, Jesulín (who has the intention of breaking all numerical records this season, and is well on his way to doing it, having already performed in ninety-six corridas), and Finito make up the cartel. Rincón draws two excellent bulls of the Marqués de Domecq, number 10 at 560 kilos and number 67 at 555, and cuts an ear from each, taking a triumphant ride through the Puerta Grande on the shoulders of the boisterous feria crowd (plate 27).

Afterwards he comments that he liked the fourth bull better: "His charge was smoother and he let me torear more at ease, more smoothly, with more temple. I am a torero who can handle tough bulls, but I also have the right now and then to enjoy a good bull!"

The next day, August 24, Manzanares and Espartaco and César Rincón are to kill a corrida of Sánchez Arjona bulls, low in the shoulder, not too big, but possibly weak in the legs. Today I end up with two tickets—are the taurine fates trying to make up for yesterday?—but manage to "flog" one of them and sit with César's business manager, Edgar Heyn.

Rincón has drawn an ugly red bull, number 55 at 462 kilos, that splinters the wood of two of the burladeros before settling down in soothing verónicas. Rincón dedicates him to the público and proceeds to do a faena full of class and sentiment, again enjoying the animal while designing a sculpted work of art. Both brave and artistic, he looks better than in 1991. His naturales succeed each other with a cadence that goes straight to the heart, with that ineffable gracia that lies at the aesthetic core of toreo.

Edgar comments: "It's his perfect sense of distances that allows the rhythm."

"It's not for nothing he loves to dance," I say as Rincón takes the bull behind his back in a pase de las flores.

"Right," says Edgar. "But watch, it's actually the bull that determines the beat."

"Yes," I say, "but it's the torero who discovers it and then choreographs it with gracia."

He tries to kill recibiendo but hits bone. Then, putting in a volapié up to the hilt, he cuts an ear. The delirious público demands the second ear but the presidente refuses.

Colmenar Viejo: August 29, 1994

Corridas in Bilbao on August 25 and 27 made me wonder if Rincón's lucky bulls in Almería were the exception that proves the rule. Only the lunches were memorable.

On August 29 *Aplausos* ran a long interview with Rincón by José Luis Benlloch. Rincón continued being proud of his faena with Bastonito, "one of the most important bulls ever to come out in Madrid," but he was also very pleased with his artistic dimension with the second Marqués de Domecq bull in Almería, which he said had surprised a number of aficionados. They were used to "seeing me with the water up to my neck, with tough bulls, but faenas like that one put you back in touch with yourself, they make you feel like a torero. Sometimes with so much battling, you can lose the pleasure of fine toreo." He did not deny his warrior half, but he wanted aficionados to know there were two sides to him. People were "accustomed to seeing me interpret the raw drama of the corrida" and wanted to continue seeing that, but for the torero, the rawness could become nerve-wracking and overwhelming. It made him very proud to give passes to a bull no one thought had any passes in him, but he liked "to relax and enjoy the smooth part" as well. "Enjoyment instead of suffering. That's the trick."

He praised the Marqués de Domecq bulls for their "mobility, their force, the fact that they usually don't fall down, [and] their capacity to transmit emotion." He liked them enough to have bought sixty vacas for his own ganadería in Colombia, the place to which he hoped some day to retire.

Benlloch noticed that Rincón used the word "suerte" often. Did he believe in that? "Yes. In this profession—even though you have to make your own—you have to have luck. Luck to draw the bull that charges on the key afternoon, luck so he doesn't wound you at the wrong time. You have to have luck."

(What kind of luck, I wondered, was Bastonito? Good luck to draw such a spectacularly aggressive animal? Bad luck that Bastonito caught him in the kill? Or good luck that the bull did not kill him?)

At the close of the interview came important news. Toward the end of the season Rincón would undergo an operation for a foot injury from being stepped on by a bull, a process that would put him out for about three months: "Around the twenty-fourth of September I'll cut my temporada." Rincón's feet were in bad shape and he had been talking about the need for the operation for some time. Although there had been rumors, this announcement was the first public indication of his intentions.

The following day José Carlos Arévalo published a very different piece titled "A Torero Named César" on the editorial page of 6T6. It was a reply to a comment made by a critic to the effect that, no matter how good César Rincón was in a recent triumph, "he's still an Indian." Arévalo, in responding, did not merely attack this single remark; rather he used the remark, which he did not dignify by quoting directly in his piece, as a pretext to denounce "tribalism" and chauvinism within the taurine world in general. The good thing about corridas, he wrote, was that they were "only tangentially competitive," since men did not compete directly with each other but instead put their individual skill and art to the test in front of the bull. And there— facing the bull—no national interests, personal interests, or love interests had any place. The test of toreo was so "authentic and definitive" that the man could have only "the attributes of his torería and the bull those of his bravery and aggressiveness."

Rincón was now waging "a double struggle," competing with his peers and trying to combat these "outbreaks of tribalism" that some critics were employing to belittle his performances and his standing in toreo. Furthermore, while Rincón was accepted by Spanish publics, he was also subjected to severe pressure, having to prove himself every afternoon without a slip.

Praising Rincón's purity of style and classicism, Arévalo described Rincón most accurately as "the true primera figura in France," as in the "first rank" in Spain, and as "the king of toreo in South America." In concluding, Arévalo made it clear he was not making excuses for Rincón. He was simply corroborating "the history written by [Rincón] in the rings" and debunking the "irrational outbreaks of tribalism futilely fabricated to impede his progress" in the taurine sphere. Against those who denied Rincón "out of mediocrity and provincialism," Arévalo was pleased to say: "Maestro, your home is also in Spain" (6T6 45:6).

On August 29, the afternoon before the appearance of Arévalo's piece, Ortega Cano, César Rincón, and Manolo Sánchez kill a corrida of Manuel San Román bulls in the old torista town of Colmenar Viejo, just north of Madrid, for the Feria de la Virgen de los Remedios. The new ring holds some ten thousand, and many aficionados from Madrid come out for the corridas. The local crowd still has the reputation of being tough—so tough they have been known to throw rocks at the toreros, or so the story goes. At any rate the toreros speak of Colmenar, where Yiyo was killed, with a mixture of respect and trepidation.

The hot afternoon is rife with the intimate ambiente of a small-town feria and palpable taurine expectation. Ortega Cano wears a flamboyant traje the color of red wine but will have a gray afternoon. César Rincón wears gray but will have much to celebrate. Manolo Sánchez, in blue, matches the sky—in color if not in depth—and close behind the ring the blue wall of the Guadarramas rises in stony relief.

Rincón's first bull creates problems on both horns with his erratic and abrupt charge, and the matador limits himself, decorously, to dispatching the unwilling beast. Manolo Sánchez does an excellent faena, kills defectively (the sword comes out on the side), yet earns an ear.

The fifth bull—born in November 1988, meaning he is now nearly six years old instead of the usual four—is reluctant to charge the horse. What can one expect to do with such an animal, defensive and wise with too many years' experience, except to kill him? Instead, Rincón proceeds to execute a memorable faena that no one could possibly have foreseen.

After low doubling passes of great authority (plate 28), Rincón backs off ten to fifteen meters and with his body provokes the bull to charge, wrapping him in the muleta and bending the bull around behind his hip. Instead of being at the mercy of a charging animal, Rincón seems to be reeling him in, and the bull obeys as if he were a trained dog. The effect on the crowd is instantaneous and profound: Rincón's dominance, mastery, and purity jolt them and the unexpected miracle of toreo lights up the ring in a succession of passes so elegantly executed they have the look of polished ritual. The powerful six-year-old 562-kilo manso of San Román gradually becomes helpless, succumbing pass by pass to Rincón's direction, until the matador relieves the baleful animal of all defensive doubt with a sword thrust up to the hilt in his withers. Exactly as he would have in Las Ventas, César Rincón opens wide the Puerta Grande of Colmenar Viejo—at the "gates of Madrid" (plate 29a).

The next day Emilio Martínez will write in *El País* that there is nothing new about "the magisterial nature of the Colombian, the highest priest of this lay religion [we call] the fiesta." Rincón "limited himself to the eternal truth of toreo: harmoniously mocking the fury of the horns with a scarlet lure, [in the way that] only he among the figuras dares to practice this gospel of the fiesta."

In the coolness after sunset, with the Guadarramas turning to silhouettes against the deepening sky of evening, César Rincón, riding out on shoulders, displays a wide, angelic smile (plate 29b).

San Sebastián de los Reyes: September 1, 1994

The fifth Victoriano del Río, number 18, Marginado, is not without his problems: he jumps and hooks violently at the end of each pass; he does not like to *humillar*, to lower his head as he follows the muleta; and he has perhaps more casta than bravura (plate 30a). But he has his merits too: he charges from a distance; in fact, he charges at a gallop; he increases in strength and bravery as the faena progresses; and, except for that odd jumping hook at the end of the pass, he has nobleza.

Rincón seems to glow in the encroaching darkness. The combination of valor, art, gracia, rhythm, and distance makes for one of the most complete faenas I have seen him do, and I write frantically in my notebook in Spanish between shots, "This is the Rincón of 'before,' as they say, who is in reality the Rincón of 'always,' the eternal Rincón who 'eternalizes' toreo and takes it to the plane of epic deeds [*gesta*] that escape the confines of time into the realm of the eternal present. When a bull such as this charges from a distance, galloping to the muleta, and Rincón awaits him, with tranquillity and with confidence, taking him smoothly in the muleta, bringing him through and around, and sending him on beyond, losing a few steps to take him again and again, the repeated fusion of the static man and the dynamic animal produces one of the most profound emotions of any human endeavor. It is hair-raising, overwhelming, captivating, and liberating. It is toreo.

"[With rare exceptions] only Joselito and Enrique Ponce can work at this level and they are both half a head taller than Rincón, their arms and legs far longer than his. Rincón's toreo, not unlike Belmonte's must have been, happens in spite of his body, and that handicap produces an unusual depth of empathy in the público. He kills in spite of the fact that his arms are not long enough for him to cross properly. And he is a torero *mandón*, controlling and sending the bull where he chooses. And he 'grows' in his toreo like Rosa Durán used to when she danced Peteneras at the old Zambra in Madrid in the '60s, or Manuela Carrasco that night she danced the dust out of the platform in the gardens of the Alcázar in Córdoba."

I am carried away as I write this in my notebook, but that is why I go to the bulls, to be carried away, to be enraptured, to find myself beside myself, to lose myself in that ex-static catharsis that great toreo can produce. I tell Gonzalo Rincón, next to me in the callejón: "You must be very proud."

They give César Rincón—who has already cut two ears in his first bull—the ears and the tail of Marginado. After his vueltas his face looks seraphic and his eyes have sadness in them, as though all the individual concerns and pains of the crowd, purged through his faena, were now contained in him (plate 30b).

The fifth bull, which Rincón himself applauds, and the sixth, from which Andrés Caballero bravely but not so aesthetically also cuts a tail,[4] are given vueltas. Everybody, including Ortega Cano, who cut two ears, and Victoriano del Río's mayoral, goes out on shoulders from San Sebastián de los Reyes "to heaven." Madrid's taurine "summer schools" in Colmenar and San Sebastián have suddenly turned César Rincón's temporada red hot (plate 30c).

Palencia: September 2, 1994

Has César's luck changed, I wonder as I drive to Palencia the next morning, or was it those good bulls of Victoriano del Río's, good and brave and dependable, like old friends?

The first touch of fall is in the air. When I left Madrid in the chilly blue morning I felt it and noticed small herds of fallen leaves rustling along the sidewalk. The afternoon sun in Palencia beats down warmly but the breeze has a cool edge. Outside the café across the street from the ring, José Antonio del Moral, Tom Weitzner, Harlan Blake, and I compare notes. I tell them about the great corrida they missed in San Sebastián and they tell me that Joselito and Enrique Ponce's mano a mano with the Victorino Martín bulls here in Palencia yesterday was not a success. None of us has any inkling that this afternoon—Espartaco, César Rincón, and Oscar Higares with bulls of Manuel Alvarez—will be grim.

The first bull, short on strength and dangerous, catches Espartaco as he goes in to kill, hitting him in the chest and face but failing to sink the horn. Then Rincón's bull—a 575-kilo sobrero of Sánchez Arjona—catches him in the second series of passes with the muleta, as he is moving out from the fence, and tosses him high in the air over his back, then whirls around and goes after him on the ground (plates 31 and 32). This bull also fails to sink his horn, but he does manage to injure Rincón, shake him up, and bloody him.

Rincón works through the pain at the fence, then, ignoring it, hobbles out and gives the uncertain animal a valiant faena, killing with one sword and a descabello to cut an ear as "all Spain" watches on television. Back at the fence he nearly collapses (plate 33).

The third bull nearly catches Oscar Higares, who, if Espartaco had not come back from the enfermería, would have had to kill four animals in a row. After his bull, an announcement is made that César Rincón cannot return from the enfermería for his second bull. Anderson Murillo gestures to me that it is his neck.

In the fourth bull Antonio Bejarano, Espartaco's banderillero, falls after putting in a pair of sticks. This time the animal does sink the horn, deep into the man's upper right thigh. As they come running with him through the callejón in front of me, I can see the blood pumping and bubbling out over his upper leg. It looks like the cornada everyone fears most. (As it turns out, the horn has penetrated upward into the pelvic region, ripping loose the interior saphenous vein.) As Espartaco lines up and kills the animal, my stomach comes and goes, bubbling like Bejarano's blood. When the sixth bull nearly catches one of Higares's banderilleros, I wonder if this corrida has been jinxed.

At the Hotel Rey Sancho, Luis Carlos, packing suitcases, tells me César has a distended ligament or ligaments in his right knee and that he will be out for at least twenty days. This is wishful thinking on Luis Carlos's part—Juanito is winking at me—which, if true, would mean Luis Carlos could leave right away for Colombia to see his wife and children.

In the hallway Gonzalo tells me César said: "Put some ice on it and we'll torear tomorrow in Bayonne. We'll at least go and see." Inside room 101 television commentator Fernando Fernández Román is talking and César, sitting on the bed with his right leg up, heavily bandaged, is listening. He has a cut on the back of his right thigh where the "pull" is and bruises all over his body, especially the neck, as Muri indicated, and the side of his forehead, where he has a big *raspón* with the skin all gone.

When Fernández Román leaves, César looks at me and says, "We'll stay here to see, and if I am up to going on to Bayonne, we'll go." I leave, saying the ritual phrase "Que te mejores, hombre," may you get better. Then I stick my head back in the room and say what I am really thinking: "Eres un torerazo"—you are one hell of a torero. He grins and shakes his head in mock disbelief.

Down at the bar, where I am having a copa with Tomás el Presidente, one of the banderilleros tells me, "Just between you and me, all he has is the puntazo in the thigh and all the rest is just theatre, in case he doesn't feel like toreando tomorrow." Somehow, after seeing the shape he is in, I doubt this piece of information. "I'll let you know what's going to happen," he says.

A few minutes later, about 10:30, Pablo Chopera tells me Rincón will torear (Bayonne is managed by the Choperas). At 11:45 I happen to notice the vans leaving. They are heading for France—now. So much for the information from my "source." Gradually I am learning that inside the taurine world you can never fully trust what you hear or read, only what you see or what you think you see. But five minutes later, the veteran critic Curro Fetén confides to me in a rare moment of complete seriousness: "They don't do it for money, they do it for themselves. ¡Están locos todos!" They are all crazy.

Bayonne: September 3, 1994

At 7:30 I wake to a morning cool and beautiful, exactly like last year, and I drive through the same lacy arabesques made by the irrigation fountains. I am securely strapped to the taurine wheel now, I think. Round and round she goes, next stop Bayonne. I think about Juanito—who has been training and working with Rincón for nearly twenty years now—talking last night at the bar about the fatigue that comes in the late summer: "Day after day and the same *cinqueño* [five-year-old bull] is trying to kill you. You have to give up everything from age ten on, just so that cinqueño can try to kill you, over and over again. You give up your studies, your family, your friends. Any kind of normal life." I wondered at the time if he was speaking for himself or for Rincón. Then I realized he did not much differentiate between himself and his matador. "Why do I leave my wife and my two children? To chase five-year-old bulls all over this bull's hide they call España. At least I gave up trying to kill them. The matador can do that. But it's still day after day for all of us. And that five-year-old bull never goes away, even if you no longer have to kill him. And if you do have to kill him, it's even worse. For the matador it is unimaginable. He dreams about those cinqueños. Many nights."

In my mind's eye, I see the big vans rumbling off into the street at midnight, heading for France. César is in the back of his, his knee up, iced, hurting, his head hurting. Everything hurting. Gladiator, I think, and traveling minstrel, rock star and "savior." A regular Hispano-Colombian traveling circus: César, the three banderilleros, the two picadores, Luis Alvarez, Luis Carlos, Juanito, and Primo. Sometimes more. But they are the ten that have to be there, the ten that are necessary to chase those cinqueños up and down the dusty bull's hide of Iberia. Toreros. The last serious men on earth.

At lunch in the Hotel Mercure in Bayonne, César tells Alain and Brigitte and me: "The trip last night was horrendous. I couldn't sleep because of the pain. The head hurt. The neck hurt. The right knee, the left leg." He laughs telling it. "There was no position I could lie in without something hurting. No matter which way I turned. Every bump in the road hurt, every turn. When we got to Bayonne this morning I couldn't put my right foot down on the ground."

"Did you take pain pills?"

"By the dozen. Nothing helped. Then later this morning we saw Dr. Bernard Vargues and he checked me over, gave me therapy, which helped a lot, and some more medicine, and said I could torear."

Later Alain would tell me that César had called him several times during the night from the van to get him to call Dr. Vargues. "I told him I couldn't call him in the middle of the night. 'This is France, not Spain. We don't call people in the middle of the night,' I said. 'I'll call him first thing in the morning.' He was in so much pain he was not thinking properly."

César is telling stories to the Briscadieu children about how Luis Carlos falls asleep all the time (because now he also has to drive one of the vans): "Luis Carlos falls asleep all the time. Driving. Dressing me for the corrida. Eating. Talking to Don Luis. He's probably asleep now. I only fall asleep in front of the bulls."

"Like yesterday," I put in.

"¡Sí, sí! That's what happened to me yesterday. I went to sleep and the hijueputa caught me." The Briscadieu girls snicker at the "hijueputa."

Somehow we get onto the subject of what is most important in life and César says abruptly: "¡El dinero!"

"¿Dinero?" I say. "No, hombre. La salud." Health.

"No, no, no, no."

"Sí, sí, sí, sí," interjects Alain.

Brigitte, who likes to mother César, rolls her eyes as if to say, "Oh, la, la."

"You can't do anything without money," César insists.

"You can't do anything without health, either," Alain and I say simultaneously. As the conversation reaches an impasse, I try to decide whether it is age or experience that makes him feel that way. This question will trouble me for a long time. What I did not yet understand was how it also troubled César.

"How much money would you give, right now, not to be in pain?" I ask him.

"Exactly my point," César says. "You have to have the money to give."

Alain and I know when we are defeated, and César contentedly returns to teasing with the Briscadieu girls.

Rincón makes the paseíllo without his montera, not because he is "new in this plaza," but because he cannot put his montera on over the wound on his forehead. All afternoon he looks physically impaired. Either his performance is doubly meritorious or he should not be performing, depending on your point of view. Or perhaps both.

The Jandilla bulls inspire little confidence, charge reluctantly, and lack strength. The fifth bull, called Hipoteca, catches Rincón but fortunately does not do him any permanent damage. The injured matador's bravery, however, appeals mightily to the crowd and even after four pinchazos he receives a grand ovation. All afternoon I am aware his reflexes are off.

In his room afterwards, he tells Dr. Vargues and Alain and me that he did not have enough strength to support himself on his right knee. "The bull caught me because I slipped. And I slipped because my knee wasn't strong enough for me to get out of his face." As I watch Dr. Vargues working on the injured knee, I think César Rincón has been lucky today.

Arles: September 11, 1994

The morning of September 10 back in Madrid, as I begin to wake up, I hear a popular song by Los del Río playing in my head. Two lines play over and over about blue bulls in the springtime in the sea. As I listen to the song, I *see* the toros azules charging through the curl of breaking waves. The blue water-bulls charge through the wave tunnels like surfers and I cape them with revoleras of foam from the crests. The color and the music have a surreal intensity and as those noble blue sea-bulls continue to charge with the smoothness of waves, I spin revolera after revolera of bubbly azure light and white spume in slow motion around my waist. Never have I had such dreams. I play the Los del Río tape all the way to Arles and the toros azules charge through my daydreams almost as intensely as they did in my dawn dream.

The following noon I wait for Luis Alvarez outside the empresario's office. It was a long trip not to see a corrida, I am thinking. Then I spot him with Luis Carlos and Juanito in a different café from the one where we had agreed to meet. Juanito tells me the Bernardino Píriz corrida in the new little ring at Ocaña the day before was the same old story: "Pedrito de Portugal cut a tail and Jesulín cut three ears. César's lote was a sovereign *mierda* [shit]." Corridas in Mérida on September 4 and in Albacete on the ninth had also been without much luck.

Up in Hubert Yonnet's office, Luis Alvarez receives the cash and I get my pass to the callejón. While I wait, I scan the local papers, which call the mano a mano between Espartaco and Rincón "le choc des stars" and "le duel au soleil."

Outside in the street the air is hot and laden with tension. Vendors have set up street stalls near the amphitheatre selling Provençal shirts and skirts, books, tapes, CDs, and pizza. Local Gypsies perform to a primitive beat and the girl who dances has no idea of how to dance or play castanets. Her mother sings, toothlessly, but with a macabre gracia.

Before five I am in the callejón setting up. It is hot, crowded, and over-policed. Espartaco in white and César Rincón in what Luis Carlos calls *burdeos*—Bordeaux, or the color of claret—line up, acknowledge the grand applause, and make the long paseíllo as the band breaks into Bizet.

Espartaco makes a good faena with the first Núñez del Cuvillo, a 540-kilo red bull, but has trouble killing it and loses an ear. Of the six Núñez del Cuvillo bulls, four are excellent, perhaps a little weak in the legs but beautiful animals, well presented, well horned, brave with good-to-great nobility, reminiscent of the corrida in Sevilla the year before when Rincón was gored. Of the four good ones, Juan Antonio Ruiz Román draws three. César Rincón draws one, number 70, a dark castaño of 500 kilos named Zalamero that comes out in second place.

Rincón begins the faena with a pass I have never seen before. He stands facing the fence, with the muleta between him and the fence, citing Zalamero, who stands farther along on the fence, perhaps ten meters away, for what looks like a pass you would use late in the faena and only with a manso that refuses to charge except along the barrera. As I am wondering what in the hell is he doing, Rincón shakes the muleta and calls, "¡Jé-jei, toro!" Zalamero charges and Rincón turns slowly 180°, the muleta picking up the bull as the man comes around to the outside. Now I see it: Eureka! The pass becomes, technically, an ayudado por alto *cambiado*, a two-handed high pass, switching the terrain from inside (tablas) to outside, but it requires a bull that is brave, comes from a distance, and has a tendency to shy away

Figure 34. Joan Simpson and Tim Bairstow, Arles, September 11, 1994. Rincón has just dedicated the Núñez del Cuvillo bull Sanguinario to them, and they are now intent on his faena.

from the wood, an unusual combination that Rincón has, of course, recognized.

The aficionados of Arles have never seen anything like it either, and they roar with approval. The music starts, and then the clapping, and everyone knows it will be a grand faena. Rincón repeatedly takes Zalamero from a distance to emphasize the animal's bravery and nobility, not breaking him down with low punishing passes, but taking him with long, smooth strokes to preserve his buoyancy, as he sculpts the kind of artistic faena that the crowd is not used to seeing from him (plate 34a). As Zalamero begins to lose steam, Rincón winds him closer around his waist, finishing with circular passes that bring the public to their feet. The sword goes in so deeply his hand seems to disappear into the morrillo, and when Zalamero crashes over (plate 34c), the Roman arena becomes a blaze of white and César Rincón takes a long, slow victory tour with both ears.

Pirata, the third bull, a 490-kilo *salinero,* an off-white animal whose coat is veined with chestnut, has perhaps an even sweeter charge than Rincón's bull, sweeter and more rhythmical. Espartaco does the best faena I have seen him do, cutting both ears and showing the critical French public that he has indeed developed in his thirties into a great torero of arte, a master of temple, of classical forms, and of a special technique he calls "the secret of the last second," waiting until the last second, past where you think it possible to wait, to pass the bull (6T6 45:36). His style has lost those hot, rough, impetuous edges with which he won over so many crowds in his youth and he has developed a sweetness, a smoothness, and an introspection that with Pirata approach the sublime (plate 34b).

Rincón dedicates the fourth bull to his devoted followers from Edinburgh, Joan Simpson and Tim Bairstow, or *los escoceses,* as the cuadrilla affectionately calls them. In any other circumstances except following those two grand faenas, Rincón would have cut an ear with this difficult bull, named Sanguinario, and Espartaco does manage an ear from the fifth bull, Catetón, which he dedicates to Rincón.

The enthusiasm of the crowd for these toreros of pundonor and arte runs so high that, after taking them on a tour of the oval on shoulders (plate 35a), they suddenly decide to carry them up and out through the old Roman gate, at the last minute turning right and heading up the dark, low interior stairway (plate 35b)—in their enthusiasm nearly knocking out both of the toreros on the old stone ceiling—and emerging at last through the ancient Roman portal into the streets and the clamoring throng (plate 35c).

Figure 35. Jacques Durand. The taurine critic for the Paris paper Libération. *I would find over time that Jacques and I agreed on many critical issues.*

Afterwards many will say it was the greatest afternoon in the amphitheatre of Arles.[5] Much discussion will ensue as to who "won" the mano a mano, but I think Jacques Durand, the perspicacious critic of *Libération*, will come closest to the truth when on September 17 he titles his review "Rincón and Espartaco upon a Shared Pedestal." Durand will declare there is no winner because the toreros nourished each other, stimulated each other, and enriched each other—unlike Rincón and Ponce or Joselito, which would be war. Instead there was a shared experience that "united the two toreros, both in the watchful silences of the crowd and in the heat of their ovations." The most unforgettable afternoon of recent years in the rings of France, it is also one of the most inspiring corridas I have seen anywhere.

I stop off at César's room briefly to discuss the fine afternoon and he explains the unusual pass that began his faena and that we will dub the Rinconcina. "I don't know if I invented it," he says, "but I have never seen anyone else do it."

I tease him about heading for old age—he has turned twenty-nine since I have last seen him—and he replies, "I'm already there!"

"Good," I say, "you'll make my work easier!"

"Yes! Yes! Mine too!" he replies. His triumph has put him in an excellent frame of mind.

It is a shame there is not more time to savor the moment, I think, but I realize I must be on the road. "See you tomorrow in Salamanca. ¡Buen viaje!" I say, and head for the parking lot.

Salamanca: September 12 and 15, 1994

I sleep in the car for an hour a hundred kilometers before Madrid and then run straight into the morning rush hour at 7:00 A.M. Dawn is about to break and the traffic has stopped out by the airport. I wonder where the vans are. Did they pass me while I slept? Traffic is stop-and-go all the way around Madrid but eventually I head to the northwest. The sun rises over the eastern end of the Guadarramas at 8:00 on the dot (in summer there is two-hour daylight saving in Spain) and bathes the chain of mountains in opalescent pink and charcoal gray.

At Sanchidrián I turn off the autopista and take the two-lane road across the plains of the Castillian breadbasket, tan and yellow in the slanting morning light. To the southwest I can see pine groves and poplars and behind them the Gredos rising like a purple wall. Hawks hunt the hayfields and solitary shepherds watch their flocks under a rainbow that arches over an approaching thunderstorm.

At 9:30 I park in the downtown underground lot and walk in the drizzle to the Gran Hotel to have breakfast. In the dining room Paco Aguado from 6T6 and Joselito are already eating. César comes in just behind me with Camilo Llinás and we have a quiet breakfast.

That afternoon Joselito cuts two ears after a colossal sword thrust on his first bull but then gets into an argument with a spectator during the faena of his second, inviting the spectator to come down into the ring. As a result the only brave bull of the afternoon, showing true Santa Coloma casta, goes to waste as Joselito kills it in a self-indulgent huff.

Up in Rincón's room in the Gran afterwards, everything is buzzing, as they are leaving at once for a corrida in Murcia. I have decided to stay in Salamanca, where Joselito and Enrique Ponce are scheduled to kill a corrida of Fraile de Valdefresno bulls, to wait for Rincón's corrida back here on the fifteenth.

I tell Tim Bairstow and Joan Simpson that when I saw Rincón on the thirteenth last year in Murcia I'd seen a man run over by an automobile. I tell them I do not want to repeat that experience, and I also say that the bulls are Núñez del Cuvillo again, and that the odds against his drawing another animal like Zalamero are virtually impossible. Tim says that they are going anyway and that he rather likes the night drives. I wish them luck and tell them that I admire their spirit.

The thirteenth is windy and gray in Salamanca, and it feels strange to be in a plaza de toros without César Rincón on the cartel. The Fraile de Valde-fresno bulls come out quite "complicated," and the best thing that happens is that Ponce cuts an uninspired ear in the sixth bull in the rain. Down in Murcia the sun shines and it is sweltering. On Tuesday the thirteenth[6] of September, César Rincón draws bull number 13, a 520-kilo Núñez del Cuvillo named Compañero, gives it an extraordinary faena, kills it straight on, being caught and tossed dramatically, his taleguilla ripped but his body unharmed, and cuts both ears and the tail. Evidently the only bad luck—or bad choice—is mine: Espartaco cuts three ears, Jesulín cuts two, and all three matadors go out on shoulders.

The next day Tim and Joan give me the details about Rincón's extraordinary performance. Finally, it seems, he drew a great bull at an important feria in Spain.

"What a terrible shame," says Joan, "that you'd pick that one not to go! After so many dreadful bulls. He was so marvelous! He was, in fact, his most perfect! And the kill! He went straight in and the bull caught him with the right horn and shook him up and down. We all thought he'd really got it this time. Especially after Sevilla and Bastonito in Madrid. But when he gets up, he never even looks at himself. He stands up, his hand goes up in the air, and the bull crashes over at his feet as if by magic. It was very dramatic, to say the least. Thirteen is his lucky number!" Joan's blue eyes glisten as she recalls the kill. "I cried then and I think I'm going to cry again now."

I ask them how they became followers of Rincón. Tim tells me they had seen their first corrida in 1988. "Out of the usual curiosity, you know, the tourist's approach. It was on the twelfth of October in Sevilla and we saw Rafael de Paula with six bulls. After that we came back in summer in 'eighty-nine and in 'ninety. It was like opening a door into another world. We thought surely we'd hate it. What a grand surprise!" Almost as an after-thought he adds, "Everyone in Edinburgh thinks we're mad, of course."

"Then," interrupts Joan, "we saw César for the first time. In Córdoba, in May of 'ninety-two. We've followed him ever since!"

"Why César Rincón?"

"Why? Because I fell madly in love with him!"

"How do you manage to get away?"

"We're both commercial writers—partners," explains Tim. "We work out of our home and we work for ourselves, so we just arrange our work sched-ule around his. It can be a bit tricky sometimes with deadlines and such, but we manage."

That night at dinner at the old Candil, over perfectly toasted roast suck-ling pig and Rioja, Michael is merciless: "Well, what did you expect, that he'd continue to draw bad bulls in honor of your not being there? Are you saying that you didn't go because of what happened the year before on the thirteenth? Sounds like you're the triskaidekaphobe to me. Surely you're not really superstitious?"

"Not really, no. I'm like my father, who always says he's not superstitious, but that he knocks on wood just in case the superstitious people are right. César is the same way about knocking on wood."

"Well, your torero certainly doesn't seem to be worried about the number thirteen. In fact, it sounds rather like he's a triskaidekaphile, if anything. But that still doesn't explain why you didn't go. Or perhaps you didn't know thirteen is his lucky number."

"How can you say thirteen is his lucky number, Michael? That bull that nearly killed him in Sevilla last year, Fugitivo, was number thirteen! It was good luck only if you figure he was supposed to die. I made an error in judgment. I figured that the odds for a good corrida were better here than there, and that in any case the chance of his drawing another good bull, specifically another Núñez del Cuvillo, was quite low. That, without factoring in a seven-hour drive each way. Plus I guess—thirteen or no—seeing that guy run over last year was still on my mind. Murcia didn't much appeal to me. After all, the drive isn't that bad. I've made far worse. I don't know. It was just, as it turned out, the wrong decision. Besides, you can't see them all."

"Ah, but you must!" says Michael, somewhere between gleefully and forcefully. "You must! You must see them all! It's the only way, old boy."

"Well, it was this time," I say, not without some dejection. "Why don't you rub it in?"

"Perhaps next time you'll think twice," says Michael.

"Perhaps I will. At least out of loyalty, if nothing else," I say, attacking the pig.

Early the next morning I dream that César tells me it was not wrong to miss Murcia, that I did not really miss anything, that he had been better in Arles, and that—but the telephone wakes me and I do not find out where the dream was leading me.

On the fifteenth, the bulls of Los Bayones do not cooperate. At least the weather is warmer, and I wonder if today will be another historic day for César Rincón, Espartaco, and José Mari Manzanares. Sevilla and Salamanca, the centers of bull breeding, ought to produce the best bulls and have the best ferias as a result, yet they seldom do. Nothing remotely historic happens.

At the front door of the hotel afterwards, when they are ready to leave, César climbs into the driver's seat of his van. I come up to the window and say, "You wouldn't have a photo of the matador, by any chance?"

César replies without a blink: "No. No. Look, I've just run out, right this minute."

"What a shame! He's such a terrific matador."

"Yes, that's true, he's the best. You should have seen him on the thirteenth in Murcia," he says as he swings the van away from the curb, heading back to France.

Plate 1. César Rincón, matador de toros. Photo taken August 11, 1995, in Béziers. Rincón is citing a bull of Juan Pedro Domecq.

2a

2b

2c

Plate 2. The cuadrilla, part one.
These are the men who were with
Rincón the whole time I followed
him. 2a: Anderson Murillo
"Muri," Colombian picador.
2b: Antonio Pinilla, Spanish
picador. 2c: Rodrigo Arias
"Monaguillo de Colombia" or
"Mono," Colombian banderillero.

3a

3b

Plate 3. The cuadrilla, part two.
3a: Curro Cruz, Spanish banderillero (formerly a matador), with
Rincón in '93. 3b: Manolo Gil,
Spanish banderillero, with Rincón in '93 and '94. 3c: Vicente
Yesteras, Spanish banderillero
(formerly a matador), with Rincón in '94 and '95. 3d: Manolo
Bélmez, Spanish banderillero,
with Rincón in '95.

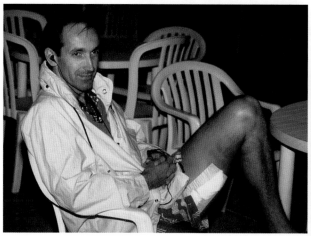

3c

3d

4a

4b

4c

4d

Plate 4. The staff. 4a: Luis Alvarez, the Spanish manager. 4b: Luis Carlos Rincón, César's brother, his sword handler and dresser. 4c: Juanito Márquez, aide to Luis Carlos and training assistant to Rincón. 4d: Edgar Heyn, Rincón's Colombian-born business manager.

5a

5b

Plate 5. The competition.
5a: Enrique Ponce, born in Valencia, trained in Jaén. 5b: José Miguel Arroyo, Joselito, from Madrid. 5c: Juan Antonio Ruiz Román, Espartaco, from Espartinas near Sevilla. 5d: José Ortega Cano, from Cartagena.

5c

5d

6a

6b

7a

7b

Plate 7. Circular pass, Mérida, September 5, 1993. The four photos show four successive moments in the same pass, making Oprimido come all the way around the matador. The wrist, the waist, and perfect rhythm.

8a

Plate 6. Mano a mano, Joselito, Palencia, September 3, 1993. 6a: Rincón with Madroño, forcing the charge. Notice how low the bull's head is, how intent he is on the receding muleta. 6b: Detail showing Madroño's tenacity. The bull is "looking for what he left behind." 6c: Joselito had an inspired afternoon. Here he gives Playero an impeccable natural.

6c

7c

7d

Plate 8. Killing, Mérida, September 5, 1993. 8a: Although Oprimido's head is high, Rincón has put the sword high up in the withers. 8b: Waiting in the callejón with Luis Alvarez for the presidente to award two ears.

8b

Plate 9. Killing, Arles, September 11, 1993. Using the descabello: Rincón will miss an instant later and the bull will charge forward, catching him. I missed the shot.

Plate 10. Achilles' thumb, Salamanca, September 15–16, 1993. 10a: Signing autographs outside the Gran Hotel before the corrida. 10b: One of the ten naturales he gives Cigarrero in spite of having cut his thumb. The bull's head is down, the muleta sweeping before him, casting the spell. 10c: Dressing the following day is made difficult, as is everything else, by the injured thumb.

10a

10b

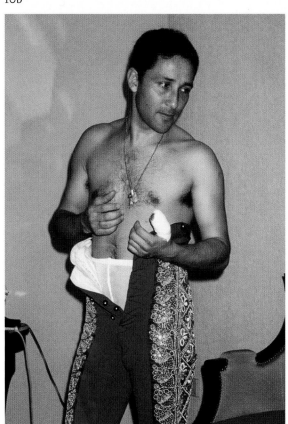

10c

11a

11b

Plate 11. Preparation for Madrid, September 21–22, 1993. 11a: On a training walk with Jorge Molina, the day of the "biblical" sky. 11b: Talavera turned out to be a waste of time and effort for Rincón, but the sky and the church were pure Goya.

12a 12b

12c

Plate 12. The day before Madrid,
September 30, 1993. 12a and 12b: In
the little "plaza" in the side yard of
his house. Killing, killing, killing.
12c: On the last training walk. From
left to right: Muri, César, Mono, and
Diego González. The weather is just
about to change. 12d: The state of the
thumb.

12d

Plate 13. Thinking about Madrid, September 30, 1993. His look says everything, especially responsabilidad.

Plate 14. Grace and danger, Madrid, October 1, 1993. 14a: Mariposito twisting back on Rincón's media verónica. 14b: Mariposito lunging upward with the horn thrust. This is the moment he gives Rincón the "closed cornada."

14a

14b

15a   15b

Plate 15. Against all odds, Madrid, October 1, 1993. 15a: Making Mariposito bend
around him in a long, low derechazo. 15b: Each pass is worth a series. A powerful,
far-sending chest pass. 15c: "You do it alone." 15d: Tranquillity and fire.

16a

Plate 16. Tienta in Vejer, October 8, 1993. 16a: Relaxing with Julio Vega,
Marismeño, friend and trainer. 16b: Rincón working a brave cow to the limit—
"breaking" himself.

15c

15d

16b

17a

18a   18b

Plate 18. "Made in Rincón," Cali, December 30, 1993, and January 2, 1994. 18a: The blind
ensabanado. Notice how the bull, blind in the left eye, cannot see Rincón. 18b: Colombiano,
his second Ambaló bull, turned out to be better. After dedicating the animal to Antoñete,
Rincón does a very characteristic faena, "made in Rincón," as the critics say. You can "see"
the temple in this pass. 18c: On January 2, 1994, the day of the missing tirantas, Rincón
came "to blow the place to pieces," as Molés would write. Rincón at his finest, toreo grande
on the right with his first Achury Viejo bull.

17b

17c

Plate 17. Disappointment in Cali, December 28, 1993. 17a: Rincón in one of the few passes he was able to make away from the fence. 17b: The Abraham Domínguez bulls quickly went to the tablas. Rincón spinning a molinete in tough terrain. 17c: Chest pass next to the fence. Even though he tries his utmost, a triumph is not possible.

18c

19a

19b

Plate 19. Mano a mano, Enrique Ponce, Cali, January 4, 1994. 19a and 19b: Dominating and breaking Sabanero, his first Guachicono. 19c: Enrique Ponce with Vengador. 19d: Both of them up on shoulders, although Ponce cannot go out the Puerta Grande, not having cut the requisite (in Cali) two ears from one animal.

20a

19c

19d

20b

20c

Plate 20. Wine of Nîmes, May 20, 1994. 20a: A verónica to Lapiceto, Rincón's first Samuel Flores. 20b: And the media verónica to finish the series. The fluid beauty of this cape work set a hot tone for a grand corrida. 20c: After cutting four ears, César allows himself a glass of fine wine.

21a

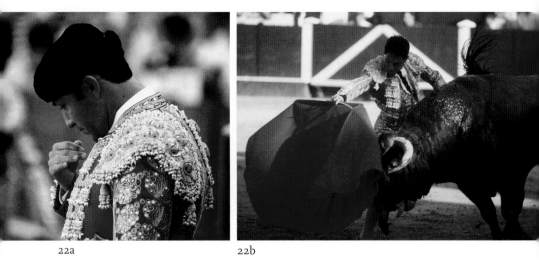

22a 22b

Plate 22. The light of Sanlúcar, June 4, 1994. 22a: Crossing himself before the fray. 22b: On this afternoon, everything seems destined to succeed: A high pass with his first bull. 22c: A right-handed chest pass with the difficult fifth bull. 22d: Into the infinite blue evening of Andalucía in June. Behind Rincón is Jesulín.

21b

Plate 21. Waiting for Rincón, Madrid, May 27, 1994. 21a: At the beginning of the faena with Querellante from the Marqués de Domecq, it looks like a triumph, but the overweight animal turns defensive. 21b: Rincón's spectacular kill causes a collective gasp from the público.

22c

22d

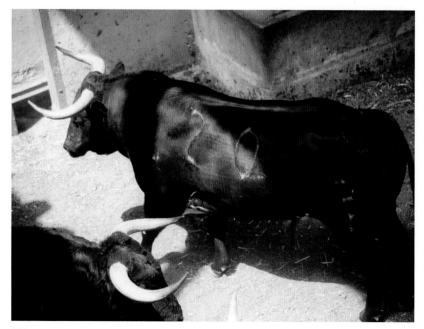

23a

24a

24b

23b

Plate 23. Bastonito, the beginning, June 7, 1994. 23a: Bastonito seen from above at the apartado. Not a large animal at 501 kilos, this Baltasar Ibán bull will nevertheless provide an object lesson in trapío. At this point no one has any idea of the fierceness of this animal. 23b: Rincón, asking the presidente's permission to dedicate the bull to the público. By now he knows what is in store for him, yet he dedicates the bull anyway.

Plate 24. Bastonito, the battle, June 7, 1994. Three successive moments in one of the decisive naturales with which Rincón "broke" Bastonito. 24a: He cites de frente and Bastonito gallops after the muleta. 24b: Rincón, leaning onto the "axis" leg, is able to control Bastonito with the cloth. 24c: Continuing to lean on that axis leg, he forces Bastonito around the axis and behind his hip, making Bastonito go where Bastonito does not want to go.

24c

25a

25b

26a

26b

Plate 26. Bastonito, the consequences, June 7, 1994. 26a: Rincón is clutching his right hand, because of the pain, to his groin. At first we all thought he was gored there. 26b: At the fence he nearly faints from pain and loss of blood. 26c: Wrapping a towel around his right hand to stop the bleeding, he carries Bastonito's ear in his left. 26d: Summoning some reserve, he discards the towel, puts the ear in his right hand, and takes his vuelta. As Arévalo will say, "There is not and there never has been—that I have seen or that I know of—a torero like him."

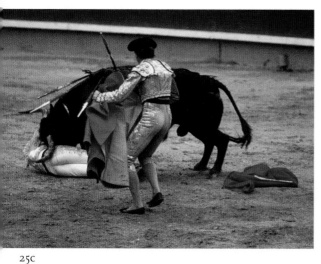

Plate 25. Bastonito, to the death, June 7, 1994. Although "broken," the bull is extremely dangerous and Rincón must still kill him. 25a: As Rincón sinks the sword so deeply that he cuts his hand, Bastonito flicks out his lethal right horn, hooking Rincón's trailing leg. 25b: Flipped onto his back, Rincón tries to roll away as Bastonito turns on him. 25c: Finally the capes arrive, but not before the man and the animal lock in a deadly embrace.

25c

26c

26d

Plate 27. Good day in Almería, August 23, 1994. Finally Rincón draws two good bulls, again from the Marqués de Domecq, and cuts an ear from each: "I also have the right now and then to enjoy a good bull!" 27a: A right-handed pass with alegría. 27b: A monumental chest pass with the left. Both with the second bull.

27a

28a

Plate 28. Domination in Colmenar Viejo, August 29, 1994. The authoritative low, doubling passes with which Rincón began, with a nearly six-year-old bull of San Román.

27b

28b

Plate 29. At the gates of Madrid, Colmenar Viejo, August 29, 1994. 29a: With the ears of the San Román bull. 29b: "Against the deepening sky of evening, César Rincón, riding out on shoulders, displays a wide, angelic smile."

29a

30a

Plate 30. Grand triumph, San Sebastián de los Reyes, September 1, 1994. 30a: Marginado, jumping and hooking at the end of the pass. The bull is so close to the camera and moving so violently, the only thing in focus is the edge of the muleta. 30b: "His face looks seraphic and his eyes have sadness in them." 30c: All three matadors go out on shoulders and Madrid's "summer schools" in Colmenar and San Sebastián turn Rincón's temporada red hot.

30b

29b

30c

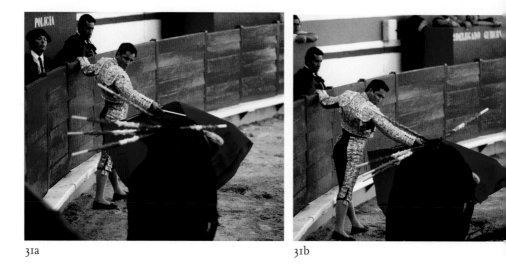

31a   31b

Plate 31. Fine beginning in Palencia, September 2, 1994. Four successive moments as Rincón characteristically begins his faena in tablas. It smells of something grand.

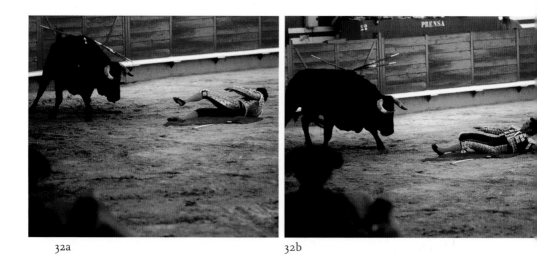

32a   32b

Plate 32. Peril in Palencia, September 2, 1994. Immediately following the pass in plate 31, while I was changing film, the Sánchez Arjona bull caught Rincón and tossed him high in the air. Rincón hit the bull's rump as he fell. 32a: The bull still turning around to gore Rincón on the ground. 32b: As the bull moves forward, Rincón rolls. 32c: Just as the animal reaches Rincón, Yesteras enters the frame to make the quite. 32d: Raking Rincón's back and neck with the horn.

31c

31d

32c

32d

Plate 33. Collapse in Palencia, September 2, 1994. After making a valiant faena and cutting an ear, Rincón has trouble keeping his feet. He will not be able to kill his second bull.

34a

34b   34c

Plate 34. Mano a mano with Espartaco, Arles, September 11, 1994. 34a: A derechazo with Zalamero, Rincón's only good Núñez del Cuvillo bull. But he was very good: the head is lowered, the animal intent on the muleta. 34b: Espartaco in an elegant natural with Pirata, the salinero. 34c: Watching Zalamero wobbling and going down.

35a

Plate 36. Drafty afternoons, Nîmes, September 17–18, 1994. 36a: César, happy as usual in France, in the Hotel Imperator in Nîmes. 36b: Putting on his dress cape for the paseo on September 18. Mono (back to the camera) and Vicente Yesteras help him with the adjustment. Note César's look of detachment.

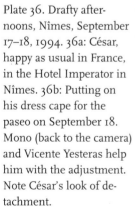

36a

35b   35c

Plate 35. Greatest afternoon in Arles, September 11, 1994. 35a: Caesar and Spartacus in the Roman arena. 35b: Going up the dark and dangerous interior Roman stairway, in the process nearly knocking the matadors senseless. 35c: "Emerging at last through the ancient Roman portal into the streets and the clamoring throng."

36b

Plate 37. Tension, Nîmes, September 18, 1994. Four moments of attempted conversation, just before the paseo, when the tension is greatest. César is trying but his mind is obviously elsewhere.

Plate 38. Monster in Logroño, September 21, 1994. Two views of Rincón with Potrico, the 675-kilo bull of El Pilar that he nearly failed to kill. This afternoon is our low point. You can actually see his lack of confidence in the body language.

39a

Plate 39. Depression, Consuegra de Toledo, September 22, 1994. 39a: The little ring at Consuegra de Toledo, with Don Quixote's windmills in the background. 39b: Lining up for the paseo. Rincón looks, well, bad.

40a   40b

Plate 40. Rainbow, Consuegra de Toledo, September 22, 1994. 40a: Was it the rainbow? What brought César back? 40b: Again, notice the change—the confidence restored—in César's body language. 40c: A powerful derechazo with the brave bull of Galache. The Rincón of always.

39b

40c

41a

41b

Plate 41. Disaster in Cali, January 3, 1995. 41a: Unloading one of Ernesto González Caicedo's bulls as night falls. 41b: Rincón looks great and the crowd loves him. How will his feet be? 41c: The spectacular entrance into the ring of the fifth bull, Opita. But he will prove to be only another manso. 41d: Mansedumbre: Opita backing away from the encounter.

42a

42b

Plate 42. Half a triumph, Manizales, January 6, 1995. 42a: Ultrasound for the still swollen feet. 42b: Directing the death of the Rocha bull. 42c: Rincón, maestro, with the accoutrements of triumph. But the thumb was injured again. 42d: The bota of Coca-Cola from a friend.

41c

41d

42c

42d

43a

Plate 43. Festival, Torre de Esteban Hambrán, May 7, 1995. 43a: César's chalice. Many of the matadors use such silver goblets. 43b: After the kill, unwinding with Julio Vega in the callejón.

44a   44b

Plate 44. Tienta at Guadalix de la Sierra, May 8, 1995. 44a: A low, stylized, extreme media verónica. 44b: A natural, pushing the cow. 44c: A pase de pecho, "breaking." Notice the curve in the cow's body. 44d: Taking her down to clip the horns so she cannot injure her herdmates in the future.

43b

44c

44d

Plate 45: Slabs of meat, Madrid, May 17, 1995. Rincón in a difficult, but typical, moment with Saltillo, the sardo, one of the out-of-type Baltasar Ibán bulls. A perfect example of Madrid's self-defeating strategy regarding huge animals.

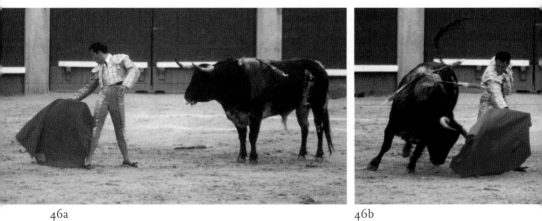

46a   46b

Plate 46. Dream of thirteen ships, Madrid, May 29, 1995. 46a: Rincón turning back to offer Emplazado the muleta backhanded on the opposite horn. 46b: Emplazado takes the lure and Rincón winds him in a complete circle, breaking open the faena. 46c: Emplazado, the bull of Astolfi, lunging upward in the pase de pecho. 46d: "The most exquisite estocada recibiendo I ever hope to see."

46c

46d

Plate 47. Fifth trip to heaven, Madrid, May 29, 1995. Rincón outside the ring near the Calle Alcalá, perilously perched on the shoulders of the crowd. Astolfo Núñez is just to the left of César's right hand. I took this photograph from atop the van. Edgar Heyn, far right, has just gone out to help get César into the van.

48a   48b

48c

Plate 48. Fiesta, May 29–30, 1995. 48a: The radiant ambassador, María Emma Mejía, and the beaming manager in suite 803 of the Foxá. 48b: Finally the matador emerges from the inner sanctum.
From left to right: César, Natalia Lorente, Edgar Heyn, and Alain Briscadieu. 48c: Fiesta, chez César.
I took this about 3 A.M. in César's wine cellar-salon. The intimacy of the triumph: Yesteras on the
left, Muri with his arm around César. Taurine history.

49a   49b

Plate 49. Tutelary divinities. The heads of the four Madrid bulls of 1991, mounted in César's wine cellar-salon. 49a: Santanerito, Baltasar Ibán. 49b: Alentejo, Murteira. 49c: Tomillero, Samuel Flores. 49d: Ramillete, Moura.

50a

Plate 50. Detachment, León, June 24, 1995. 50a: The little altar. The Bible open to Psalm 91. The image in the back against the wall is San Judas Tadeo, Saint Jude. The photograph is of César's mother and sister. 50b: Before a corrida, even when he smiles, César wears a trancelike stare. The more trancelike, the better the afternoon will usually be. 50c: Killing his first Victoriano del Río, cutting his first ear. The trance pays off.

49c

49d

50b

50c

51a

51b

Plate 51. State of grace, León, June 24, 1995. 51a: Unhinging the fierceness of Exquisito. 51b: Lit with an inner fire. 51c: Even with the sword in to the hilt, Rincón's expression does not change. 51d: "I realize that my wish for a state of grace is coming true."

52a

51c

51d

52b

52c

Plate 52. Half-luck, Pamplona, July 10 and 14, 1995. 52a: The rowdy peñas on the sunny side. Although many aficionados do not like Pamplona because of this behavior, the atmosphere is unique. For a torero to triumph, he must overcome the crowd's riotous nature as well as the bull's. 52b: Rincón connects again in Pamplona, with Sabedorito, a brave Cebada Gago bull, cutting an ear. But the corrida is suspended because of a downpour. 52c: Soñador, from El Torreón, is too fat and cannot keep his feet. Rincón's derechazo is splendid but the animal is already starting to cave in.

53a 53b

Plate 53. Disdain, Béziers, August 11, 1995. 53a: Rincón saluting after the death of his first Juan Pedro Domecq. 53b: Praise from Espartaco in the callejón after killing his second. 53c: Natural del desdén, using only the tip of the muleta and the play of the wrist.

54a

Plate 54. Cape work, Dax, August 14, 1995. 54a: Defending his throne in France against Joselito and Enrique Ponce, Rincón begins strongly with Lagartero, his first Victoriano del Río. Citing for a chicuelina. 54b: Making the chicuelina.

53c

54b

55a   55b

Plate 55. King of France, Dax, August 14, 1995. 55a: Pase de pecho to Lagartero. 55b: End of the faena with Lagartero. 55c: After trying to kill recibiendo, he puts this devastating volapié into the bull.

Plate 56. Rascally Horns, Bilbao, August 24, 1995. Two of the fine pases de pecho, the first with the left hand, the second on the right. Note the length of horn of this Samuel Flores bull.

55c

57a

57b

Plate 57. Thievery, Almería, August 26, 1995. 57a: Rincón, in a very posbelmontino pase de pecho, brings the bull as far around to the opposite shoulder as possible, with the good second bull of El Torreón. But the presidente denies the ear. 57b: In the van afterwards, Rincón is unhappy with the presidente's decision.

Plate 58. Everyone triumphs, San Sebastián de los Reyes, August 28, 1995. After another great afternoon with the Victoriano del Río bulls, Ortega Cano, Pepín Liria, and César Rincón on the shoulders of the crowd.

59a

59b

59c

Plate 59. Tribute to a grand aficionada, Bayonne, September 3, 1995. 59a: Citing to kill Hacendoso, number 13, of the Marqués de Domecq. 59b: Coming to retrieve his montera from the Condesa de Barcelona. 59c: On the shoulders of the crowd again. Taurine truth, as Curro Fetén said.

60a

Plate 60. Showdown in Dax, Enrique Ponce, September 10, 1995. This was to be the duel in the sun. 60a: Enrique Ponce, the most important figura of the decade, waiting in the wings. 60b: César Rincón, the Caesar of the Americas, getting ready for the paseo.

61a

Plate 61. Blowout in Dax, September 10, 1995. 61a: Rincón with the Alcurrucén bull Cumbrealta. The sun still shines. 61b: Ponce in a nearly identical pass with Cigarrito as the first drops preceding the downpour begin to fall. You can see raindrops on the lens.

60b

61b

62a

Plate 62. Ear of the season, Logroño, September 25, 1995. 62a: On the twenty-second the Martín Arroyo bulls are so bad, I begin to create fantasies. This is Rincón, "hiding" behind his cape, thinking of the faena he would like to do if only the bulls would charge. 62b: On the twenty-fifth Rincón cuts the last ear of our season, winning the prize for the best faena of the feria, in spite of the presidente's refusal to award the second ear.

62b

63a

63b

63c

Plate 63. Against the Magnificent Seven, Bogotá, December 17, 1995. 63a: A strong doubling pass with Darío Restrepo's fine bull Gavilán. 63b: A rain of flowers for the returning hero. 63c: "Theseus has come home."

Plate 64. End of the saga. There would be no more hiding behind the cape as the bull entered the ring, no more waiting in the sun. Now was the time to breed bulls and make himself whole.

Nîmes: September 17 and 18, 1994

The morning of the seventeenth, after picking up my passes for César's corridas, I have a café au lait down from the Maison Carrée, one of the best-preserved Roman buildings in the world. A band plays a pasodoble to make one's blood boil but the weather is cool and far too breezy. The more I come to Nîmes—a touch of New Orleans, a hint of Sevilla, a chunk of Rome, a very tasty bouillabaisse—the more I appreciate it, but the weather is almost as antitaurine as the posters on all the streetlamps that say "La corrida devant la justice." Yet it is hard to buy a ticket at any price, and the streets— where paellas bubble, sausages fry, music plays, bars overflow—are full of the ambiente of feria.

I chat with Jacques Durand about the corrida in Arles on September 11, and he confirms to me his impression that Rincón and Espartaco, almost by design, shared equally in the glory that afternoon. A band struts by outside playing "When the Saints Go Marching In," and we come out to watch. I have never heard it better, not in Pamplona, not in New Orleans, but the north wind is rising and the temperature is dropping.

Setting up in the callejón, I talk with Ivon Parés, the photographer for *Aplausos,* about the corrida in Arles. "Did you know," he says, "that's the only time they've ever taken anybody out through the Roman gate?"

"No, I did not know that. It makes it that much more of an honor, then."

"Exactly."

"You know, Ivon," I say, "in Spain some critics are saying that Espartaco has dethroned César Rincón in France."

"That is just Spanish jealousy. Nobody who saw the corrida can say that one was definitively better than the other. They were both superb. The rest is all personal taste."

"That's right," chimes in Luis Carlos Rincón, who has overheard our conversation as he puts together the muletas. "Some of the critics are always looking for any excuse to bad-mouth the Colombiano. It never fails. It's too bad, but that's how it is. We just have to learn to live with it. And it's especially wrong because César and Juan Antonio are good friends. There's no one César respects more."

The cartel could not be better—Victorino Martín bulls for Manzanares, Espartaco, and Rincón—but the drafty afternoon does not live up to its promise and the best bull of the day is the local cowboys' bull stew, *boeuf des gardians,* that Luis Carlos, Alain, and Tim and Joan and I have for dinner that night while we discuss what a generally disastrous afternoon it has been (plate 36a).

On the morning of the eighteenth the mano a mano of Joselito and Enrique Ponce is blown to pieces by the mistral, and that afternoon when César Rincón, Julio Aparicio, and Finito de Córdoba line up for the paseo (plate 36b), the north wind continues to howl. I notice people in the arena wearing overcoats. Although César appears animated in the callejón, I can sense that the combination of wind and responsabilidad has done its work (plate 37).

The José Luis Marca bulls turn out to be magnificent, but the wind blows so hard during the first four that the matadors can only defend themselves. The corrida should have been canceled.

When the fifth bull comes into the ring, not only is he the best bull, but the wind drops. Julio Aparicio does an inspired, overly theatrical faena on his knees as though he had a sign from the taurine gods—and perhaps he did—reaping two ears in the only important triumph in the entire Feria des Vendages. Nevertheless, César Rincón is the clear triunfador of the temporada in Nîmes, and that night he is presented with a triple magnum of Lanson champagne on which is etched "Hommage à / césar rincón / Pour sa temporada / 1994 à Nîmes."

Logroño: September 20 and 21, 1994

The mistral blows for the fourth day as I make my way back across the Mediterranean coast of France, and a heavy snow has fallen in the Pyrenees. In the badlands of Aragón the earth becomes tawny and the sky is high and blue. Monasteries, Moorish towers, and stones the color of iron ore dot the landscape. Thirty kilometers east of Zaragoza a church, a ruined castle, and the silhouette of the black bull of Spain—for years the commercial emblem of Osborne sherry and brandy—stand astride the hills.[7] A minaret rises in the town square.

Going past Zaragoza you can barely glimpse the towers of the cathedral amid the clumps of mid-rise apartment buildings. Then as you leave town, running parallel to the hills along the Ebro that stretch like a circus line of white elephants northward toward Navarre, you return to bleak and desolate country. At Alagón the road swings out from the Ebro to the west, and in the campo fires burn in the distance below the peak of Moncayo—mystical and warlike, as the poet Antonio Machado wrote—rising in blue and white relief against the flame-colored sky. I arrive in Logroño just before dark.

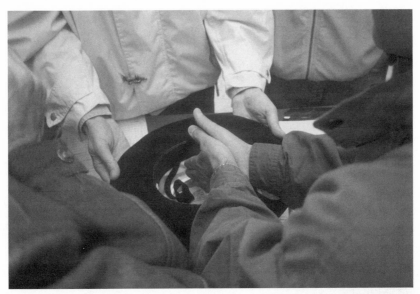

Figure 36. Luck of the draw, Logroño. September 20, 1994. The cigarette papers go into the hat. Rincón's representative, Monaguillo, will draw numbers 19 and 27. The ganadero believes number 27 is the bull of the corrida, but the bull will break a horn. Not even the luck of the draw works sometimes.

At the sorteo, on this morning of September 20, they "patch" the corrida of Luis Algarra—one bull broke a horn in the unloading—with a bull of Veiga Teixeira. We draw numbers 19 and 27, both Algarras, and the ganadero tells us 27 is the bull of the corrida. As Curro Vázquez, César Rincón, and Enrique Ponce line up for the paseo, it feels as if it could rain any minute.

Number 27, the ganadero's favorite, has broken a horn while being put into the *chiqueros,* the individual pens, so Rincón faces a Veiga Teixeira, number 97 at 510 kilos, a bull with a smooth charge on the right horn only. Bothered by the wind, Rincón nevertheless makes a valiant faena on that side and kills with a pinchazo and a good estocada that earns him a petition for the ear, a vuelta, and the best ovation of the afternoon.

The rain begins during Enrique Ponce's bull, which is soso. Ponce's faena gets better as it progresses, but most people are scrambling to get out of the rain. It has not rained a drop all summer in Logroño, but today is the first afternoon of feria, and down it comes as though the corrida were a rain dance.

Rincón's second, the Algarra at 520 kilos, turns out to be a full-blown manso that he has to chase. Rincón attempts a faena, but everything gets waterlogged and his knee bothers him from running after the bull. After the bull goes down, César looks up at me under my small umbrella as if to say, "What are we doing here?"

Ponce's second bull breaks a horn against the burladero, and the people who are still in the plaza begin to leave. All I can think of is a big steaming bowl of *pochas* and some fine, fruity young Rioja to accompany the white beans and warm the body and gladden the soul.

Natalia Lorente, Rincón's longtime friend and now the taurine interviewer for Antena-3, brightens the sorteo the following morning, cheering up the somewhat morose cuadrilla. The corrida of El Pilar bulls looks huge and "serious" up front. Rincón draws a black bull, number 40, named Renacuajo, which weighs 539 kilos, and a gigantic castaño, number 36, named Potrico. Potrico weighs 685 kilos but he is not fat. (Potrico means ironically "little colt," but the secondary meaning of the word, "torture rack," seems more fitting.)

Today, September 21, marks the last day of summer, the Fiesta de la Vendimia, or grape harvest, and the feast day of San Mateo. It also happens to be

Figure 37. Natalia Lorente and Luis Carlos Rincón, Logroño, September 21, 1994. Natalia will brighten up the sorteo but not César's luck. In the photo Natalia and Luis Carlos study the possible lots. Mono will draw a 685-kilo bull named Potrico that will give Rincón trouble.

Figure 38. Antonio Pinilla in a bind, Logroño, September 21, 1994. Potrico has gotten under the rear of the horse and is upending it in the photograph. Pinilla, going over, can't get his foot out and will be caught under the horse for some time. Somehow he gets loose without injury.

Charles Patrick Scanlan's sixtieth birthday. Despite the birthday festivities at lunch, we are all freezing as we head for the plaza de toros, and I am grateful for the scarf and gloves Charles Patrick has loaned me. In spite of the weather, the ring has filled to see César Rincón, Jesulín, and Manolo Sánchez. Even Televisión Española has come. At least today the sun is shining.

When Potrico trots onto the sand, he looks as big as the proverbial cathedral. Everything starts well as Rincón gives the huge beast seven verónicas and a media. Then Potrico slams into the rump of Pinilla's horse, pitching them over and briefly pinning Pinilla underneath. For a moment the situation looks grim, then Pinilla wiggles free and picks the bull twice more to grand applause. Vicente Yesteras puts in two spectacularly placed pairs of banderillas and takes his corresponding bow. Rincón, obviously seeing a bull for a triumph, dedicates to the público.

But Potrico charges in erratic waves, hesitating, then rushing, and he now refuses to put his head down. As the bull becomes more and more distracted, he begins to crowd the matador, and Rincón cannot recenter the charge. A few passes work smoothly, but he takes too long trying to teach the animal to follow the cloth. As time passes, the man begins to "doubt" the animal, and by not standing still he draws the animal's attention to himself (plate 38).

As he lines Potrico up for the kill the first aviso sounds. He hits bone twice and then gets in half a sword. Potrico goes down but suddenly rises like a Cape buffalo coming out of the bush. He kneels again but gets up when Manolo Gil misses with the puntilla. Then the second aviso goes off, meaning Rincón has only two minutes left.

Potrico, standing, defends himself every time Rincón approaches with the descabello, making quick forward rushes to catch him. Twice he nearly succeeds. He is going back alive! I think. But Potrico kneels again, and this time Manolo Gil nails him.

Renecuajo is a complete manso and Rincón limits himself to lining him up and killing him. The crowd gives him a bronca. It is unlike Rincón to choose this option, and he seems full of doubt and lacks his usual will. It is the worst performance I have seen him give. And "all Spain" is watching. From the tendido they yell at him: "¡Fuera! Get out of here! Go home!" And they whistle at him and boo.

In Jesulín's bull they continue to yell at him: "Go home, César!" Jesulín cuts an unaesthetic ear, but he gets to the público, and as he takes his vuelta, César Rincón watches him from the callejón. Jesulín has just broken El Cordobés's record for most corridas in a season (121 in 1970) and still has dozens of contracts to go.

By the time the sixth comes in, the light has gone and I am cold. Manolo Sánchez goes on his knees and gives a beautiful series of derechazos, beginning a grand faena, very smooth, very torera, with naturales de frente and a beautiful abaniqueo. He also cuts an ear, a very well deserved ear that, had the bull died sooner, would probably have been two.

When Manolo Sánchez leaves the ring, they shout "¡Torero!" Jesulín is mobbed outside by his fans and has to be protected by the police. They boo Rincón as he leaves and throw cushions at him. As I leave the plaza, I feel as though I may be freezing.

Consuegra de Toledo: September 22, 1994

Two dozen buzzards circle high overhead above the car and John Fogerty sings "Walk on the Water." South of Burgos the weather has cleared and the hay is baled and stacked high. The fields have been burned and the stubble around the edges still smolders. César Rincón did not walk on the water yesterday, I am thinking. He barely walked on the land. Will he do it today?

When I asked Luis Alvarez why they did not cancel this last corrida for today, September twenty-second, he told me: "I wanted to cancel, and I called the empresario at Consuegra to tell him César was not in good shape. But the man was practically crying, saying it would ruin him. He said he had already changed the bulls and the dates for us, and that if Rincón didn't come, it would be a disaster for him." His words trail off and he shrugs: La responsabilidad.

At 4:00 showers race across the fields of La Mancha, spitting bolts of lightning like summer storms off the Gulf of Mexico. At Tembleque sudden hail falls, rattling hard against the roof of the car and the glass, and I remember that I have left my umbrella in Madrid. When I get to the Hotel Contreras at Madridejos, the storm is over and I find Primo and the cuadrilla but no César. He arrives alone in his Mercedes at 4:20 for a corrida at 5:00. Twenty minutes later we are all in the van, riding over to Consuegra de Toledo, a rural town backed by a high castle and a string of windmills straight out of *Don Quixote* (plate 39a). In the van it is quiet. César and Luis speak briefly of the bulls yesterday in Logroño. César has seen a tape made from television and he is not happy about his performance.

The Francisco Galache bulls for César Rincón, Julio Aparicio, and Pepín Liria come out charging for the most part. The first one is the exception: he appears weak in the legs and Luis Alvarez yells to Rincón, "¡Que no ve!"—he can't see. But Rincón does not attempt much with the animal. He seems to be in Colombia already, or anywhere but in Consuegra. His eyes have looked vacant all afternoon and his energy level strikes me as low, without any enthusiasm. It makes me wonder if the hepatitis is coming back (plate 39b).

Aparicio cuts an ear from a fine looking *lucero,* an animal with the "morning star" on his forehead. Pepín Liria, in the rain and cold under a rainbow (plate 40a), bravely cuts both ears from his bull.

Was it the rainbow? Or did César Rincón get pricked with a jealous pride? He comes out a different person, centered, concentrated, vibrantly emotional and transmitting that emotion to the público, who instantly love him. After a faena as electric as the storm that has just broken around us (plates 40b and 40c), he drives in hard for the kill but hits bone, then gets in a good sword and drops the animal on the second descabello. With a more effective sword he would have cut at least two ears, but now he must be content with one. It does not matter. He takes a slow, triumphant vuelta and the kids and the old people swarm to him, throwing in hats and botas of wine in old-fashioned pueblo style.

I have followed Rincón closely with the camera, free to move in the callejón in this small town ring where the "rules" are less strictly enforced. The excitement of the physical proximity of the animal, the pulsing emotion from the crowd behind me, and the adrenaline rush of the matador himself have enveloped me. When he finishes the vuelta I pronounce to him the ritual but heartfelt phrase "¡Bien, torero!"

His eyes shine with their normal brightness now and he turns to shake my hand, strongly, saying: "Gracias, Alain," calling me as he always does by the French version of my name. Our season is over, I think, and I realize how cold it has turned.

For me there is little left in this incomplete season, now that César Rincón has headed for Colombia to have his feet operated on. The small bones have multiple fractures that have knitted poorly and the surgeon is going to rebreak the bones and set them, in effect reconstructing both his feet, especially the right. He will be in a wheelchair for some time. On September thirtieth I fly north to see Alain and Brigitte Briscadieu at their Bordeaux townhouse.

One evening we watch a documentary with old French footage of César's first tienta with Paco Camino. I cannot help noticing the unfinished wooden floors of that ill-fated house in the Barrio de Fátima, the walls with no paint, the almost squalid condition of the little white dog Príncipe. César, who looks very small and thin, is eating soup and talking about how his mother is always at his side (and she is there beside him). "I dedicate everything to her," he says to the camera.

Then come scenes of October 12, 1991. César is in the airport at Bogotá, hiding behind the police cordon. He is saying, "How can this be?" People are reaching and stretching to touch him as though he were the Virgin. Mono and Muri and Camilo Llinás are with him. Girls are hugging and kissing him and he has that vacant stare. Then Francia and Paolo, Luis Carlos's little children, run up to hug him and he responds to them. His sister Rocío is there too, and everyone looks very preoccupied. Millions of people—literally millions: the crowds remind me of the films of Germany and Italy during and just before the war—are waiting, waving banners, screaming "¡Torero! ¡Torero!" He tries to speak and a drunk yells in his face, "¡Monstruo! ¡Monstruo!" The degree to which the people of Colombia have responded to his triumphs in Spain in 1991 impresses me greatly and at the same time it depresses me. Alain and I look at each other and shake our heads.

That Sunday night after the corrida in Floirac we listen to Fernando Fernández Román's interview with César Rincón on Radio Nacional de España, but the transmission is poor and all we hear him say is "multiple fractures" and that he is "in bed with his feet up" and that he "will be inactive for at least two months." But we know that.

On my last night back in Madrid, over dinner at Casa Botín, Edgar Heyn tells me that César's feet were worse than they had thought but that the operation has evidently gone well. On the flight home the next day, I have a very unfinished feeling about everything.

The year-end ranking in *6T6*, never based solely on statistics, came out in November: Ponce, Joselito, Manzanares, Espartaco, Jesulín, and Rincón. My own ranking for the year, were I asked to make one, would have been Ponce, Joselito, Rincón, Espartaco, Manzanares, Jesulín. At any rate, more than with rankings, I was concerned with whether Rincón could recover from the operation on his feet. I got the feeling that his career was on the line.

Emilio Martínez in *El Ruedo* on September 20 thought that, in spite of Rincón's great triumphs in Almería, San Sebastián de los Reyes, Colmenar, Palencia, and France, his continued effort to perform with maximum purity had left "his body and soul broken." He compared Rincón to the *ecce homo*, the figure of Christ that Pilate scorned with the Latin words for "lo, the man," an allusion that means by extension a broken or lacerated person.

I believed, slightly to the contrary, that his spirit was capable, but about his severely castigated body I could not be so positive. The only thing I knew for sure was that it was not yet finished.

1995

On December 27, 1994, I run into Irish aficionados David and Marlene Fitzpatrick in the Miami airport. David says, so quietly amid the airport uproar that I can barely hear him, "They say he's not coming to Cali."

"David," I say, "I know him pretty well by now. If he can possibly torear, he will." When I get on the plane I pick up the Colombian *El País* and there is the notice: "Viene Rincón." He will arrive from Madrid today, it says. The unanswered question is, will he be able to torear on the twenty-ninth?

Cali: January 3, 1995

The morning of the twenty-eighth, Jorge Molina and I go to the plaza for the sorteo of Guachicono bulls for this afternoon, where Gonzalo Rincón informs us that César will test himself this afternoon at Darío Restrepo's ganadería near Bogotá.

Two hours later the Colombian matador Enrique Calvo el Cali tells us he has just talked to César. "I don't think he is going to make it for the first corrida or two." The situation is becoming a soap opera of suspense.

On the morning of the twenty-ninth, *El País* announces that José Gómez, Dinastía, will substitute today for Rincón, whose "medical team" has not given him permission to perform. It is not yet known whether Dinastía will substitute in any further corridas.

That afternoon Ortega Cano and Pepín Liria pardon two fine bulls of Guachicono, and Ortega Cano and Dinastía both dedicate bulls to the absent Rincón over the radio.

On the thirtieth the Plaza de Toros de Cali has its annual luncheon, which Jorge Molina and I attend. Among the ganaderos and the journalists, Luis Alvarez shows up, a big Havana wedged in his teeth. "César will be able to torear on January third," he claims. "His feet are going to be fine. At any rate it's the bull that uses his feet, not the matador."

The real taurine expectation centers on the cartel of January 3: bulls of Ernesto González Caicedo for Curro Vázquez, César Rincón, and Enrique Ponce, the cartel of the feria. On the evening of January first, Jorge Molina and I meet at the corrals with Ernesto and his daughter Nanda to watch the unloading of the bulls. Everyone feels on edge because the Santa Coloma casta of these thoroughbreds is famous for its "nervy" character, which means the bulls have to be handled very carefully so they will not injure themselves or each other. The unloading is quiet and tense but proceeds without incident (plate 41a), while behind us the last of the sun's rays sets the ragged edge of the western Andes—los Farallones de Cali—aflame in a portentous light.

The following afternoon we observe the magnificent animals in the corrals, all cárdenos, very *parejos* (all the same size), with an average weight of about 500 kilos. Ernesto comes up to announce that he has just talked to César, who is driving—alone—from Bogotá in his new Toyota minivan. We all look at each other and shake our heads about his driving alone, not a recommended procedure in Colombia, where the *muchachos,* the rural guerrillas, can block the roads and seize you at any time.

On the morning of January third I see Ernesto at the sorteo and ask him how he is. "Asustado," he replies. Scared.

"How scared, Ernesto? The same way a torero is? Stage fright? Responsabilidad?"

"Responsabilidad," he answers. "Responsabilidad. Maybe more afraid than the torero. Because you have no control whatsoever. It's completely out of your hands."

After the sorteo Nanda remarks, "César got the best lote, numbers 49 and 61. The other good one is Ponce's, number 57."

Everyone mumbles the ritual word: "Suerte!"

To say that there is great expectation for this corrida—the return of César Rincón and the return, after a five-year absence, of the Ernesto González Caicedo bulls, plus the número uno of Spain, Enrique Ponce—is like saying the Andes is a mountain range (plate 41b). The corrida is being televised in

Colombia and in Spain. The weather alternates between cloudy and sunny and a mild breeze blows. No aficionado could reasonably expect that the corrida will turn out to be as dreadful as it does.

Curro Vázquez draws the only tractable animal, the first, and does an artistic faena that would have been worth an ear, had he killed well. The bull dies an exemplary, brave death.

Number 61, Manchas Blancas, 486 kilos, Rincón's first, fools everyone in the beginning, including the matador, who dedicates it to the público. But then the bull refuses to take the muleta. Rincón calls him and the animal does not respond. "¡Hijueputa!" he snaps at the bull, loud enough for all to hear. "¡Qué malo es!" he complains.

Since the bull will not charge, Rincón must move around him, more than he would like. The pain in his feet soon becomes a visible limp as Manchas Blancas keeps backing away from him. Rincón hits bone twice, gets an aviso, then puts in a "comfortable" sword, somewhat low. Manchas Blancas draws whistles as he is dragged out by the mules, and the matador, visibly annoyed, receives applause.

Curro Vázquez's second bull seems good at first, taking three varas in style, but in the beginning of the faena he shuts off the charges as though someone had flipped a switch, and our hopes for the corrida decline further. As the mules pull him out, the crowd starts the favorite local chant to castigate the breeder: "¡Ganadero pícaro!"

The fifth bull—number 49, Opita, 532 kilos—comes into the ring like the finest and bravest bull you have ever seen (plate 41c). His entrance is worthy of a taurine film, but as soon as Rincón's cape appears, he begins to turn away. Anderson Murillo can only pick him with a *carioca,* blocking the bull's exit with the horse's body. Rincón, in spite of an enormous effort, can do nothing with him. The rowdy section in the sun begins to chant: "¡Ganadero, hijo de puta!"

Rincón has trouble because Opita refuses to line up (plate 41d). After two pinchazos, the bull tries to kick Rincón. He backs down, retreating like a horse that will not enter the gate, paws the sand, and finally turns his back. When he does turn and charge, Rincón deftly puts in a half sword recibiendo and then, after an aviso, another half sword. The crowd applauds mildly for Rincón, who looks very resigned. Now the chant rises from the entire crowd like thunder through a tropical storm: "¡Ganadero pícaro! ¡Ganadero pícaro!" When Opita's carcass is dragged out, it receives a full bronca.

Number 57 comes in beautifully but refuses Enrique Ponce's cape. Ponce looks over at Rincón and shrugs, making a face as though he smelled something rotten. Then he says a number of things to Rincón that I cannot hear but that I can imagine.

Afterwards Nanda comments: "Well, they were parejos, all right. They were all equally bad. They had every possible defect of Santa Coloma bulls."

Ernesto can only mutter: "For twenty-five years I've been a ganadero and nothing like this has ever happened to me."

When we get to Ernesto's house that evening, César has already arrived but must leave soon for a corrida in Manizales the next day. He takes Jorge Molina by the shoulder and says: "You come to my room to see me before the corrida while I'm dressing. You don't stay at all. You come with a cameraman"—indicating me—"and you don't stay five minutes. Is that any way to treat an old friend? You can't do that. It's not good, it's not educated; in fact, it's bad manners and it's a terrible way to act. How would you like it if I did that to you? We didn't even get to say hello. Is that how you want our friendship to be?" As César looses this tirade at Jorge he is smiling and by the end he is almost laughing. Everyone tries to joke—with about the same degree of success.

Figure 39. Ernesto González Caicedo (right) and Iñigo Sepúlveda, Cali, January 3, 1995. After Ernesto's debacle, Iñigo and he commiserate at Ernesto's house.

Then César voices what we are all thinking: "No one in Spain ever calls the ganadero names. No matter how bad the bulls are, they only whistle at the bull. The bull gets a bronca, even. But no one insults the ganadero. They have no right to treat Don Ernesto that way. The público of Cali, of Colombia, has yet to learn the etiquette of the plaza de toros."

Ernesto puts on a brave front but confesses to Spanish ganadero Iñigo Sepúlveda: "I don't know what to do about my bulls today. Such a *desgracia* [misfortune] has never happened to me."

Iñigo, who is a plastic surgeon, replies: "As a doctor, I always read up when I have a problem. As a ganadero, though, it's different. I don't think you can read up on this. I think you just have to feel it out on your own."

Ernesto, who is a retired pulmonologist, can only nod his head.

Manizales: January 6, 1995

In Manizales on January fourth, the Ernesto Gutiérrez bulls charge well and César Rincón, Juan Mora, and Manolo Sánchez all take a triumphant ride on shoulders. Rincón creates an uproar with a *gran faena* in the fourth bull, and one critic writes the next day in *El Tiempo* that Colombians can relax now because the "César of always" is back and will triumph here in Colombia as well as in Spain.

On January fifth, Enrique Ponce has a great faena in Manizales with bulls of La Carolina and César Rincón traps a manso in the tablas and passes him back and forth the way he did with the manso of Samuel Flores in the Beneficencia in 1991. Jorge Molina and I listen to the corrida on the radio and it does indeed seem he is "back." It feels strange to listen to a corrida: you can hear the olés and the music, the crowd shouting "¡Torero! ¡Torero!" and the announcer exclaiming in a feverish voice reminiscent of a soccer match that Rincón has broken all the molds of toreo. Evidently the faena is heroic and his feet work fine. The only negative note we hear is that a bull of Mondoñedo has severely gored Ortega Cano in the back up in Cartagena de Indias.

At dawn on the morning of Reyes, January 6, tropical birds are screaming their praises to the morning sun and Jorge and I are having coffee at Ernesto's house. By seven on a cloudy, cool morning we are out of town, headed for the corrida in Manizales. I ride in Jorge's four-wheel-drive vehicle with him and his friend Marta Borrero, with Julio César at the wheel. Close behind us come Ernesto and his daughter Nanda with their driver.

We head north on the two-lane toll road that borders the muddy Cauca

River. The narrow road quickly clogs with trucks, buses of all sizes and colors, motorcycles, bicycles, and other assorted motorized contraptions, as well as horses, burros, chickens, turkeys, and cattle.

On the left the Cordillera Occidental backs fields of sorghum, hot peppers called *ají*, corn, and sugarcane. On the right the Cordillera Central rises into the clouds. Zebu and Angus graze peacefully and the flat-topped samán trees give the landscape a bucolic quality not unlike East Africa. Fortunately we see no signs of the problems that the day before led the *Washington Post* to call Colombia the most dangerous country in the world.

At nine we stop at the Parador Rojo near Uribe for coffee and cornmeal cakes called *arepa*. An hour later we are ascending through the pineapple fields near Pereira and then, as we wind up out of the city, we come into coffee plantations dotted with banana palms and mimosas. The mountain road twists and turns and the heavy traffic moves very slowly, especially around a bus that has overturned in a curve. At eleven-thirty we pass the Río Chinchiná and Jorge describes how on November 1, 1985, the Nevado de Ruíz, which rises 5,400 meters, blew its top, catapulting entire glaciers down the river and completely destroying the town of Armero. At noon we arrive in Manizales for its fortieth feria. The altitude reads 2,100 meters and the temperature has dropped to a pleasant 22°.

At the Hotel Carretero César is having his feet, which are visibly swollen, and his shoulder and hip treated with ultrasound and liniment (plate 42a). "I feel like a train ran over me," he says with a smile.

We hear that Ortega Cano, who had flown a few days before from Cali to Manizales to torear, had sent his cuadrilla and his mother by bus to save money but that the bus was ambushed. Gracias a Dios no one was hurt. The other news is that Ortega Cano's grave goring in the back was "clean" and did not affect any of his major organs. He is in the intensive care unit after an operation but is expected to recover. It was his twenty-second goring.

The corrida of Rocha Hermanos bulls turns out to be an escalera, and a less than good one at that. César Rincón draws the best lot, but if one of his bulls looks "very serious," the other one more than compensates. His first, which weighs 488 kilos and has "bananas" for horns, charges well, especially on the right horn, and César does an artistic, well-constructed faena that pleases the crowd greatly. Rincón looks today—as opposed to three days ago in Cali—like the maestro he is. His sense of theater, his "stage presence," has returned, even his humor. He puts in a superb sword, after a pinchazo, then sits on the estribo to watch the animal expire, directing him, telling him "Careful!" when he gets too close, showing him where to die (plate 42b). In Spain I have never seen this comic side to his toreo, but it works very well in Manizales.

He looks as relaxed and as composed as ever I have seen him, but although he has cut an ear (plate 42c), he has also sprained his "Achilles' thumb" while killing, reinjuring the same flexor tendon that he hurt killing Bastonito. The médicos will not let him come back out because he cannot close his thumb and forefinger.

"And your feet?" I ask César back at the hotel.

"They're fine. Fine. Couldn't you tell?"

When he took the vuelta with the ear, someone had thrown him a *bota*, a leather wine bag, and he had taken a very long drink (plate 42d). "What was in that bota?" I ask.

He swivels his eyes around at me and says: "Coca-Cola! It was a friend."

"What did the doctor say about your thumb?"

César examines the thumb as if it were a defective piece of merchandise. "Eight or ten days. But we'll see about that."

Next morning, as I settle in for the flight to Miami, I recall a story Nanda and Ernesto told about César when he was much younger and once got tipsy out at their finca. Nanda thought it was *aguardiente,* the local "firewater" made from anise-flavored cane liquor, and Ernesto believed it was whiskey, but the two agreed he had been very amusing. According to Nanda, he went around saying, "Just don't anybody fuck around with me. Don't anybody start anything with me. I'm fine. I'm fine, but don't mess with me. I'm just going for a little walk."

Inside the drumming roar of the jet engines I can hear the chants: "¡Torero! ¡Torero!"

I called Jorge Molina to see how Rincón had been on the twenty-second in Bogotá. "He was *pesado* [heavy, boring]. His feet were bad. His thumb was swollen and bandaged. He killed poorly. But the worst thing was his feet. He can't get away from the bull. There was one time he had to throw the muleta in the bull's face to distract him. I don't know who's running this operation. He's going to Venezuela now, and on March fourth he's going to kill six bulls in Medellín." He neglected to tell me that Rincón had failed to kill one of his bulls.

In February Jorge's brother Alvaro told me Rincón had sent a second bull back alive in Bogotá on February fifth. "He dedicated it to a guy in the press from the Grupo Santo Domingo, the group that owns the Cervecería Bavaria and Radio Caracol. César switched patrons from Postobón, the Ardila

Lulle group, when their contract expired. The Grupo Santo Domingo is not popular with everybody in Bogotá and they say the bronca was the worst since the days of the dictator Rojas Pinilla. They say César was so affected by it he couldn't kill the bull. And they say Luis Alvarez did it for a few pesetas more."

Later Jorge explained: "It was not a few pesetas. It was a lot of money. Supposedly it was a million dollars." The second bull he had failed to kill was another impossible manso from the ganadería of Ernesto González Caicedo. The review I later read in the French taurine magazine *Barrera Sol* said Rincón had been magnificent with the impossible animal—"as in his most beautiful days"—but unable to kill it when at the end of the faena the bull had turned tail and refused to hold still (77:35). Regardless, I thought I knew how César must feel about such a turn of events, especially in his hometown.

I also asked about the upcoming corrida in Medellín and Jorge told me not to come. "The bulls will be small and César is not in shape. It's not worth the trip. Besides, all this political mess—and that's all it is, Colombian politics—it's not what you are interested in. And it's not what toreo is about either. This is the first case I know of like this—commercial patronage of a torero. In my opinion it has hurt César."

On March 6 Jorge called to tell me about the corrida in Medellín. "It was good. Three of the bulls charged. His feet seem to be healed and he killed well. He's at or close to a hundred percent. The ring was full—to celebrate fifty years of the Plaza de la Macarena of Medellín—and he went out on shoulders. He got a vuelta with an Ernesto Gutiérrez bull, an ear from the Vallejuelos and two ears from Ernesto's bull."

"Two from Ernesto's bull?"

"Yes. It was a good bull—another Ebanista—and César was above the level of the animal."

Jorge put Nanda on briefly. She said, "My father feels much better now, and César was César—the César of always."

Ernesto's bull. Two ears (three with the Vallejuelos) and carried out on shoulders. You cannot see them all. But you must.

Sevilla: April 26, 1995

On the cold and windy afternoon of April 23, Francisco Rivera Ordóñez— son of Paquirri and Carmina Ordóñez; grandson of Antonio Ordóñez and Carmen González Lucas, sister of Luis Miguel Domínguín; great-grandson of Cayetano Ordóñez, Niño de la Palma, the model for Pedro Romero in *The Sun Also Rises*—takes his alternativa from Espartaco, cutting a well-deserved ear.

The second bull catches Espartaco during the kill, running a horn between his legs and pitching him high in the air. He comes down on his head and neck, and his body lies face up on the sand while shouts and cries fill the ring. When they carry Espartaco out, it is as though he were a rag doll.

Rivera Ordóñez cuts another ear from his second bull, creating an excellent impression in his first corrida as a matador. This is the young man who at age ten, when told that his father had just been killed by a bull at Pozoblanco, said: "Now I know that I must be a torero."

Suerte and muerte are strange bedfellows in the taurine world. After the corrida we hear that Espartaco has suffered "only" a serious concussion and a severe luxation of the right elbow, but it is the beginning of a difficult time for him.

On April 25 at the Colón I run into Luis Alvarez, who laments that there are only three bulls for tomorrow's corrida. "The vets rejected bull after bull. It was a nightmare. I don't know if there will be a corrida."

Tim and Joan have arrived and Joan is raving about César's performance in Arles on April 15. "He only cut one ear in the second bull, because he had to use the descabello, but the faena was marvelous. Definitely a two-ear faena. The crowd were mad for him."

The morning of the twenty-sixth I manage to work my way into the corrals. The weather hangs damply over the plaza and the air feels chilly. I find Edgar Heyn, who explains: "Out of thirteen Los Guateles bulls, they passed three! It's crazy. You sign a contract and the vets are free to destroy it. You never know what you're going to get in this plaza."

César Rincón ends up with number 27, a Sánchez-Ybargüen of 533 kilos, in first slot and number 22, a Los Guateles of 579 kilos, in fourth.

"What about his feet?" I ask Edgar. "Luis says they're fine. Are they?"

"Now they are. They weren't in Colombia, but now they are."

The weather clears by corrida time and the afternoon has warmed as César Rincón, Enrique Ponce, and Fran Rivera Ordóñez make the televised paseo. But the climate of the público of Sevilla feels more like the early morning, except toward the local matador Rivera Ordóñez.

César Rincón's cape floats this afternoon. His verónicas glide and his chicuelinas wrap around his body like a second skin. But the first bull quits early in the faena and the second limps visibly. César kills flawlessly to polite applause.

Figure 40. Francisco Rivera Ordóñez. In the callejón. Fran was the new sensation of the 1995 season, with a very strong beginning in Sevilla.

Enrique Ponce, who has yet to triumph in Sevilla, draws more difficult bulls and gets tossed for his insistence. He does not even earn applause.

Rivera Ordóñez, who is launching his career, seems inspired and infused with confidence and bravery. Once again he comes close to the Puerta del Príncipe, losing an ear in his first with the sword and cutting two in the last bull.

Up in suite 435 of the Colón many people have squeezed in. César, whom I have not seen yet, greets me with an abrazo.

"You know," I say, "as far as I'm concerned, the second bull was crippled and the presidente was blind."

"You said it! Sevilla's Sevilla. They're not going to do me any favors," he replies with a soft shrug of the shoulder.

César looks to be in top form, jokes a lot, and carries on a televised interview. Still we are all a little disappointed that Rivera Ordóñez stole the show. César had drawn dangerous mansos on the eighteenth, a day with lots of wind, so now he is leaving Sevilla empty-handed again.

Torre de Esteban Hambrán: May 7, 1995

The morning I leave Sevilla, the sky is that impossible color of blue and there is a sweet crispness in the air. Jacaranda and bougainvillea are in bloom and I am remembering the paella down at Matalascañas with the

Atlantic flat and shining silvery in the hot sun and the corrida of Miuras when we got back; and the home-cooked lunches at the Colmao behind John's; and the big taurine lunches in the Laurel with John and Michael Wigram and Charles Patrick Scanlan; and always the evenings at the Bodegón after the bulls when everyone is there, arguing about the corrida. Springtime, fine weather, friends, and los toros. And the air of Sevilla in Feria. There is nothing that can compare to it—except for the bulls, which so often seem to lack casta and strength and the wildness that makes them bulls.

An hour later I am driving the red Renault, which now has more than 30,000 kilometers on it, the majority of which are mine, through the hills north of Sevilla, among black-trunked cork oaks and fields of purple and yellow wildflowers. Poppies the color of fresh blood dot the landscape. At Santa Olalla del Cala a gilded saint with a halo is being carried from the church. There is a crowd out front and the Guardias are watching impassively from the shade.

At three I cross the deep green Tajo, and as I crest the ridge beyond I watch the great blue barrier of the Gredos rising in the north. Turning northeastward toward Madrid, I run parallel to the range, which is jagged like a wall encrusted with glass, arriving at Valmojado where Mirabeleño, Juan Mora's father, has told me his son and César Rincón will dress for the festival.

There is only one hostal. Inside it is hot and noisy and the men of the pueblo are playing dominos and cards. They are slapping down the dominos and smoking and yelling above the noise of the TV, which is turned up enough to be heard over the yelling. I decide to go on to Torre de Esteban Hambrán, where the festival is to take place.

Torre is an old-time pueblo right out of the Spain of the '60s. The plaza de toros is down through a gulch and across the waterless "river." Cars with blaring loudspeakers advertise the festival "with the greatest toreros of all time." Inside the narrow callejón there is trash, including a ripped-up heartthrob magazine. One torn page reads "José [Ortega Cano] and Rocío [Jurado] in the intimacy of their finca." Cigarette boxes, plastic water bottles, rocks. "Cosas," I think, "cosas de España," the things of Spain, as the set phrase has it.

This pueblo belongs to that vaguely defined area west of Madrid known as the Valle del Terror. I have been near here before, at San Martín de Valdeiglesias where they cracked the windshield of the van.

Luis Carlos shows up in an effusive mood, gives me an abrazo, and begins to put together the muletas. Then César and Juan Mora and everyone else arrive and things become simultaneously hectic and slowed down, pueblo-style.

Rincón's first animal causes him difficulty, but he outsmarts and subdues the animal, which they drag out with a tractor. "Modern mules," cracks Edgar.

Juan Mora's first bull acts at first as though he cannot see. Mora says so over his shoulder to us in the callejón: "Pero no ve. ¡Me cago en la leche!" But then the bull charges and he can see and Juan Mora straightens up and begins to pass him.

Rincón cuts an ear from his second after a risky faena, invading the novillo's territory to force him to charge, then slamming a good sword into the *rinconcito*—a spot down from the cruz, effective but less risky[1]—and yelling everyone off, walking the bull backward in a spectacular, though imperfect, kill (plate 43).

"How did you know the kill would be so effective? Could you feel something?"

"No, just the position and the angle. It's a matter of experience, there's no mystery to it. And sometimes you're wrong."

Juan Mora's second animal charges better and Mora cuts both his ears. "Bien, Juan," encourages Rincón when Mora comes back into the callejón.

Juan Mora waggles his head from side to side, as if to say not *so* good, really. He laughs. "I put it in the rinconcito, just like you."

As I head into Madrid in thick traffic under an orange sunset with puffy, Goyaesque clouds, I realize that once again the burning question is Madrid. César Rincón's only corridas of note, of the six so far in Europe, were the one in Arles and one in which he cut an ear in Valencia on March 17. As always, it seems, Madrid will make or break his season. His feet seem fine and his morale is high. The bulls today were not good, and if they were shaved, as they should be for a festival, you could hardly tell it. Yet César Rincón and Juan Mora enjoyed themselves like novilleros in the campo and the público was appreciative.

Guadalix de la Sierra: May 8, 1995

The following day, I drive north on the Burgos road and turn off at Guadalix de la Sierra to find Victoriano del Río's ranch. I follow directions but get lost twice anyway. Eventually, deep into the dirt roads of the campo, I find a sign that reads: "Ganado bravo. Do not proceed." I head back, running into César's van, and follow them to the little plaza de tienta.

Julio Vega el Marismeño is with César, as are Muri and Mono, the ganadero and his wife Alicia, Colombian ganadero Darío Restrepo and his wife Raquel, Victoriano's sons (one of them picks, while the other is learning the muleta), plus friends of Victoriano. At one point Julio yells at the son with the muleta: "Don't *ever* bend over—not even sitting on the toilet!"

Being a natural trainer, Julio trots out to show him, and the vaca goes after him. "¡Me cago en tu estampa!"² exclaims Julio, and then proceeds to subject her to his cloth while we all laugh at his gracia.

Altogether there are five vaquillas. After one, César comes back to the burladero breathing hard, slams in beside me, and says, "Man, she made me suffer. ¡Qué mala! ¡Ay, qué mala!" The afternoon is filled with curses, shouts, epithets, jokes, complaints, lamentations, advice, lessons on toreo, unending competition, and good-natured rivalry. One vaquilla charges very well and César practices his most difficult form of toreo, what he calls "breaking," stretching the pass to the absolute physical limits possible (plate 44). Julio coaches him as he does a series of ten derechazos, then an equal series of naturales. "Take her, take her. More, more, more—*ahí* [there]. Take her, take her, take her, bien torero, bien, ahí. Get her, get her, get her, now, more, *rómpete* [break], rómpete ahí! Bien, torero. Bien. Bien."

Rain is coming down hard beyond us. Along the edge of the sierra toward Madrid, the sky has turned dark purple and grids of lightning go to ground like electric trees. But no rain falls on us. After the fifth vaquilla I say to César, "If you want a laugh, let me do a muletazo sometime. I haven't done one to a live animal in about thirty years. But I have this sudden urge."

"You should have said something sooner," he replies. "I think the ganadero is finished." No sooner have we gone into the little house next to the ring to eat than the heavens burst in a downpour so loud we cannot hear ourselves talk.

One of the people I meet at the tienta is Astolfo Núñez, a ganadero and aficionado from San Cristóbal, Venezuela. After we eat I drive Astolfo back downtown to his hotel. Eventually we take refuge from the deluge in the taurine inner sanctum of the Hotel Victoria. As we sit there like wet dogs, trying to dry out with a copa, Gonzalito, a well-known apoderado and old-time taurino, sits down and asks me: "You know who Fran [Rivera Ordóñez] looked like in Sevilla, who he reminded me of? Not his father. Not his grandfather." Gonzalito, who has a heavy (lisping) Andalusian accent, looks at Astolfo and then back at me. "He looked like César. Yes thir. Like César Rincón. No arguments please. In these matters I am a thycologist!"

Madrid: May 17, 1995

On the cartel with Julio Aparicio and Jesulín, on the seventy-fifth anniversary of Joselito el Gallo's death, César Rincón cuts an ear from each of his Laurentino Carrascosa bulls out in Talavera with a much nicer crowd than two years before. What encourages me the most, much more than his salida a hombros, is Rincón's perfect footwork in the face of a difficult fourth bull that constantly turns around on him. He also kills it very well, and all I can think, watching the sword slip in perfectly, is: I hope he can do that tomorrow with the Baltasar Ibán bulls in Madrid.

Going into the ring at Las Ventas the next day, I spot a group of Colombians near the entrance to Seven, but it is not just Colombians who have turned out on this perfect, sunny afternoon to see César Rincón confirm the alternativa of José Ignacio Sánchez, a young new matador from Salamanca, in the presence of Joselito. José Miguel Arroyo, Joselito, who is the principal figura from Madrid, has not appeared in San Isidro since 1992, so he creates a great deal of expectation. But the greater draw of the day, after last year's duel with Bastonito, is César Rincón with the bulls of Baltasar Ibán. In fact, of the thirty-nine matadors coming to Madrid for San Isidro, there is no doubt, to judge by the articles in all the papers and taurine magazines, that Rincón in Madrid with the Baltasar Ibán bulls is the highest possible draw. Together with Joselito he creates a cartel of maximum expectation. *6T6* runs a double-page spread on Rincón in Las Ventas, reminding everyone that Rincón is a pure torero in the line of Belmonte, and ending by saying that his faenas "create a toreo the theory of which we knew, but the practice of which we had forgotten" (60: center section).

Before the corrida Rincón told an interviewer: "Every time I watch the faena [with Bastonito] on video, I get a knot in my throat, because I see those moments when he was trying to gore me. I remember his strength and his intentions and it gives me goose bumps" (*El Mundo,* May 17, 1995).

Corrida de expectación. . . . For some reason, perhaps explicable only to the taurine gods, the Ibanes—beautifully presented, astifinos and with awesome trapío—come out mansos, dangerous, broncos, and, with the exception of the sixth bull, *infumables.* As the taurinos say, unsmokable.

The first bull, for José Ignacio Sánchez, does not have a single pass. Neither does Saltillo II, César Rincón's bull, a *sardo*—with mixed black, red, and white hair—weighing 544 kilos, a beautiful but impossible animal with which Rincón can do nothing (plate 45). Joselito's bull is equally terrible. Rincón's second, a black named Peluquero, weighing 556 kilos, turns out to be still more dangerous and unpredictable. Then late in the faena the animal simply lies down and refuses to charge. Joselito begins a good faena with the fifth but the bull begins to chop at the muleta, destroying the matador's designs. José Ignacio Sánchez does good work with the last bull, which is complicated but not impossible, and takes a deserved vuelta.

Afterwards César says to me: "What a disappointment! What terrible, terrible bulls. The only good thing I did all day was that media verónica in my quite on the sixth. Who would have expected such mansos, and so dangerous, and such a lack of mobility?" His voice trails off at the end like a man going under water.

Michael Wigram and I listen to José Miguel Arroyo saying almost the same words in the Hotel Victoria: "I'm very disappointed. Only the sixth was not intoreable." He will tell Luis Nieto at *ABC*: "This ganadería I thought was one of the spiritual reserves among the brave bulls of Spain. Who the hell can figure it out?"

César Rincón will tell Nieto that his bulls did not remind him at all of Bastonito. From among his fifteen or so corridas of Ibanes, these were "the worst," and he felt "very sad, just as the público must as well" (May 18, 1995). Later he will admit that he was furious about the out-of-type slabs of meat sent to Madrid.

San Isidro drags on and on as usual, and the only detail worthy of note is that Enrique Ponce cut a heroic ear from a buoyant but manso Samuel Flores on May twenty-third. That same day *6T6* comments: "This year César Rincón's date with the cycle of San Isidro has a special importance. For the Colombian—and for the afición of Las Ventas—not to go out on shoulders through the Puerta Grande is almost like a failure" (62:13). In the interview that follows, Rincón complains again about out-of-type bulls and points out that Bastonito weighed only 500 kilos. He knows that he is up against the wall of Madrid's unreasoning love affair with fat bulls, whether they can stand up and charge or not. Indeed, Bastonito had nearly been sent back for being too small.

How to explain the debacle of the Ibanes? Pablo Lozano, the man who selects the corridas for San Isidro, explains it this way: "I pick six bulls, the best in the ganadería, according to their presence and appearance, for any particular corrida. Then what happens is that [the vets] reject four of them.

So I'm left with the biggest ones, which turn out bad. Then you find out that the bulls rejected by the vets were used in another ring, where they charged exceptionally well. Those are the rules and the results are obvious" (*El País*, May 23, 1995).

Such is the panorama as César Rincón looks forward to his second corrida in Madrid, with Marqués de Domecq bulls on the twenty-ninth.

Madrid: May 29, 1995

On the twenty-eighth in Córdoba César Rincón kills a corrida of violent and dangerous Jódar y Ruchena bulls with Enrique Ponce and Jesulín. His bulls come out so bad that he almost sends his second back alive. Jesulín draws the best animals but cannot "round them out." Ponce cuts one ear.

At dinner with Astolfo and his wife Aura afterwards, I wonder if César, who has departed in a bad mood for Madrid, feels as disillusioned about his chances tomorrow in Madrid as I do. Does nearly not killing his second bull concern him? Or did he nearly fail to kill it because his attention is already on the corrida in Madrid? Or could it be something else?

Suddenly, sitting there at the table and for no reason I can discern, I am overwhelmed by the loneliness of the figura del toreo, a loneliness made all the more unbearable by the adoring troop of Colombians that follows him everywhere, trying earnestly not to bother him.

Driving up to Madrid the next day, I think back to May 25, John Fulton's sixty-third birthday, which we celebrated with a tienta out at Manuel Fernández-Palacios's ranch near Jerez. One of the last vacas was a castaña with a sweet charge that reminded me of the brave red cow that had broken her horn at the tienta at Borja Domecq's ranch two years before.

I was in the burladero with John, taking pictures of matador Vicente Salamanca, who was working the red cow. At some point I looked at John and raised my eyebrows. "You wanna?" he says.

"I don't have a muleta."

"Use Vicente's. ¡Vicente, Vicente, que va éste! ¡Dale la muleta! [He's coming out! Give him your muleta!]." As senior matador, John commands, but he also asks the ganadero's permission.

"¡Hombre, claro!" says Manolo Fernández-Palacios. "Do you want us to clip her horns first?"[3]

"No, leave her," I say and, without giving it another thought, I trot out and take Vicente's muleta. I find out the four horsemen of fear—death, injury, the público, and looking ridiculous—tend to vanish once you commit.

Having noticed that the vaca went through well on the left, I cite for a natural, easing up to her and extending the muleta out toward her large watchful eyes. "¡Coge, bonita!" I call out, as though I did this all the time.

As I say it, I shake the muleta and the vaca charges as if by command. She lowers her head and I lead her past, somewhat to my astonishment, and turn to make the next pass. Again she comes, just as she is supposed to, and I sweep the muleta in front of her, smelling her familiar bovine scent and feeling the heavy animal weight of her body as her flanks brush against me. I lean into the pass, taking her out as far as I can, and her long body fills the space in front of me. But she follows the cloth like a puppy on a leash, turning at the end when she loses it. She takes the third natural, crowding me a little, and I take two steps forward, reversing the muleta, and give her a pase de pecho, bringing her under my left arm and releasing her from the slavery of the lure. She stops, turns, and looks at me as if to say, "What now?"

It is hard for me to believe it has gone so smoothly. In spite of several years of training in the early '60s, I was never able to link a full series of passes with an animal. But there are two differences: I never had a vaquilla this good, and even though I lack extended physical training now, I have toreo much more firmly "in my head." My concentration on Rincón's technique has given me a kind of vicarious knowledge of terrains I never had before. Through my scrutiny of him as a torero, day after day, faena after faena, I have learned as though I were his shadow apprentice. As the maestro Pepe Luis Vázquez said: It's all in your head.

A second series comes off as well as the first, and while I have no illusions that I look like César Rincón or Enrique Ponce, I do manage to extend the muleta out and then bring it all the way through in each pass. The little vaca's charge is sweet and I develop a feeling for her that is difficult to describe. She is attacking me, in effect trying to kill me. Yet she does it with a gentle violence born of instinct rather than of malice. I admire her tenacity and bravery and, as with the other castaña at Borja Domecq's, I feel an unexpected empathy with an animal that makes me think long and hard about the bond between the bull and the matador who kills him. And if it feels this exhilarating to pass a small cow in front of friends, what must it feel like to link a series of naturales with a mature bull in the midst of an ecstatic plaza de toros?

After the second series, the ganadero orders the vaca out, and as I walk on air back to the burladero, I can hear John yelling, "¡Bien, torero, bien!"

Figure 41. An aficionado, May 25, 1995. The tienta on John Fulton's birthday at Manuel Fernández Palacios's ranch. As Pepe Luis Vázquez said, "It's all in your head." John, my maestro, seemed more pleased than I.

John, my maestro of thirty years, seems more pleased than I am at my success.

The last animal is a larger and more difficult black vaca. I pass her too, although she causes me problems, looking for my body behind the lure, and ends up driving a hoof into my right instep.

After the tienta we adjourn to Manolo's rustic ranch house, where Vicente Salamanca prepares venison stew and rice with coconut, the latter a recipe from his native Colombia. We celebrate John's birthday and my "debut" into the inky blue Andalusian night. John is pleased that I have done well and out on the porch he tells Manolo: "I taught him how to do that thirty years ago! He never moved an inch! Some maestro, eh, ganadero?"

Manolo smiles at John, shaking his head, and remarks, "What afición you have, John!"

John's look intensifies as he answers quietly, "I've got enough afición for twenty novilleros!" Manolo's bulls bellow around us in the dark, and the pain in my foot, which will last for months, reminds me of César Rincón's physical problems. How much afición must he have?

The sun shines hotly on this May 29 and Las Ventas del Espíritu Santo has filled to capacity to see Emilio Muñoz, César Rincón, and Manolo Sánchez with bulls of the Marqués de Domecq. But the expectation cannot be compared to Rincón's previous corrida. Joselito is missing. And no one expects the bulls of the Marqués to produce a Bastonito. Furthermore, two bulls of El Sierro have been "patched" into the corrida with four of the Marqués. Still, Rincón will torear in Madrid. As I take my seat in the third row of contentious Tendido Seven, across the way over the toriles I spot first the ganadero Lucas Caballero and then his wife María Emma Mejía, the Colombian ambassador, and I am again reminded of what Rincón means to Colombia.

I hardly ever leave a corrida, even in bad weather, as there is almost always something to be learned, even in the worst ones, but I can feel the imminent stirrings of abandonment just before Emplazado, a 563-kilo burraco from the Hermanos Astolfi, replacing the crippled fifth bull from El Sierro, trots in. He is tall, long in body and horn, and carries himself well—in fact his trapío is impressive—but I know better than to hope he will have two passes in him. The bull's original inclination is to flee any sign of movement, and the crowd begins making unpleasant noises. Vicente Yesteras shakes a cape at him and the animal bolts like a dairy cow to the side, head down, front feet splayed. Monaguillo comes up from the other side and shakes his cape. Emplazado turns and runs to the far side of the ring. When Monaguillo pursues him, the animal runs in circles to escape. The crowd starts to heat up for another rejection. Finally the bull charges Yesteras's cape twice, then races over to Rincón's, ripping it loose from his hands and continuing in a circle around the ring in the style of a classic *manso perdido,* a hopeless manso.

The picking is chaotic but Pinilla manages to work in three varas, none of them too long or too severe, as Emplazado's unpredictable charges account for more ripped capes. In the quite the animal unexpectedly switches horns, cutting in on Rincón, very nearly nailing him with a mighty upward thrust, destroying yet another cape.

Emplazado is a manso but he is a strong and interesting manso. As the picking proceeds he seems to be getting better, more centered on the horse. Or perhaps I am dreaming. The Astolfi bulls come from the encaste of Núñez, bulls that sometimes develop from manso-acting to brave. Emplazado makes me wonder if that is the case with him as he rips loose two more capes from Emilio Muñoz and from César Rincón, then takes the third pick.

In front of me a bearded regular of Tendido Seven declares to whoever is listening that the animal is a worthless manso. "Let's watch," I say to his back. "This is a Núñez bull; he just might come up."

Rincón stays out in the ring for the banderillas at the beginning and I watch his face, impassive as a mask, for some sign one way or the other. Vicente Yesteras puts in his usual spectacular banderillas to applause. Manolo Bélmez, the new tercero replacing Manolo Gil this year, also gets in a good pair. In the third attempt, Yesteras makes his characteristic broad, side-stepping leap across the animal's path, but as he begins to drive down the sticks, Emplazado thrusts upward, wrenching around to follow the man's body, and Yesteras must pull back to avoid the horn. Emplazado is definitely dangerous.

Emplazado means "summoned one" but in taurino it means a bull that stands his ground in the center of the ring without charging. Which Emplazado will this one prove to be?

As he goes out for the faena Rincón walks slowly and I know he is thinking as hard as he can. His eyebrows are arched quizzically and he looks anything but resolved. He must not like the bull, I am thinking.

The first passes look indecisive, and some of the more loutish in Seven begin to whistle when Rincón backs away from the animal. The bearded man in front says: "El toro no sirve y el hombre no puede"—the bull is inadequate and the man is incapable.

Then Rincón straightens, standing directly in front of Emplazado, and I notice they are almost the same height. Rincón cites de frente, putting his leg forward, and Emplazado lowers his head and charges. Then the animal charges again. The wind interferes and the noisemakers whistle because Rincón does not cross on every pass. He is trying to ligar the passes, and you cannot cross and ligar at the same time, but the would-be puritans and defenders of the faith hoot anyway, assuming that they know how to torear better than the maestro de Bogotá.

Rincón begins a new series, linking three derechazos, to olés from across the ring, then finishes with a fourth, unlinked because he needs to cross, and a deep pase de pecho.

The following series, a trincherazo, six derechazos, and two pases de pecho, starts in silence, is broken by whistles from the persistent few, but finishes to olés and an ovation that begins to drown out the protesters. In Madrid one must torear two beasts at the same time. As Rincón walks away from the bull, I say to the bearded man, "Pues el toro está sirviendo y el

hombre está puediendo, como dicen los mejicanos"—well, the bull is working out and the man is handling him (it loses a little something in the translation).

The bearded man, as if to prove that everyone with an abono in Seven is
not descended from Robespierre, turns around and says, "Yes, you were
right."

"He just had to persuade the bull to take the muleta, little by little."

The next series—all of this takes place over in Two, across the ring—
begins with another trincherazo, followed by five derechazos, two of them
long, low, running the hand, and eliciting thunderous olés. But then, instead of giving the sixth derechazo, Rincón pivots slowly around, from the
waist, without moving his feet, and offers Emplazado the muleta backhanded on the opposite horn. Emplazado takes the lure and Rincón winds
him in a slow, complete circle around his body, vanquishing the bull's reti-
cence, breaking the faena wide open, and bringing the house down around
himself (plates 46a and 46b). Finishing with a pase de pecho, he flaunts his
waist in the animal's face, turns, and walks away. Madrid—even Tendido
Seven—is his.

The ring hums, buzzes, and fidgets with excitement as Rincón switches
to the left, giving Emplazado six naturales, all de frente, the last three linked
and building to a strong climax. Another pase de pecho (plate 46c), once
again the subtle flaunting of the waist, and a huge ovation follow, as the
público of Madrid loses itself in ecstatic contemplation of the torero's
voluntad, willpower incarnate.

Rincón backs off and cites, and Emplazado, bent now to the hero's heart,
charges as though the man had transferred some of his own spirit to the
animal. A pase de las flores behind his back and a quick look up at the crowd
as if to say, you see, he's mine now, mine and yours. Two long, low derechazos and the fusion of man and animal is almost complete. When Rincón
repeats his flaunting desplante, the público rises in unison to applaud and
the other beast belongs to him as well.

I know what he is going to do. "Ayudados," I say to the bearded man's
back and Rincón crowns his faena with four perfect ayudados.

"Watch," I tell the bearded man, "he will want to kill it recibiendo."

César then lines Emplazado up and summons him one final time as an
image from García Lorca's "Romance del Emplazado" (Romance of the
Summoned One) flashes through my mind: "Un sueño de trece barcos," a
dream of thirteen ships.

César summons and Emplazado charges, impaling himself at the moment of union as the matador kills him with the most exquisite estocada recibiendo I ever hope to see (plate 46d). Thirteen ships, indeed—César Rincón, I realize, is about to cut his twelfth and thirteenth ears in the most demanding plaza de toros in the world.

Emplazado falters but does not go down, his bravery continuing to increase even as he dies. César steps between the still-high horns and slips the sword out. Emplazado wobbles, makes a half-hearted charge, slides along the tablas, and dies at the fence in Tendido One. The ring blurs with handkerchiefs under the blue heaven of Madrid like a whiteout on a sunny day.

César clutches the ears of Emplazado above his head like the double axes of the Mother Goddess of Knossos, and after the last bull a multitude chanting "¡Torero! ¡Torero!" carries him around the ring on shoulders like a deity. Astolfo Núñez runs alongside, holding to César as though he were the Cristo del Gran Poder. The crowd jumps up and rips the tassels from César's suit, nearly pulling him down, and he is swept on a riptide through the Puerta de Alcalá for the fifth immortal time (plate 47).

It has been three years since I made the decision to write this book and four since Rincón's historic breakthrough. That passage of time seems like the blinking of an eye and like an eternity. And I know that this fragment of sacred time stolen from the bowels of the labyrinth is the moment I have been awaiting. I and César Rincón and Las Ventas del Espíritu Santo and all Colombia. The next day *El País* will quote María Emma Mejía: "He is truly our best ambassador."

In Suite 803 at the Foxá, the incondicionales have gathered and the hallway is jammed back to the elevator. Even adjacent rooms for the cuadrilla have filled with people. Inside the suite, a smoky pandemonium reigns. The radiant ambassador sits on the sofa with the beaming manager (plate 48a). Her husband listens to Gonzalo Domecq, the ganadero of Marqués de Domecq. Everyone hugs and kisses, and the atmosphere has something of the formal gaiety of a New Year's Eve party or a political victory celebration, except that it remains distinctly taurine.

Ana Elvira Gutiérrez, who started the Peña César Rincón in 1986, years before he broke through, huddles with Colombian ganadero Darío Restrepo and his wife Raquel. Natalia Lorente glows among the males. Ganadero Felipe Rocha speaks quietly with Santiago Tobón, the empresario of Medellín. Meanwhile Manolo Sánchez, a friend and sometime business associate of César, prepares and distributes what he calls sangría de Pamplona, which disappears as fast as he can make it.[4]

Finally, from the inner sanctum of the bedroom the matador appears to applause and cheering (plate 48b). In the feast-or-famine planet of the bulls, this evening is the ultimate feast. César Rincón has done it again. Colombia has done it again. The small Colombian hero—precisely the height of Simón Bolívar—has restored himself to his rightful pedestal. Once more Theseus has prevailed in the Madrepatria and myth has again become flesh.

At midnight we adjourn in a caravan to César's house for a proper celebration (plate 48c). Only later will I learn that soon after his arrival at the hotel, in the middle of Alberto Lopera's live radio broadcast to Colombia, César suddenly prostrated himself in front of his altar and, weeping, began to kiss the images and the photograph of his sister and mother. "One goes to the plaza not knowing whether one will return. I have become emotional because I have returned a triunfador after having truly risked my life," he said. A dream of thirteen ships.

A few minutes later the tears began again and he explained: "I'm thinking about the faena, about the olés, and my hair stands on end. I'll have to tell it thousands of times tonight but right now, remembering it alone, I can permit myself this emotion, because I'm reliving it just for me."

Meanwhile, as Alberto Lopera remarked in his broadcast: "¡Colombia está de fiesta!"

The food, the wine, the company, all are as they should be, and the mounted heads of the four Madrid bulls of 1991 oversee the celebration in César's *bodega*—his wine cellar-salon—as though they were tutelary deities (plate 49). The next morning in *El País* there will be a photograph of the evening. On the left, looking on with unfeigned admiration, is Gonzalo Rincón. In the background appears an exuberant Luis Alvarez and on the wall one of the horned gods. On the right, in the foreground, stands a smiling Manolo Sánchez. In the center are Vicente Yesteras (under the looming bull's head) and César, about to embrace.

Long before I get back to my hotel for a few hours' sleep, the papers have hit the street. César Rincón confessed to Emilio Martínez of *El País* that his fifth salida a hombros in Madrid was more important than the ones in 1991 "because they know me now and they demand more of me, and because it proves I'm not finished, as some have said."

Figure 42. At the Mayte Awards Banquet. The Mayte Award is one of the most prestigious of the year. César won the 1995 award for his faena and estocada with the bull of Astolfi. At the banquet, José Carlos Arévalo explains a fine point to the manager and the matador. As usual the critic talks.

José Antonio del Moral in *Ideal* wrote: "When we all thought the afternoon had sunk, a miracle occurred."

Javier Villán suggested in *El Mundo* that the empresarios of Las Ventas give Rincón an "eternal, blank contract" to save them from disaster, pointing out that not only had he saved the honor of toreo, he had also prevented a serious public altercation. Villán named César Rincón "El Pacificador de Las Ventas."

Barquerito, writing a summation of San Isidro in *Diario 16* on June 13, titled his piece "Rincón Soars Again." In fact, César Rincón was the triunfador of San Isidro, the only matador to cut two ears from a bull and go out on shoulders in one of the most tedious San Isidros anyone could remember. Only nine ears were cut by matadors from 138 bulls. César Rincón won the Mayte Prize, and virtually every other prize as well, including the Casa de Córdoba Prize for the best estocada. As Barquerito put it, "From the beginning of the Spanish temporada there was a strong rumor the torero from Bogotá was in fine shape." He continued, "A triumph in San Isidro has the effect of a magic potion and it has given Rincón wings." César Rincón, he thought, had back "his aura of '91."

José Carlos Arévalo praised Rincón's intelligence, ability, and valor. The combination—ignoring the protests from Seven—changed the bull's behavior from an uncertain manso to a dangerous *bravucón*, a bluffing bull that charges hard but unpredictably, and then finally into a brave and moving animal. Those "successive metamorphoses" were brought about by "the miraculous art of toreo." For Arévalo, toreo "is a geometry with soul." The protestors in Seven would never get beyond the commonplaces and would never "discover the heart of toreo, the soul of its geometry, what differentiated absolutely the eternally repeated acts [*suertes*] of toreo" (6T6 64:3). Precisely what I was trying to say to the bearded man in front of me that shining afternoon.

Madrid: June 15, 1995

After the bull of Astolfi and the fifth trip to "heaven," I knew that whatever else happened, César Rincón and I had now come full circle. Finally, I began to believe I had a satisfactory ending to the book, to the quest, to the journey into the Minotaur's lair. That triumph was sufficient, I knew, but I wanted him to have another outstanding season, another "state of grace" that would bring the glory of the confirmed figura to bear on his historic temporada in 1991.

After Madrid, Barquerito's "magic potion" seemed to work very effectively. On June 3 in Vic-Fézensac, César Rincón cut three ears from the difficult Portuguese bulls of Oliveira Irmaos, and on June 5 in Nîmes he earned three more from a corrida of Samuel Flores while Espartaco and Ponce cut one each. Arévalo wrote that in Nîmes they declared César Rincón "king of toreo." If he had been any better, "they would have burned the plaza in his honor" (6T6 65:15).

Now came the corrida of the year, the Beneficencia, the cartel set since the end of April: César Rincón and Enrique Ponce, mano a mano with bulls of Sepúlveda in a special benefit for the indigenous peoples of the Cauca River in Colombia. With Rincón the clear triunfador in San Isidro again this year and Ponce missing that limelight only through a faulty sword, it seemed a cartel designed by the taurine gods themselves. The expectation was palpable, the tickets were sold out days before, and Televisión Española was to broadcast live to Latin America.

On *Tendido Cero*, Fernando Fernández Román's weekly taurine television show, Rincón said it would be a kind of world cup of toreo. Fernández Román compared it to a world heavyweight championship bout. In an interview on June 5 in *Aplausos*, Luis Alvarez predicted a new stage in world toreo, noting that this was the first time Rincón and Ponce had faced each other alone in Spain. Rincón allowed that—contrary to rumor—he and Ponce were good friends, but that "in the plaza, things change, in the plaza it will be all-out. You'll see."

Enrique Ponce and César Rincón had, in fact, just celebrated a kind of mano a mano in a tienta at Ponce's ranch in Jaén. They worked for hours, toreando males and females until eleven at night. Ponce joked with José Carlos Arévalo about fear in the hotel before a corrida: "In toreo there are many hotel fears, Sevilla hotel fear, Bilbao hotel fear, Mexico City hotel fear, but none of them can compare to Madrid hotel fear."

In spite of the jokes and the camaraderie with Rincón, Ponce admitted that "Rincón will throw himself into it like a dog" (6T6 63:27–28). Presumably so would Enrique Ponce. As he told Rubén Amón at *El Mundo*, "Madrid scares me more than Rincón does, but the presence of this torero, whom I know so well, is always an incentive. We have confronted each other in Colombia and there has always been rivalry, so this is one more opportunity to measure ourselves in a plaza de toros." He ended the interview, published the morning of the Beneficiencia, by saying that if the bulls helped out a little, "it could be an historic corrida."

At 6:30 in the Patio del Desolladero, where aficionados gather before the corrida, Alain Briscadieu remarks: "The maestro of Bogotá is nervous."

"But," I say, "he always does best when he's nervous." I can imagine him, pacing and irritable as a caged cat, then slowly sliding into his trance. What Alain does not know is that César had to dress twice because one of his stockings split. Nor does he know about the sudden urge to vomit that sent Rincón running for the bathroom. Neither do we find out until later that because of a taxi driver's bad advice, his van barely made it to the plaza on time.

But none of it matters: the Sepúlvedas disappoint and frustrate César Rincón and Enrique Ponce, the entire plaza of Las Ventas, including His Majesty Juan Carlos I, and millions of aficionados in Europe and America watching on television, as only a corrida of mansos can do. This afternoon Iñigo Sepúlveda's bulls prove almost as disastrous as Ernesto González Caicedo's a few months ago in Cali.

The mood at the Foxá afterwards is subdued. César gives me a weary look and says, "What a disaster! Thank God for the bull of Astolfi."

César Rincón and Enrique Ponce have once again foundered on the rocks of mansedumbre and nothing between them is remotely settled.

León: June 24, 1995

On June 22 I speak to Gonzalo Rincón, to Luis Alvarez, and to César. It turns out that from the original corrida of Sepúlvedas that Iñigo had picked, only one was admitted by the veterinarians. They rejected about ten bulls altogether, ending up with a corrida of overweight and out-of-type bulls that was destined to fail. Still, everyone is very happy that César is getting all the San Isidro prizes. Gonzalo comments, "You know he needed two salidas a hombros, two big triumphs. One is enough for the Spaniards, but César needed two. Gracias a Dios for the prizes!" We agree to meet in León on the twenty-fourth for the corrida of Victoriano del Río bulls, which promises to be very good.

I come up early on the twenty-third and by midafternoon I am north of Madrid. In the wheat fields above Tordesillas the weather turns nasty. The wheat and the sky look like Dorothy's Kansas, flat and scary, and the poplars along the watercourse dance in the wind.

At lunch the next day Curro Fetén tells me about seeing Rincón in Colombia when he was just beginning. "I saw him many times in Colombia. In those days nobody from Spain went to Colombia. But I did and I wrote taurine *crónicas* [reviews]. I wrote the crónica of his alternativa in the Bogotá paper *El Tiempo,* and I said, 'This torero will be a figura,' and I was right!"

"What was it you saw in him then?"

"¡Hombre!" he exclaims caustically. "¡Hombre! Lots of entrega. And especially great afición. He'd been doing it since he was eight! And of course true valor. ¡Casi na!"

Up in César's room before the corrida, the atmosphere is relaxed. Juanito is laying out two trajes de luces or, as the taurinos are wont to say, *vestidos*— suit or dress or, perhaps best of all, vestment.

"Why do you lay out two vestidos, Juanito?"

"So the matador can select," he says. Then he adds, "And also, just in case something should go wrong with one of them. You remember the missing tirantas in Cali?"

Figure 43. Curro Fetén, León, June 24, 1995. Curro holding forth at lunch at the Adonías restaurant. He is holding court and talking on his cell phone at the same time. Court jester of the taurine critics until his recent death, he also had a fine mind.

César has just arrived from Madrid. Luis Alvarez is taking a power siesta on the bed as we wait. When César notices that Luis is asleep, he motions for me to take his picture. It is some form of comic revenge, and César laughs when I take the picture. "Make sure that goes in the book!" Meanwhile he sips a Coke and watches a Clint Eastwood spy film on television.

The Bible on César's altar (plate 50a) is open to his favorite passage, from Psalm 91:

> He is my refuge and my fortress. . . . Thou shalt not be afraid for the terror by night; nor the arrow that flieth by day; nor for the pestilence that walketh in darkness; nor for the destruction that wasteth at noonday. A thousand shall fall at thy side, and ten thousand at thy right hand; but it shall not come nigh thee. . . . Thou shalt tread upon the lion and adder: the young lion and the dragon shalt thou trample under feet.

Just now he is more interested in the Clint Eastwood film and I notice the glassy detachment that begins to veil his eyes as he watches (plate 50b). As he dresses, he complains of indigestion: "It kept me up most of the night. Maybe it was the shrimp we had." Luis awakens as though he had set an alarm. Going down in the elevator, César burps and laughs. "That's better. Coca-Cola. It's the best product of your country."

César Rincón dedicates the life of his first, a bull that no one else seems to think is worth anything, and then proceeds to force him to charge against his will. It is César Rincón at his most masterful, and the genteel público of León shows itself to be grateful and appreciative (plate 50c). As Rincón takes his vuelta with the ear, you can feel the emotion charging the air.

Ortega Cano's Victoriano del Río bull looks to be the bull of the corrida, and the matador eventually plays to the gallery on the sun side, managing some good passes. A fine sword thrust earns him the ear.

Espartaco gets into serious trouble with the fifth, which bursts into the ring like an invading army. The matador's knee refuses to respond and he is nearly caught several times. After the corrida he will "cut" his season for several weeks. In the callejón his father repeats over and over, like a mantra: "He cannot go on like this. And with what this man has been in toreo. . . . But he cannot go on like this."

The last bull, Exquisito, number 51 at 521 kilos, also rockets into the ring. These Victorianos have plenty of casta, and the ganadero remarks to me, as the bull tries to rip the cape from Rincón's hands, that this animal is both brave and dangerous.

Then Rincón, as cool under pressure as I have ever seen him, proceeds to unhinge the bull's fierceness with the subtle movements of the cloth.

As we watch the faena progress from punishing doubling passes at the fence to artistic derechazos and naturales in the center of the ring, Victoriano says: "At first I was worried because the bull could have caught him any number of times. But when he took him out of his querencia at the fence, the bull lost his advantage and gave in to César. He as much as said, 'I can't beat you.' And that takes valor."

"Valor or technique?"

"No, no. Valor. All the figuras know the technique. Valor."

Luis says: "It was that crossing in front of him and taking him out to the center. Especially taking him out away from the fence. That's what did it. That's where he broke him."

Victoriano adds: "He got exactly the right distance. The right technique comes from the right distance. I think César could cut the ears off an old Guardia Civil! There's no other torero I know of who could cut the ears from

Figure 44. Victoriano del Río, León, June 24, 1995. Victoriano is very pleased by his bulls this afternoon and by César Rincón.

this bull, eh? Not just handle him but cut the ears. Because with this bull, if you doubted him for one second, he'd eat you alive."

The palpable danger of Exquisito, which no one in the tendidos misses, makes this one of César Rincón's finest moments. The only reason it lacks the greater drama of a Bastonito is that the bull—of which Victoriano is justly proud—does not quite manage to lay a horn on him. Instead Rincón subjugates him, subjects him, subdues him, gradually, pass by pass, until the animal submits, yields, gives up, and finally returns in defeat to the fence (plate 51a). As the battle seesaws in the matador's favor, the público goes wild, giving itself unconditionally to César Rincón, as bent to his will as Exquisito is. Caught up in the emotion in the callejón, I try to shoot away, but at times I become so lost in the drama and in the exposed and guileless truth of his toreo that I am forced only to watch as he incarnates the ultimate paradox of toreo: If you do not put yourself in danger, you incur greater risk. César Rincón's performance, deep in his self-created labyrinthine terrain of risk, is spellbinding, riveting, fascinating in the most literal sense of the word, a revelation from which you cannot turn away.

When he comes to the fence for the killing sword, the emotional charge radiates from his face like the aura of a holy man and his eyes are lit with an inner fire (plate 51b). As he lines up for the kill, I whisper to Juanito: "¡Qué monstruo!"

And Juanito whispers back: "No, not a monster. Rincón."

Chills run up and down my back, adrenaline floods through me, and César Rincón drops the animal almost instantly with an off-center but stunningly executed and effective sword (plate 51c). The plaza boils over into a state of delirium, the presidente quickly awards two ears, and all the grandeur of toreo comes once again to César Rincón as the *capitalistas*—the men who wait to hoist the triumphant matador on shoulders, for which they receive a generous tip from the matador's manager—hoist him up on shoulders. As I follow him around the ring, shooting, I realize that my wish for a state of grace is coming true (plate 51d).

Afterwards Paco Aguado tells me: "Important! Better than in 'ninety-one. His head is better. And that's how I'm going to write it. Important, I'm telling you." Later he will write that the bulls "gave up, seeking the tablas, cowed by the show of surety and strength of the Colombian. Without doubting them a single time, which was already heroic enough, and without losing a single step in the struggle, César subjected them both to an overdose of pundonor. He is in his sweetest moment, better we might say than in his revelation in '91. Now he has more weight, more head, a drier and more considered truth. He is a torero to follow in '95" (6T6 67:18).

Next morning the *Diario de León* titles its review "Colombia Conquers León," describing César Rincón's performance as writing "one of the most beautiful pages" in the city's taurine history.

Pamplona: July 10 and 14, 1995

A few days later, deep in France, standing in the rock shelter that is both a prehistoric cave and a medieval chapel, I remember that morning in grade school, in the library by myself, when I learned and wondered at the name Magdalenian man. Below flows the Vézère, a meandering tributary of the Dordogne. Ducks paddle in the still water against the cliff. Hawks and buzzards circle overhead and cicadas strum the song of summer. Trout and pike cruise the currents, as they did when someone here and upstream in the Salle des Taureaux at Lascaux began it all in this lush and verdant region called the Périgord.

The area centering around Les Eyzies-de-Tayac calls itself the world capital of prehistory, settled continuously for more than 200,000 years. Here some fifteen or twenty thousand years ago, or perhaps even thirty thousand at nearby Chauvet and Cussac, a specific conjunction of elements occurred: man and animal, art and religion. Here in the Chapel of the Magdalene, I am reminded that such a conjunction—specifically man revering animals through art—is still very much alive in toreo. What happened, I can only wonder, on this small stretch of stream near Les Eyzies to bring about that explosion of prehistoric art, virtually all of which is dedicated to animals: mammoths, horses, bison and bear, woolly rhinos, ibex, reindeer, and bulls? Above all, bulls, the great aurochs of antiquity, the direct forebear of the toro bravo.

Below flows the Vézère. Ducks paddle in the deep water against the cliff.

Up in room 1016 in the Iruña Park Hotel, I knock gently on the door. It is five in the afternoon but no one is in the room except César, who is still in bed for his siesta.

"Did I wake you?"

"No, no," he says, his sleepy tone telling me I had. "Come in, come in."

"I brought you two presents from France. First this book that shows the paintings of the aurochs of twenty thousand years ago. You would love to see these caves. They were the first artists of el toro. It's amazing how much those ancient bulls look like the bravos of today."

"Hombre," he muses, slowly turning the pages. "It's true they are similar. And what artists to paint them like that twenty thousand years ago!"

"I also brought you this image of the *virgencita negra* from Rocamadour."[5]

César takes the small wooden image of Mother and Child, turns it in his hands, rises from the bed, and places it on his altar. Then he turns and gives me an abrazo, saying, "What a nice *detalle* [gesture or gift]. Gracias, hombre."

"It's for luck."

"May God hear you."

"Suerte, matador."

In the ring an hour and a half later the weather is cool and the sky threatens rain. But the bands play with their usual abandon and I am sure that the Prince of Tropical Heat will warm things up (plate 52a).

Rincón's first bull is Sabedorito, number 24, a dark chestnut Cebada Gago that weighs 500 kilos but looks bigger with his magnificent trapío. Sabedorito—the bull that gored two people severely in the morning run, including fifteen centimeters of his left horn into the neck of a local runner—draws expressions of admiration when he comes into the ring, slamming into a burladero and splintering his left horn. Rincón cites from the center of the plaza and delivers six verónicas, advancing into the bull's terrain with each succeeding pass and finishing with a media verónica. Tropical heat, indeed: the crowd noise coalesces into raucous olés.

Sabedorito shows a preference for the fence, so after dedicating the bull's life to the público, Rincón takes the animal back to the center of the ring, where he proceeds to construct two series of derechazos, low, rhythmic, always leaving the muleta in front of the bull's nose, so that the animal has nowhere to go but after the cloth. The rhythm, turning four passes into one, convulses the crowd. Once again Rincón has connected in Pamplona (plate 52b).

Although Sabedorito nearly catches him in the face, Rincón goes in absolutely straight to kill. "He went in straighter than a candle," José Antonio del Moral will say to me after the corrida. "Straighter than a candle, throwing himself on the horns, leaving himself open to be killed. And that's how I'll say it in my crónica!" With Sabedorito's ear, César Rincón makes a triumphant tour of the ring, halfway to a Puerta Grande that he obviously intends to open. And I know that he will. I can feel it and so can everyone else in the ring.

Juan Mora has trouble with the second bull, and Sergio Sánchez, a local torero, cuts an ear earned more with bravery than with art. But as Sánchez begins his triumphal tour, lightning and thunder and rain surround and engulf us, turning the arena into a swimming pool. After a fifteen-minute delay, the presidente cancels the corrida.

Back in his room at the Iruña Park, César is not altogether happy. "I had more confidence in the second—he had a better *reata* [branch of the family tree]. Anyway la virgencita brought me luck."

"A suspension is luck?"

"No, hombre. But at least I cut an ear from the first."

"That's true," I say. But, luck or no luck, I can read the frustration in his eyes.

On the fourteenth Rincón, Jesulín, and Rivera Ordóñez are to perform with an overweight corrida (600–655 kilos) of El Torreón. César says to me before the corrida: "It's going to be the same old story. With these weights! There's no way these pieces of lard will charge. Look at the weights of the Cebadas, in the five-hundreds and they had great mobility."

"Someday maybe they will learn."

"Yes, they will, but who knows when that will be? And in the meantime, we can't have a triumph. That's the problem."

Rincón's first bull, Soñador, black, 600 kilos, comes out weak and fat and will not charge (plate 52c). Isabelo, his second, weighs 645 kilos and is manso. Neither of the other matadors has much luck either. As Carlos Ruiz-Villasuso will write in 6T6, it was a corrida "aborted by its own flesh . . . a disaster which with 100 kilos less [per bull] would have been a good corrida de toros" (70:16).

The Eye of the Storm: August 3–October 5, 1995

After Pamplona I returned briefly to Pensacola, where, on the third of August, Hurricane Erin's northeast winds of 100+ mph, driving directly across a couple of miles of open water on Escambia Bay, bent the windows and glass doors of my house almost to the breaking point. Rain drove horizontally through the seals and my rooms took in water like an ailing ship.

I did not realize it at the time, but in some ways Erin set the tone for the two tempestuous months to follow. César Rincón would continue his state of grace in spite of bad bulls—with important triumphs in Manzanares (two ears, triunfador), in Barcelona (three ears to Ponce's one), and again in La Coruña (three ears, triunfador)—and I would return to Spain to continue my quest. As Hemingway said, you cannot put everything you would like into a book about the bulls—but these are the highlights from César Rincón's stormy season, what I think of as the tip of the volcano.

On the way out to El Escorial on August 10, I stop at César's house and Luis Carlos tells me that the vets have rejected the entire set of bulls and that he does not know if there will be a corrida. Luis Alvarez has suffered a stress attack and is hospitalized with very low blood pressure. Taurine life as usual.

For once the corrida starts late, but the bulls of Palomo Linares—finally approved by a new set of vets (there's a switch)—for César Rincón, Julio Aparico (his father is the empresario), and José Ignacio Sánchez prove to be uncooperative.

The corrida lacks interest, but the afternoon itself turns lovely and soft, the sky clears, and the band plays. It feels fine to be back in taurine country.

After the corrida I streak north for Gijón under a full moon, winding up the craggy Sierra Cantábrica on a serpentine autopista, across suspension bridges and through immense culverts that burrow for kilometers through the bowels of mountains.

Down the long north slope the moonlight gleams like snow and tiny villages glow with a few dozen lights beneath the peaks. Just as I am about to lose myself in a reverie of the world of the ancient Astures, I pass an industrial plant that looks like an Erector set from hell, a furniture store larger than the villages above, and a nuclear smokestack silhouetted against the sky. Coming into Oviedo by night reminds me of someplace in West Virginia and there is a red haze as thick as fog. I make it to bed in the Begoña Park in Gijón by four. In my head Willie Nelson is singing "On the Road Again."

At five-thirty the next afternoon, August 11, I find a pensive César wrapped in the towel from his shower, waiting for Luis Carlos to arrive to dress him. I give him some photos, which he calls "beautiful," and he seems to mean it. I remember the first photos I showed him in Cali in 1993 and what he commented then: "You have to take many photos to get a good one. I know from family experience."

His first Martín Lorca bull, at 510 kilos, charges fiercely into the ring, destroys a burladero, and nearly gores Rincón, who trips but manages to roll to safety. The animal is wildly bronco but Rincón tames his violence with a perfectly placed muleta and cuts a hard-earned ear.

Rivera Ordóñez cuts an ear from the third by pure guts. Rincón's second animal, from Auxilio Holgado, weighing 650 kilos, has a face like a cow and the shoulder height of a steer. He reminds me of those killer village bulls Hemingway described in *Death in the Afternoon,* and Rincón despatches him as expeditiously as possible. Once again his luck in the sorteo has kept him from a double triumph. Ponce draws a *bobo,* a fool that will charge blindly, and proceeds to cut both ears.

I spend the corrida in the callejón with Alfonso Alcázar and Oscar Rentería, who are broadcasting the bad luck to Colombia, then hit the road for Béziers far into France. At eleven-thirty I cross the fjord at San Vicente de la Barquera and go through the old town, lit up and jammed with summer people in the full moon of August. After midnight I circle the gas fires and surreal landscape outside Bilbao. At 5 A.M., running parallel to the Pyrénées, I find myself in a thick, disorienting fog near Saint-Gaudens and in Toulouse there is no sunrise, only a gradually lightening gray. Beyond Carcassonne, deep into Cathar country, the sun appears suddenly, radiantly, and my fatigue dissipates in the purity of the Mediterranean light.

At the sorteo in Béziers the bulls look very good and I have time to chat with César's new banderillero, Manolo Bélmez, whose real name is Manuel Gómez Porras but who, like many taurinos, has taken the name of his town, this one being in the province of Córdoba. Manolo seems very cheerful. Mono is his usual circumspect self and Vicente Yesteras limps about and complains of various pains. At lunch Juanito explains to me how he doubles and sews shut all of Rincón's muletas, so there are four layers, two exteriors and two linings, instead of one of each, all sewn together at the bottom. "It weighs more but it works better. We've been doing it for years. Now Ponce and others are stitching theirs together too, so they won't open."

At 5:45 I am in the callejón with the French critic Jacques Durand. The plaza has filled to capacity to see Espartaco, César Rincón, and Joselito with Juan Pedro Domecq bulls, and the ambiente crackles with expectation.

Rincón's first bull weighs 530 kilos and charges the way a toro bravo should charge. Everyone in the plaza understands instantly that this hard-charging, burladero-wrecking animal is exactly what César Rincón wants.

I watch from very close as the torero winds the repeated charges of this fearsome beast around his waist, first on the right, then on the left, until there is virtually nothing left of the animal's power; then when that transfer of power from animal to man is complete, I watch the matador bury the sword up to the hilt (plate 53a). In this sunlit homeland of ancient dualism, who can fail to realize that the god of light has struck down the god of darkness in the pure catharsis of the Cathars? Jacques Durand and I merely exchange looks as César Rincón—the *perfectus*—takes his triumphant tour with both of the horned god's ears, while the tendidos go wild.

Joselito uncharacteristically ruins a great faena with a bad sword, and Espartaco cannot make his bad knee work (plate 53b).

The fifth bull, a big castaño (they show his weight as 535 kilos but he looks much bigger) disproves the adage about good fifth bulls and Rincón can do little with him. Disappointed, he returns to the fence for the killing sword. But something changes his mind and he does another faena—this time with the bull charging—and cuts a third ear!

That night at dinner I tell César: "What remains of your first faena in my mind's eye is that last series of naturales." I can still see him, offhand, indolent, disdainfully in control of the bull, using only the tip of the muleta and the play of his wrist to bring the animal past his waist (plate 53c). "You could almost call them naturales del desdén."

"Sí, naturales del desdén. I like that!" He beams. "Naturales del desdén."

I also ask him about his second faena in the fifth bull.

"Hombre," he says, "when I went to get the sword it occurred to me I had tried everything except giving him the muleta very low. I went back out and put my hand way down and he took it. So I did another faena."

After dinner the mood is as mellow as it ever gets among the taurine folk, and the only thing that spoils it for César Rincón is the news that Enrique Ponce has also cut three ears in Dax.

At 5:45 the next afternoon in Bayonne I still do not have a pass, and tickets are unavailable at any price. Finally Olivier Baratchart, the agent for the ring, solves the problem just fifteen minutes before the corrida starts. Once I am inside the callejón the tension of waiting—just part of the constant "game"—begins to melt away.

Rincón's first Gabriel Rojas bull, a long, skinny *chorreao*, a bull with vertical stripes, has no faena. El Cordobés cuts a deserved ear in the third, firing up the crowd with good toreo plus his usual comic antics. The fourth bull breaks a hoof and is sent back, but the sobrero from Andrés Ramos, a big dark six-year-old chestnut with the face of a gnu, turns out to be a very unpredictable, dangerous manso. Rincón whips the bull into shape, converting the animal's violence into rhythm, giving what they call an "authentic lesson in tauromachy" and cutting an important ear. Litri has a "gray afternoon."

On the fourteenth in Dax, the Victoriano del Río bulls charge well. Rincón, defending his throne in France, particularly against the strong campaigns of Joselito and Enrique Ponce, needs a triumph (plate 54). In his first bull, Lagartero, number 49, he makes an extraordinary faena, both powerful and artistic, using a great variety of passes crowned by circulares that bring the crowd to its feet. He cites eight separate times to kill the bull recibiendo but Lagartero refuses to budge. Finally he puts in a shallow sword, then a devastating volapié (plate 55).

Although he receives only one ear because of the delayed kill, the triumph is huge, culminating in a standing ovation. In the callejón—again I am with Alfonso Alcázar and Oscar Rentería of Radio Caracol, who this time can relay a triumph to Colombia—there is a complete consensus that he would have cut a tail had he put that final sword in to begin with. 6T6 will call it an "apotheosis" in their review titled "The King of France Torears" (75:23). Juan Mora and Rafi de la Viña each cut an ear as well but, in the strangely cogent logic of the taurinos, they are lesser ears.

After Rincón's second bull I leave the ring early, crossing the splendidly kept, splendidly green park across from the hotel, where children are playing simple games. There are flowering trees as in springtime and many flowers in small, orderly beds, instead of flowers of blood sprouting from the dark, leathery hides of toros bravos. There is grass, not dust, underfoot. People walk reasonably about the park, not screaming or cheering or rising as one in panic or in ecstasy. Young people flirt and fight with each other without dancing with death or posturing in fear or running for their lives. It is very orderly, very French.

I enter the garden of the Splendid where a hundred people sit quietly on the terrace and I sense with complete certainty that no one I know is here, that everyone I know is back at the ring, watching a bull and a man trying to destroy each other. It seems lonesome here, and inside at the bar, despite the music and the beauty of the young people, I feel alienated, realizing what a true heretic I am, I and all my "Cathar" compañeros. When Colombian friends arrive from the ring, I invite them to champagne.

That evening a celebration ensues, with all the cuadrilla and with what we call the "cuadrilla moral." Dinner—after congratulating the maestro in his private apartment in the outskirts of Dax, away from the crowd at the Splendid—takes place at two huge tables in a nearby couscous place, with raucous singing in Spanish and French and Scots, continuing into the night while the Briscadieu girls dance sevillanas as though they had been born on the Guadalquivir.

César tells me before the corrida on the fifteenth, again in Dax, that his first Núñez del Cuvillo comes from the same reata as the bull he cut the tail from in Murcia the year before. But when the bull comes in, he does not "transmit." Like all the rest, this animal has trouble keeping his feet. Rincón "nurses" him—keeping the muleta at middle height, performing with excellent temple—then kills well, cutting an ear. The crowd claps in unison and the matador takes a triumphant vuelta but I read disappointment in his eyes.

The fourth bull looks better, charges from a distance, but "comes down" in the middle of the faena. Rincón kills him well and cuts another ear, but the triumph with less than perfect bulls comes as an anticlimax to his string of magnificent French afternoons. As José Antonio del Moral remarks afterwards at the bar of the Splendid: "Today they made presents of two ears to your torero."

This is the afternoon that César talks to Tim and Joan and me about the death of his mother and sister, something that he has never brought up on his own before. But all is not morbid and there's much joking, including a supposed rundown of the sex life of the cuadrilla. César teasingly says: "Here everybody hooks up, from Chief Pluma Blanca to Lengüi,[6] everybody but me! Because in these matters I am very judicious—isn't that right?" (The question is directed to Brigitte Briscadieu.)

That night we all go to the Feria de Dax. The fiesta goes on all night, but I head for the hotel at three, exhausted by the ride on the French merry-go-round.

In Pontevedra's Feria de la Peregrina on August 16 with treacherous bulls of João Moura (and one of María José de Pereda), César Rincón and Enrique Ponce (and Jesulín) have a difficult but triumphant afternoon in a televised corrida. During the faena, full of gracia and rhythm, Rincón's first bull, the Pereda, "backwashes," catching him under the right thigh and flipping him high in the air. Rincón lands on his neck and back, but gets up furious and continues the faena, putting in a three-quarter sword and cutting two ears as the crowd chants "¡Torero! ¡Torero! ¡Torero!" and throws him flowers, Colombian flags, stuffed animals, and pieces of clothing. Afterwards in the callejón he quips, "There are no small 'enemies.'"

Rincón's second bull, a 545-kilo red animal named Faminito, the best presented of the afternoon, falls in the first pass of the faena and then falls several more times. Rincón works him patiently and does not force the animal. Faminito repays him by stepping with his full weight on Rincón's left foot, which makes him literally "hopping mad." But Rincón is inspired and, setting himself between the horns, he extracts a faena from an animal that seems impossible.

Then at the end of a long derechazo, Faminito hooks up with his right horn and catches Rincon, shaking him half a dozen times before flipping him to the ground. It looks as though he has been gored under the rib cage but, as in Algeciras in 1993, the horn has caught in the material around his waist and has not penetrated. Rincón rises and the público, shaking off its fright, again chants "¡Torero! ¡Torero!"

But the Moura bull has learned and now pursues the man, chasing him across the ring with a fury that he has not shown before. When Rincón goes in to kill, the bull absolutely ignores the cloth and almost catches him at the fence. Another deep pinchazo produces the same result, and Rincón gets a warning from the presidente. Finally he drops the animal with a well-aimed descabello. Seldom have I seen a bull go from weak and falling to such a state of concerted aggression. The crowd gives the matador a huge ovation and he tries to smile through his pain.

Rincón explains in the callejón that he grabbed on to the horn and held himself off but that he took a terrible beating in his gut in the process. "I had this tremendous lack of 'air.' That bull had enormous sentido—he waited for me and I had no strength at all. I thank God I'm still here. You have to risk your life, always, but I gave the bulls too little importance and that's why they caught me." Rincón asks permission to retire instead of waiting for his Puerta Grande, and Enrique Ponce, not to be outdone, cuts his second ear from another difficult Moura and rides out on shoulders. At the end of the corrida I am left wondering whether César Rincón's state of grace allowed him to triumph over an impossible animal or whether, even in a state of grace, the price he must pay to continue performing at peak is constant injury.

The next afternoon, in Madrid, César tells me he is not in good shape and will miss corridas in Antequera on the nineteenth and Ciudad Real on the twentieth. The plan is to reappear on the twenty-first in Bilbao. Meanwhile he is to stay in bed with his foot up. He is also having a problem breathing due to contusions of his diaphragm.

On August 22 in Almería César Rincón, Joselito, and the local torero Ruiz Manuel take on the Santa Coloma bulls of La Quinta. The weather is windy and cloudy but without the extreme heat for which Almería is famous. Rincón's foot looks less swollen, but yesterday in Bilbao, taking off his stockings after a fruitless corrida with Buendía bulls, he pulled off the scab and today it still appears quite raw.

Ignoring the pain in his foot, Rincón strings together a half dozen passes with his first bull, the only noteworthy work of the afternoon. The wind and the lack of casta of the bulls prevent virtually anything else. During the second bull, some fool yells out: "Go back to Colombia and sell drugs!" Rincón gestures for the fool to come down into the ring, but the fool is also a coward. When the bull is dead, the crowd applauds until Rincón comes out from the fence to take a bow. The público in Almería is famous for being good-natured and they do not want César Rincón to think that the cowardly fool is anything other than that.

Next day, driving back to Madrid, I pass five separate accidents, all of them spectacular high-speed catastrophes. High summer is in high gear and what the taurinos euphemistically call the *toro de la carretera* everywhere wreaks havoc.

After the sorteo in Bilbao on the twenty-fourth, Samuel Flores stops by César's room in the Hotel Ercilla and tells us: "Your first one, number 50, looks good and his mother was good. He'll charge, but don't punish him too much. Your second, number 13, has more horn but his reata is very good—they've almost all been good. He could have a lot of raza. Just go easy on the first one. And may we all go out on shoulders!"

Rincón's first, named Pitanguero, weighs 575 kilos and looks good, but he has a weak right front hoof and is manso as well. Rincón tells Anderson Murillo to go easy on him, but Murillo bears down hard and Rincón yells: "Good! Enough! ENOUGH! That's ENOUGH!" The animal soon takes to the fence and all Rincón can do is kill him, getting an aviso in the process.

When Rincón's second bull comes into the ring, people gasp at the size of his horns. What was it the ganadero said, he has more horn? More indeed: the animal's name is Cuernos Pillos, Rascally Horns. Unfortunately he too has a weak right forefoot, but he is brave and magnificently presented, with horns only a Samuel Flores can have. Rincón's faena frightens everyone, especially since Cuernos Pillos cuts in on the left. On the right the bull charges but does not lower his head all the way, making the matador's work harder and riskier. An idiot above me yells at him to cross, and Rincón looks up and says in a low but audible voice, "Hijueputa." His deep pases de pecho highlight this emotional standup slugfest of a faena, with the passes well linked, and Rincón cuts a very legitimate ear (plate 56).

Back at the Ercilla, César remarks: "What a fright! I was really scared! Those were the most horrendous horns I have ever seen!"

At 1:30 A.M. I arrive at César's house outside Madrid. The vans roll in at 3 A.M. and César has brought number 13's rascally horns home with him to have mounted. I leave my car there, riding in the van, and we arrive a little after 6 A.M. on August 25, the day after Saint Bartholomew's Day, in Almagro, where San Bartolomé is patron saint. That afternoon Manzanares, César Rincón, and Pepín Liria try valiantly but the Sepúlvedas do not lend themselves to much arte.

Felipe Lafita sends a good string of Torreón bulls to Almería for the corrida on the twenty-sixth. Unlike the out-of-type animals in Pamplona, these weigh a hundred kilos less and they charge.

Today in Almería you can probably cook the proverbial egg on the side-

Figure 45. Wedding picture, Almería, August 26, 1995. The incongruity of this photograph is typical of the taurine sphere.

walk. As usual here in this festive ring, all the matadors have to take a bow before the paseíllo, and César Rincón defers to Curro Romero: "Go ahead, maestro. Go ahead. No, no, you first, maestro, please." (Curro will waste two good bulls.)

After cutting an ear in his first bull, Rincón dedicates the life of his second—number 26, a well-presented black animal weighing 546 kilos—to the público and does a heroic faena, starting on his knees and continuing on both horns (plate 57a). He quickly subjects this bull, which looks insistently at the man, by lowering his hand and forcing the animal to follow the cloth around his body time after time. Clearly, after killing well, Rincón deserves at least one ear, for which there is a clamorous petition, but the presidente denies the ear. The crowd derides the "authority," then screams insults at him, but the man remains as stubborn as he is wrong.

In the van going back to the hotel, first comes the ranting and then the cursing of the "imbecile in the palco." "Hijueputa" and "thief" echo back and forth, and everyone agrees that the second faena was better than the first (plate 57b). Then a total silence falls, the silence of impotent indignation, and all I can hear is the gasoline sloshing in the tank.

At the Gran Hotel, César, Luis, Marismeño, and I get out. There is a crowd of people cheering a wedding and then cheering César Rincón. They pose together spontaneously for a quick photograph: the ritual killer of bulls and ensurer of fertility in his traje de luces and the bride and groom in their wedding finery. The fiesta rolls around us in the sultry evening and the beat of the fiesta and of the temporada throbs on.

In the tertulia Rincón speaks of the fine casta of the Torreón bulls, and taurine journalist Manuel Molés observes that "the presidente lacked the sensibility of an aficionado." Rincón agrees, remarking with characteristic stoicism: "The truth is it makes one rather sad." But an aficionado in the audience counters, telling him not to worry, that he is "the truest torero we have seen in Almería."

At twelve-thirty that night we find ourselves at a gas stop in Huercal-Overa, a little east of nowhere, pulled up alongside a truck full of pigs. The jokes in the van, which seem never to stop, take on a new tone. Outside in the stench, César autographs his publicity photos for the local fans. As we pull out, "Lengüi" puts in a new salsa tape. We are still four hours from Madrid but at least now the pigs, which we have smelled for some kilometers, are behind us.

At six I drop Luis off at his house, not far from César's, and get on the autovía back into Madrid. As I go to sleep at seven, I am thinking about what a true figura César Rincón has become and about how Curro Romero fits into a traje de luces like sausage into a casing. If Curro bent too far, I think, which he is careful not to do, he would split his suit the way a sausage casing splits if you bend the sausage too far. I reckon it must be fatigue that brings such thoughts. Or maybe it was the pigs.

Next afternoon, August 27, we are in Arenas de San Pedro at the foot of the rock wall of the Gredos Mountains. It is hot and picturesque. Storks nest in the high places, and there is a well-preserved Roman bridge.

The bulls of La Cardenilla—for César Rincón, Finito, who will cut the only ear, and Rivera Ordóñez—are terrible, even for a pueblo, with very little casta. And they are vicious mansos. The first one catches Rincón in the right thigh as he goes in to kill. Back in the callejón he says to me: "He was a *morucho.*[7] He didn't want to charge at all."

"Just as well the hijoputa wasn't astifino."

"Just as well. He'd have given it to me," he says as Luis Carlos puts ice on the spot.

"A hole in your taleguilla and your leg doesn't hurt, right?"

"No, not at all."

"I saw your face."

"Sí, claro."

The Red Cross attendant asks: "A puntazo, no?"

"A hard blow," says César. "It's swelling up."

After he dispatches his second bull, we take him into the infirmary, where Dr. Antonio Crespo Neches examines him, determining that there are several breaks in the muscle wall and a good-sized hematoma caused by a "closed cornada," one that penetrates without breaking the skin.

"It's very sore," César finally admits to the doctor. As he can barely walk without support, Colombian matador Guillermo Perla Ruiz and I help him to the van and "home" to room 106 of the Hotel Los Galayos, which is close by. In the darkened room César kneels and kisses the images on his altar.

That night on the Extremadura road, as I head back toward Madrid, around Navalcarnero, the toro de la carretera suddenly charges. I am driving along at the usual highway speed in the left lane, music on, window open, and suddenly the car is going sideways, completely out of control.

The Renault careens down the highway, rakes the aluminum barrier rail on the left side of the road, bounces off, slides across into the opposite railing, bounces again, then spins around, slamming broadside into the right-hand railing and eventually coming to a stop against it.

At some point I become aware that I am lying in the back seat, having broken through the front seatback. There is a man at the window, saying something. Eventually I hear: "Can you get out? It smells of gasolina." That word galvanizes me to the extent that I can be galvanized, and I push my way forward, kick open the door, and slide out.

All I remember about the man is that he is short, with a large round head, wears a radiantly white shirt and dark pants, and has long, silky white hair. "Come here," he says. "Look at this. Somebody hit you from behind. Make sure you tell the police about it."

I look at the rear of the car. On the right rear fender there is an indentation as though someone had hit it with a baseball bat. The dent tapers as it goes forward, and inside the dent in my red fender there is a thick streak of white paint.

When I look up, the man is gone, vanished into thin air. I have no idea where he went or how he left. The police arrive, check me out for injuries—fortunately, I have nothing but bruises and small cuts—write down my version of the events, examine the dent and the white paint, concur with my unknown friend's analysis, call the tow truck, and wait with me until it arrives.

Our mutual conclusion is that someone came up very fast behind me in the left lane—perhaps without lights, certainly without blinking—came up too fast, in fact, and nipped my right rear extremity with his left front extremity as he changed lanes, just enough to put me out of control as he went by. (Later examination will show that the blow beneath the white paint was severe enough to bend the automobile's frame.) One of the officers avers: "The hijoputa is probably in Madrid by now."

The police are very sympathetic, almost apologetic for what has happened, as they escort me to the tow truck. I leave the remains of the car at the garage in Navalcarnero and take a taxi into Madrid.

In the afternoon I take a taxi out to San Sebastián de los Reyes. César and the cuadrilla appear stunned when they arrive at the patio de caballos and hear the story. César shakes his head. "El toro de la carretera." Luis nods and remarks funereally: "El negro toro de la noche." Mono mumbles something about my being caught and not gored, and about suerte, but no one jokes, not even Anderson Murillo.

The Victoriano del Río bulls seem to ensure success in this ring. Rincón does a grand faena, highlighted by one of his backhanded circulares and ayudados, puts in an effective sword, and cuts two thoroughly deserved ears. The faena generates great emotion through Rincón's special "truth," and the maestro of Bogotá, consistently lowering and "running" the hand, seems very much at the top of his form.

The fifth, an ugly burraco, creates problems, charging erratically and looking for the bodies behind the capes. Rincón imposes himself on the beast, taking him out of his querencia near the fence, making the bull go where he does not want to go, forcing a faena where none seems to exist. He puts in a superb sword and cuts the third ear.

Ortega Cano, Pepín Liria, and Rincón all go out on shoulders, although the afternoon clearly belongs to Rincón, and for a while I forget how shaken up I feel (plate 58).

With the car replaced, I drive to Palencia on September 2. On a cool sunny afternoon Rincón does a splendid faena with the fourth bull, including inspired naturales. When he puts in a fine sword in the toriles, where the bull goes when he knows he is beaten, the crowd insistently demands both ears. But the presidente refuses to concede the second and cheats Rincón out of another Puerta Grande. The phenomenal bronca for the presidente is little consolation.

In room 403 of the Hotel Rey Sancho, a heartthrob magazine that wants exclusive photos of César Rincón's thirtieth birthday (September 5) brings in an early birthday cake with a little black bull on it. They intend to publish the pictures on his birthday, and soon the whole affair gets out of hand, helped by the fact that the temperature in the room, which is overcrowded, must be near the boiling point. In the heat and the crowd it is difficult to speak to César, but when I get the chance, I tell him: "That was a hell of a sword you put into the fourth, maestro."

He grins sheepishly and says, "Yes. It was pretty good, wasn't it?"

At the bar later Curro Fetén, in his annual state-of-the-temporada conversation with me, says: "Rincón is better than any other torero active today. César and Fran. Fran is entrega. César is *la verdad torera* [taurine truth]. If he were Mexican, he would storm the world. But he's Colombian, so they pay him no heed—like the presidente today. I've seen them all, all the great American toreros, César Girón, Carlos Arruza. There's no comparison! I'm a little drunk or I wouldn't be telling you this. But back in 1982 when he took his alternativa in Bogotá," he says, repeating what he told me in León, "I wrote in *El Tiempo* that César Rincón would be one of the greats! Here's the rundown: For arte, Antonio Ordóñez, Pepín Martín Vázquez, and Manzanares. For maestría, Luis Miguel Dominguín. For entrega, Fran Rivera Ordóñez. And for verdad, César Rincón. You can take it to the bank!"

Next morning, Sunday, September 3, as I head for Bayonne at a slightly lower speed than the two previous seasons—I think of it as having lost some of my sitio—I pass a tractor-trailer that has run off the road, has overturned, and is burning in a field. A nauseating smell of burning rubber and metal pervades the air. El toro de la carretera has struck again.

At the Hotel Mercure, Luis Carlos tells me Olivier Baratchart says no passes are available and the plaza is sold out. The cartel for the last corrida of the season—César Rincón, Juan Mora, and Rivera Ordóñez with bulls of the Marqués de Domecq—is understandably a sellout. But when I arrive at the plaza de toros, there is no problem getting a pass. Olivier Baratchart smiles benignly, buys me a glass of champagne, hands me a pass, and says: "You know there is never a problem for friends." Right, I think, I knew that.

All the bulls refuse to charge except for the fourth, Hacendoso, number 13, and with that happily charging animal César Rincón creates an uproar. Starting at the fence with six passes with his feet together, Rincón follows by running to the center of the ring and citing from twenty meters away. Hacendoso charges at a gallop. The effect is seismic. Rincón, with his innate sense for distance, tempo, rhythm, and cadence, and Hacendoso, with his long-distance charge, rattle the foundations of the ring. When a torero is in a state of grace, the grace imbues the crowd, and when he draws a bull that storms the muleta from afar, the resulting emotion saturates the público. How right Curro Fetén has proved to be: for verdad taurina, César Rincón. An accurate sword and the long, slow, dramatic death of a brave animal, resisting to the end, create an emotional finale in which the brave bull receives tremendous applause and the matador the utterly justified prize of two ears. César Rincón's brindis to the mother of the King of Spain and the presence of three Saudi princes in the barrera, who inevitably bring to mind the Reyes Magos, only add to the greater glory of Caesar (plate 59).

That evening in the tertulia, Rincón handles the crowd. Rafael el Gallo once remarked that in life one torears everything: "En la vida todo se torea." That is precisely what César Rincón does with the tertulia crowd. When someone asks him about the fool in Almería who shouted at him, Rincón patiently responds: "It's my intention that Colombia be identified with other things. I simply do not believe that all of us Colombians are drug dealers."

To a question about how he plans his faena, Rincón explains: "I never have a preconceived faena. You have to work with every animal in a different way to create that particular harmony that we call taurine beauty." It is true, and it is a mark of his brilliance as a torero. His faena was markedly "danced," very harmonious, with an "edge" of salsa in the long four-beat derechazos, exactly synchronized in the few naturales the bull allowed. Timing—and tempo—become supremely important in César Rincón's tauromachy when he draws a fine animal: he allowed the bull that slow, dramatic, emotion-laden death, that *muerte de bravo,* in spite of the literal time it took. Timing for effect was more important than the literal passage of time. Hacendoso, number 13, clearly deserved that respect.

César Rincón's thirtieth birthday turns out to be an ugly, rainy afternoon back in Palencia. But the band plays "Cumpleaños Feliz" when he takes his vuelta with the ear of his first Marqués de Domecq, and he looks genuinely pleased.

Rincón's second bull appears fat and refuses to charge. It is the only bad bull of the afternoon, his birthday *regalito*—a little present, said ironically of a terrible bull—in the rain, and Rincón is no longer happy.

Then Manolo Sánchez dedicates the fifth to Rincón to celebrate, a nice detalle, I think. But irony compounds irony and the bull looks to be one of the best of the season, far superior to the torero, who kills poorly but cuts an ear anyway because he has many local fans.

Figure 46. Talking to aficionados, Bayonne, September 3, 1995. The tertulia after the corrida is important to aficionados. For a matador to be successful, he must be able to torear in the tertulia as well as in the ring. As César does here.

The sixth bull is even better and El Cordobés does a grand faena, one that makes all the critics take serious notice of his artistic ability. He cuts an ear, which should have been two, and he and Manolo Sánchez go out on shoulders, while César Rincón walks. No one even bothers to comment on what Rincón would have done with either of the last two animals, but it makes me wonder if he is paying for his good luck in France.

The duel of the season—César Rincón and Enrique Ponce, mano a mano with bulls of Alcurrucén on the tenth of September in Dax—approaches, and the hype and the pressure mount. For the occasion the matadors talk about each like boxers. Enrique Ponce reportedly remarks: "If I were Rincón, I wouldn't sleep very well." And Rincón is said to have said: "I wish him all the luck in the world. He's going to need it."

Spirits are high at the sorteo and the competitive atmosphere is palpable. Pierre Molas, who is bowing out after twenty years of running the plaza, has conceived this cartel as his swan song. He acts as though I were an old friend, gives me a pass to the callejón without blinking, and hands out champagne and oysters as though it were his daughter's wedding.

Clearly it is meant to be the corrida of the year in France. The ring is splendidly bedecked and the afternoon is soft and calm with a gentle breeze off the Atlantic. The bulls of Alcurrucén looked superbly "presented" this morning at the sorteo. And two of the most important toreros of the decade are to face each other in this "duel in the sun" for the taurine scepter of France: the Caesar of the Americas, king of France, and champion of Madrid versus the most important figura in contemporary toreo. Enrique Ponce is resplendent in a suit of soft Corinthian while César Rincón wears the muted olive he wore in Madrid the day he cut two ears from the bull of Astolfi: Grecian red against Spanish green (plate 60). As they make the paseo you can hear the tension humming around the ring.

The first bull, a burraco bearing the name Cumbrealta and the number 56, repeatedly charges the horse from a distance but does not seem to see well at close range. On his own he charges Murillo's horse spectacularly, three times from a distance, then turns and without provocation attacks Pinilla's mount across the way.

In the muleta Cumbrealta continues to prove himself a whirlwind of bravery, but the distraction caused by his faulty vision prevents Rincón from linking up passes in his accustomed style. After a three-quarter sword and one descabello, the matador receives a grand ovation but not the ear he probably deserves for having overcome the formidable obstacle of the bull's uncertain charges. Ah well, there will be two more, I think. Surely Luis Alvarez put the bull he liked least first (plate 61a).

Cigarrito, number 63, a large castaño, perhaps 550 kilos (they do not always post the weights in France), looks as brave as the first, is possessed of a violent charge, and has no problem seeing. He too attacks the horse in a hair-raising manner, taking three picks, although with slightly less alegría than the first. As Cigarrito slams into the horse the last time, I notice fast-moving storm clouds gathering in the western sky, with thunder and lightning.

When Enrique Ponce starts his faena, the sky turns much darker and a gale whips up. A single dark cloud, with visibly spiraling currents, charges the ring like a bull of heaven, and I can see heavy raindrops circling like hornets in the eye of the spiral (plate 61b). The rain falls so suddenly that I am soaked before I can get my umbrella open, and the callejón floods with ankle-deep water. The sky looks dark as night and the rain hardens into hail.

The ferocity of this isolated tropical-style thunderstorm feels every bit as intense as the worst moments of Hurricane Erin.

I abandon the callejón to try to keep my cameras dry while Enrique Ponce calmly cuts both ears from Cigarrito. Alain Briscadieu, looking as if he had fallen in a swimming pool, says afterward Ponce would have cut only one ear if it had not rained. Others say if it had not stormed, he would have cut the tail.

The corrida is suspended, the arena a quagmire. People wander around as if in shock. César is furious that Luis put the burraco first. Outside the ring, the freakish storm has uprooted two old giants. They have toppled, exposing enormous tangled roots and leaving huge holes in the ground, but no one is injured.

Was there so much emotion, so much expectación, in the ring that we called down the storm, I wonder, watching a horizon-to-horizon rainbow arc from the ring to the river. Right about now Enrique Ponce and César Rincón should be going out on shoulders. Is the rainbow a sign of atonement from the taurine gods or nature's accidental suit of lights? Whatever else it is, it highlights the frustrating anticlimax of the taurine season.

Next day in Aranda de Duero the Portuguese bulls of Cabral de Ascenção come out mansos and infumables. César Rincón and Julio Aparicio can do virtually nothing and the local hero, Conrado Muñoz, draws the only decent animal and cuts ears. After the corrida I have dinner with Luis Alvarez and two Colombians, Carlos Pinzón and Eduardo Caba, who are planning to mount the first Festival Taurino Mundial, the first World Charity Corrida, in December in Bogotá. The event will benefit disadvantaged children and César Rincón will be the host matador.

We discuss the difficulties of being a top matador, and Luis trumps everyone by quoting empresario Eduardo Lozano, who once said, "It's easier to be pope than to be a torero," and El Viti, who once remarked, "To be a torero is impossible and to be a figura is a miracle."

Next day at lunch Carlos Pinzón, who falls somewhere between a taurine journalist and the Jerry Lewis of Colombia (as children's charity sponsor, not as comedian), gives me his version of Rincón's debacle in Bogotá the winter before: "César had already sent a bull back alive in his previous corrida, so the público was not exactly with him. Then he dedicates his bull to this journalist in the unpopular group that was now sponsoring him and some clown yells '¡Sapo!' [toad]. Somebody else picks it up. Soon the whole ring is chanting '¡Sa-po! ¡Sa-po! ¡Sa-po!' César freezes, thinking they are yelling at him—and in a way they are, because if he hadn't dedicated the bull to this guy, there would have been no bronca. Anyway César 'lost his papers,' broke down, and couldn't kill the bull. Juan Mora dedicated *his* bull to César, who was still broken up, but it didn't help. Afterwards César said he'd never perform in the Santamaría ring again. But the Festival in December will be his homecoming, the return of the hero, the prodigal son. And all of it to benefit handicapped children. You've got to come."

"I'll be there," I say, thinking, I wouldn't miss it for the world.

On September 16 in Nîmes, Manzanares, Espartaco, and Rincón kill a corrida of Atanasio Fernández, patched with Veiga Teixeira bulls from Portugal. Manzanares cuts an ear from the bravest of the Atanasios and César Rincón cuts an ear in the sixth. Espartaco's knee keeps him in trouble all afternoon. What should have been a good afternoon seems somehow flat. Alain Briscadieu sums it up: "This business of the bulls," he says with the Gallic sagacity of Roland's lieutenant Olivier, "c'est compliqué, c'est très compliqué."

That night Jorge Molina and Andrés Holguín, fresh from Colombia, Alain, Tim and Joan, and I end up in the catacombs of old Nîmes, in an ancient underground nightspot called the Cave of the Poet. There amidst mountains of champagne bottles we encounter two members of Rincón's cuadrilla. As it is something like 4 A.M., the one with whom I "have the most confidence" sidles up to me in a decidedly impaired state, his face partially averted, and says: "You won't tell the maestro, will you? He would kill us!"

Next noon the Colombians, Tim and Joan, and Alain and I meet at the Bar Hemingway in the Imperator and lunch in that beautiful garden, discussing Rincón's impending triumph over Joselito and Enrique Ponce. But it is not quite to be: the José Luis Marca bulls come out complicated, difficult, mansos. Rincón cuts the only ear from the first, but by the end of the afternoon, everyone is grumbling about another season in Nîmes with nothing but decepción.

After two corridas of disastrous bulls in Salamanca, I leave Madrid early on September 22 on a perfect fall morning. A pale red glow tinges the eastern horizon and the air has the clarity that comes with autumnal weather. Maybe, I muse, the weather—and the mood—have changed. But by the time I get to Logroño the muggy, breezy air has turned solidly gray. At the hotel Herencia Rioja, César seems apathetic. Even Alain Briscadieu is subdued. Perhaps he is right: C'est compliqué.

The Martín Arroyo bulls—Joselito's own bulls—come out worse than the bulls in Salamanca. Rincón's first, a manso perdido, reminds me of a wildebeest. Why does Rincón dedicate this animal to the público? He appears ill at ease with the bull, which goes to the fence and "waits for him," and the crowd whistles at his inability to kill it quickly.

Joselito gets an aviso with his bull. Enrique Ponce draws a morucho that flees from him, and kills it with a sword and eleven or twelve descabellos.

In Rincón's second bull a dispute arises over the picks. He wants to change the tercio after one pick but the presidente refuses. After the second pick the bull, a big castaño, falls down and will not get up. Finally Rincón and Vicente Yesteras grab him by the horn and hoist him up. It is a horrible spectacle, a horrible afternoon. The crowd whistles again at César Rincón and they whistle more at the bull.

Try as they might, neither Joselito nor Enrique Ponce can do anything. The three most important figuras in the taurine world, having sold out the ring, can do nothing in the face of these casta-less animals. The afternoon turns almost as frigid as the crowd. Ay, I think despondently, these sad ferias of the north: gray sands, gray air, gray bulls, gray toreros (plate 62a).

On the twenty-fourth a group of us drive over to Valladolid to see Joselito kill six bulls. It is an historic afternoon. Joselito is at his finest—inspired, complete, elegant, brave, a maestro. He cuts an ear from the second (Núñez del Cuvillo), two ears from the third (Núñez del Cuvillo; the bull is awarded a vuelta for his bravery), two ears from the fifth (Jandilla), and two ears from the sixth with a strong petition for the tail (Algarra). These seven ears will stand Joselito in great stead when the year-end ranking comes.

The same afternoon, far to the south in Lorca, César Rincón cut two ears from a bull of José Luis Pereda and two more from a Baltasar Ibán. I am sorry to have missed it but glad to have seen Joselito's historic triumph.

At the sorteo in Logroño on the twenty-fifth the sky weeps lightly, a sad drizzle blowing out of the north. Rincón draws one El Pilar, to go first, and one Puerto de San Lorenzo, to go fourth. No one seems particularly happy about the animals, but I tell Luis: "The sobrero is left over from that great corrida of Cebada Gago on the twenty-third. He could be very good."

"Sí, hijo, sí," says Luis wearily. Behind us Oscar Chopera, running the apartado, bellows: "¡Silencio!"

The Puerto de San Lorenzo falls in the picking and the presidente sends him back. As we wait for the sobrero, I say to Barquerito, next to me in the barrera of Tendido Seven, "Nacho, if this Cebada Gago comes out like the fourth or the fifth the other day . . ." Barquerito nods and we watch the 527-kilo animal, named Escandaloso, trot into the ring, his head high, his morillo arched up, his trapío very evident. He looks spectacular but quickly shows a tendency to flinch away from movement.

In spite of Vicente Yesteras's cape work, the picking becomes an ordeal as the bull continues to flee every encounter. The crowd whistles. Rincón's face registers studied indifference. Eventually the animal centers on the horse and Murillo manages a decent pick. Something about this bull reminds me of the bull of Astolfi. While Rincón gives him tentative verónicas, as if he were trying to teach the animal how to charge, I am wondering: Will this one come up?

The banderillas, one at a time, become a further ordeal as the bull pursues Monaguillo and Manolo Bélmez repeatedly. Escandaloso proves to be somewhat manso, to be sure, but with plenty of raza and with definite danger.

Will César Rincón strike out in Logroño yet again or can he somehow subjugate this difficult bull? He does not dedicate the life of Escandaloso to anyone, and his face, if it shows anything, shows, in one arched eyebrow, only resignation.

He opens with five doubling passes, taking the bull masterfully from the fence toward the center. In the sixth pass, the animal cuts in severely on the right, "warning" him and nearly catching him in the groin.

As Rincón tries unsuccessfully a series with the left, someone calls him *payaso,* clown. Visibly annoyed, he mumbles back something with "hijueputa" in it, and I can see him harden.

As though beginning anew, Rincón follows with three confident, bruising derechazos, each lower than the last, the bull following the cloth in spite of his tendency to cut in with that horn, and the ring springs to life.

Three more derechazos, wrapping the bull around his leg, and a pase de pecho bring forth an ovation, and the plaza lights up like a bonfire in the gray afternoon.

Four more extreme derechazos, with the hand very low, and the olés explode out of the tendidos like rifle fire. The band plays, even the sun comes out.

Figure 47. "Two ears!" *Luis Alvarez and Manolo Chopera. I took this photograph on September 1, 1996, in Bayonne. Although outside the period covered in the book, it exemplifies the situation in which César Rincón and Luis Alvarez found themselves many times. In Logroño, finally, he should have been awarded two ears. The prize for best faena is, however, some consolation.*

Then follow three epic derechazos de frente and a pase de pecho. As the matador walks away from the chest pass, Escandaloso charges and Rincón feeds him the muleta, making another long chest pass, winding the bull under his arm and across his chest in the most classic style, only to walk away, his back turned, as if he had planned it that way all along. Truth and beauty in improvisation. Dance. Rincón.

Two naturales, two ayudados, two more naturales, and a pase de pecho so close the bull bumps the man as he goes through, and the faena is complete.

Four more derechazos, low and slow to show total domination, and the afternoon is complete, the feria is complete, the season is complete.

As Rincón gets ready to kill, a loutish voice rings out: "¡Colombia! ¡Vete a la mierda!"[8] Rincón never even looks up but I know he has heard it. Everyone in the plaza heard it.

As he profiles to kill, the voice comes again, louder: "¡Colombia! ¡Vete a la mierda!" This time people boo and shout down the offender. Rincón, apparently untouched, sinks a magnificent sword high up, threading the "eye of the needle." A roar goes up from the público and Escandaloso staggers and falls, regains his feet, wobbles toward the fence, and collapses.

Incomprehensibly but not unpredictably, the presidente grants only the first ear. After Rincón's triumphant vuelta the light fades and I realize that my season in the sun with César Rincón is over (plate 62b).

Two evenings later in Madrid, 6T6 hosts a dinner for César Rincón in the Plaza Mayor. To open, Luis Alvarez announces that even though the presidente denied César the second ear, they have just called from Logroño to tell him he has won the prize for the best faena of the feria. (Later 6T6 will announce that the Faustino Martínez winery is also awarding César Rincón his weight in their Gran Reserva 1965, his birth year.)

Many of the staff of 6T6 are present, as well as some from Radio España. The evening is warm, humorous, and sentimental. José Carlos Arévalo stands at one point, clinking his spoon on his wine glass, and directs himself to César: "You are of the tribe. You are one of us. This is your house. You are one of the greats of our epoch. You are a gran figura and we are all of the same tribe of afición. Your tribe."

Fernando Fernández Román goes on at length about the "faith we had in you before you became who you are: César, now and always."

César is very moved. "In my country I have never had this kind of tribute. Here among you, I consider myself Spanish. Sometimes I have felt ill treated in this country—I cannot forget '¡Colombia, vete a la mierda!'—but never by you. . . . I thank all of you with all my heart."

One of the last nights I was in Spain, I ran into the taurine critic Vicente Zabala, who told me: "Rincón is the purest of all. How he torears and how he lowers the hand! Rincón and the Valencian, those are the two that matter."

When 6T6 did their year-end rankings, they gave Enrique Ponce number one, Joselito number two, and César Rincón number three. Later I would find out that there were fierce discussions about who should be two and who should be three. Evidently there was plenty of sentiment to give number two to César Rincón. At any rate, 1995 for César Rincón has to be considered, even with all the bad bulls, a phenomenal season, almost as good as 1991, even if his rating was again one rung under where I thought it should have been.

6T6 pointed out that Rincón was the leader in the big plazas, "the ones that bring money and ranking." They judged that his season, from Madrid on, had been "unstoppable," and they described him as the most belmontista of current toreros, one who had arrived at an "aesthetic peak" that placed him in the category of "sublime virtuoso" (84:32).

A short time later the Assemblée Nationale in Paris received César Rincón—the first torero ever so honored—to recognize his professional trajectory. For the fifth year in a row, Rincón was declared the triunfador of the season in France.

José Carlos Arévalo summed up the entire season well, creating his own frankly subjective escalafón in which the leaders were "Joselito and Manzanares, Muñoz and Rincón, *in practically all of his actuaciones.* And Ponce, in some of his triumphant afternoons" (*6T6* 84:3; my emphasis). Obviously there were substantial differences of opinion.

Michael Wigram liked Enrique Ponce.

José Carlos Arévalo liked Joselito.

I liked César Rincón.

What was clear at the end of this stormy and competitive temporada was that it had been a formidable year, undoubtedly the greatest I had ever seen, and that greatness was due to the competition among the three of them.

What stood out the most? César Rincón with the bull of Astolfi, the fifth time he opened the Puerta Grande in Madrid. As José Luis Ramón of *6T6* remarked, that Puerta Grande was "the one most firmly bolted shut" (84:16).

The night before I fly home, I crawl into bed early, around midnight. I open the *Herald Tribune,* the first copy of an English-language paper I have seen in two months, and read that a killer hurricane named Opal is bearing down on Pensacola.

Santa Fe de Bogotá: December 17, 1995

It is raining when I arrive late on December 14 at El Dorado Airport in Santa Fe de Bogotá. Next morning at the Hotel Tequendama I meet Luis Alvarez and we have a lunch of *ajiaco,* a stewed hen with three kinds of potatoes, corn, and avocado. Luis says authoritatively: "They make the best ajiaco in the world right here in the Tequendama." With Luis are José Nelo, Morenito de Maracay, representing Venezuela, and Víctor Mendes, the matador from Portugal. Denis Loré, the matador from France, also joins us. The international cast from the eight active taurine countries is assembling for the first Festival Taurino Mundial.

On the sixteenth at breakfast, as Denis Loré and his banderillero Lauri Monzón and I chat about the food and the weather and the upcoming festival, Manolo Mejía arrives with a retinue. Denis says he looks like an Aztec prince. The most important figura in Mexico at the moment, he will represent his country in the festival.

That afternoon there is a training session in front of the Santamaría ring. Adriana Eslava, the flamboyant one-eyed daughter of Pepe Cáceres (she lost her eye in a shooting), is there to do media interviews with the toreros.

I have a long talk with Víctor Mendes. He is well educated, speaks Portuguese, Spanish, French, and English, and was a law student when the leftist revolution hit Portugal in the mid-'70s. Mendes is well aware of the chauvinism of some of the Spanish taurinos. "The Spaniards would like for me and Rincón and the Mexicans and everybody else to slip and get a big one in the culo. It's not everybody, of course, just some of them. But enough." Víctor Mendes thinks César Rincón an unusual case. "The Spaniards aren't making him rich for nothing."

Enrique Ponce, it turns out, is not coming. Carlos Pinzón arrives at the plaza with the news. "He sent a medical certificate. He has a high fever—flu. Fernando Cámara will take his place for Spain. Fortunately he is here in Bogotá." The malas lenguas get to work at once, fabricating theories about why Ponce is not coming.

On the seventeenth, the day of the festival, the sun actually shines, at least for a while. At the sorteo they say that this prickly sun will bring rain. With eight matadors, eight cuadrillas, eight ganaderos (each has donated one bull), and a host of hangers-on, the sorteo is crowded and confusing.

Lauri Monzón is superstitious and does not want to draw for Denis Loré. Denis cannot draw his own—that is really asking for bad luck. "Will you draw for us?" they ask me.

"Sure," I say, suddenly not at all sure of how I feel about that responsabilidad.

The bull I draw for Denis Loré, the youngest in seniority of the matadors, is a Fuentelapeña bull, owned by Abraham Domínguez. After the drawing—which, by the time I put my hand in, has become purely symbolic since there is only one paper left to draw—Abraham tells me: "This bull is going to be the best of the afternoon. You drew the right one!"

At lunch back at the hotel, Darío Restrepo is clearly nervous. César Rincón has drawn his bull. "Oh, what a responsabilidad!" he wails. "God will that he charge. If the bull will just help a little—he's from the Núñez bloodline and he could be good—César will do the rest. God will that he charge!"

By 3:00 the sun has hidden in the thick Andean clouds. A constant fine drizzle, which reminds me of the weather in Bilbao, shines in the glare. The ring is nearly full, with well over ten thousand spectators.

Things do not start auspiciously. Morenito's bull comes in with a lot of *nervio*, typical of Ernesto González Caicedo's bulls, but quits after the banderillas, going to toriles to "hole up."

Víctor Mendes's bull slams into the horse, knocking it over with the unexpected charge of a dangerous manso. The horse hits its head on the estribo as it falls, and the bull returns repeatedly to the stricken animal. It soon becomes clear that the horse is mortally wounded. They administer the coup de grace with the puntilla and cover the horse with its peto.

Víctor Mendes puts in banderillas as best he can with the bull going insistently to the dead horse. You hear that, before the peto was introduced in 1928, a bull would take up a querencia where he had killed a horse. That is precisely what this animal does, becoming extremely dangerous. Mendes handles the animal with a professional expertise that comes of dealing with intractable animals for many years. He puts in a well-placed sword, tells everyone around him to take it easy, and then hits a bull's-eye descabello as the animal charges him.

Víctor Mendes receives an ovation and flowers from the público. They also throw flowers for the dead horse and applaud when the mules drag it out. Above us some of the women in the tendido are crying.

Then the crowd begins the now familiar chant: "¡Céééééésar! ¡Céééééé-sar! ¡Céééééésar!" When he goes out for a bow, they throw so many flowers that it takes the ring attendants some time to clear the ring. It is, as in a García Márquez novel, a rain of flowers. Now César Rincón will take on the seven knights from foreign lands, a brilliantly conceived strategy—if he can prevail.

Darío Restrepo's bull, number 4, named Gavilán, weighs 468 kilos and comes into the ring at a gallop, attacking the burladero in front of us.

Rincón steps out behind him, calls him, and cites, making six impeccable verónicas and a media.

Murillo picks the hard-charging animal carefully and Rincón asks for the change. Gavilán is brave and noble, with a good left horn and a right horn as sweet as those sea-bulls in my dream. This time he has been lucky in the draw.

César Rincón dedicates to the público of the Santamaría and opens with strong, classic doubling passes, one knee on the ground. I have never seen him look more confident (plate 63a).

The faena that follows is vintage Rincón: derechazos and naturales in that purest of post-Belmonte style, the matador's leg forward, his chest exposed, winding Gavilán around and around his turning waist as he sculpts with his scarlet cloth a labyrinth of diminishing time and space that imprisons Gavilán more securely than chains.

There is delirium in the tendidos and more flowers shower down upon the sand as César Rincón continues, now dancing through molinetes and pases de las flores, linking them to yet more derechazos, finishing each series with exquisitely timed desplantes. I do not know who is more suffused with emotion, the matador performing for his adoring público or the público enraptured with their messiah. Along the callejón the faces register high emotion—above all Darío Restrepo's. God has granted his wish.

Rincón raises the sword and throws himself on Gavilán. The thrust proves to be mortal but Rincón allows the bull his time to die, with no turns from the banderilleros to speed up the process. The delay may cost him the tail, but the respect he shows the animal is more important. As Rincón takes his vuelta with Gavilán's ears—amid thunderous repetitions of "¡Torero! ¡Torero!"—I hear Luis Alvarez say to no one in particular, "I'm going to smoke another *puro*. ¡Me cago en la leche!" A rain of carnations and other flowers follows (plate 63b). Theseus has come home (plate 63c).

The rest of the festival is anticlimactic. Manolo Mejía's bull is weak in the legs. He dedicates it to César Rincón, for being the host matador, but can do little of merit, killing poorly.

During the faena of Freddy Villafuerte, the matador from Peru, some fool explodes a big chunk of fireworks, scaring everyone in the plaza. They have to carry one wounded person out, running with him through the callejón as though it were a cornada.

José Luis Cobo from Ecuador dedicates his Rocha bull, which looks like a

Figure 48. Darío Restrepo, Bogotá, December 17, 1995. God granted Darío's wish. His bull charged and César Rincón vanquished the Magnificent Seven.

prancing gnu, to Carlos Pinzón, but Cobo seems to lack sitio and kills poorly.

Fernando Cámara represents Spain well. He performs elegantly with a horrid little bull and cuts a well-deserved ear. (It's just as well Enrique Ponce didn't come, I am thinking, if this is what he would have drawn.)

Abraham Domínguez's bull comes out bucking like a rodeo bull, and Denis Loré gives him a kneeling larga and five verónicas and a media. He takes him to the horse with walking chicuelinas and dedicates to the público. The bull charges well and Denis Loré is torerísimo, killing efficiently and cutting an ear.

All's well that ends well—César Rincón has indubitably vanquished the foreign knights. At the ceremonies afterwards at the Tequendama, Carlos Pinzón sums it up. He thanks "those eight stars who have helped fifteen thousand handicapped children. A big hand, ladies and gentlemen, for all of them, for César Rincón and the Magnificent Seven!"

The celebration that follows is a grand taurine event. The high points for me are a long conversation with Ernesto González Caicedo and Abraham Domínguez, and the endless fervent discussion that lasts into the wee hours with, among others, Luis Alvarez, Manola Mejía and his manager

Mariano González, Víctor Mendes, and Adriana Eslava, who believes fiercely that her father has not been given his proper place in taurine history. It is one of those long-drawn-out, emotional, hypertaurine nights that stay with you for years. Except for the party after the bull of Astolfi, it was the social highlight of the seasons I spent with César Rincón.

On the plane coming home I reflect on the last days in Bogotá, after the festival. Particularly I remember my day out at César's ganadería. The majesty and sweet silence of the Andean landscape, the beauty and the grandeur of the bulls in the campo, and the hospitality of Efraín Olano and his Andalusian wife María—contrast strongly with the disorder, the grime, and the constant tension of Bogotá.

The peace and beauty are marred by the death of Ramito, Rincón's prized Marqués de Domecq semental, killed by his rival, Nueva Ropa. César is disconsolate, not merely because the animal was worth perhaps eighty thousand dollars, but also because he is virtually irreplaceable. Nueva Ropa and Ramito fought and Nueva Ropa pushed his antagonist off the edge of a ravine. When I arrive at the finca, they are just bringing him down. That evening as I leave to return to Bogotá, they are loading up his headless, bloated, bloody carcass, skinned out now for the taxidermist at César's request.

Another sad memory is the late afternoon I went with Ricardo Chinza, César's former driver and childhood companion, to see the little house of Hermógenes Martínez in the south end of Bogotá, where the family tragedy took place. Although there is no visible sign of the fire, a sadness still pervades the atmosphere thirteen years later. No one in the barrio has forgotten.

After our visit we adjourn to the Casa San Isidro, up on Montserrate where Gonzalo Rincón used to take photographs of newlyweds. As we are getting on the cable car, we hear of the crash of American Airlines flight 965 to Cali. Taurine critic Vicente Zabala was on that flight, coming to cover the feria.

For that which befalleth the sons of men befalleth beasts. Mortality, I write in my notebook, is the lesson of the corrida. If it were not, there would be no glory, no alegría. The essence of life is death; the essence of death is life. And the corrida provides lessons in order and rhythm that no other spectacle or endeavor can equal. In the very real death within the corrida and in the defying of very real death within the corrida, we learn virtually every lesson of life. Every emotion, every sense of religion, every ceremony and ritual are there, if we are willing to learn, to be open, to seek and to find. Even perhaps how to deal with flight 965 or the tragedy of María Teresa Ramírez and Sonia Rincón.

Jorge Molina has given me a copy of a little-known interview with Federico García Lorca made on April 8, 1935, by the Italian journalist Giovanni Papini, and I read it for the first time on the flight coming home.

Papini asks García Lorca what he thinks about foreigners disposed to seeing this bloody game of toreo as proof of the cruelty of the Spanish people, and García Lorca replies: "Not all foreigners are that imbecilic."

He tells Papini that the corrida is really "a religious mystery, a sacred rite" and that the torero is a kind of "priest from pre-Christian times." What does the bull "represent in man's conscience? Primitive and savage energy and at the same time the ultrapotency of fertility. He is the beast in all his dark power; the male with all his sexual force."

But man, García Lorca continues, must subdue these forces. He must "kill within himself that underlying animal nature"; he must overcome "the brute that exists within him." That is what the corrida is about: "The victory over the sensual and ferocious beast is the visible projection of an interior victory." So the corrida portrays "the superiority of the spirit over matter, of intelligence over instinct, of the smiling hero over the foam-flecked monster" (215–16).

As I read this I remember what President César Gaviria said to César Rincón at his 1991 homecoming: "The fiesta brava, beyond the mere spectacle, symbolizes man's capacity for transformation and purification. Courage, intelligence and art against strength, brutality and fear. Death serves as a pretext so that life can be affirmed." Man, Gaviria said, "ought to divest himself of his original animal nature and discipline the force of his intelligence. Both the bull and the tauric elements of the toreo die."

All cultures have had their beast slayers. Gawain and Percival, Siegfried/ Sigurd, and Saint George come quickly to mind. Some have even had bull slayers: the Babylonian hero Gilgamesh kills the bull-of-heaven in the earliest myth we have; the Persian hero-god Mithra sacrifices a white bull-of-heaven with a sword. But of these mythical heros, Theseus is the one who best fits what García Lorca and Gaviria were expressing. When Theseus goes within the labyrinth and kills the half-man, half-bull, thereby saving his country, he is doing exactly what García Lorca and Gaviria are describing.

That is what César Rincón does, except that he does it in life instead of in myth. His ritual is real, his sacrifice literal. As the matador, every time he enters the labyrinth of the ring, he saves us from the Minotaur's curse; he saves us from the animal itself and from our own animal nature. His mission is grace. He is our exemplar. César Rincón also "saves" his country. And he had just proved it, yet again, against the Magnificent Seven.

As I reflect on these ideas, I remember that original dream in which the black bull of fear had made César into a hero, the only hero left, the last serious man in the world. He was the doer; I was honored to be the recorder. And now it was no longer a dream.

Epilogue

Metamorphosis

During the years it has taken to write this book, I have continued to follow César Rincón's career. In spite of a number of important triumphs, the European seasons of 1996–99 were hard for him, and he sustained so many injuries that his father remarked to me: "He's going to be made of Teflon. They're turning him into a bionic torero." Yet through these difficult seasons in Europe, he always maintained himself as the Señor de las Américas, with more triumphs than anyone and a number of pardoned bulls.

Then in May 1999 César Rincón bought the prestigious ganadería of El Torreón from the architect Felipe Lafita. Rumors had circulated for some time that the young figura Julián López el Juli was interested in this prime 570-hectare property near Santa Cruz de la Sierra in the province of Cáceres. But El Juli and Felipe Lafita failed to come to terms, and César Rincón bought the entire estate, including all the bulls, cows, and sementales, reportedly for 700 million pesetas (more than $4 million).

When the news broke, all I could think was that it was what had to happen. He had already bought a smaller finca two years before at nearby Navalmoral de la Mata. With the acquisition of one of Spain's finest ganaderías—encaste Domecq, the same as his ganadería in Colombia—he was passing almost inevitably into the ranks of matador-ganaderos, beginning the new cycle that attracts many figuras, metamorphosing from bull slayer into bull breeder. As Rincón expressed it in July 1999, "The world of the bull is our world, the one we live from, so we must take care of it." Not that it would be easy. "In any profession the great thing is to maintain oneself, that I know well. To arrive is difficult, to maintain is almost a miracle. It's the same for an important ganadero as for a figura del toreo. To create a ganadería is very complicated. Mine is already done. Now it's up to me to sustain it" (6T6 264:28).

In August he announced he would retire at the end of the season, or at least take a "sabbatical," and that he would not perform in the 2000 season in the Americas or in Europe.

On May 23, 2000, César Rincón debuted in Las Ventas del Espíritu Santo as a ganadero, bringing a splendid set of novillos, brave, well presented, and with excellent juego. In the sixth bull Javier Castaño, a novillero from Salamanca, cut two ears—a feat only one matador accomplished during this San Isidro—and went out on shoulders. César Rincón, in his barrera, looked ecstatic. Afterwards he remarked: "It was beautiful to triumph again in a plaza where I had had so many successes as a matador, but it felt very different" (6T6 309:15).

Not long after, when I spoke with him, he reiterated the pride and satisfaction he had felt, and added: "I am very contento, with the ganadería and with living here."

"Do you remember what you said in 'ninety-one about being able to retire at the right moment and being able to enjoy the money you hoped to earn? Is this that moment?"

"Yes, I believe it is."

"Are you thinking about coming back as a matador?"

"The truth is, I'm not. I want to concentrate completely on breeding the best bulls I can. Here and in Colombia."

But César did not tell me quite the whole story. In September he finally went public, revealing on the radio that he had suffered a serious recurrence of the hepatitis C. "I have begun treatment," he told Manuel Molés on September 10, 2000. "I've had this disease for years, and I noticed it was getting worse. I decided to stop and put myself in the hands of the doctors, who are the only ones who can cure me."

Looking back on his situation and his terrible cornada in Palmira in November 1990, he commented: "I say 'fortunately' I have hepatitis C, because some charitable soul donated blood. The transfusion was so urgent, there was no time to screen the blood, and the screened blood they had on hand wasn't compatible. Then in 'ninety-two I found out I had hepatitis."

The yearlong treatment, using Interferon and Ribavirin, has about a 60 percent cure rate, as well as seriously debilitating side effects. "It's going to be a tough year, but I am very aware that my health is the most important thing and that I have to drop everything for my health."

Two weeks later he made a clarification: "I did not know I had the disease until the 'ninety-two season, and at that point in my career I made the decision not to quit and to handle the hepatitis as best I could. Last year I decided it was time to get serious about my health, and I announced my retirement. I did not want [news of the recurrence] to get out, since it really has nothing to do with my profession. I don't know how it leaked out."

He reiterated that he was "not even thinking about coming back or anything like that. I am concentrating on taking care of myself because my health is the most important thing" (6T6 326:3).

In an interview the following February, César Rincón explained more details about the evolution of his disease. It was difficult, he said, because in 1992 there were two alternatives, to begin treatment and stop performing or "to continue my career when I was in my best moment." He decided "to put aside the disease and continue," admitting that he had to make "an enormous effort so that no one would notice." Every year he had tests, and every year the "disease continued and got worse." Last year "the doctors told me I had to quit toreando, that it was time to chose my health rather than my profession" (*Diario 16*, February 6, 2001).

When I read that admission, some of the doubts I had had along the way were confirmed. I could only marvel all the more at the magnitude of his accomplishment, including the concealment. I realized that all the triumphs—the four salidas a hombros in Madrid, the epic battles with Mariposito and Bastonito, with the bull of Astolfi, the state of grace in León in 1995 and all through France, the indultos in the Americas—all had been achieved, to some degree or other, in spite of the disease. He had chosen to go on, not to give up, until he was literally forced to stop. What was it he said that day in Bayonne in 1994 when I asked him how much he would give not to be in pain? *Exactly my point. You have to have the money to give.*

On May 13, 2001, almost ten years to the day since Rincón's breakthrough with Santanerito, an *El Mundo Magazine* cover story appeared titled "Rincón de Tristeza"—corner of sadness, or Rincón in sadness. The cover shows a chemo-diminished César in a chair, backed by the high cloud-streaked sky of his finca in Cáceres. The subtitle reads "La mala suerte del torero César Rincón"—the bad luck of torero César Rincón. He stares at his white terrier, or at nothing. Inside, along with photos of his triumphs, there is one showing him and his bride Sandra Briceño in Bogotá on their wedding day, December 13, 1997. (They are separated and she lives in Colombia with their son.)

He complains of devastating side effects from the medication: migraines, exhaustion, depression, dry skin, chills. He asks himself if it is worth continuing. "It's not that I don't want to live, but I ask myself how long I can continue this. . . . I cry over anything, everything affects me too much."

Even if he survives the disease, he does not think about returning to the ring. He tells of making three passes with an animal recently: "By the third one, I was finished." The interviewer cannot resist asking whether he would like to have died in the ring rather than to die an old man. César replies: "I would like not to die." Amid the speculations, memories, and emotions that his comments stir in me, there arises one sobering certainty. Barring a medical miracle, the saga of César Rincón, matador de toros, is finished (plate 64). The last time we spoke he sounded like the César "of always." His voice was weak but his spirit was undiminished. "The treatment," he said, "is going well and I am very hopeful." All I could do now was wish him, as I had so many afternoons: "¡Suerte, matador!"

Notes

Prologue

1. If a matador performs well, he is awarded one ear as a symbolic trophy. If he has a great success he is given two. On rare occasions (and not in all rings), he can also be awarded the tail.

2. Other taurine countries where corridas are occasionally given, or have been given in the past, include Cuba, Guatemala, Nicaragua, Costa Rica, Panama, Bolivia, Uruguay, Brazil, Italy, Lebanon, Egypt, Algeria, Morocco, South Korea, Japan, Canada, and the U.S.A. Some form of taurine ritual in ancient times has been documented all across Eurasia and as far south as Madagascar (Bishop 447–55).

Chapter 1

1. Formerly the village or town square, evolving in time into the round of the ring—i.e., the circling of the square.

2. Literally terrain, figuratively territory, as in the bull's terrain and the torero's terrain; the immediately reachable area, especially in the case of the bull. This concept is in constant evolution in modern toreo as the torero encroaches more and more on the bull's terreno.

3. Present participle of *torear,* working or playing the bull.

4. Hemingway seems to have invented the forms "pic," "pic-ing," and "pic-ed" for the suerte de varas, and most subsequent writers in English have followed his lead. Since one of the first meanings of the verb "to pick" is to pierce, I see no reason not to use the logical English cognate "pick," both as a noun and as a verb, thereby avoid the awkward hyphenation of such forms as "pic-ing." Kenneth Tynan used the forms "pick" and "picking" in *Bull Fever.*

5. It is doubtless an exaggeration to give Belmonte the entire credit for the evolution of modern toreo, and some critics have used an idealized notion of Belmonte's toreo to criticize contemporary toreros. Be that as it may, Belmonte was clearly the

guiding genius of change. For a technical discussion, see the series of six letters by José Carlos Arévalo and Michael Wigram to Mr. Tunku Varadarajan in *6T6* 104–9.

6. Again I am simplifying. For a superb discussion of the intricacies of the development of modern toreo, see José Alameda's classic work *El hilo del toreo*.

7. *Cargando la suerte* has become a much disputed term. Arévalo and Wigram have proved that the use of the term for stepping into the pass, or advancing the outside or contrary leg, which amounts to the same thing, is not historically altogether correct (see the letters to Varadarajan, especially the third and fourth in *6T6* 106–7). Still, the use of the term to mean advancing the leg is so widespread that it will probably continue, even if it is wrong.

Regardless of what it is called, the movement is considered basic to modern toreo, although the notion currently prevalent, especially in the Madrid ring, that the matador should put the leg forward in *every* pass is clearly absurd to anyone who understands how passes are linked. The elder maestro Antoñete defines *cargar la suerte* as "substituting linear toreo with depth and profoundness by loading your weight onto the contrary [outside] leg" (Molés 23). In conversation in December 1996 the young maestro Joselito (no relation to the Joselito of the golden age) told me, "It's not advancing the leg; it's leaning on the axis leg." He went on to explain how a certain matador sometimes advanced the contrary leg but in fact managed to *descargar* la suerte by rocking his weight back onto the inside leg. Needless to say, these theoretical discussions can become infinite, but such is the stuff of afición.

Chapter 4

1. Actually they were freed the evening of the twentieth in Colombia, but by then it was the morning of the twenty-first in Spain, so for César Rincón it was all the same day.

Chapter 6

1. *Narcotráfico* is, of course, drug traffic, and *terrorismo* is obviously terrorism, but in Colombia the two sometimes become confused and confusing since, at this time, some of the direst acts of terrorism were being perpetrated by the Medellín drug cartel.

2. "Planet of the bulls," a much used phrase coined by the critic Antonio Díaz-Cañabate.

Chapter 8

1. Corrida in which two matadors kill three bulls each; an intentional competition.

2. Remember, that is the gross. From that Rincón himself has to pay his manager's share (usually 15 percent) and the salaries and expenses of all his staff: sword handler and assistants, banderilleros and picadores, driver of the van, and that's only the beginning. And do not forget Hacienda, Spain's version of the IRS. Nice work if you can get it and the bull does not kill you, but the gross does not go straight into the matador's pocket.

3. Not valid, weak. An inválido, usually weak in the legs, is dispatched in the corrals behind the ring in the presence of a representative of the proper authority.

4. *Encaste* refers to a crossing or mixing or "refreshing" of castas, and *casta* means genotype, a group or class sharing a specific genetic makeup or strain, as well as the aggressiveness resulting from that strain. To make matters more confusing, *encaste* is often used for *casta,* but the crossing of castas is such that this usage is perhaps inevitable.

5. *Chicuelina:* a cape pass named for the artistic matador Chicuelo, who invented it. In the verónica the matador's body accompanies the directional swing of the cape, but in the chicuelina the matador's body turns in the opposite direction, against the flow of the pass, so that the cape wraps around the matador's body as he spins.

6. *Revolera:* a finishing pass with the cape that begins as a one-handed pass, a larga. As the bull charges by, following the end of the cape, the matador switches hands behind his back, drawing the cape out from under the bull's muzzle, and swirls it around his waist.

7. According to the *reglamento taurino,* the laws governing the corrida, if the majority present requests the ear by waving handkerchiefs, the presidente must accede to the request. The second ear, however, is entirely at the presidente's discretion, at least according to the reglamento.

Chapter 9

1. Hasta el cuarenta de mayo, no te quites el sayo. "Ne'er shed a clout till May be out" is a close English version, as my friend Perdita Hordern has informed me.

2. "Torears" is inevitable. It is either "torears" or "fights," and "fights" has all the wrong connotations. We simply have to accept the verb "to torear." Much as it might pain us, the alternative is worse. Hemingway was the first to realize this: "torear, that is the only word for all the actions performed by a man with the bull" (*Death in the Afternoon* 69).

3. More ink has been spilled trying to define *trapío* than perhaps any term used to describe the bull. The *Oxford Spanish Dictionary* calls it power, but it is more than that. It is also presence or, as Barnaby Conrad writes in his *Encyclopedia of Bullfighting,* "the general physical aspect of the fighting bull" (242). Trapío is visual. If a bull looks aggressive and bravo and as though he will charge anything, he has trapío, regardless of his actual size.

4. What Brett Ashley is fascinated by in *The Sun Also Rises* and calls "those green trousers" (165). They are not always green, of course, but the knee-length breeches (rather than trousers), which date back to the eighteenth-century matador's costume, at once the essence of Spanish, especially Andalusian, style and of the French influence from the court of Versailles, are in modern times always tight, precisely so they will not get ripped off or otherwise endanger the matador. They were ripped in this instance because that is how close the horn came to Rincón's gut: snaggingly close.

5. *El Sol* was the Republican paper from before the Spanish Civil War. It did not survive, then or now.

Chapter 12

1. Espartaco led the 1991 season with 80, Víctor Mendes was second with 77, and Rincón was third with 71. Quantity and quality can be separate issues, but Espartaco's record is amazing. He led the escalafón eight times, in 1982 and in 1985 through 1991, seven straight years, in the process breaking Joselito el Gallo's record of six years running and Domingo Ortega's record of seven years total. In the seven years 1985–91, he performed in 624 corridas, killed 1,172 bulls, and cut 1,026 ears and 54 tails. (See the announcement in 6T6 6:10–11.)

2. Both Espartaco and Rincón were eventually fined five million pesetas each. Espartaco paid; Rincón appealed. Nine years after the events, the Tribunal Supremo confirmed the fine (El País, November 21, 2000). How this decision will affect contracts in the future is unclear.

3. On October 20, 1974, the Mexican matador Manolo Martínez and Paco Camino had appeared in a corrida televised to the whole taurine world. The bulls of Carlos Núñez were laughable—one was completely disabled by the picador and had to be put out of its misery—and no one was well served, least of all the fiesta brava.

Chapter 13

1. Toreros say the worst soledad of all is in the ring. Joselito, just before he was killed in the ring in Talavera de la Reina in 1920, told the taurine writer José María de Cossío, "No one is as alone as I am" (Pérez Mateos 37).

2. A bridge on the Boyacá River was the site of Simón Bolívar's decisive defeat of the Spanish royal army on August 7, 1819. Taking Bogotá several days later, Bolívar liberated New Granada, subsequently Colombia.

Chapter 14

1. "Windmill" pass, done on the right or left by spinning, as in a chicuelina, in the direction opposite to or away from the charge, in the process wrapping the muleta around the torero's body.

Chapter 15

1. Sitio here means terrain, the same "place" in front of the bull, which is not so much a literal place as a position relative to the bull, the position that causes the bull to charge.

Chapter 17

1. Javier Villán reproduced some of them before they disappeared.

Chapter 19

1. In 1996 Darío Piedrahíta, Pedro Domingo, or, as he prefers, "Dapie," published his own account, El otro . . . Rincón: Su verdadera historia (The other . . . Rincón: The true story), denying all of the above, attempting to justify his actions, and claiming credit for virtually everything Rincón had accomplished. This thoroughly incred-

ible version ends with a long invented telephone conversation between César Rincón and his father, in which father and son plot to ruin the former manager.

Chapter 20

1. The alternativa must also be confirmed in the principal rings of national capitals such as the Santamaría in Bogotá and the Plaza México. The *confirmación* is identical in ceremony to the alternativa.

Chapter 22

1. His younger brother Curro Girón was very popular in Spain but did not achieve the artistic mastery with which César Girón is generally credited. I saw them both in the '60s and thought César to be a more profound torero.

Chapter 23

1. The six bulls are divided into three pairs, according to their supposed characteristics, and then drawn by lot.

2. Taurinely a bull with sentido is one that "understands," i.e., one that seeks out the matador behind the lure.

3. The rule is clear: If a majority of the crowd petitions the *first* ear of any bull, the presidente is obliged to grant it. Rincón cut an ear in his first and had a clear majority petition for the *first* ear of his second animal. Yet the presidente refused to grant the ear.

4. *Torista,* as opposed to *torerista,* is afición that centers primarily on the animal, preferring large, fearsome beasts to more manageable animals. The distinction is essentially false, as true afición should center equally on the man and the animal.

Chapter 24

1. The first and second banderilleros alternate the cape and the sticks, putting in two pairs (the first and the third) on one bull, handling the cape in the other. The third banderillero, the tercero, puts in the second pair on each bull.

2. A reverse molinete starts as a natural and finishes by spinning backward away from the bull at the end of the pass.

3. Literally, the milk. Sometimes euphemistically, semen. Usually negative and vulgar. Used in reverse here to express the ineffable; cf. in English "the real shit."

4. Literally, the Host, the consecrated wafer of the Eucharist. Spanish can be profoundly blasphemous. The term is used to express extreme displeasure or annoyance and extreme admiration. Joselito meant that the experience was awesome.

5. The taurine world, in the diminutive. The same as the planeta de los toros, but more familiar, less grandiose.

6. Since the vacas will only be bred and never sent to the ring, they may be passed until they drop. It does not matter that they "know Latin."

7. Literally, I shit in the milk. Unrenderable in English except literally. Connotes severe disapproval.

8. César Rincón's triumphs now demand closer coverage of the Colombian

corridas than ever before. A number of Spanish critics covered—and continue to cover—the season.

9. Two ears from one animal applies in only a few rings, although the practice is becoming more and more accepted.

Chapter 25

1. Cuckold in English. Far more offensive in Spanish. Literally, he-goat.

2. This sculpture now resides permanently at the exit of the international terminal of Barajas Airport in Madrid, where it greets all visitors with its ancient intrinsic message, connecting the rise of civilization with the bulls since earliest antiquity.

3. The program had spelled Bastonito's name wrong, so Bastoncito was the name used in some reviews.

4. Andrés Caballero, who had been brave but awkward, did not come close to deserving the tail, but the crowd was not about to let the local torero be outdone.

5. One famous (but unnamed) matador with cartel in Spain and in France was quoted by Emilio Martínez in *El Ruedo* as saying: "In France it is much more difficult to cut ears than in Spain, except in Madrid. The seriousness of the bull used there and especially the knowledge of [the French] aficionados are unequaled." Martínez called that judgment "absolutely certain and representative of the current state of affairs in the fiesta" (September 20, 1994).

6. Remember, Tuesday the thirteenth is the unlucky day in Spain, rather than Friday.

7. Some misguided people in the government wanted to remove these horned totems from the Spanish roads, but the public outcry was enormous and the *toro de la carretera*, the bull of the highway, remains in place to remind all travelers that they are in the country of ineradicable taurine rituals.

Chapter 26

1. From *el rincón de Ordóñez*, the Ordóñez spot, so called because Antonio Ordóñez used it so frequently.

2. Literally, "I shit on your picture." Very Andalusian—estampas are usually religious images.

3. They customarily clip the animals' horns after a tienta to keep them from injuring each other later in the campo.

4. A bottle of *cava* (Spanish sparkling wine), half a glass of Spanish brandy, half a glass of Cointreau, on ice.

5. Little black Virgin. This black virgin belongs to the medieval tradition that includes the Moreneta, from the Montserrat hills above Barcelona.

6. Chief White Feather, or Luis Alvarez, and Harold Enrique Torres. Torres, from Bogotá, his new driver, called Lengüi for his habit of sticking his tongue out the side of his mouth when concentrating.

7. A half-breed, a bull that is genetically half bravo and half domestic.

8. *Mierda* is literally shit. Unrenderable in English except as "go to hell," but stronger.

Bibliography

ABC (Madrid).

Abella, Carlos. *Paco Camino: El Mozart del toreo*. Madrid: Espasa Calpe, 1994.

Alameda, José. *El hilo del toreo*. Madrid: Espasa Calpe, 1989.

Anuario Taurino Internacional 1992: Temporada 1991. Bilbao: Ediciones Eguía, 1992.

Aplausos (Valencia).

Armiñán, Jaime de. *Juncal*. Madrid: Espasa Calpe, 1989.

Barrera Sol (Irún).

Bishop, C. W. *The Ritual Bullfight (Smithsonian Report for 1926)*. Washington: United States Government Printing Office, 1927.

Blasco Ibáñez, Vicente. *Sangre y arena*. Madrid: Espasa Calpe, 1990.

Caballero, Antonio. *Toros, toreros y públicos*. Bogotá: El Ancora, 1992.

Campbell, Joseph, with Bill Moyers. *The Power of Myth*. New York: Doubleday, 1988.

Cau, Jean. *Las orejas y el rabo*. Barcelona: Plaza y Janés, 1962.

———. *Por Sevillanas*. Madrid: Espasa Calpe, 1988.

Conrad, Barnaby. *Encyclopedia of Bullfighting*. Boston: Houghton Mifflin, 1961.

Diario 16 (Madrid).

Espectador, El (Bogotá).

Evans, Nicholas. *The Horse Whisperer*. New York: Dell, 1996.

Extremadura (Mérida).

Fondeviole-Stefanuto, Geneviève. *Le voyageur de San Jude*. Mont-de-Marsan: Lacoste, 1993.

Frazer, Sir James George. *The Golden Bough: A Study in Magic and Religion*. Abridged ed. New York: Macmillan, 1950.

Fulton, John. *Bullfighting*. New York: Dial, 1971.

García Lorca, Federico. *Obras completas*. 3 vols. Madrid: Aguilar, 1988.

García Márquez, Gabriel. *News of a Kidnapping*. New York: Knopf, 1997.

González Valencia, María Fernanda. *Tauromaquia: Rito, juego y fiesta*. Thesis, Pontificia Universidad Javeriana, Bogotá, 1993.

Hemingway, Ernest. *Death in the Afternoon*. New York: Scribner's, 1932.
———. *Ernest Hemingway: Selected Letters 1917–1961*. New York: Scribner's, 1981.
———. *The Sun Also Rises*. New York: Scribner's, 1926.
Ideal (Granada).
International Herald Tribune.
Iragorri, Juan Carlos, and Germán Bernate. *César Rincón: Perfil de un hombre de casta*. Bogotá: Ediciones Gamma, 1992.
Josephs, Allen. *White Wall of Spain: The Mysteries of Andalusian Culture*. Ames: Iowa State University Press, 1983. Reprint, Gainesville: University Press of Florida, 1990.
Leibold, John. *This Is the Bullfight*. New York: A. S. Barnes, 1971.
Libération (Paris).
Lopera, Alberto. *Colombia: Tierra de toros*. Madrid: Espasa Calpe, 1989.
Los Angeles Times.
McCormick, John, and Mario Sevilla Mascareñas. *The Complete Aficionado*. Cleveland: World, 1967.
Michener, James A. *Iberia*. New York: Random House, 1968.
Molés, Manuel. *Antoñete: El maestro*. Madrid: El País Aguilar, 1996.
Mundo, El (Madrid).
Olano, Antonio D. *Yiyo*. Madrid: Delfos, 1985.
Oxford Spanish Dictionary. Oxford: Oxford University Press, 1996.
País, El (Bogotá).
País, El (Madrid).
Papini, Giovanni. *Gog: El libro negro*. Mexico City: Porrúa, 1984.
Pérez Mateos, Juan Antonio. *El toreo: Una visión inédita*. Madrid: Alianza, 1995.
Piedrahíta, Darío. *El otro . . . Rincón*. [Bogotá?]: Privately printed by author, 1996.
Plato. *Critias*.
Ruedo, El (Madrid).
6 Toros 6 (Madrid).
Sol, El (Madrid).
Stanton, Edward F. *Hemingway and Spain: A Pursuit*. Seattle: University of Washington Press, 1989.
Sur (Málaga).
Taurino Gráfico 1991, El. Madrid, 1991.
Tendido (Mont-de-Marsan).
Tiempo, El (Bogotá).
Tynan, Kenneth. *Bull Fever*. New York: Harper, 1955.
Vanity Fair.
Villán, Javier. *César Rincón: De Madrid al cielo*. Madrid: Espasa Calpe, 1992.
Wigram, Michael. "The Rise and Fall of San Isidro." In *Valor y Arte 1997*, 65–66. New York: Club Taurino of New York, 1997.
Ya (Madrid).
Zumbiehl, François. *El torero y su sombra*. Madrid: Espasa Calpe, 1987.

Index of Terms

I have listed the first, usually italicized (unless in dialogue) usage of the Spanish taurine (and related) terminology by page numbers. Either a translation, an endnote, or the context will make the meanings clear should the reader need such a reference.

a puerta cerrada 141
a un tiempo 157
abaniqueo 178
abarrotado 196
abono 87
abrazo 40
actuación 72
adorno 245
afición 7
aguantar 103
alarde de valor 227
alegre 38
alegría 38
aleonado 54
alguacil 40
altarcito [diminutive of *altar*] 85
alternativa 43
ancianito 192
andanada 53
apartado 167
apoderado 8
apodo xvi
arte 10
astifino 69

autopista 184
autovía 184
aviso 14
ayuda 72
ayudado, ayudando 26
ayuntamiento 91

bache 153
bamba 96
banderilla 11
banderillero 12
barrera 30
becerro 117
belmontista 15
bobo 330
bodega 318
bos taurus Africanus 3
bos taurus Ibericus 3
bos primigenius 5
bota 302
bragado 192
bravucón 320
bravura 80
brindis 53

Allen Josephs is university research professor and professor of Spanish at the University of West Florida, Pensacola. A past president of the Ernest Hemingway Foundation and Society, he is the author of *White Wall of Spain: The Mysteries of Andalusian Culture*, *"For Whom the Bell Tolls": Ernest Hemingway's Undiscovered Country*, several books on Federico García Lorca, and numerous articles on Hispanic culture in scholarly journals, as well as the *Atlantic*, *Boston Review*, *New Republic*, and the *New York Times Book Review*.